GW01607506

Books by J. H. Avery

OBJECTIVE TESTS IN ORDINARY LEVEL PHYSICS
(*with A. W. K. Ingram*)
OBJECTIVE TESTS IN ADVANCED LEVEL PHYSICS
(*with A. W. K. Ingram*)

Books by M. Nelkon

ADVANCED LEVEL PHYSICS (*with P. Parker*)
ADVANCED LEVEL PRACTICAL PHYSICS (*with J. Ogborn*)
SCHOLARSHIP PHYSICS
MECHANICS AND PROPERTIES OF MATTER
PRINCIPLES OF ATOMIC PHYSICS AND ELECTRONICS
REVISION NOTES IN PHYSICS
Book II. Optics, Sound, Heat, Properties of Matter
GRADED EXERCISES AND WORKED EXAMPLES IN PHYSICS
(with Multiple Choice Questions)
REVISION BOOK IN ORDINARY LEVEL PHYSICS
ELEMENTARY PHYSICS, Book I and II (*with A. F. Abbott*)
ELECTRICAL PRINCIPLES (*with H. I. Humphreys*)
ELECTRONICS AND RADIO PRINCIPLES (*with H. I. Humphreys*)
SOLUTIONS TO ORDINARY LEVEL PHYSICS QUESTIONS
BASIC MATHEMATICS FOR SCIENCE

All published by Heinemann Educational Books

Mathematics of Physics

Fourth Edition

by

J. H. AVERY, M.A.

Formerly
Senior Science Master,
Stockport Grammar School

and

M. NELKON, M.Sc.(Lond), F.Inst.P., A.K.C.

Formerly
Head of the Science Department,
William Ellis School, London

HEINEMANN EDUCATIONAL BOOKS
LONDON

Heinemann Educational Books Ltd
22 Bedford Square, London WC1B 3HH

LONDON EDINBURGH MELBOURNE AUCKLAND
SINGAPORE KUALA LUMPUR NEW DELHI
IBADAN NAIROBI JOHANNESBURG
PORTSMOUTH (NH) KINGSTON

ISBN 0 435 68047 1

First published 1954
Reprinted four times
Second Edition 1964
Reprinted once
Third Edition (SI), 1973
Reprinted twice
Fourth Edition 1980
Reprinted 1982, 1987

Printed and bound in Great Britain by
Biddles Ltd, Guildford and King's Lynn

Preface to Fourth Edition

In this edition we have added a selection of worked examples at the end of the book which cover different branches of the subject. We are very grateful to the Oxford Delegacy of Local Examinations for permission to reprint past questions. More logarithm examples have been added to the main text in place of the section on the slide rule and minor changes have been made where necessary. In an earlier reprint additional questions were added to the exercises on the calculus and on the motion of charges in electric and magnetic fields.

PREFACE TO THIRD EDITION

The text and subject matter of the original editions have been revised and SI units introduced throughout. In addition to replanning the original material, chapters have been added on SI units, differential equations, oscillations and waves, statistics and probability.

It is hoped that the book will be useful particularly to students taking the newly introduced Physics-and-Mathematics Advanced level course examined by the Oxford Delegacy; to those students taking Nuffield Advanced level Physics course without taking an A-level Mathematics course; and to Biology and Chemistry students at schools and technical colleges.

We are indebted to R. J. Williams, William Ellis School, for his contribution in the Statistics and Probability section, to M. Milford, Trinity College, Glenalmond, for constructive criticisms of the earlier books, and to John Osborne, Westminster School, for reading parts of the new edition and for valuable suggestions. We are also grateful to R. P. T. Hills, D. Deutsch and I. Robertson of Cambridge University for their assistance in reading and checking parts of the proofs.

In addition to the Examination Boards listed in the Preface to the first edition we are grateful to the Oxford Delegacy for Local Examinations for permission to reprint questions (denoted by the symbol (*O.*)) set in the past papers of the Physics-and-Mathematics examinations. Each Exercise is followed immediately by the Answers.

PREFACE TO FIRST EDITION

It is well known that without a knowledge of mathematical skills only a limited appreciation of Physics can be gained. This book is written for A-level students of Physics such as biologists, medical students and others who do not also take Mathematics to that level. It deals with the technique of Algebra, Trigonometry, Calculus and Mechanics necessary for A-level Physics, and their application in the subject. In general a knowledge of O-level Mathematics has been assumed, but certain aspects of Algebra are revised and emphasised, and the Trigonometry section is designed for a student with no previous knowledge of the subject. No attempt has been made to adopt the rigorous approach or the method of treatment that would appeal to the pure mathematician. It is hoped that the book will also enable mathematical students to appreciate how mathematical principles are applied to Physical problems, and be useful for students who find difficulty with the mathematical items in A-level Chemistry.

The authors are indebted to O. M. Slaney, Esq., B.A., Llandovery College, for reading the manuscript and making valuable criticisms and suggestions. Numerous examples have been given in the text to assist the student, and thanks are due to the following Examination Boards for kindly giving permission to reprint questions set in past papers: London University (*L.*), Northern Joint Matriculation Board (*N.*), Oxford and Cambridge (*O. & C.*), Cambridge Local Examinations (*C.*), Welsh Joint Board (*W.*).

Contents

1.
An Introduction to SI Units

SI ('Système International') units of length, mass and time are respectively the internationally agreed standards for the *metre* (m) the *kilogramme* (kg) and the *second* (s). It follows that the units for velocity and acceleration are respectively metre per second (m s^{-1}) and metre per second squared (m s^{-2}).

The SI unit of force is the *newton*, which is that force which causes a mass of 1 kg to accelerate at 1 m s^{-2}. From the relationship work = force × displacement, the unit of work (and thus also of energy) is obtained—a '*joule*'. In the subject of '*Heat*', exchanges of energy are studied and the joule is the correct unit to use for this. Power is the rate of dissipation of energy and so the unit is the joule per second, named the '*watt*'. These and some other important SI units are given in Table 1 below. Note that when units are named after famous men of science a large letter is used for the abbreviated form but a capital letter is not used when the unit is written in full. Thus we refer to a newton (N) and a hertz (Hz) etc. When writing units in full the Royal Society uses the plural when necessary (e.g. 5 newtons) whereas the Association for Science Education uses the singular (e.g. 5 newton). In this book we follow the latter usage.

TABLE 1

Quantity	Units	Name and Symbol	
Velocity	m s^{-1}	—	—
Acceleration	m s^{-2}	—	—
Force	kg m s^{-2}	newton	N
Work and energy	kg m^2 s^{-2}	joule	J
Power	kg m^2 s^{-3}	watt	W
Momentum	kg m s^{-1}	—	—
Frequency	s^{-1}	hertz	Hz

Electrical units are based on the above and in addition the ampere. This is defined as that constant current, which if maintained in two straight parallel conductors of negligible circular cross-section and placed one metre apart in vacuum, would produce between these conductors a force equal to 2×10^{-7} newton per metre of length. Table 2 summarises the more important electrical units.

TABLE 2

Quantity	Name and Unit Abbreviation	Definition	Units
Current	ampere (A)	See above.	A
Quantity of charge	coulomb (C)	Ampere second	A s
Potential difference	volt (V)	(i) Energy per unit charge. (ii) Power per unit current.	$\mathrm{J\,C^{-1}}$ $\mathrm{W\,A^{-1}}$
Resistance	ohm (Ω)	P.d. per unit current	$\mathrm{V\,A^{-1}}$
Magnetic flux density	tesla (T)	That field producing a force of 1 N on a conductor 1 m long perpendicular to the field and carrying 1 A	$\mathrm{N\,m^{-1}\,A^{-1}}$
Magnetic flux	weber (Wb)	That quantity of which the rate of change gives e.m.f.	V s
Capacitance	farad (F)	Charge per unit potential difference.	$\mathrm{C\,V^{-1}}$
Inductance	henry (H)	(i) Induced e.m.f. per ampere per second. (ii) Magnetic flux per ampere.	$\mathrm{V\,s\,A^{-1}}$ $\mathrm{Wb\,A^{-1}}$
Reactance and impedance	ohm (Ω)	$\dfrac{\text{r.m.s. voltage}}{\text{r.m.s. current}}$	$\mathrm{V\,A^{-1}}$

In addition to the four basic units mentioned above, measurements in other branches of science require further agreed standards. These are the kelvin (K), the candela (cd) and the mole (mol). The definitions of these are:

Kelvin: this measures thermodynamic temperature and is 1/273.16 of the thermodynamic temperature of the triple point of water. It is the same magnitude as one degree Celsius (°C). The symbol is K (*not* °K).

Candela: this is used when measuring luminous intensity and is defined as that luminous intensity, observed in a perpendicular direction to the surface, when viewing a surface of 1/600 000 $\mathrm{m^2}$ of a black body at temperature of freezing platinum under a pressure of 101 325 $\mathrm{Nm^{-2}}$. The symbol is cd.

Mole: This is used to measure the amount of substance and is formally defined as the amount of substance which contains as many elementary units as there are carbon atoms in 0.012 kg of carbon-12. The units must be specified and may be atoms, molecules, ions, electrons, photons etc. The reader will recognise that the mole is thus a quantity with which he is already familiar under the names 'gramme molecule', 'gramme atom', 'gramme ion' etc. The symbol is mol.

Two other basic units complete the requirements—the *radian* and the *steradian*; these are defined and discussed on p. 104 and pp. 111–13.

Submultiples:

The basic SI units are not always the most suitable ones in which to express a magnitude. For instance the mass of the Earth is about

5 980 000 000 000 000 000 000 000 kg

and that of an electron about

0.000 000 000 000 000 000 000 000 000 000 91 kg

Such quantities may be expressed much more simply by using what is termed the 'standard form'. The mass of the Earth would be written 5.98×10^{24} kg and that of an electron, 9.1×10^{-31} kg. Guidance on this type of conversion is given below.

This is the best method to use as the quantities are then (*a*) in SI units and (*b*) expressed in a way that can help to eliminate arithmetical errors. In some cases however prefixes are used before the SI unit to indicate that a power of ten has been omitted from the statement. For example an electric current of 2×10^{-3} A is often written 2 mA, the 'm' meaning 'milli' and signifying that 10^{-3} A was the unit used. Table 3 gives a list of submultiples in common use.

TABLE 3

For large quantities			For small quantities		
Multiple	Prefix	Symbol	Multiple	Prefix	Symbol
$\times 10$	deka-	da	$\times 10^{-1}$	deci	d
$\times 10^{2}$	hecto-	h	$\times 10^{-2}$	centi-	c
$\times 10^{3}$	kilo-	k	$\times 10^{-3}$	milli-	m
$\times 10^{6}$	mega-	M	$\times 10^{-6}$	micro-	µ
$\times 10^{9}$	giga-	G	$\times 10^{-9}$	nano-	n
$\times 10^{12}$	tera-	T	$\times 10^{-12}$	pico-	p
			$\times 10^{-15}$	femto-	f
Note: the first two are rarely used			$\times 10^{-18}$	atto-	a

Other Units:

At times older units which are often more familiar will be encountered. For instance time will often be reckoned in minutes, days and years. Many such units are so familiar that definitions are unnecessary. Table 4 gives a list of some additional units which due to usage will survive for a long time.

Conversion to Standard Form

All quantities used in calculations should be expressed in *basic* SI units, submultiples should not be used. In addition, if the numbers are large or small the standard form (see p. 3) will contribute to accuracy. The rules for the conversion are:

(i) If necessary first eliminate the submultiple (see Table 3 p. 3) e.g. For 252 kV write 252×10^3 V; for 74 μg write 74×10^{-9} kg (notice the 'trap' here—that for *masses* the base unit already has a kilo-prefix and conversions must always allow for this).

(ii) When this is done, move the decimal point to the left or the right a suitable number of places and alter the power of ten by that number; if the point is moved to left increase the power of ten and if it is moved to the right reduce the power of ten. Thus the examples given under (i) above become

$$252 \times 10^3 \text{ V} = 2.52 \times 10^5 \text{ V} \quad \text{and} \quad 74 \times 10^{-9} \text{ kg} = 7.4 \times 10^{-8} \text{ kg}$$

Now refer to p. 3 and look at the shift of the decimal point which was carried out to express the masses of the Earth and of an electron in standard form.

This method of expression is also of value when comparing the values of physical constants for different substances. For example the linear expansivities per °C for aluminium and iron are 0.000 025 5 and 0.000 011 9 respectively. This does not convey immediately any idea of their relative magnitudes, but when the coefficients are expressed as 25.5×10^{-6} and 11.9×10^{-6}, a clear picture is obtained.

This form of expression is of value when giving lists of values as not only does it enable the reader to comprehend the quantities more easily but it saves space. It is also of value when calculations involving the quantities are performed for it reduces the time needed for the calculation and makes the likelihood of error much smaller. The examples below illustrate the procedure to be adopted.

When plotting graphs it is sometimes useful to relate the scale used to the actual values by a multiple of ten for it facilitates plotting as well as calculating.

TABLE 4

Quantity	Name of unit	Symbol	Notes
Mass	tonne	t	= a 'metric ton' i.e. 1000 kg
	Unified atomic mass	u	= $\frac{1}{12}$ of the mass of the atom of the nuclide ^{12}C
Length	ångström	Å	10^{-10} m
	light-year		= distance travelled by light in 1 year
Time	minute	min	
	day	d	
	hour	h	
	year	a	
Pressure	pascal	Pa	= N m^{-2}
	bar	b	= 10^5 N m^{-2}. (Commonly used in meteorology especially mb)
Energy	kilowatt hour	kWh	= 3.6×10^6 J (the 'unit' used for electricity accounts)
	electron volt	eV	= 1.602×10^{-19} J
Conductance	siemens	S	= Ω^{-1}
Activity	curie	Ci	= 3.7×10^{10} disintegrations per second
Dynamic viscosity	poise	P	= 10^{-1} N s m^{-2} (To convert values in P to SI divide by 10)

EXAMPLES

1. Evaluate $\dfrac{0.00048 \times 0.0081}{270 \times 0.000004}$.

The expression may be written

$$\frac{48 \times 10^{-5} \times 81 \times 10^{-4}}{270 \times 4 \times 10^{-6}},$$

i.e. $$\frac{\overset{\overset{12}{}}{\cancel{48}} \times \overset{\overset{3}{\cancel{9}}}{\cancel{81}}}{\underset{\underset{10}{\cancel{30}}}{\cancel{270}} \times \underset{1}{\cancel{4}}} \times 10^{-3} = 36 \times 10^{-4} \text{ or } 0.0036.$$

2. Calculate the area of the Earth in m² assuming that its radius is 6.38 Mm.

$$\text{Radius} = 6.38 \times 10^6 \text{ m}$$

$$\therefore \quad \text{Area} = 4\pi r^2 = 4\pi \times (6.38 \times 10^6)^2$$

$$= 4\pi \times 6.38^2 \times 10^{12}$$

$$= 5.12 \times 10^{14} \text{ m}^2$$

No.	Log.
4	0.602 1
π	0.497 2
6.38	0.804 8
6.38	0.804 8
	2.708 9

3. What will be the extension in mm of 2 m of steel wire (Young's modulus $= 2.0 \times 10^{11}$ N m^{-2}) of cross-section area (c.s.a.) 1 mm² when a mass of 10 kg is supported?

$$\text{Young's modulus} = \frac{\text{Force (in N)}}{\text{c.s.a. (in m}^2)} \div \frac{\text{Increase in length}}{\text{Original length}}$$

By substituting the values given (after conversion to basic SI) we obtain

$$2.0 \times 10^{11} = \frac{10 \times 9.81}{10^{-6}} \div \frac{x \times 10^{-3}}{2}$$

where x is the required increase in length (in mm).

Hence $$\frac{x \times 10^{-3}}{2} \times 2.0 \times 10^{11} = 9.81 \times 10^7$$

$$\therefore \quad x = \frac{9.81 \times 10^7}{10^8} = 0.981 \text{ mm}$$

4. Rewrite the following table of values of cubical expansivities in such a way that a comparison can more easily be made.

Material . .	Ethanoic acid	Pentanol	Pentane	Water
Coefficient .	0.001 07	0.000 93	0.001 59	0.000 053

Since water has the lowest value the decimal point is adjusted so that the value is 5.3×10^{-5}. Hence all values are adjusted similarly:

Material . . .	Ethanoic acid	Pentanol	Pentane	Water
Coefficient $\times 10^{-5}$	107	93	159	5.3

EXERCISES 1

(1) Express in standard form eliminating denominators where necessary:

Examples: (i) $0.000\,82 = 8.2 \times 10^{-4}$

(ii) $\dfrac{1}{0.004} = \dfrac{1}{4 \times 10^{-3}} = 0.25 \times 10^{3} = 2.5 \times 10^{2}$

(*a*) 2830 (*b*) $\dfrac{1}{0.0025}$ (*c*) 0.000 009 (*d*) 800.04

(*e*) $\dfrac{1}{80\,000}$ (*f*) $\dfrac{10^4}{0.02}$ (*g*) $\dfrac{0.02}{10^4}$ (*h*) $\dfrac{0.0086}{10^{-7}}$

(*i*) $\dfrac{10^{-6}}{0.002}$ (*j*) $\dfrac{10^6}{0.002}$ (*k*) $\dfrac{0.000\,38}{190\,000}$ (*l*) $\dfrac{380\,000}{0.000\,19}$

(*m*) $\left(\dfrac{0.000\,000\,4 \times 2\,000\,000}{0.000\,016}\right)^2$

(2) Express the following in base SI units (using standard form where necessary to avoid very large or very small numbers).

Examples: (i) 28 g = 0.028 kg

(ii) $40\ \mu\text{V} = 40 \times 10^{-6}\ \text{V} = 4 \times 10^{-5}\ \text{V}$

(*a*) 400 g (*b*) 0.02 mg (*c*) 89 cm (*d*) 6 mm (*e*) 4 ms
(*f*) 70 μA (*g*) 20 kV (*h*) 6.7 MΩ (*i*) 0.4 Tm (*j*) 45 ns
(*k*) 7 min (*l*) 4 light year (*m*) 4.3 eV (*n*) 2 500 Å (*o*) 0.7 mV
(*p*) 78 kW (*q*) 1.018 μC (*r*) 47 kΩ (*s*) 50 pF (*t*) 43 nm
(*u*) 14.4 eV (*v*) 0.07 light year (*w*) 5896 Å (*x*) 42 μg (*y*) 1620 year

(3) A mass of 5000 kg is raised 80 mm in 2s. What is the power required in kW? (assume $g = 10\ \text{m s}^{-2}$).

(4) If a man of mass 80 kg can work for a few second at 600 W what is the shortest time in which he can run up a staircase of 15 steps measuring 30 cm (tread) by 20 cm (riser)? (Assume $g = 10\ \text{m s}^{-2}$ or $10\ \text{N kg}^{-1}$.)

(5) If a mercury barometer stands at 770 mm what is the atmospheric pressure in Pa? (Assume the density of mercury to be 13 600 kg m^{-3} and $g = 10\ \text{m s}^{-2}$.)

(6) Calculate the mass of an iron rod of diameter 4 mm and length 214 cm if the density of iron is 7700 kg m^{-3}.

(7) What is the resultant force needed to cause a car of mass 1 tonne to accelerate at 1 km h^{-1} s^{-1}?

(8) If the value of the charge on an electron is 1.6×10^{-19} C, what is the mean value of the number of electrons passing a given point in a millionth of one second when a current of 4 μA is flowing?

(9) What is the mass of a copper solenoid of 5 cm diameter and having 100 turns of wire of diameter 1 mm? The density of copper is 8400 kg m^{-3}.

(10) A radio transmitter is listed as broadcasting on a wavelength of 1500 m or 200 kHz. What value do these quantities give for the speed of radio signals?

(11) Calculate the mass of the earth in tonne given that its diameter is 1.274×10^4 km and its mean density is 5.517×10^3 kg m^{-3}.

(12) How many km away is a star which is at a distance of 47 light-years? Assume that there are 365 days in a year. (Speed of light $= 3 \times 10^8$ m s^{-1}.)

(13) The moon is 3.84×10^5 km away from the earth. What is the average speed of a body which takes three days to cover this distance? Give your answer in km h^{-1}. How long would it take to get there at a speed of 100 km h^{-1} (i.e. the cruising speed of many cars).

(14) A pair of Young's slits 0.5 mm (x) apart produce interference fringes of width 0.8 mm (y) at a distance of 0.80 m (D). What is the wavelength (λ) of the light? [$\lambda = xy/D$.]

(15) Assuming that the number of molecules in a mole is 6.023×10^{23} calculate the mass of the molecule of hydrogen (relative molar mass = 2). Hence find the mass of the hydrogen atom. Assuming that the one electron in this atom contributes $\frac{1}{1840}$ of the mass of the atom, calculate the mass of an electron.

(16) Rewrite the following tables so that the values can be compared more easily:

Substance	Pentanol	Ether	Mercury	Pentane	Water
Compressibility (per bar)	0.000 0894	0.000 1452	0.000 003 82	0.000 314	0.000 0489

Substance	Ethyne	Methanol	Ethanoic Acid
Heat of formation in J mol^{-1}	− 200 000	+ 215 000	+ 442 000

Metal	Aluminium	Copper	Wrought Iron	Mercury
Resistivity (Ω m)	0.000 000 027	0.000 000 018	0.000 000 14	0.000 000 95

Answers

1. (*a*) 2.830×10^3 (*b*) 4×10^2 (*c*) 9×10^{-6}
(*d*) 8.0004×10^2 (*e*) 1.25×10^{-5} (*f*) 5×10^5
(*g*) 2×10^{-6} (*h*) 8.6×10^4 (*i*) 5×10^{-4}
(*j*) 5×10^8 (*k*) 2×10^{-9} (*l*) 2×10^9
(*m*) 2.5×10^9

2. (*a*) 0.4 kg (*b*) 2×10^{-8} kg (*c*) 0.89 m
(*d*) 6×10^{-3} m (*e*) 4×10^{-3} s (*f*) 7×10^{-5} A
(*g*) 2×10^4 V (*h*) 6.7×10^6 Ω (*i*) 4×10^{11} m
(*j*) 4.5×10^{-8} s (*k*) 420 s (*l*) 3.78×10^{16} m
(*m*) 6.88×10^{-19} J (*n*) 2.500×10^{-7} m (*o*) 7×10^{-4} V
(*p*) 7.8×10^4 W (*q*) 1.018×10^{-6} C (*r*) 4.7×10^4 Ω
(*s*) 5×10^{-11} F (*t*) 4.3×10^{-8} m (*u*) 2.3×10^{-18} J
(*v*) 6.62×10^{14} m (*w*) 5.896×10^{-7} m (*x*) 4.2×10^{-8} kg
(*y*) 5.10×10^9 s

3. 2 kW
4. 4 s
5. 1.048×10^5 Pa
6. 0.207 kg
7. 278 N
8. 2.5×10^7
9. 0.104 kg
10. 3×10^8 m s^{-1}
11. 5.97×10^{24} kg
12. 4.45×10^{14} km
13. (i) 5340 km h^{-1}, (ii) 160 day (over 5 months!)
14. 5×10^{-7} m
15. 1.66×10^{-27} kg; 9.03×10^{-31} kg
16. (i) Values $\times 10^5$ are 8.94, 14.52, 0.382, 31.4, 4.89
(ii) Values $\times 10^{-5}$ are -2, $+2.15$, $+4.42$
(iii) Values $\times 10^9$ are 27, 18, 140, 950

2.
Indices

Summary of Rules Applying to Indices

1. x^n is the short way of writing down x n times with multiplication signs throughout. Thus $x^5 = x \times x \times x \times x \times x$.

2. $x^{1/m} = \sqrt[m]{x}$; thus $x^{1/2} = \sqrt{x}$; $x^{1/5} = \sqrt[5]{x}$.

3. $x^{-n} = \dfrac{1}{x^n}$, so that $\dfrac{1}{x^{-n}} = x^n$; thus $x^{-4} = \dfrac{1}{x^4}$; $\dfrac{1}{x^{-7}} = x^7$.

4. $x^{-1/m} = \dfrac{1}{x^{1/m}} = \dfrac{1}{\sqrt[m]{x}}$; $\dfrac{1}{x^{-1/m}} = x^{1/m} = \sqrt[m]{x}$.

   Thus $x^{-1/5} = \dfrac{1}{\sqrt[5]{x}}$; $\dfrac{1}{x^{-1/3}} = \sqrt[3]{x}$.

5. $x^\circ = 1$.

6. $x^a \times x^b = x^{a+b}$. This holds for *all* values of a and b, positive, negative, integral and fractional.
   Thus $x^7 \times x^{10} = x^{17}$; $x^{-7} \times x^{10} = x^3$; $x^{1/2} \times x^{-1/4} = x^{1/4}$.

7. $x^a \div x^b = x^{a-b}$. This is really an extension of rule 6 above because $x^a \div x^b = {}^ax \times x^{-b}$. It holds for all values of a and b.

8. $(x^m)^n = x^{m \times n}$ for all values of m and n.
   Thus $(x^4)^7 = x^{28}$; $(2x^3)^2 = 4x^6$; $(3x^4)^{1/2} = \sqrt{3}.x^2$.

EXAMPLES

1. Simplify $\dfrac{9a^2bc}{4ab^7c} \times \dfrac{2}{3}a^{-1}b^5c^{-3}$.

$$\frac{9a^2bc}{4ab^7c} \times \frac{2}{3}a^{-1}b^5c^{-3} = \frac{9a^2bc \times 2b^5}{4ab^7c \times 3ac^3} = \frac{3a^2b^6c}{2a^2b^7c^4} = \frac{3}{2bc^3}$$

There are several other ways in which the expression can be simplified one which may appeal to the student is:

$$\frac{9a^2bc}{4ab^7c} \times \frac{2}{3}a^{-1}b^5c^{-3} = \frac{9 \times 2}{4 \times 3} \times a^2bc \times a^{-1}b^{-7}c^{-1} \times a^{-1}b^5c^{-3}$$

$$= \frac{3}{2}a^0b^{-1}c^{-3} = \frac{3}{2bc^3}.$$

2. Simplify $\left(\frac{4v^2}{u^6}\right)^{3/2}$.

$$\left(\frac{4v^2}{u^6}\right)^{3/2} = 4^{3/2}v^{2 \times 3/2} \times u^{-6 \times 3/2} = (\sqrt{4})^3\, v^3u^{-9} = \frac{8v^3}{u^9}.$$

Rationalization of Surds

Since it is permissible to multiply the denominator and the numerator of a fraction by the same quantity—provided it is not equal to zero—then

$$\frac{1}{\sqrt{x}} = \frac{1 \times \sqrt{x}}{\sqrt{x} \times \sqrt{x}} = \frac{\sqrt{x}}{x}.$$

This may not seem much simpler but when actual numbers are used it does provide an easier method of solving. Thus if we know that

$\sqrt{3} = 1.732$ we can find $\frac{1}{\sqrt{3}}$ as follows:

$$\frac{1}{\sqrt{3}} = \frac{\sqrt{3}}{3} = 0.577.$$

A number which cannot be evaluated, such as $\sqrt{3}$ or $\sqrt{5}$, is called a *surd*, and the process of removing the root sign from the denominator of a fraction, as we have just illustrated, is called 'rationalising' the surd.

The Binomial Theorem

An expression which contains two quantities separated by a plus or minus sign (i.e. two 'terms') is called a 'binomial'; $(1 + x)$, $(2 - 3a)$, $(mx + c)$ are binomials. When such an expression is raised to the nth power $(n + 1)$ terms are found in the answer (known as the 'expansion').

Thus $(1 + x)^2 = 1 + 2x + x^2$,
$(1 + x)^3 = 1 + 3x + 3x^2 + x^3$.

And in general, when x is numerically less than 1,

$$(1 + x)^n = 1 + nx + \frac{n(n-1)}{1 \times 2}x^2 + \frac{n(n-1)(n-2)}{1 \times 2 \times 3}x^3 + \ldots$$

If x is small the terms involving x^2, x^3, etc., may be neglected in comparison with the other two terms and the expression becomes

$$(1 + x)^n = 1 + nx.$$

Also $$(1 + x)^{-n} = 1 - nx,$$

i.e. $$\frac{1}{(1 + x)^n} = 1 - nx, \text{ when } x \text{ is small.}$$

Thus αt is a small quantity

$$\frac{1}{1 + \alpha t} = (1 + \alpha t)^{-1} = 1 - \alpha t.$$

Similarly when x is small

$$\sqrt{1 + x} = (1 + x)^{1/2} = 1 + \frac{x}{2},$$

and $$\frac{1}{\sqrt{1 + x}} = (1 + x)^{-1/2} = 1 - \frac{x}{2}.$$

This finds application in a number of problems, especially those relating to expansivities and change of density with temperature.

If two quantities a, b are both very small,

$$(1 + a)(1 + b) = 1 + a + b, \text{ to a good approximation,}$$

because ab is small enough to be neclected.

Thus $$\frac{1 + a}{1 + b} = (1 + a)(1 + b)^{-1} \simeq (1 + a)(1 - b) \simeq 1 + \overline{a - b}.$$

When 'correcting' the barometric height to 0°C, we encounter the expression $\frac{1 + \alpha t}{1 + \gamma t}$, where αt, γt are both very small.

This can be simplified as follows:

$$\frac{1 + \alpha t}{1 + \gamma t} \simeq (1 + \alpha t)(1 - \gamma t) \simeq 1 + \alpha t - \gamma t = 1 + (\alpha - \gamma)t.$$

EXAMPLES

1. The density of mercury at 0°C is 13 595.5 kg m^{-3} and its cubic expansivity 18.18×10^{-5} per °C. What will be its density at 10°C?

If ρ_t is the density at t°C and ρ_0 that at 0°C then

$$\rho_t = \frac{\rho_0}{1 + \alpha t}$$

where α is the cubic expansivity.

$$\therefore \quad \rho_{10} = \frac{13\,595.5}{(1 + 18.18 \times 10^{-5} \times 10)} = \frac{13\,595.5}{1 + 0.001\,818}$$

$$= 13\,595.5\,(1 - 0.001\,818)$$

$$= 13\,570.8 \text{ kg m}^{-3}$$

2. The string of a simple pendulum is lengthened by 1 part in 1000. What is the relative change in the periodic time?

If t and t' are the periodic times corresponding to length l and $l + \frac{l}{1000}$, then

$$t = 2\pi\sqrt{\frac{l}{g}} \quad \text{and} \quad t' = 2\pi\sqrt{\frac{l + \frac{l}{1000}}{g}}$$

$$\therefore \quad t' = 2\pi\sqrt{\frac{l(1 + \frac{1}{1000})}{g}} = 2\pi\sqrt{\frac{l}{g}}\,.\,(1 + \tfrac{1}{1000})^{1/2}$$

$$\therefore \quad t' = t(1 + \tfrac{1}{1000})^{1/2} = t(1 + \tfrac{1}{2}\,.\,\tfrac{1}{1000}) = t(1 + \tfrac{1}{2000}).$$

i.e. the periodic time is increased by 1 part in 2000.

DIMENSIONS

In Table 1 on p. 1, the units used for various important mechanical quantities are listed. Notice that only the three internationally agreed units are required. The 'dimensions' of a physical quantity relate to the manner in which these three basic units appear in the derived unit. The unit of mass is denoted by $[M]$, that of length by $[L]$, and that of time by $[T]$. Thus the dimensions of force are $[MLT^{-2}]$. Those of density are $[ML^{-3}]$. The square brackets denote that it is the dimensions of the quantities which are being expressed.

A ratio has no dimensions. Thus an angle is dimensionless; so also is temperature.

The relationships connecting quantities can sometimes be deduced by applying the rules of mathematics to the dimensions of the quantities concerned. This is known as the 'method of dimensions'. Before it can be applied, experimental data must be available so that it is clearly understood what are the relevant factors. As an example consider the case of a simple pendulum. Suppose experimental evidence tells us that the only factors which affect the periodic time (t) are the length of the pendulum (l) and the value of the acceleration of free fall at the spot (g). In other words the mass of the bob, the angle of swing, the diameter of the string, etc., all have no effect.

If we may write the equation in the form

$$t = kl^x g^y$$

where k is a constant, then the dimensions on the right-hand side must be the dimensions of time. But the dimensions on the right side are

$$[L^x L^y T^{-2y}] = [L^{x+y} T^{-2y}].$$

If these are to be the dimensions of time, i.e. $[T]$,

$$x + y = 0 \quad . \quad . \quad . \quad . \quad . \quad . \quad . \quad (1)$$

and $$-2y = 1 \quad . \quad . \quad . \quad . \quad . \quad . \quad . \quad (2)$$

Hence $$y = -\tfrac{1}{2} \quad \text{and} \quad x = +\tfrac{1}{2}.$$

$$\therefore \quad t = kl^{1/2} g^{-1/2} = k\sqrt{\frac{l}{g}}$$

k can be determined experimentally and is actually 2π.

A study of the proof given above will reveal that the equations (1) and (2) were obtained by equating the powers of $[L]$ and of $[T]$ on each side of the equation. Had $[M]$ appeared a third equation could have been obtained. In general three equations are obtained but clearly never more than this are deducible. Hence for a problem to be completely soluble by this method there must not be more than three unknowns. A further example of the method will now be given:

EXAMPLE

Assuming that the frequency (f) of a uniform stretched wire depends only on the mass per unit length (m), the length of the wire vibrating (l), and the force stretching the wire (F), find the relationship between these quantities.

$$\text{Let } f = km^x l^y F^z.$$

$$\text{Then } [f] = [m^x l^y F^z]$$

$$\therefore \quad [T^{-1}] = [M^x L^{-x} \times L^y \times M^z L^z T^{-2z}]$$

$$= [M^{x+z} L^{-x+y+z} T^{-2z}].$$

Hence, equating indices on l.h.s. and r.h.s.,

$$x + z = 0 \quad . \quad . \quad . \quad . \quad . \quad . \quad (1)$$

$$-x + y + z = 0 \quad . \quad . \quad . \quad . \quad . \quad . \quad (2)$$

$$-2z = -1 \quad . \quad . \quad . \quad . \quad (3)$$

From (3), $z = \frac{1}{2}$, which on substituting in (1) gives $x = -\frac{1}{2}$.
Hence from (2) $y = x - z = -\frac{1}{2} - \frac{1}{2} = -1$.

$$\therefore \quad f = km^{-1/2} l^{-1} F^{1/2}$$

$$\therefore \quad f = \frac{k}{l}\sqrt{\frac{F}{m}}.$$

LOGARITHMS

It is assumed that the student has already been introduced to the use of logarithms, and the following notes should be regarded as revision; they do not represent a full treatment.

1. If $10^x = y$ then we say 'x is the logarithm of y to the base 10', or in algebraic notation $\log_{10} y = x$.

Thus when we look under '2' in our log-tables we find 0.3010, by which is meant that $10^{0.3010} = 2$.

2. A logarithm consists of two parts—(*a*) a characteristic and (*b*) a mantissa:

(*a*) the characteristic is the number which precedes the decimal point; this is used to 'locate' the decimal point in the anti-logarithm;

(*b*) the mantissa is the number following the decimal point in the logarithm, and it is obtained from our 'log-tables', which could better have been named 'mantissae-tables'.

Thus the logarithm of 20 is 1.3010 and of 200 is 2.3010, etc. The justification for these is

$$20 = 2 \times 10 \quad = 10^{0.3010} \times 10^1 = 10^{1.3010}$$
$$200 = 2 \times 100 = 10^{0.3010} \times 10^2 = 10^{2.3010}.$$

3. For numbers which are of value less than one, negative characteristics are used, denoted by a 'bar' placed over the characteristic. Thus $\log_{10} 0.2 = \bar{1}.3010$, the reason being that

$$0.2 = 2 \times \frac{1}{10} = 2 \times 10^{-1} = 10^{(-1+0.3010)}.$$

Similarly $$\log_{10} 0.002 = \bar{3}.3010.$$

Note that the mantissa is *always positive.*

It is actually true to say that because $\log_{10} 0.2 = \bar{1}.3010$ it is also equal to -0.6990, but the second form is rarely used. It does occasionally find use in the study of pH values in physical chemistry.

4. From the foregoing it is evident that physical quantities expressed in a form like 2×10^{11} (which is the value for Young's modulus for steel in N m^{-2}) can be put into logs very quickly, as the index of ten is the characteristic. This is another, though slight, advantage of the use of this form of expression. [Note that it is only true so long as there is only one digit to the left of the decimal point, and that must not be a cipher. Thus log (20×10^{11}) is *not* 11.3010 but 12.3010.] Similarly negative indices can be put quickly into logarithmic form. Thus log (2×10^{-6}) is $\bar{6}.3010$.

5. Two numbers are multipled by adding their logarithms together and looking up the antilogarithm of the result. The justification for this is the fact that $10^x \times 10^y = 10^{x+y}$ (see p. 11).

Two numbers are divided by subtracting the logarithm of the divisor from that of the dividend, and finding the antilogarithm of the result. The justification for this is the fact that $10^x \div 10^y = 10^{x-y}$ (see p. 11).

6. If a number is raised to the nth power the logarithm should be multiplied by n and the antilogarithm evaluated, e.g.

$$\log(3^{1.4}) = 1.4 \log 3.$$

7. If the mth root is required the logarithm should be divided by m and the antilogarithm evaluated. If the characteristic is negative it must be increased in value until it equals the nearest multiple of the divisor (m), so that the characteristic of the log of the answer is always a whole number. To offset this change and restore the log to its correct value, the mantissa must have the same amount added to it (the characteristic was increased negatively so the mantissa is increased positively). Thus to evaluate $\sqrt{0.2}$ we proceed as follows:

No.	Log
0.2	$\bar{1}.3010$
$\sqrt{0.2}$	$\bar{1}.6505$

Antilog. = 0.4472
Answer 0.4472.

[$\dfrac{\bar{1}\cdot 3010}{2}$ is regarded as $\dfrac{\bar{2}.^{1}3010}{2}$, i.e. the extra '1' is 'carried'.]

Similarly to evaluate $^{3}\sqrt{0.2}$, $\bar{1}.3010$ must be divided by 3. The $\bar{1}$ is changed to $\bar{3}$ and the 0.3010 to $0.^{2}3010$ to offset this change.

Thus $$\frac{\bar{1}.3010}{3} = \bar{1}.7670.$$

$$\text{Antilog } \bar{1}.7670 = 0.5848.$$

Hence $$^{3}\sqrt{0.2} = 0.5848.$$

8. When a complex calculation is undertaken look carefully at it and choose the simplest approach. If it is a quantity such as

$$\frac{328.1}{19.3} \times \frac{6.73}{0.005} \div \frac{4.9}{\pi(0.2)^2}$$

recast it thus

$$\frac{328.1 \times 6.73 \times \pi \times (0.2)^2}{19.3 \times 0.005 \times 4.9},$$

then add together the logs of the top line (allowing for the occurrence of log 0.2 twice because it is squared in the expression); then add together the logs of the divisor and subtract the result from that obtained for the top line. Look up the antilog. The result is 586.5 and the full working will be found in the margin.

No.	Log
328.1	2.5160
6.73	0.8280
π	0.4971
0.2	$\bar{1}.3010$
0.2	$\bar{1}.3010$
	2.4431
19.3	1.2856
0.005	$\bar{3}.6990$
4.9	0.6902
	$\bar{1}.6748$
	2.4431
	$\bar{1}.6748$
	2.7683

The Technique of Calculation

Always inspect your answer to see that it is reasonable. It should satisfy two tests:

(i) If a physical quantity is being obtained it should be of the right order. For example, if an experiment to determine the acceleration of free fall has been performed check that the result is about 10 m s^{-2}. Do not be content to accept a result like $g = 100$ m s^{-2} without considering its likelihood.

(ii) An *estimate* of the value of the answer should be made when the final expression has been formed and the calculated result should be of the same order as this value. Thus if the expression discussed in note 8 above were being evaluated the estimating process would proceed roughly as follows (probably done mentally—depending on the experience of the calculator)

$$\frac{328.1 \times 6.73 \times \pi \times (0.2)^2}{19.3 \times 0.005 \times 4.9} \simeq \frac{300 \times 7 \times 3 \times 4 \times 10^{-2}}{20 \times 5 \times 10^{-3} \times 5}$$

$$\simeq \frac{300 \times 4}{5 \times 10^{-1} \times 5} \text{ (21 and 20 struck out)}$$

$$\simeq \frac{3000}{5} \text{ (4 and 5 struck out)} = 600.$$

The result of 586.5 is thus accepted as reasonable.

This rapid estimate should be done before the more accurate calculation as it may expose an error in the expression. Thus if it was discovered that a rough evaluation of the result of an experiment to determine the acceleration of free fall gave 0.1, an error in a decimal place would be suspected, and it should be tracked down before undertaking the final calculation. If a rough value of, say, five was obtained then a more serious error must be sought.

Common errors made in calculations, which can often be found by this rough estimate, are:

(1) The substitution of quantities in inconsistent systems of units, e.g. millimetre for metre, and especially the omission of 'g' in your expression.

(2) The substitution of diameter instead of radius. This leads to answers of twice, a half, four times (if quantity is squared) or a quarter of the correct value.

(3) Omission of π (this leads to answers of about a third or three times the correct one).

The method of tabulating the numbers and the logs side by side in the margin is not essential once you have become really confident in the use of logs. Until you are really confident, however, it is a method to be recommended as not only can you personally check your working more easily, but your instructor can help you if necessary.

Many sets of mathematical tables provide square-root tables, square tables, reciprocal tables, etc. All of these are of value at times. Note the following points:

1. When using square-root tables it is necessary to estimate the answer before using the tables. As an example we may need the square root of 0.912 and of 0.0912. 0.912 is best regarded as 91.2×10^{-2} which we can see is about 9.5×10^{-1} or about 0.95. 0.0912 is about 9×10^{-2} which will have a root of value about 3×10^{-1}. Inspection of tables gives under 912 the values 9550 and 3020. Obviously therefore

$$\sqrt{0.912} = 0.9550 \quad \text{and} \quad \sqrt{0.0912} = 0.3020.$$

2. When using reciprocal tables do not forget to subtract the 'differences'. The decimal point must be placed by inspection.

The use of a calculator eliminates most of these difficulties.

Napierian Logarithms

Napier was the first to point out the value of using logarithms to the base 'e', where e is the number obtained by summing the series

$$1 + \frac{1}{1} + \frac{1}{1 \times 2} + \frac{1}{1 \times 2 \times 3} + \frac{1}{1 \times 2 \times 3 \times 4} + \ldots$$

which is 2.7183 . . . (See equation (5), p. 159, and put $x = 1$)

It is shown on p. 20, that

$$\log_e a = 2.3026 \log_{10} a,$$

but in practice Napierian logarithms, as they are called, are obtained from special tables.

Note that '$\log_e a$' is now symbolized by '$\ln a$'.

Extension of the Use of Naperian Logarithms to Greater and Smaller Values

If the value of ln 31 is required, proceed as follows:

$$\begin{aligned}\ln 31 = \ln (3.1 \times 10) &= \ln 3.1 + \ln 10 \\ &= 1.1314 + 2.3026 \\ &= 3.4340\end{aligned}$$

Similarly
$$\begin{aligned}\ln 0.031 = \ln (3.1 \div 100) &= \ln 3.1 - 2 \ln 100 \\ &= 1.1314 - 4.6052 \\ &= -3.4738\end{aligned}$$

This is not $\bar{3}.4738$ since the mantissa (0.4738) is also negative.

CHANGING THE BASE OF A LOGARITHM

A logarithm is an index (see page 16). When we say that $\log_{10} 2 = 0.3010$ we mean that

$$10^{0.3010} = 2.$$

Any number can be raised to an appropriate power to obtain a given number and we can thus have logs to any base we like. If we chose the base 4 the log of 2 would be 0.5 because $4^{0.5} = \sqrt{4} = 2$. We can therefore write $\log_4 2 = 0.5$. The use of Napierian logs is important in science and it is often necessary to 'change the base of the logs', i.e. to look up a log in 'ordinary' ($\log_{10}$) tables and deduce the log to another base (usually e). The rule is

$$\log_b x = \log_a x \times \log_b a.$$

So if $a = 10$ and $b = e$, $\log_e x = \log_{10} x \times \log_e 10$.

Now $\log_e 10 = 2.3026$ and hence $\log_e x = 2.3026 \log_{10} x$.

Proof of the rule:

Let $\log_a x = y$ and $\log_b x = z$

$$\therefore \quad a^y = x \quad \text{and} \quad b^z = x$$

$$\therefore \quad a^y = b^z$$

Taking logs to base b

$$y \log_b a = z \log_b b.$$

But $\qquad \log_b b = 1.$

$$\therefore \quad y \log_b a = z.$$

$$\therefore \quad \log_a x \times \log_b a = \log_b x$$

which is the rule quoted above.

Logarithmic Series

Any series of the form $a_0 + a_1x + a_2x^2 + \ldots + a_nx^n + \ldots$ to infinity where a_0, a_1, a_2 etc. are constants, is known as a 'power series' and if the sum of such a series to n terms is S_n it is clear that sometimes S_n will steadily increase as the number of terms increases but in certain cases the sum approaches a limit, i.e. S_∞ has a definite value. In this case the series is said to be 'convergent'. One such convergent series is given on p. 19 for e. It is possible to express a logarithm in the form of a power series, provided we start with $(1 + x)$ rather than x. (The student should apply the reasoning given below to the series for $\ln x$ and show that this does not succeed.) Let

$$\ln(1 + x) = a_0 + a_1x + a_2x^2 + \ldots$$

when $x = 0$ the l.h.s. $= \ln 1 = 0$ (since $e^0 = 1$) and r.h.s. $= a_0$, hence

$$a_0 = 0.$$

Now differentiate the series with respect to x. From p. 157,

$$\frac{\mathrm{d}}{\mathrm{d}x}[\ln(1 + x)] = \frac{1}{1 + x}$$

and the differential coefficient of r.h.s. $= a_1 + 2a_2x + 3a_3x^2 + \ldots$ (p. 124).

By putting $x = 0$ in this equation we have

$$\frac{1}{1+0} = a_1 \quad \text{i.e. } a_1 = 1.$$

By differentiating a second time and putting $x = 0$ we have

$$\frac{-1}{(1+0)^2} = 2a_2 + 0 + \ldots \quad \text{i.e. } a_2 = -\tfrac{1}{2}$$

By successive application of this process we can evaluate all the coefficients and arrive at the complete series; thus

$$\ln(1 + x) = x - \frac{x^2}{2} + \frac{x^3}{3} - \frac{x^4}{4} + \ldots + (-1)^{n+1}\frac{x^n}{n} + \ldots$$

This is true if $-1 < x \leqslant +1$.

If instead of x we wrote $(-x)$ in this expression we obtain

$$\ln(1 - x) = -x - \frac{x^2}{2} - \frac{x^3}{3} - \frac{x^4}{4} - \ldots - \frac{x^n}{n} - \ldots$$

and the condition $-1 < -x \leqslant +1$ applies. We can more easily compare this condition with the former one if we rewrite it

$$-1 \leqslant x < +1.$$

We can now make use of both of these series as follows:

$$\ln(1 + x) - \ln(1 - x) = \ln\left(\frac{1+x}{1-x}\right),$$

from log theory.

$$\text{Hence} \quad \ln\left(\frac{1+x}{1-x}\right) = \left(x - \frac{x^2}{2} + \frac{x^3}{3} - \frac{x^4}{4} + \ldots\right)$$
$$- \left(-x - \frac{x^2}{2} - \frac{x^3}{3} - \ldots\right)$$
$$= 2x + 2\frac{x^3}{3} + 2\frac{x^5}{5} + \ldots$$
$$= 2\left(x + \frac{x^3}{3} + \frac{x^5}{5} + \ldots\right)$$

For this to be true the condition for each series must apply simultaneously and thus $-1 < x < +1$. It is this series which is used to calculate 'natural' logarithms for the numbers lying between -1 and $+1$.

For example supposing we wish to evaluate ln 2. To apply the series

$$\text{for } \ln\left(\frac{1+x}{1-x}\right) \text{ we must make } \left(\frac{1+x}{1-x}\right) = 2$$

i.e. $$1 + x = 2(1 - x)$$

$$\therefore \quad x = \frac{1}{3}.$$

Hence

$$\ln 2 = \ln\left(\frac{1+\frac{1}{3}}{1-\frac{1}{3}}\right) = 2\left[\frac{1}{3} + \frac{1}{3} \times \frac{1}{27} + \frac{1}{5} \times \frac{1}{243} + \frac{1}{7} \times \frac{1}{2187} + \ldots\right]$$

$$= 2\,(0.333\,33 + 0.012\,35 + 0.000\,82 + 0.000\,065 + \ldots)$$

$$= 2 \times 0.346\,57$$

$$= 0.693\,14$$

i.e. ln 2 to four figures is 0.6931.

Evaluation of Four Figure Logarithms to the Base 10

It is shown on p. 20 that

$$\log_{10} x = \frac{\ln x}{\ln 10}.$$

Thus to evaluate logs to the base 10 we need ln 10. The obvious method of putting $\dfrac{1+x}{1-x} = 10$ gives $x = \dfrac{9}{11}$ but this leads to a series which converges rather slowly and many terms have to be evaluated if four significant figures are required. This is avoided by putting

$$\frac{1+x}{1-x} = \frac{n+1}{n} \quad \left(\text{this implies that } x = \frac{1}{2n+1}\right)$$

and hence obtaining the alternative form for the ln series:

$$\ln(n+1) - \ln = 2\left(\frac{1}{2n+1} + \frac{1}{3}\frac{1}{(2n+1)^3} + \frac{1}{5}\frac{1}{(2n+1)^5} + \ldots\right)$$

If now we put $n = \frac{10}{8}$

$$\ln \tfrac{10}{8} = \ln 10 - \ln 8$$

$$= \ln 10 - 3 \ln 2$$

i.e. $$\ln 10 = 3 \ln 2 + \ln \tfrac{10}{8}$$

Now to evaluate $\ln \frac{10}{8}$ we put $\frac{x+1}{x-1} = \frac{10}{8}$. Hence $x = \frac{1}{9}$ and the series converges rapidly so that, proceeding as for the evaluation of ln 2 above we obtain

$$\ln \tfrac{10}{8} = 0.2231_4$$

Thus
$$\ln 10 = 3 \times 0.6931_4 + 0.2231_4$$
$$= 2.3025_6$$
$$= 2.3026 \text{ (to four significant places)}$$

We can now write $\log_{10} x = \frac{\ln x}{2.3026}$ and hence by using the series for $\ln \left(\frac{1+x}{1-x}\right)$ or for $\ln \left(\frac{n+1}{n}\right)$ and dividing the sum by 2.3026 the 'common' logarithms are found. $\frac{1}{2.3026} = 0.4343$ and it is often convenient to use

$$\log_{10} x = 0.4343 \ln x.$$

EXAMPLES

1. Write down the log of 10 to the base 100.
If x is the log of 10 to the base 100, then

$$\log_{100} 10 = x$$

Hence
$$100^x = 10$$

Now
$$\sqrt{100} = 100^{1/2} = 10$$

$$\therefore \quad x = \frac{1}{2} = 0.5$$

2. Evaluate (i) $\log_5 25$ and (ii) $\log_5 0.2$

(i) Let
$$\log_5 25 = x$$
Then
$$5^x = 25$$
So
$$x = 2$$

(ii) Let
$$\log_5 0.2 = y$$
Then
$$5^y = 0.2$$
But
$$0.2 = \frac{1}{5} = 5^{-1}$$
So
$$5y = 5^{-1}$$
$$\therefore \quad y = -1$$

3. Simplify $\log_4 8 + \log_4 0.5 - \log_4 2$

Since we add logs in multiplying numbers and subtract logs in dividing numbers, then

$$\log_4 8 + \log_4 0.5 - \log_4 2 = \log_4\left(\frac{8 \times 0.5}{2}\right)$$

$$= \log_4 2$$

Now $$4^{1/2} = \sqrt{4} = 2.$$

So $$\log_4 2 = \frac{1}{2} = 0.5$$

4. Simplify $4 \ln 3 - \ln 27 + \frac{1}{4} \ln 1296 - \ln 9$

We have $$4 \ln 3 = \ln 3^4 = \ln 81$$

$$\tfrac{1}{4} \ln 1296 = \ln 1296^{1/4} = \ln(\sqrt[4]{1296}) = \ln 6$$

So $$4 \ln 3 - \ln 27 + \tfrac{1}{4} \ln 1296 - \ln 9$$

$$= \ln 81 - \ln 27 + \ln 6 - \ln 9$$

$$= \ln\left(\frac{81}{27} \times \frac{6}{9}\right) = \ln 2$$

5. Write down the first four terms of the expansion of $\ln(1 + 2x)$ and state the condition for which the series is valid.

Using the expansion for $\ln(1 + x)$, instead of x we write $2x$,

$$\therefore \quad \ln(1 + 2x) = 2x - \frac{(2x)^2}{2} + \frac{(2x)^3}{3} - \frac{(2x)^4}{4} + \dots$$

$$= 2x - 2x^2 + \frac{8x^3}{3} - 4x^4 + \dots$$

The conditions are that $-1 < 2x \leqslant +1$

i.e. $$-\tfrac{1}{2} < x \leqslant +\tfrac{1}{2}$$

6. Evaluate to 4 places decimals $\log_{10} 3$

$$\log_{10} 3 = 0.4343 \ln 3.$$

To evaluate $\ln 3$ put $\dfrac{1 + x}{1 - x} = 3$. Hence $x = \frac{1}{2}$

$$\therefore \quad \ln 3 = \ln\left(\frac{1 + \frac{1}{2}}{1 - \frac{1}{2}}\right) = 2\left[\tfrac{1}{2} + \frac{(\frac{1}{2})^3}{3} + \frac{(\frac{1}{2})^5}{5} + \dots\right]$$

$$= 1.0986.$$

$$\therefore \quad \log_{10} 3 = 0.4343 \times 1.0986$$

$$= 0.4771$$

THE ELECTRONIC CALCULATOR

Fig. 2.1 shows one form of a hand electronic calculator, whose battery can be re-charged from the mains.

With the power ON, and by pressing keys in the lower half of the keyboard, any of the digits 0 to 9 can be displayed on the rectangular screen at the top of the panel. A key at the bottom provides a decimal point when required. Ten significant figures can be displayed, with a space on the left for a minus if needed and two spaces on the right for powers of 10 (called exponents) as explained later.

The operations of division (÷), multiplication (×), addition (+) and subtraction (−) are performed by pressing the appropriate keys on the right. The result is displayed by pressing the key = at the bottom. The decimal point floats; for example, 36.2 × 68.7 = is displayed as 2486.94.

The key EXP on the left of the display screen at the top enters powers of 10 or exponents. For example, $2315 = 2.315 \times 10^3$, which is therefore entered as 2.315 EXP 3. The display is 2.315 03, the exponent being shown on the extreme right. Similarly, 6.025×10^{23} is entered as 6.025 EXP 23; the display is 6.025 23. The fraction 1/3 is displayed as 3.333333333 − 01 because the multiplying factor here is 10^{-1}.

FIG. 2.1 Electronic Calculator—Front panel.

The function of the keys on the left of the lower half of the keyboard is as follows:

M *Memory key*. A displayed number can be retained by pressing this key and subsequently recalled for use at any stage by pressing the key again.

+/− *Change Sign key*. Any number displayed can be reversed in sign by pressing this key. For example, for $-3 + 5$, press +/− 3 + 5 = ; for $-3 - 5$, press +/− 3 − 5 = . For 3.2×10^{-8}, press 3.2 EXP +/− 8; the display is 3.2 − 08. If the +/− key is pressed after the EXP key it will affect only the sign of the exponent or power.

CE *Clear Entry key*. This clears the display of the last entry only (erasure key).

C *Clear key*. This clears all the calculations except for the memory and sets the number in the display to zero for a new calculation.

Special function keys

The top half of the keyboard contains special function keys.

Algebraic functions

$1/x$ Reciprocal (or Inverse) of the number displayed. For 1/32, for example, press 32 then $1/x$. The figure 0.03125 appears.

$\sqrt{x}$ Square root of the number displayed. For $\sqrt{28.42}$, for example, press 28.42 then $\sqrt{x}$; the figure 5.331041174 appears, which is 5.33 to two decimal places.

Trigonometric functions

sin, *cos* and *tan* keys enable these trigonometric values to be displayed. For tan 60°, for example press 60 then *tan*; the display is 1.7320508 which is 1.732 to three decimal places.

arc is the key for inverse trigonometric functions. To find θ where $\sin\theta = 0.5642$, for example, press 0.5642, then arc, then sin. The display is 34.3467562 which is 34.3° to one decimal place.

DEG RAD is the key which enables degrees to be changed to radians, or vice-versa, if required at any stage of a trigonometric calculation.

Logarithmic functions

log This is the key for the common log or log to the base 10. For log 9.81, for example, press 9.81 log; the display is 9.916690071 − 01, which is 0.9917 to four decimal places.

ln This is the key for the natural logarithm or log to the base *e*. For ln 224, for example, press 224 ln; the display is 5.411646052 which is 5.412 to three decimal places. The display for ln 0.032 is −1.117795108 or −1.118 to three decimal places.

e^x This key raises e to the displayed power x.

Two-variable function keys

y^x This is the key for y raised to the power x. For π^2, for example, press π, then y^x, then 2, then = ; the display is 9.86960441. For 2.652^3, press 2.652, then y^x, then 3, then = ; 18.6517917 is displayed.

$x \leftrightarrow y$ This is the key for 'exchange', that is, it reverses the factors x and y. For example, suppose $3^{1.4}$ is required and an entry error is made by 1.4 y^x 3, which is actually 1.4^3. Then, by pressing this key, x and y are exchanged so that we now obtain $3^{1.4}$ as originally required. As a simple example, an entry error in 3 ÷ 8 is corrected by 8 ÷ 3 $x \leftrightarrow y$ = , which displays 0.375.

Brackets

The brackets (parentheses) keys are used to separate groups of figures in calculations. For example:

(i) 6.9 × 8.7 − 4.2 × 5.3 is entered as 6.9 × 8.7 − (4.2 × 5.3) = . The display is 37.77.

(ii) $\dfrac{6{\cdot}4}{6.9 \times 8.7 - 4.2 \times 5.3.}$ To calculate this fraction, note that we need the reciprocal of the answer in (i) × 6.4. So we key in 6.9 × 8.7 − (4.2 × 5.3) = $1/x$ × 6.4 = . The display is 1.694466508 − 01, which is 0.169 to three decimal places.

Further details of calculators are outside the scope of this book and must be obtained from specialist works.

Significant Figures

Since the electronic calculator described has a 10 digit capability, calculations can be performed to this number of significant figures. The real significance, of course, cannot be greater than that of the original data used in the calculation. Hence the final answer must be rounded off to that number of significant figures in agreement with the data.

The slide rule is an analogue device—numbers represented by distances along the rule—and its accuracy is limited to the ability to read lengths accurately. Typically this might be 1 mm in 25 cm or one part in 250. This limits the slide rule accuracy to the third significant figure in most cases and in a long calculation the cumulative errors will make it worse than this. With the electronic calculator, however, one is working digitally to so many significant figures, that one avoids cumulative errors. The calculator is quick and easy to use, and is recommended for awkward or difficult calculations.

EXERCISES 2

Indices

(1) Simplify the following using only positive indices in your answers:

(i) $a^9 \times a^4$ (ii) $b^9 \div b^4$ (iii) $c^9 \times c^{-4}$ (iv) $(d^9)^4$ (v) $(e^4)^9$

(vi) $(f^{-5})^{-2}$ (vii) $\sqrt{\dfrac{1}{g^{-2}}}$ (viii) $(h^{3/2})^{-2}$ (ix) $i^{3/4} \times i^{2/3}$ (x) $j^{3/4} \div j^{2/3}$

(xi) $\left(\dfrac{k^{4/7}}{k^{3/7}}\right)^{-2/3}$ (xii) $(5l^2)^3$ (xiii) $(4m^3n^6)^2 - (2m^2n^4)^3$

(xiv) $p^{17}k \times k^{-1}p^{-17}$ (xv) $10^5 \times 10^7$ (xvi) $10^{12} \times 10^{-3}$

(xvii) $10^{-27} \div 10^5$

(2) Express the following without using fractional indices (e.g. $x^{2/5} = \sqrt[5]{x^2}$). Use only positive indices in your answers.

(i) $a^{2/5}$ (ii) $\dfrac{1}{l^{1/2}}$ (iii) $2\pi\left(\dfrac{l}{g}\right)^{1/2}$ (iv) $(8m)^{2/3}$ (v) $64p^{5/6}$ (vi) $(64p)^{5/6}$

(vii) $z^{-2/3}$ (viii) $\dfrac{1}{y^{-3/4}}$

(3) Express the following using only positive fractional indices:

(i) $\sqrt{4x}$ (ii) $\sqrt[3]{p^4}$ (iii) $\sqrt[5]{k^{-8}}$ (iv) $\sqrt{9/a}$ (v) $\dfrac{1}{\sqrt[7]{q^9}}$ (vi) $\sqrt[8]{p^{-4}}$

(vii) $\sqrt[4]{v^{-8}}$ (viii) $\sqrt[3]{\dfrac{27}{64x^9}}$.

Binomial Theorem

(4) Evaluate without using tables:

(i) $(1.003)^5$ [regard it as $(1 + 0.003)^5$] (ii) $\sqrt{1.003}$, (iii) $\sqrt[3]{1.003}$

(iv) $\dfrac{1}{\sqrt{1.003}}$ (v) $\dfrac{1}{1.001}$ (vi) $\dfrac{2}{2.01}$ (vii) $\dfrac{1}{0.998}$ (viii) $\dfrac{4}{3.996}$

(ix) $(0.997)^5$ (x) $\sqrt[3]{0.998}$ (xi) $(1 + 0.006)(1 - 0.01)$ (xii) 0.995×1.003

(xiii) $\dfrac{0.995}{1.003}$ (xiv) $\dfrac{1}{0.997 \times 0.996}$

(5) An oil has density 800 kg m^{-3} at 15°C and a cubical expansivity of 9×10^{-4} K^{-1}. What will be its density at 5°C?

(6) A brass scale calibrated at 15°C was used to measure a length at 25°C. The reading taken was 755.50 mm. What was the true length? The linear expansivity of brass = 1.89×10^{-5} K^{-1}.

(7) The height of a mercury barometer read with a steel scale is 754.0 mm at 20°C. What will it read at 0°C? (Linear expansivity of steel 0.000 012 K^{-1}, expansivity of mercury 0.000 182 K^{-1}) (*O. & C.*) [*Hint.* $h_0\rho_0 = h_t\rho_t$, or $h_0 = h_t\rho_t/\rho_0$.]

(8) A mercury barometer with a brass scale reads 765.30 mm at 20°C. What would the reading be at 0°C, the atmospheric pressure remaining the same? (Cubical expansivity of mercury = 0.000 181 K^{-1}, linear expansivity of brass = 0.000 019 K^{-1}) (*L.*)

(9) A 'seconds pendulum' designed for use at 15°C has a steel bob supported by a very fine steel wire. What will be the periodic time at 0°C and at 30°C? (Linear expansivity of steel = 0.000 012 K^{-1}. A 'seconds pendulum' has a periodic time of exactly two seconds.)

(10) The height of the mercury column in a barometer provided with a brass scale correct at 0°C is observed to be 749.0 mm on an occasion when the temperature is 15°C. Find (*a*) the true height of the column at 15°C, (*b*) the height of a column of mercury at 0°C which would exert an equal pressure. Assume that the volume expansivities of brass and of mercury are respectively 0.000 054 and 0.000 181 K^{-1}.

Surds

(11) Given that $\sqrt{2} = 1.414$ and $\sqrt{3} = 1.732$ find the values of the following *mentally*, writing down only the answers:

(i) $\dfrac{1}{\sqrt{2}}$ (ii) $\dfrac{2}{\sqrt{2}}$ (iii) $\dfrac{3}{\sqrt{3}}$ (iv) $\dfrac{6}{\sqrt{2}}$ (v) $\dfrac{6}{\sqrt{3}}$ (vi) $\dfrac{10}{\sqrt{3}}$

(12) Given that $\sqrt{2} = 1.414$ and $\sqrt{3} = 1.732$ rationalize the following and evaluate (without using tables):

(i) $\dfrac{2.5}{\sqrt{2}}$ (ii) $\dfrac{1}{\sqrt{2}} + \dfrac{1}{\sqrt{3}}$ (iii) $\dfrac{10.1}{\sqrt{3}}$ (iv) $\dfrac{1}{\sqrt{2}} - \dfrac{1}{\sqrt{3}}$ (v) $\left(\dfrac{4}{3}\right)^{3/2}$

(vi) $\sqrt{12}$ (vii) $\sqrt{8}$ (viii) $\dfrac{1}{\sqrt{12}}$ (ix) $\dfrac{1}{\sqrt{8}}$ (x) $\dfrac{1}{\sqrt{18}}$

(xi) $\dfrac{1}{\sqrt{27}}$ (xii) $\sqrt{48} + \sqrt{162}$

Dimensions

(13) Write down the dimensions of the following (omit any with which you are unfamiliar):
(i) Momentum, (ii) kinetic energy, (iii) potential energy, (iv) surface tension, (v) Young's modulus, (vi) frequency, (vii) pressure, (viii) moment of inertia.

(14) Assuming that the velocity of sea-waves (v) depends only on the wave-length (λ), the density of the water (d) and the acceleration of free fall (g), show that $v = k\sqrt{g\lambda}$ where k is a constant.

(15) Assuming that the periodic time (t) of a very light spring depends only on the load in kg (m) which is oscillating, the acceleration of free fall (g) and the spring constant (k)—i.e. the load per metre in kg m^{-1} needed to cause a static extension—show that $t \propto \sqrt{m/kg}$.

(16) Show that the dimensions of the coefficient of viscosity, η, are $[ML^{-1}T^{-1}]$; use this fact in the following deductions:

(i) Assuming that the terminal velocity (v) of a sphere of radius (r) depends only on a force (F) known as the 'viscous drag', the coefficient of viscosity (η), and r, show that $F \propto \eta rv$ (*Stokes's law*).

(ii) Assuming that the volume of liquid (V) delivered per second by a capillary tube depends only on its radius (r), the coefficient of viscosity (η) of the liquid, and the pressure gradient along the tube (p), show that $V \propto pr^4/\eta$.

(17) What is meant by the dimensions of a physical quantity? Explain, with examples, how the method of dimensions can be used to test the validity of an equation.

Find how the period of vibration of a drop of liquid depends upon the radius, the density, and the surface tension, assuming that no other quantities are involved. (*C.*)

Technique of Calculation

[*Preserve the solutions to this Exercise for use below* (*see* Qn. **26**).

(18) Using square-root tables evaluate:

(i) $\sqrt{291.3}$ (ii) $\sqrt{0.002\,913}$ (iii) $\sqrt{0.000\,2913}$ (iv) $\sqrt{21 \times 10^5}$
(v) $\sqrt{6.8 \times 10^{-3}}$ (vi) $\sqrt{0.000\,112}$

(19) Using reciprocal-tables evaluate the reciprocals of the following:

(i) 35 (ii) 0.0075 (iii) 1.27 (iv) 3.2×10^{-2} (v) 15 550
(vi) 5×10^{-8} (vii) 0.6714 (viii) 21.25 (ix) 17.5 (x) 11.3
(xi) 8.4

(20) Using logarithms evaluate:

(i) $\sqrt[3]{20}$ (ii) $\sqrt[3]{2}$ (iii) $\sqrt[3]{0.02}$ (iv) $\sqrt[4]{29}$ (v) $\sqrt[4]{0.29}$

(21) Evaluate the following (*a*) very approximately using mental arithmetic, (*b*) carefully, using appropriate tables:

(i) $29.62 \times 0.008\,31$ (ii) $0.2962 \div 0.0831$ (iii) $\dfrac{16\pi}{3.85} - \dfrac{12.6}{900}$

(iv) $\dfrac{892.7 \div 68.1}{\pi(0.137)^2 \times 8.2}$ (v) $2\pi\sqrt{\dfrac{123}{981}}$ (vi) $\dfrac{23.1^2 - 6.2^2}{2 \times 23.1}$

(22) If $g = \dfrac{4\pi^2(M + S/3)}{kT^2}$ calculate the value of g when $M = 0.4335$, $S = 0.004$, $k = 1.46$ and $T = 1.09$.

(23) Calculate the value of $\dfrac{52.25}{47.75} \times 2.00 \times \dfrac{\pi \times (0.0345)^2}{168.5}$.

(24) Calculate the value of $87.78\left(\dfrac{7.7^2}{3} + \dfrac{0.5^2}{4}\right)$.

(25) Evaluate

(i) ln 2 (ii) ln 20 (iii) ln e (iv) ln 10 (v) ln 23.78 (vi) ln 0.0341
(vii) ln 527.2 (viii) ln (10^8) (ix) ln 9.5 (x) ln 0.01

Use of the Calculator:

(26) Using a calculator perform the calculations set in examples 18, 19, 21, 22, 23 above and check your answers with those obtained using tables.

(27) The following table of values was obtained in an experiment on (i) a carbon filament lamp, (ii) a tungsten filament lamp. Complete the table.

I (A)	0.44	.40	.355	.32	.282	.239	.21	.17	.14	Carbon
V (V)	236	219	203	187	175	152	139	121	106	
V/I (Ω)										
I (A)	0.24	.23	.22	.21	.20	.185	.175	.165	.15	Tungsten
V (V)	225	210	191	172	162	147	135	117	100	
V/I (Ω)										

[Preserve the completed table for use in Qn. 8, on p. 65.]

(28) The following table shows the results of an experiment designed to verify the maximum power theorem. Complete the table.

Resistance R (Ω)	0	5	10	20	30	40	45	50	55	60	70	80	90
Current I (mA)	48.5	42.3	40.9	35.5	31.3	28.1	26.7	25.4	24.2	23.1	21.3	19.7	18.5
I^2R (W)													

[Preserve the completed table for use in Qn. 9, on p. 65.]

Theory of Logarithms

(29) Write down the logs to the base 2 of:

(i) 4 (ii) 8 (iii) 64 (iv) 0.5 (v) 0.25

(30) Write down the logs to the base 3 of:

(i) 81 (ii) $\sqrt{3}$ (iii) $\frac{1}{9}$ (iv) 0.577 (v) $\dfrac{1}{\sqrt[4]{3}}$

(31) Write down the logs to the base 5 of:
(i) 25 (ii) 0.2 (iii) 125 (iv) $\frac{1}{25}$ (v) 0.0016

(32) Evaluate:

(i) $\log_3 27$ (ii) $\log_4 16$ (iii) $\log_4 0.25$ (iv) $\log_2 32$ (v) $\log_7 49$
(vi) $\log_2 0.25$ (vii) $\log_{1.2} 1.2$ (viii) $\log_2 1.414$.

(33) If $\log_{10} 2 = 0.301$ and $\log_{10} 3 = 0.477$ evaluate (without using tables):
(i) $\log_{10} 6$ (ii) $\log_{10} 12$ (iii) $\log_{10} 9$ (iv) $\log_{10} \frac{2}{3}$ (v) $\log_{10} 1.5$
(vi) $\log_{10} 36$ (vii) $\log_{10} 0.5$ (viii) $\log_{10} \frac{1}{6}$ (ix) $\log_{10} 0.25$ (x) $\log_{10} 0.75$

(34) Express in the simplest form:
(i) $\log_{10} 7 - \log_{10} \frac{7}{3} - \log_{10} 3$
(ii) $\log_5 7 - \log_5 \frac{7}{3} - \log_5 3$
(iii) $\log_8 45 - 2 \log_8 5$
(iv) $3 \log_4 2 - \log_4 4 + 2 \log_4 3 - \log_4 18$
(v) $5 \ln 2 + \frac{1}{2} \ln 25 - 2 \ln 20$
(vi) $\ln e + 2 \ln e + 3 \ln e$
(vii) $2 \log_5 x - \log_5 x^3$
(viii) $3 \log_7 (x - 1) - \log_7 (x^2 - 2x + 1)$
(ix) $\log_{12} 144 - \log_3 81 + \log_2 4$
(x) $5 \log_x y - 2 \log_x (2y) + 3 \log_x \left(\frac{1}{y}\right)$

Logarithmic Series

(35) Write down the first four terms of the following series and state the conditions of validity where appropriate.
(i) $\ln (1 + 3x)$ (ii) $\ln (1 - 2x)$ (iii) $\ln (1 - 0.5x)$ (iv) $\ln 1.1$
(v) $\ln \left(1 + \frac{x}{3}\right)$ (vi) $\ln 0.9$ (vii) $\ln (1 + 0.2x)$ (viii) $\ln 4$

(36) Evaluate $\log_{10} 4$ to three places of decimals.

(37) Given that $\log_e 2 = 0.6931$ and $\log_e 10 = 2.3026$ without further use of tables find the values of $\log_e 100$ and $\log_e 50$.

Using the above and the expansion of $\log_e (1 + x)$. When $x = -\frac{1}{50}$ calculate to four significant figures the value of $\log_e 7$. (*O.*)

Answers

1. (i) a^{13} (ii) b^5 (iii) c^5 (iv) d^{36}
(v) e^{36} (vi) f^{10} (vii) g (viii) $\frac{1}{h^3}$
(ix) $i^{\frac{17}{12}}$ (x) $j^{\frac{1}{12}}$ (xi) $\frac{1}{k^{\frac{2}{21}}}$ (xii) $25l^6$
(xiii) $8m^6n^{12}$ (xiv) 1 (xv) 10^{12} (xvi) 10^9
(xvii) $\frac{1}{10^{32}}$

2. (i) $\sqrt[5]{a^2}$ (ii) $\frac{1}{\sqrt{l}}$ (iii) $2\pi\sqrt{\frac{l}{g}}$ (iv) $4\sqrt[3]{m^2}$
(v) $64\sqrt[6]{p^5}$ (vi) $32\sqrt[6]{p^5}$ (vii) $\frac{1}{\sqrt[3]{z^2}}$ (viii) $\sqrt[4]{y^3}$

3. (i) $2x^{\frac{1}{2}}$ (ii) $p^{\frac{4}{3}}$ (iii) $\frac{1}{k^{\frac{8}{5}}}$ (iv) $\frac{3}{a^{\frac{1}{2}}}$
(v) $\frac{1}{q^{\frac{9}{7}}}$ (vi) $\frac{1}{p^{\frac{1}{2}}}$ (vii) $\frac{1}{v^2}$ (viii) $\frac{3}{4x^3}$

4. (i) 1.015 (ii) 1.0015 (iii) 1.001 (iv) 0.9985
(v) 0.999 (vi) 0.995 (vii) 1.002 (viii) 1.001
(ix) 0.985 (x) 0.9993 (xi) 0.996 (xii) 0.998
(xiii) 0.992 (xiv) 1.007

5. 807 kg m^{-3} 6. 755.64 mm 7. 751.4 mm 8. 762.8 mm

9. 1.999 82 s at 0°C and 2.000 18 s at 30°C

10. (*a*) 749.2 mm, (*b*) 747.2 mm

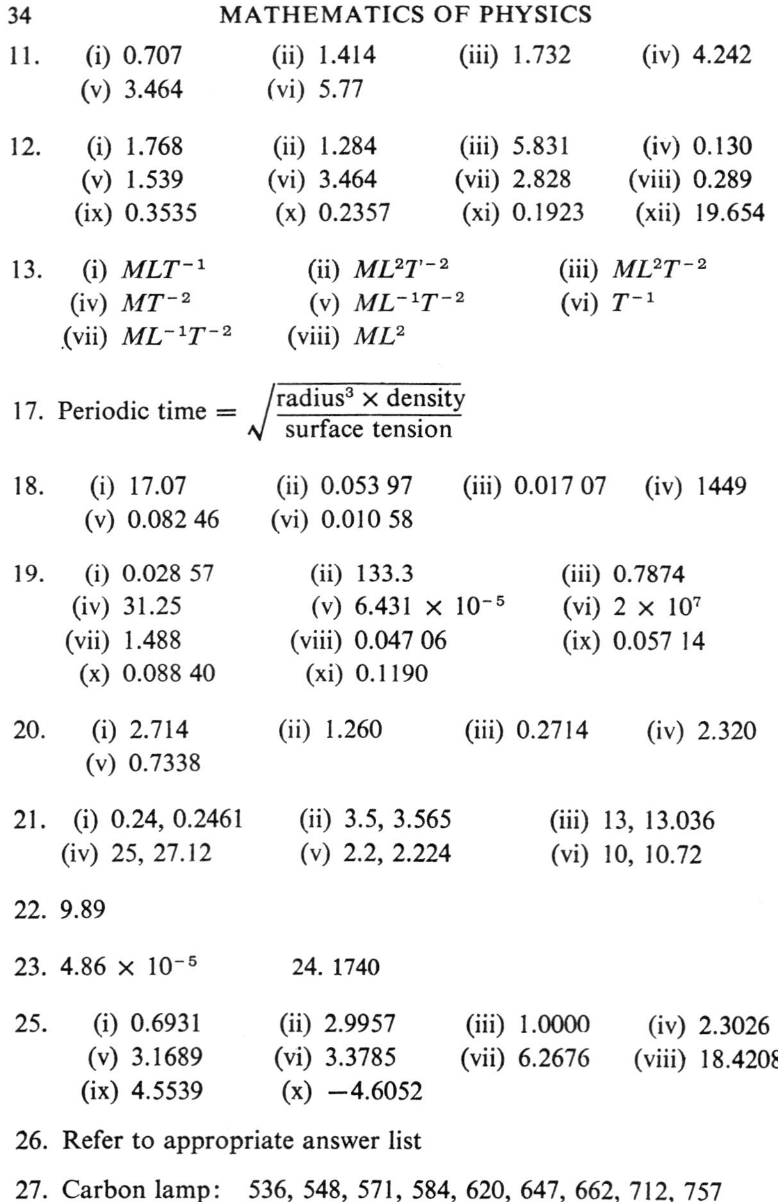

11. (i) 0.707 (ii) 1.414 (iii) 1.732 (iv) 4.242
(v) 3.464 (vi) 5.77

12. (i) 1.768 (ii) 1.284 (iii) 5.831 (iv) 0.130
(v) 1.539 (vi) 3.464 (vii) 2.828 (viii) 0.289
(ix) 0.3535 (x) 0.2357 (xi) 0.1923 (xii) 19.654

13. (i) MLT^{-1} (ii) ML^2T^{-2} (iii) ML^2T^{-2}
(iv) MT^{-2} (v) $ML^{-1}T^{-2}$ (vi) T^{-1}
(vii) $ML^{-1}T^{-2}$ (viii) ML^2

17. Periodic time $= \sqrt{\dfrac{\text{radius}^3 \times \text{density}}{\text{surface tension}}}$

18. (i) 17.07 (ii) 0.053 97 (iii) 0.017 07 (iv) 1449
(v) 0.082 46 (vi) 0.010 58

19. (i) 0.028 57 (ii) 133.3 (iii) 0.7874
(iv) 31.25 (v) 6.431×10^{-5} (vi) 2×10^7
(vii) 1.488 (viii) 0.047 06 (ix) 0.057 14
(x) 0.088 40 (xi) 0.1190

20. (i) 2.714 (ii) 1.260 (iii) 0.2714 (iv) 2.320
(v) 0.7338

21. (i) 0.24, 0.2461 (ii) 3.5, 3.565 (iii) 13, 13.036
(iv) 25, 27.12 (v) 2.2, 2.224 (vi) 10, 10.72

22. 9.89

23. 4.86×10^{-5} 24. 1740

25. (i) 0.6931 (ii) 2.9957 (iii) 1.0000 (iv) 2.3026
(v) 3.1689 (vi) 3.3785 (vii) 6.2676 (viii) 18.4208
(ix) 4.5539 (x) −4.6052

26. Refer to appropriate answer list

27. Carbon lamp: 536, 548, 571, 584, 620, 647, 662, 712, 757
Tungsten lamp: 938, 914, 869, 820, 810, 795, 772, 709, 668

28. Values of I^2R (all times 10^{-2}) 0, 0.895, 1.67, 2.52, 2.94, 3.16, 3.21, 3.23, 3.22, 3.18, 3.18, 3.10, 3.08

29. (i) 2 (ii) 3 (iii) 6 (iv) -1
(v) -2

30. (i) 4 (ii) 0.5 (iii) -2 (iv) -0.5
(v) -0.25

31. (i) 2 (ii) -1 (iii) 3 (iv) -2
(v) -4

32. (i) 3 (ii) 2 (iii) -1 (iv) 5
(v) 2 (vi) -2 (vii) 1 (viii) 0.5

33. (i) 0.778 (ii) 1.079 (iii) 0.954 (iv) $\bar{1}.824$
(v) 0.176 (vi) 1.556 (vii) $\bar{1}.699$ (viii) $\bar{1}.222$
(ix) $\bar{1}.398$ (x) $\bar{1}.875$

34. (i) 0 (ii) 0 (iii) $\log_8(\frac{9}{5})$
(iv) 0 (v) $\ln 0.4$ (vi) 6
(vii) $-\log_5 x$ (viii) $\log_7(x-1)$ (ix) 0
(x) $\log_x 0.25$

35. (i) $3x - \dfrac{9x^2}{2} + 9x^3 - \dfrac{81}{4}x^4;\ -\frac{1}{3} < x \leqslant +\frac{1}{3}$

(ii) $-2x - 2x^2 - \dfrac{8x^3}{3} - 4x^4;\ -\frac{1}{2} \leqslant x < +\frac{1}{2}$

(iii) $-\dfrac{x}{2} - \dfrac{x^2}{8} - \dfrac{x^3}{24} - \dfrac{x^4}{64};\ -2 \leqslant x < +2$

(iv) $0.1 - 0.005 + 0.000\dot{3} - 0.000\,025$

(v) $\dfrac{x}{3} - \dfrac{x^2}{18} + \dfrac{x^3}{81} - \dfrac{x^4}{324};\ -3 < x \leqslant +3$

(vi) $-0.1 - 0.005 - 0.000\dot{3} - 0.000\,025$

(vii) $\dfrac{x}{5} - \dfrac{x^2}{50} + \dfrac{x^3}{375} - \dfrac{x^4}{2500};\ -4 \leqslant x < 4$

(viii) $\dfrac{6}{5} + \dfrac{18}{125} + \dfrac{486}{15\,625} + \dfrac{4374}{78\,125}$

36. 0.6021

37. 4.6052, 3.9121; 1.9459_5

3. Formulae and Equations

Quantities are of two types—constants and variables. The value of a variable is dependent on the values of the other quantities affecting it, one at least (often more) of these quantities being variable.

For instance $$T = 2\pi\sqrt{\frac{l}{g}}.$$

The connection between the quantities involved is expressed by an equation, such as that given above, and because an equation is a statement it is a grammatical sentence, having a subject, a verb and an object. It is called an equation because the verb is always 'equals'. To save space and to enable mathematical processes to be applied to it this sentence is usually written in 'shorthand', i.e. in algebraic symbols.

If in an equation a single variable is isolated on the left-hand side (l.h.s.), as is the case above, this variable will naturally be the subject. The object is the right-hand side (r.h.s.). In such a case the equation is known as 'a formula' for the quantity on the l.h.s. Thus the subject of the above equation is T, and a formula for T is

$$T = 2\pi\sqrt{\frac{l}{g}}.$$

The quantity, T, is also known as the 'dependent variable' in the above equation because its value depends on those substituted in the r.h.s.

Sometimes an equation is not given in the most convenient form for our purposes and it is necessary to rearrange it, i.e. we may require a formula for one of the other variables involved. The process of rearrangement is known as the 'transformation of the formula' and the important processes by which it can be effected are as follows:

1. (i) Add the same quantity to both sides.
   (ii) Subtract the same quantity from both sides.

These two rules are often summarised in the rule: 'A quantity may be transferred from one side of an equation to another provided the sign of that quantity is changed."

Thus if $y = x + a$, then $y - a = x + a - a$;

hence $y - a = x$,

i.e. subtracting a from both sides is equivalent to transferring it from r.h.s. to l.h.s. and changing its sign.

Be careful to transfer whole terms and not parts of them when applying this method, i.e. always relate what you do to the fundamental rules (i) and (ii) above.

For example if $y = \sqrt{x + a}$

$y - \sqrt{a}$ DOES NOT equal $\sqrt{x}$.

2. (i) Multiply each term in an equation by the same quantity.
   (ii) Divide each term in an equation by the same quantity.

Thus if $y = x - \frac{a}{2}$, then $2y = 2x - a$.

Similarly if $\frac{A}{B} = \frac{C}{D} + E$, the *correct procedure* is to multiply through out by the L.C.M. of the denominators, i.e. BD. This leads to

$$AD = CB + BDE.$$

The student is warned about the dangers of 'cross-multiplying'. The process is a shortened version of rules (i) and (ii) given above, but unless applied with great discrimination leads to unsound mathematics and wrong answers. In the expression

$$\frac{A}{B} = \frac{C}{D},$$

multiplying throughout by BD leads to the expression

$$AD = BC$$

in which the denominators have crossed the equals sign and entered the numerators of the opposite sides. Applied to such expressions this is a quick way of obtaining the necessary result. But if applied to an expression such as

$$\frac{A}{B} = \frac{C}{D} + E,$$

it will lead to the wrong result unless the r.h.s. is given a common denominator first. Thus

$$\frac{A}{B} = \frac{C + DE}{D}.$$

Hence $AD = BC + BDE.$

(It is not unusual to find students applying cross-multiplication to the original expression and obtaining $AD = BC + BE$, which is of course incorrect.)

3. Raise both sides to the same power, e.g. square both sides, cube both sides, etc.

Thus since
$$T = 2\pi\sqrt{\frac{l}{g}}$$
$$T^2 = 4\pi^2 \cdot \frac{l}{g}$$
$$\therefore \quad g = \frac{4\pi^2 l}{T^2}.$$

EXAMPLES

1. If $y = mx + c$ find an expression for m.
$$y = mx + c.$$
$$\therefore \quad y - c = mx.$$
$$\therefore \quad \frac{y - c}{x} = m.$$
Hence
$$m = \frac{y - c}{x}.$$

2. Make S the subject of the formula $T = 2\pi\sqrt{\frac{M + S/3}{kg}}$.
$$T = 2\pi\sqrt{\frac{M + S/3}{kg}}.$$
Squaring both sides we obtain
$$T^2 = 4\pi^2\left(\frac{M + S/3}{kg}\right).$$
Multiplying both sides by $\frac{kg}{4\pi^2}$ we obtain
$$T^2 \cdot \frac{kg}{4\pi^2} = M + S/3$$
$$\therefore \quad T^2\frac{kg}{4\pi^2} - M = S/3$$
$$\therefore \quad S = 3\left(\frac{T^2 kg}{4\pi^2} - M\right).$$

3. The formula for the periodic time (T) of a simple pendulum of length l in m is $2\pi\sqrt{\frac{l}{9.81}}$ s. What is the length of a pendulum which has a periodic time of 2 s?

$$T = 2\pi\sqrt{\frac{l}{9.81}}$$

$$\therefore \quad T^2 = 4\pi^2 \cdot \frac{l}{9.81}$$

$$\therefore \quad l = \frac{9.81\, T^2}{4\pi^2}$$

Substituting the given values we obtain

$$l = \frac{9.81 \times 4}{4\pi^2} = \frac{9.81}{\pi^2} = 0.993 \text{ m}$$

SOLUTION OF EQUATIONS

Linear Equations Involving only One Variable

In linear equations the variable only occurs raised to unit power (i.e. there are no terms involving it squared, cubed, square-rooted and so on).

The method of solution consists in isolating the variable on the l.h.s. so that only constants appear on the r.h.s. This is done by applying the rules for transforming formulae given on pp. 36–37.

EXAMPLES

1. Solve $2x - 3 = 5(7 - 2x) - 2.$

$$2x - 3 = 5(7 - 2x) - 2$$

$$\therefore \quad 2x - 3 = 35 - 10x - 2$$

$$\therefore \quad 2x + 10x = 33 + 3$$

$$\therefore \quad 12x = 36$$

$$\therefore \quad x = 3.$$

2. 10 g of dried ice at 0°C are added to 50 g of water at 20°C contained in a vessel of heat capacity 40 J K^{-1}. Calculate the final temperature given that the specific heat capacity of water is 4200 J kg^{-1} K^{-1} and the specific latent heat of ice is 336 000 J kg^{-1}.

Let θ be the temperature of the mixture at the end of the process. Then:

(i) energy absorbed by 10 g of ice melting = 0.010 × 336 000 J, (ii) energy absorbed by 10 g of water so formed in warming from 0°C to θ

$$= 0.010 \times 4200 \times \theta \text{ J}.$$

Hence total energy absorbed is $0.010 \times 336\,000 + 0.010 \times 4200 \times \theta$.

i.e. $$3360 + 42\theta \text{ J}$$

The energy given out is:

(i) by the vessel cooling from 20°C to $\theta = 40(20 - \theta)$, (ii) by the water cooling from 20°C to $\theta = 0.050 \times 4200(20 - \theta)$.

Hence total energy given out $= 40(20 - \theta) + 0.050 \times 4200(20 - \theta)$

i.e. $250(20 - \theta)$ J.

Since total energy absorbed must equal total energy emitted,

$$3360 + 42\theta = 250(20 - \theta)$$
$$= 5000 - 250\theta$$
$$\therefore \quad 292\theta = 1640$$
$$\therefore \quad \theta = \frac{1640}{292}$$
$$= 5.6°\text{C}.$$

3. Find the position and nature of the image formed by a diverging lens of focal length 10 cm of an object 30 cm away.

If the 'real is positive' sign convention is used (refer to a text-book on Optics if this is not understood) the equation which applies is

$$\frac{1}{v} + \frac{1}{u} = \frac{1}{f}$$

where v, u and f have the usual significance.

In this case v is required (and it is therefore left as the unknown variable and allocated no sign. The sign will appear as a result of the calculation and will give the nature of the image)

$u = +30$ cm (object is real)

$f = -10$ cm (diverging lenses have negative focal lengths).

As all quantities are in cm it is not necessary to convert to metre (the conversion factor would 'cancel out'). But if the student is ever in any doubt the full conversion to SI should be made. In this case, of course, the answer resulting would then be in metres.

Substituting:

$$\frac{1}{v} + \frac{1}{+30} = \frac{1}{-10}$$
$$\therefore \quad \frac{1}{v} + \frac{1}{30} = -\frac{1}{10}$$
$$\therefore \quad \frac{1}{v} = -\frac{1}{10} - \frac{1}{30} = \frac{-3 - 1}{30} = -\frac{4}{30}$$
$$\therefore \quad \frac{v}{1} = -\frac{30}{4}, \quad \text{or} \quad v = -7.5 \text{ cm}$$

Hence the image is virtual and is 7.5 cm from the lens.

Quadratic Equations

A quadratic equation always includes a term involving the square of the variable and usually also contains a term involving the variable raised to the first power as well as a constant term. The general equation of the quadratic therefore becomes

$$ax^2 + bx + c = 0.$$

The solution to this is $x = \dfrac{-b \pm \sqrt{b^2 - 4ac}}{2a}$.

If $b^2 - 4ac$ is negative the equation has no real solutions.

If no simpler method presents itself this formula for x must be used to solve a quadratic, but often the l.h.s. will factorize and lead to a quick method of solution. Thus we should not apply the formula to the equation $2x^2 + 5x - 3 = 0$ as it factorises to $(2x - 1)(x + 3) = 0$; this solves to give $x = +\frac{1}{2}$ or -3.

In Physics we sometimes find cases in which only one of the two roots of the relevant quadratic has any real significance, and as always, the answer should be carefully related to the Physics of the problem. The worked example on page 42 illustrates this point.

Applications of Quadratics to Optics

Two points are important here:

(i) If the variable is the distance of the object from the lens or mirror the two solutions are often the object distance and the corresponding image distance. This is to be expected as by the principle of conjugate foci the object and image positions are interchangeable. This only applies when both object and image are real as otherwise a sign change comes in and the result then gives the required answer as one root, and the answer for a virtual object as the other root.

(ii) The relevant equation can often be obtained more rapidly (and with less chance of error) by applying Newton's formula. This states that if the distances of the object and image from the first and second principal foci respectively are x and y, then

$$xy = f^2,$$

where f is the focal length. The magnification is given by

$$m = \frac{y}{f} = \frac{f}{x}.$$

It is often found that the use of one of these expressions leads more rapidly to a solution than the use of the better known relationships involving u and v. When values for x and/or y have been obtained it is necessary to remember that these are not distances from the lens but from the appropriate foci.

EXAMPLES

1. A camera lens must be moved 2 mm when changing focus from 'infinity' to 1.2 m. What is the focal length of the lens in mm?

Let the focal length of the lens be f (in mm). When focussed for infinity the film is f from the lens. When focused for 1.2 m the film must be slightly farther from the lens because as the object moves towards the lens the image moves away. Thus when the object is at 1.2 m the image is at $(f + 2)$ mm. [If an error were made at this stage and the image distance given as the value $(f - 2)$, the derived equation would have no real roots and the student would thus know that an error had been made.]

Hence, using the 'real is positive' sign convention, we obtain when substituting in $\frac{1}{v} + \frac{1}{u} = \frac{1}{f}$,

$$\frac{1}{f+2} + \frac{1}{1200} = \frac{1}{f}$$

$$\therefore \quad 1200f + f(f + 2) = 1200(f + 2)$$

$$\therefore \quad 1200f + f^2 + 2f = 1200f + 2400$$

$$\therefore \quad f^2 + 2f - 2400 = 0$$

$$\therefore \quad (f + 50)(f - 48) = 0$$

and $$f = -50 \text{ or } +48.$$

Now if the first solution were valid the lens would be diverging and could not produce a real image of a real object, i.e. it could not be a camera lens. This solution is therefore rejected and the value of +48 mm for the focal length is accepted.

An alternative method of solution using Newton's equation is as follows: When the object is at 1200 mm the image is 2 mm from the second principal focus.

$\therefore$ when $$x = (1200 - f), \quad y = 2$$

Substituting in $$xy = f^2 \text{ we obtain}$$

$$(1200 - f) \times 2 = f^2$$

$$\therefore \quad f^2 + 2f - 2400 = 0$$

This is the same equation as that obtained above but is reached more quickly.

2. A converging lens of focal length 10 cm produces a real image 45 cm from the object. How far is the lens from the object?

With the usual symbolism $v = 45 - u$ and thus

$$\frac{1}{(45 - u)} + \frac{1}{u} = \frac{1}{10}$$

$$\therefore \quad 10u + 450 - 10u = 45u - u^2$$

$$\therefore \quad u^2 - 45u + 450 = 0$$

$$\therefore \quad (u - 30)(u - 15) = 0$$

$$\therefore \quad u = +30 \quad \text{or} \quad +15 \text{ cm}$$

If Newton's equation is used

$$xy = f^2 = 100$$

and $$x + y + 20 = 45$$

i.e. $$x + y = 25$$

$$\therefore \quad x(25 - x) = 100$$

$$\therefore \quad x^2 - 25x + 100 = 0$$

$$(x - 5)(x - 20) = 0$$

and $$x = +5 \quad \text{or} \quad +20 \text{ cm}$$

Hence $$u = 15 \quad \text{or} \quad 30 \text{ cm}$$

Simultaneous Equations

If two variables in a given equation are unknown, no solution is possible, but if a second independent equation involving the two variables can be formed from the data, the value of each unknown can be found. Such a pair of equations is called a pair of 'simultaneous equations'. If three unknowns appear, three equations are in general needed for a solution, and so on. The method of solution consists of manipulating the equations so as to obtain one equation involving only one of the unknowns—a process known as 'elimination'. The most *direct* method is that of substitution from one equation to the other, as in Example 1, part (i), below. Another common way is that given in Example 1, part (ii), below. Other shorter ways can often be found in individual cases and much of the interest in mathematics lies in 'spotting' these quick methods.

EXAMPLES

1. Solve

$$3x + 2y = 13 \quad \ldots \quad (1)$$

$$6x - y = 16 \quad \ldots \quad (2)$$

Method (i): From (2) $y = 6x - 16$. Substitute this value in (1).

Then $$3x + 2(6x - 16) = 13$$

$$\therefore \quad 3x + 12x - 32 = 13.$$

Whence $$x = 3.$$

Substituting this value for x in $y = 6x - 16$ we have

$$y = 18 - 16 = 2.$$

Answer: $x = 3, \quad y = 2.$

Method (ii): Multiplying equation (2) by 2 we obtain

$$12x - 2y = 32 \quad \ldots \quad (2)$$

Also, $$3x + 2y = 13 \quad \ldots \quad (1)$$

Adding (1) and (2),

we obtain $$15x = 45,$$

i.e. $$x = 3.$$

Substitute $x = 3$ in equation (2) to obtain $y = 2$.

2. Find the value of q from the following equations:

$$\begin{cases} 2p + 3q + r = 4 & \quad (1) \\ 3p - 2q - r = 5 & \quad (2) \\ p - 4q + 4r = 18 & \quad (3) \end{cases}$$

As only q is required p and r are eliminated. First r is eliminated between (1) and (2) by addition:

$$5p + q = 9 \quad \text{. . . . . (4)}$$

r is now eliminated between (2) and (3) by multiplying (2) by 4 and adding; thus:

$$\begin{cases} 12p - 8q - 4r = 20 & \quad (2\text{A}) \\ p - 4q + 4r = 18 & \quad (3) \end{cases}$$

Adding. $$13p - 12q = 38 \quad \text{. . . . (5)}$$

Finally p is eliminated between (4) and (5) by multiplying (4) by 13 and (5) by 5 thus:

$$\begin{cases} 13 \times 5p + 13q = 117 & \quad (4\text{A}) \\ 5 \times 13p - 60q = 190 & \quad (5\text{A}) \end{cases}$$

Subtracting, $$73q = -73$$

$$\therefore \quad q = -1.$$

Use of Simultaneous Equations in Physics

The technique discussed briefly above will find application in any problem in which there is more than one unknown. The elimination process to be adopted varies from one problem to another and it is always worth giving careful thought to this matter. In some problems an unknown must be introduced to reach a solution, though in fact the question does not ask for its value (see Example 1 below). In this case it is obviously sensible to eliminate this unknown and retain the quantity required.

EXAMPLES

1. A wire has resistance 0.82 Ω at 14°C and 0.96 Ω at 69°C. Find the temperature coefficient of resistance for the material of the wire.

The relevant equation is

$$R_\theta = R_0(1 + \alpha\theta)$$

where R_θ is the resistance at temperature θ (in °C),
R_0 is the resistance at 0°C.,
and α is the required coefficient.

It should be noticed immediately that the statement involves R_0 which is not given in the question, and this must therefore be introduced as an unknown, though it is not required in the answer. Substituting the two sets of conditions into the equation we have

$$0.82 = R_0(1 + 14\alpha) \quad . \quad . \quad . \quad . \quad (1)$$

and

$$0.96 = R_0(1 + 69\alpha) \quad . \quad . \quad . \quad . \quad (2)$$

R_0 is eliminated by dividing* equation (2) by equation (1) thus:

$$\frac{0.96}{0.82} = \frac{R_0(1 + 69\alpha)}{R_0(1 + 14\alpha)} = \frac{1 + 69\alpha}{1 + 14\alpha}$$

$$\therefore \quad 0.96(1 + 14\alpha) = 0.82(1 + 69\alpha)$$

$$\therefore \quad 0.96 + 13.44\alpha = 0.82 + 56.58\alpha$$

$$\therefore \quad 43.14\alpha = 0.14$$

$$\therefore \quad \alpha = \frac{0.14}{43.14} = 0.000\,32\ \text{K}^{-1}$$

2. The positive pole of a 10 V battery of internal resistance 1 Ω is joined to the negative pole of a 6 V battery of internal resistance 3 Ω. The other two poles are also connected by a wire. The combination so formed is connected to the ends of a 9 Ω wire. What current will flow through this wire?

(This is an example of the application of Kirchhoff's laws, which invariably produce simultaneous equations. If the reader is unfamiliar with these laws he should consult a suitable text-book on Electricity.)

Let the current in the 9 Ω wire be x and that in the 10 V battery y. Assume that the directions are as marked in Fig. 3.1.

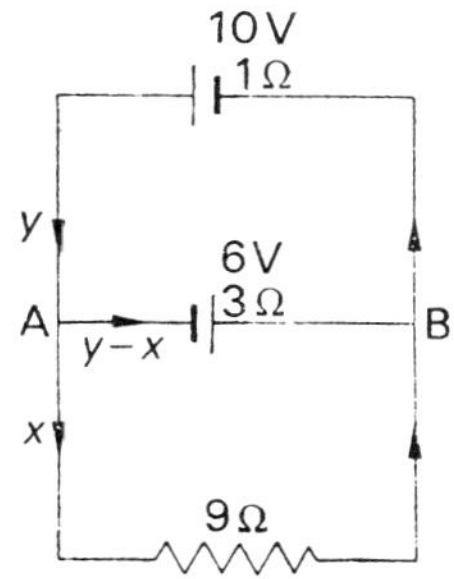

FIG. 3.1 Circuit analysis by Kirchhoff's Laws.

Applying Kirchhoff's first law to the junction A we obtain the current in AB as $(y - x)$.

Now apply the second law to each 'battery and 9 Ω circuit'. The equations obtained are

$$10 = 1 \times y + 9x \quad . \quad . \quad . \quad . \quad . \quad (1)$$

$$6 = 3(y - x) - 9x \quad . \quad . \quad . \quad . \quad (2)$$

---

* Note that R_0 is NOT eliminated by subtracting equation (2) from equation (1).

[The minus sign operates on $9x$ because we have assumed the current in the 6 V battery to be in the opposite direction to that in the 9 Ω wire.]

Simplifying these equations we obtain

$$y + 9x = 10 \quad . \quad . \quad . \quad . \quad . \quad (1)$$

$$3y - 12x = 6 \quad . \quad . \quad . \quad . \quad . \quad (2)$$

Multiplying (1) by 3 we obtain

$$3y + 27x = 30.$$

Subtracting (2) from this gives

$$39x = 24$$

$$\therefore \quad x = \frac{24}{39} = 0.6$$

$$\therefore \quad \text{current is } 0.6 \text{ A}$$

Note that we eliminated y because we did not need its value.

Further Discussion of Solution of Problems by Kirchhoff's Laws

It is generally best to apply the first law when the circuit diagram is being labelled as this reduces the number of equations involved. In the following example the diagram was first drawn (Fig. 3.2), then the main current was marked as x, and the other currents were all then put in, giving them what appeared to be the most likely direction and only introducing a new unknown for current when the first law failed to provide a value in terms of the previously selected unknowns. Thus the current in the 4 Ω arm did not need a new unknown once x and y were chosen, but the junction B did need a new one (z) before the current in BC could be inserted. By working through the diagram in this way the circuit was fully labelled using only three unknowns and thus three independent equations had to be formed by applying the second law (there is no point in applying the first law any more). In forming these equations it is necessary to avoid forming as the third equation one which is deducible from the first two. In the solution given below the second law is applied to circuits ABD, CBD and EABC. Had we used ABD, CBD and ABCD the third equation would not have been independent. It would further not have used all the data (the e.m.f. and internal resistance of the cell would have been omitted) and thus was unlikely to lead to a solution. It is also worth noting that if on solving the equations a current has a negative value, this means that it is flowing in the opposite direction to that marked. It is not necessary therefore to spend time trying to decide the true directions—just insert what *at first glance* seems most probable.

EXAMPLE

ABCD is a Wheatstone's net with the cell, e.m.f. 1.7 V and internal resistance 8 Ω, connected across A and C. The galvanometer is connected across B and D and has resistance 10 Ω. The resistances in AB, AD, BC, DC are respectively 2, 4, 20 and 5 Ω. Find the currents flowing in the cell and in the galvanometer.

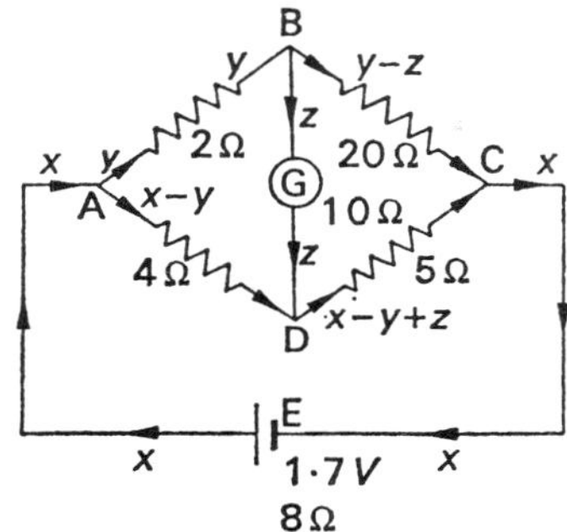

FIG. 3.2 Wheatstone's net.

Applying Kirchhoff's second law to the circuits ABD, CBD and EABC respectively we obtain:

$$\begin{cases} 4(x-y) - 2y - 10z = 0 & \quad (1) \\ 5(x-y+z) + 10z - 20(y-z) = 0 & \quad (2) \\ 8x + 2y + 20(y-z) = 1.7 & \quad (3) \end{cases}$$

These equations simplify to

$$\begin{cases} 4x - 6y - 10z = 0 & \quad (1\text{A}) \\ 5x - 25y + 35z = 0 & \quad (2\text{A}) \\ 8x + 22y - 20z = 1.7 & \quad (3\text{A}) \end{cases}$$

If equation (1A) is multiplied throughout by 2 and subtracted from (3A) the result is $34y = 1.7$. Whence $y = \frac{1}{20}$.

This value is substituted in (1A) and (2A) to give

$$\begin{cases} 4x - \frac{6}{20} - 10z = 0 & \quad (4) \\ 5x - \frac{25}{20} + 35z = 0 & \quad (5) \end{cases}$$

Hence

$$\begin{cases} 40x - 3 - 100z = 0 & \quad (4) \\ 20x - 5 + 140z = 0 & \quad (5) \end{cases}$$

Elimination of x gives $z = \frac{7}{380}$ and substitution of this value in (4) leads to $x = \frac{23}{190}$, i.e. $x = 0.121$ and $z = 0.0184$.

Answer: Currents in the cell and the galvanometer are 0.12 and 0.018 A respectively.

EXERCISES 3

Transformation of Formulae

(1) Make 'x' the subject of the following formulae:

(i) $y = mx + c$ (ii) $y = \sqrt{mx + c}$ (iii) $y = \frac{3}{x} + 5$ (iv) $y = \sqrt{x + 1}$

(v) $y = \frac{1}{x + 1}$ (vi) $y = x^{-1/2}$ (vii) $y = \frac{3}{x} + \frac{1}{2x}$ (viii) $y = 2x^2 - 5$

(ix) $y = \frac{1}{(2x^2 - 5)}$ (x) $y = \frac{1}{\sqrt{x - 2}}$ (xi) $y = \frac{x - 2}{2x}$ (xii) $y = \frac{x - 1}{5x}$

Questions 2–9 introduce well-known equations in Physics; the topic is given in brackets after each one.

(2) Make g the subject of the formula $T = 2\pi\sqrt{\frac{I}{mgh}}$.

(Periodic time of a compound pendulum.)

(3) Make k the subject of the formula $T = 2\pi\sqrt{\frac{h^2 + k^2}{gh}}$.

(Periodic time of a compound pendulum.)

(4) Make h the subject of the formula $\gamma = \frac{r}{2} \cdot \rho g \cdot \left(h + \frac{r}{3}\right)$.

(Surface tension by capillary rise.)

(5) $\frac{1}{v} + \frac{1}{u} = \frac{2}{r}$; construct a formula for r.

(Spherical mirror.)

(6) Make T the subject of the formula $f = \frac{1}{2l}\sqrt{\frac{T}{m}}$.

(Frequency of a note from vibrating string.)

(7) Make r the subject of the formula $V = \frac{R}{R + r} \cdot E$.

(Terminal p.d. of a cell of internal resistance r.)

(8) Make e the subject of the formula $E = \frac{F/A}{e/l}$.

(Young's modulus).

(9) Make x the subject of the formula $f = \frac{1}{2l}\sqrt{\frac{w + x}{m}}$.

(Sonometer tuning.)

(10) The bore of a capillary tube is d cm where $d = 2\sqrt{\dfrac{m}{\pi l D}}$, m being the mass of mercury, in g, which occupies l cm of the tube; $D = 13.6$ g cm^{-3}. Find the length of the tube occupied by 0.25 g of mercury in a tube of bore 1 mm.

(11) A cell of e.m.f. $(E) = 4.5$ V and internal resistance $(r) = 0.5\ \Omega$ gives a p.d. (V) of 3 V across an external resistance of value R. What is the magnitude of R? (Use the equation given in question 7 above).

(12) The formula for the impedance (Z) in alternating current theory is $\sqrt{R^2 + \left(2\pi fL - \dfrac{1}{2\pi fC}\right)^2}$ where R is the resistance (in Ω), f the frequency (in Hz) L the inductance (in H) and C the capacitance in farad. In a given circuit it is found that the impedance is equal to the resistance when f is 50 Hz and L is 10 mH. What is the value of C?

Linear equations:

(13) Solve the following equations:

(i) $5x + 6 = 5 + 4x$ (ii) $7(a - 2) = 4 + a$

(iii) $\dfrac{1}{v} + \dfrac{1}{10} = \dfrac{1}{20}$ (iv) $7.2\left(r + \dfrac{1}{8}\right) = 15.3$

(v) $300(25 - t) = 250(t - 3)$ (vi) $\dfrac{1}{35} - \dfrac{1}{25} = \dfrac{1}{f}$

(vii) $\dfrac{240}{R + 20} = 0.01$ (viii) $\dfrac{1}{v} - \dfrac{1}{3v} = \dfrac{1}{30}$

(ix) $\dfrac{1 + 10\alpha}{1 + 20\alpha} = \dfrac{3}{4}$ (x) $\dfrac{1 - r}{r} = \dfrac{3}{5}$.

(14) 100 g of water at 80°C are poured into a copper vessel of mass 150 g at an initial temperature of 10°C. What is the final equilibrium temperature? (Specific heat capacities of water and copper are 4.2 J g^{-1} K^{-1} and 0.4 J g^{-1} K^{-1} respectively.)

(15) A cell of e.m.f. 1.1 V supplies a current of 0.25 A when a resistance of 0.4 Ω is connected across its teminals. What is the internal resistance of the cell?

(16) A galvanometer with f.s.d. 0.5 mA has a resistance of 25 Ω What shunt is needed to convert it into an ammeter with f.s.d. 10 A?

(17) A uniform metre rule of mass 100 g has a 150 g mass attached at the 30 cm mark, and a 250 g mass at the 80 cm mark. Where must the rule be suspended so that it will balance?

(18) A piece of wire has resistance 3.78 Ω at 0°C and 4.61 Ω at 100°C. What is its temperature coefficient of resistance?

(19) A metre bridge gives a balance point at the 60 cm mark when two resistors differing by 2 Ω are included in the gaps. What is the value of the larger resistance?

(20) A metre bridge gives a balance point at the 48 cm mark when resistors differing by 3 Ω are included in the gaps. What is the value of each resistance?

(21) Describe the method and explain the theory of a practical determination of the frequency of a tuning fork which does not assume the velocity of sound, or the frequency of another fork.

If the frequency of a tuning fork is 550 Hz where will the first and second resonance positions be located in a resonance tube whose end correction is 3.5 cm? Assume that the velocity of sound in air at 0°C is 330 m s^{-1} and that room temperature is 20°C. (*L.*)

Quadratic Equations:

(22) Solve the equations:

(i) $x^2 + 4x - 5 = 0$	(ii) $6p^2 + 13p + 6 = 0$
(iii) $12l^2 - 31l + 20 = 0$	(iv) $36z^2 - 60z + 25 = 0$
(v) $R(3 - R) + 4 = 0$	(vi) $(29 - a)^2 = 0$
(vii) $h(h + 1) = 1$	(viii) $3u^2 - 5u - 11 = 0$.

(23) A converging lens of focal length 10 cm produces a real image 45 cm from the object. How far is the lens from the object? Explain the *two* answers obtained.

(24) A diverging lens of focal length 25 cm produces an image 80 cm from the object. Draw a diagram of the arrangement. Where is the image formed? Explain both answers.

(25) Assuming the usual equation for a converging lens prove Newton's formula, $xy = f^2$, for real images.

(26) A resistance is connected in parallel with one which is 2 Ω more in value. The effective resistance of the pair is $1\frac{7}{8}$ Ω. What are the values of the separate resistances?

(27) Lamps of intensity 4 cd and 9 cd are placed 2 m apart. Where must a screen be placed between them so that it is equally illuminated on both sides?

(28) A stone is thrown vertically upwards with an initial velocity of 15 m s^{-1}. How long does it take to reach a height of 5 m? Assume that the acceleration of free fall is 10 m s^{-2}.

(29) A bus which takes $1\frac{1}{2}$ min longer for a 2 km journey averages 18 km h^{-1} less than a car. What is the speed of each?

Simultaneous Equations:

(30) Solve the following sets of simultaneous equations:

(i) $5x - 3y = 7$
$3x + 5y = 11$

(ii) $3p + 2q = 5p - q = 13$

(iii) $2k + 3m = 6.3$
$3k + 2m = 5.2$

(iv) $2m + 3n = 2$
$6m + 8n = 5$

(v) $7l - z + 21 = 0$
$l - z = -5$

(vi) $m + n + 4 = 3m - 2n$
$= 2m - 3n - 3$

(vii) $a + b + c = 4$
$3a - b - 2c = 7$
$4a + 3b + c = 20$

(viii) $I_1 + I_2 + I_3 = 0$
$3I_1 - 2I_2 - 2I_3 = 1.25$
$-8I_1 + 7I_2 - 4I_3 = 3.95$

(ix) $p + q - 4r = -2$
$3p - 5q + 4r = 26$
$5p + 2q + r = 17$

(x) $x + y + z = 0.6$
$x = 15yz = y + z$

(31) A platinum wire has a resistance of 10 Ω at 80°C. What will be its resistance at 50°C? (Temperature coefficient of platinum is 38×10^{-4} °C^{-1}.)

(32) If a gas at constant pressure has volume v_1 at temperature t_1°C, and v_2 at t_2°C, show that it follows from Charles's law that the ratio of v_2 to v_1 is $(273 + t_1)/(273 + t_2)$.

(33) A battery is connected in series with an ammeter of negligible resistance and a variable resistance R. When R is 9 Ω, the ammeter reads 1 A, and when R is 4 Ω it reads 2 A. What is the e.m.f. and the internal resistance of the battery?

(34) Two cells of negligible internal resistance are connected in series and their terminals joined to an external circuit of a resistance of 1750 Ω and a galvanometer. The latter reads 2 mA when the positive pole of the one cell is joined to the negative of the other, and this value falls to $\frac{2}{7}$ mA when one of the cells is reversed. What are the e.m.f.'s of the cells?

(35) Two cells are connected to a high external resistance and a reflecting galvanometer. When the cells are joined in series the spot is deflected three times as far as it is when the cells oppose each other. Find the ratio of the e.m.f.'s of the cells.

(36) A column of dry air is trapped in a uniform tube by a thread of mercury 5 cm long. The tube is held vertically (i) with the sealed end uppermost, (ii) with the open end uppermost; it is found that in the first position the air column is 8 cm longer than when the tube is horizontal whilst in the second case it is 7 cm shorter than when horizontal. What is the atmospheric pressure?

(37) The second and third resonance positions of a tube responding to a fork of frequency 256 Hz were 965 mm and 163 mm. What were (i) the speed of sound under the conditions of the experiment, (ii) the end correction for the tube?

(38) A 1.5 V cell of internal resistance 4 Ω is used to supply a Wheatstone's bridge of which the wire has resistance 2 Ω. The gaps are closed by resistances of 4.00 and 2.00 Ω and a galvanometer of resistance 20 Ω used. What current will flow through the galvanometer when contact is made between the slide and the midpoint of the wire?

(39) State Kirchhoff's laws relating to the currents in networks of conductors. Two cells of e.m.f. 1.5 V and 2 V respectively and internal resistances 1 Ω and 2 Ω respectively are connected in parallel to an external resistance of 5 Ω. Calculate the currents in each of the three branches of the network. (*N.*)

(40) State Kirchhoff's laws for a network of electrical conductors. The resistances of a Wheatstone bridge arrangement are AB 100, BC 10, CD 6, DA 601 Ω in that order. A battery of e.m.f. 2 V and negligible resistance is applied between the points B and D. Find the current through a galvanometer, of 100 Ω resistance, connected between A and C. (*C.*)

(41) Explain the term *resonance*, giving examples from more than one branch of Physics. What conditions are necessary for resonance to occur?

A tuning fork produces resonance in an air column open at both ends when the length of the column is 31.0 cm and also when it is 64.0 cm. If the temperature of the air is 10°C find (*a*) the frequency of the fork, (*b*) the end correction for the column. Describe the motion of, and the changes in pressure in, the air in the longer column while it is sounding. [Velocity of sound in air at 0°C = 332 m s^{-1}.] (*L.*)

Answers

1. (i) $x = \dfrac{y - c}{m}$ (ii) $x = \dfrac{y^2 - c}{m}$ (iii) $x = \dfrac{3}{y - 5}$

(iv) $x = y^2 - 1$ (v) $x = \dfrac{1 - y}{y}$ (vi) $x = \dfrac{1}{y^2}$

(vii) $x = \dfrac{7}{2y}$ (viii) $x = \sqrt{\dfrac{y + 5}{2}}$ (ix) $x = \sqrt{\dfrac{1 + 5y}{2y}}$

(x) $x = \dfrac{1 + 2y^2}{y^2}$ (xi) $x = \dfrac{2}{(1 - 2y)}$ (xii) $x = \dfrac{1}{(1 - 5y)}$

2. $g = \dfrac{4\pi^2 I}{T^2 mh}$

3. $k = \dfrac{1}{2\pi}\sqrt{T^2 gh - 4\pi^2 h^2}$

4. $h = \dfrac{2\gamma}{r\rho g} - \dfrac{r}{3}$

5. $r = \dfrac{2uv}{u + v}$

6. $T = 4mf^2 l^2$

7. $r = R\left(\dfrac{E - V}{V}\right)$

8. $e = \dfrac{Fl}{AE}$

9. $x = 4f^2 l^2 m - w$

10. 2.341 cm

11. 1.0 Ω

12. 1014 μF

13. (i) $x = -1$ (ii) $a = 3$ (iii) $v = -20$

(iv) $r = 2$ (v) $t = 15$ (vi) $f = -87.5$

(vii) $R = 23\,980$ (viii) $v = 20$ (ix) $\alpha = 0.05$

(x) $r = 0.625$

14. 71.25°C

15. 4.0 Ω

16. 0.001 25 Ω

17. The 59.0 cm mark

18. 0.0022 K^{-1}

19. 6 Ω

20. 36 Ω and 39 Ω

21. 12.0 cm and 43.1 cm

22. (i) $x = -5$ or $+1$
(ii) $p = -\frac{2}{3}$ or $-\frac{3}{2}$
(iii) $l = +\frac{5}{4}$ or $\frac{4}{3}$
(iv) $z = +\frac{5}{6}$
(v) $R = +4$ or -1
(vi) $a = +29$
(vii) $h = +0.6$ or -1.6
(viii) $u = +2.9$ or -1.3

23. Object at 30 cm or 15 cm and image at 15 cm or 30 cm respectively (illustrates the principle of conjugate foci).

24. Object at 100 cm; virtual image at 20 cm.

26. 3 Ω and 5 Ω

27. At 0.8 m from the 4 cd source. What is the significance of the solution -4?

28. 0.38 s

29. 48 km h^{-1} and 30 km h^{-1}

30. (i) $x = 2, y = 1$
(ii) $p = 3, q = 2$
(iii) $k = 0.6, m = 1.7$
(iv) $m = -0.5, n = +1.0$
(v) $l = -\frac{8}{3}, z = +\frac{7}{3}$
(vi) $m = -1, n = -2$
(vii) $a = 2, b = 5, c = -3$
(viii) $I_1 = 0.25, I_2 = 0.45, I_3 = -0.7$
(ix) $p = 4, q = -2, r = 1$
(x) Either $x = 0.3, y = 0.2, z = 0.1$ or $x = 0.3, y = 0.1, z = 0.2$

31. 9.13 Ω

33. 10 V and 1.0 Ω

34. 2 V and 1.5 V

35. 2:1

36. 750 mm Hg

37. 338 ms^{-1}, 25 mm

38. 3.1 mA

39. 29 mA, 265 mA, 294 mA

40. 5.1 mA

41. 512 Hz, 1 cm

4. Graphs

A graph summarises data pictorially so that the main features of the relationship between two variables can be seen at a glance. Usually there is an equation which gives the relationship between the variables, and this equation may be linear or non-linear. The linear equation always leads to a graph which is a straight line (that is in fact the significance of the word 'linear'), whereas other types of equation lead in general to curves. The linear equation and its graph are of exceptional importance in Physics and will therefore be discussed first.

The Linear Relationship—'Straight-line' Graphs

The general form of the linear equation is $y = mx + c$ in which y is the dependent variable (see p. 36), x the independent variable, and m and

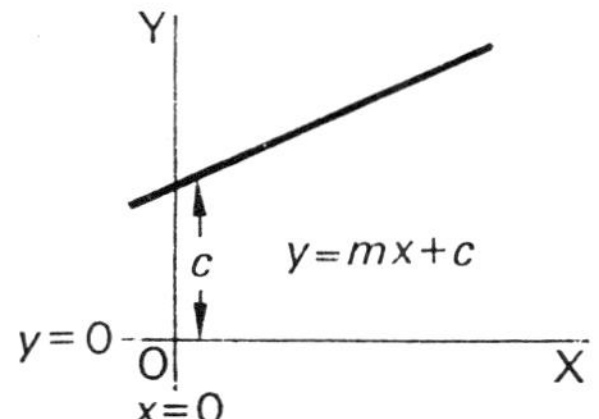

FIG. 4.1 Linear graph

c are constants. The graph of this equation is shown in Fig. 4.1. The intercept on the Y-axis is c and the gradient of the line is m.

(1) *The intercept* (c)

If we give x a value of zero, the equation $y = mx + c$ reduces to $y = c$. Thus c is the value of y corresponding to $x = 0$. It is thus the intercept on the axis of Y, i.e. it is the *intercept on the line* $x = 0$ *measured in the units of the Y-axis*. In plotting graphs from experimental data the range of the horizontal axis is sometimes altered so that the distribution of points over the graph paper is improved; the line which is drawn, and labelled 'Y-axis', is not then the true Y-axis because it does not coincide with the line $x = 0$. *The intercept on this false axis will not be c.* This is a pitfall to beware of when analysing experiments graphically. Notice that it is not necessary to show the zero on the Y-axis to obtain c as once the line $x = 0$ is drawn the actual point of intersection of the graph with the Y-axis can be read off in units of that axis. (See p. 58.)

If the intersection of the selected axes is not the point $x = 0, y = 0$, the intercept is best found by evaluating m (see below) and substituting this value together with the co-ordinates (i.e. x and y values) of any point *on* the line, in the equation $y = mx + c$.

(2) *The gradient* (m)

If we transpose the equation $\quad y = mx + c$

we can obtain
$$m = \frac{y - c}{x}.$$

Since we have already seen that c is the intercept it is evident that m is the value of PQ/QR in Fig. 4.2. It is important to notice that PQ is the difference between two values of y, and QR the difference between two values of x. These quantities will therefore be measured in the units of the Y-axis and the X-axis respectively. (See Examples below.)

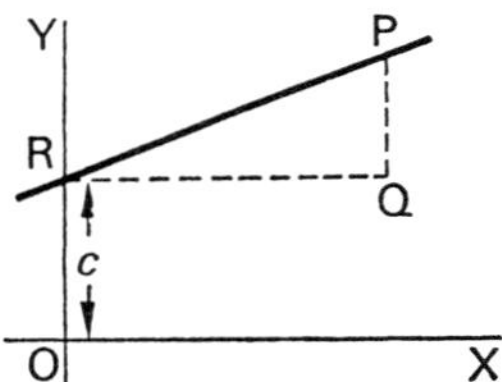

FIG. 4.2 Gradient and intercept

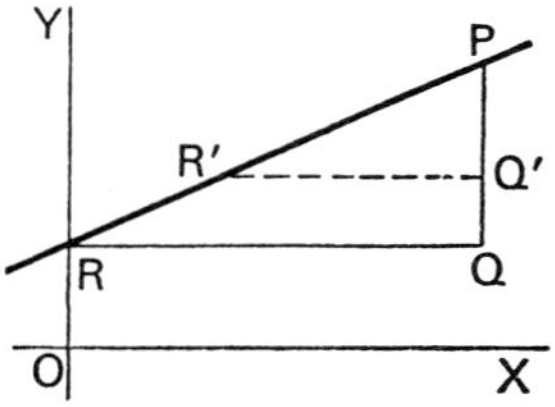

FIG. 4.3 Determination of gradient

By the geometry of similar triangles (see Fig. 4.3) it will be found that PQ/QR equals PQ′/Q′R′ and hence the gradient can be found from any triangle like PQ′R′, and the origin need not be shown for this purpose. Nevertheless the points P and R′ should be chosen to be as far apart as convenient, as this leads to greater accuracy in the result. Do not forget that PQ′ and Q′R′ must be measured in units of the axes to which they are parallel.

(3) *Deduction of the equation of variation from the graph*

Once the experimental results have been plotted and the straight line drawn it is only necessary to obtain the intercept and the gradient from the graph, by the methods given above, in order to write the equation for the variation.

Sometimes the general equation of variation is known and the actual value of the constants is required. In this case the student sometimes finds difficulty in deciding which axis to make his Y-axis in order to obtain the correct gradient, or perhaps having plotted the graph to fit his paper conveniently he finds he cannot decide whether the gradient of his graph is the value of m or its reciprocal. There need be no difficulty here if the equation given is recast (see p. 36) so as to *make the subject of the formula the quantity plotted along the Y-axis.*

Thus, for example, if the results of an experiment with a constant volume air thermometer were plotted, the Y-axis might be the pressure

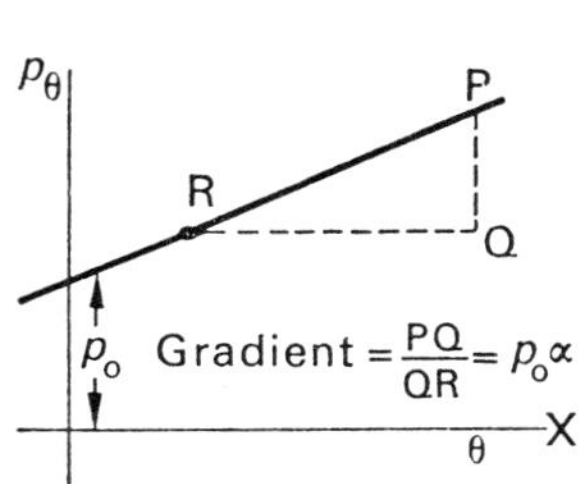

FIG. 4.4 Graph of pressure against temperature of gas

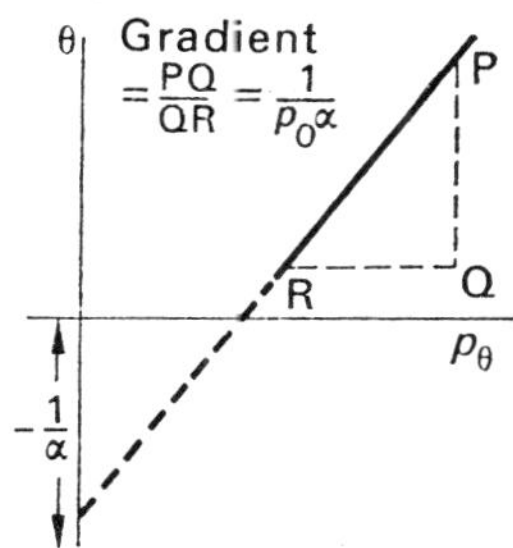

FIG. 4.5 Graph of temperature against pressure of gas

axis or the temperature axis, i.e. either like Fig. 4.4 or Fig. 4.5. The equation connecting these quantities is

$$p_\theta = p_0(1 + \alpha\theta)$$

and this simplifies to $\quad p_\theta = p_0\alpha\theta + p_0$

Compared with $\quad y = mx + c$

this shows that if p_θ is the dependent variable (i.e. plotted along the Y-axis) then the gradient is $p_0\alpha$ and the intercept p_0. If however the Y-axis has been made the temperature axis as in Fig. 4.5, then the equation should be recast as follows:

$$\theta = \frac{1}{p_0\alpha} \cdot p_\theta - \frac{1}{\alpha}.$$

If this is compared with

$$y = mx + c,$$

we see that the gradient is $1/p_0\alpha$ and the intercept $-1/\alpha$.

Labelling the Axes

Though graphs deal only with magnitudes, these values depend on the units used to measure them and must therefore be stated. Two possible ways are available:

(i) State the unit after the quantity, e.g. 'mass in kg'.

(ii) Use an oblique, placing the unit after the stroke, e.g. 'mass/kg'.
The justification for this follows from the argument that 4 kg means 4 × a kilogramme. Hence the magnitude (i.e. 4) is mass/kilogramme.

EXAMPLE

Fig. 4.6 shows the graph of the results obtained in an investigation of the variation of the resistance of a piece of copper wire with temperature, through the range 14°C to 100°C.

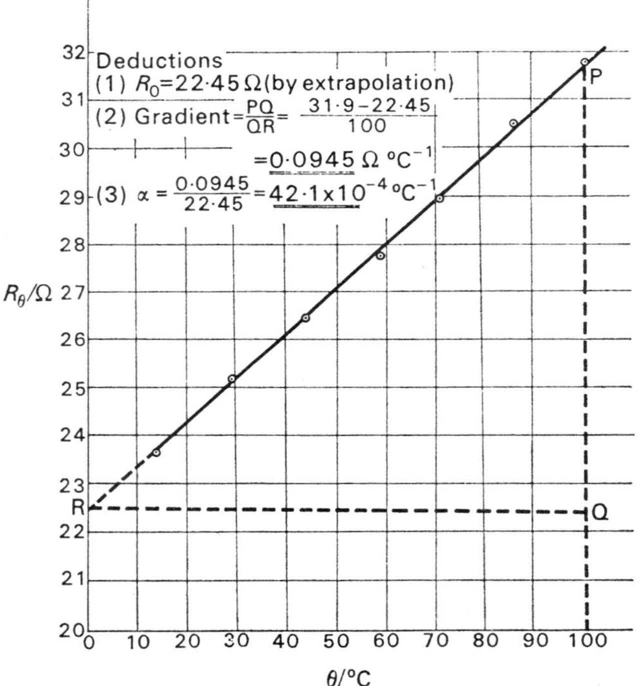

FIG. 4.6 Graph of resistance against temperature for copper

The relationship is seen to be linear. It is also to be noted that we have to assume that the linear relationship holds from 15°C to 0°C; for we have to produce the line back to intersect the Y-axis before we can find *c*. (The extension of the relationship outside the observed values is a process known as 'extrapolation'.) The value of *c* is found to be 22.45 Ω. A moment's reflection should show you that it is not necessary to show the zero of the resistance scale in order to obtain this value.

Next the value of *m* is found as follows: the ordinate corresponding to

100°C is drawn and its value found to be 31.9 Ω. The value of c (22.45 Ω) is now subtracted from 31.9 and the answer divided by 100°C. This gives the value of m as 0.0945 Ω °C^{-1}.

Thus we have the equation for R_θ, the resistance of this wire at θ°C, as

$$R = 0.0945\theta + 22.45\ \Omega.$$

The deduction of the value α is given on the graph, and this quantity is known as the 'coefficient of the increase of resistance with temperature'.

Non-linear Relationships

Many relationships are non-linear, but most of those dealt with at the level with which we are concerned are nevertheless fairly simple ones—such as quadratic or reciprocal relationships. In such cases the graph of the dependent variable (y, say) against the independent variable (x, say) is not a straight line, but a curve. A quadratic relationship leads to a parabola, a reciprocal relationship to a hyperbola.

If the equation is of one of these types it is possible to obtain a straight-line graph from experimental observations by the process known as 'changing the variable'. This is a mathematical term and does not in any way imply that the quantities being varied in the experiment were altered.

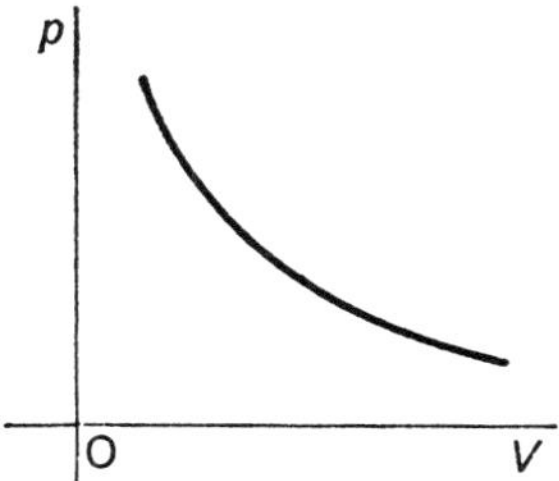

FIG. 4.7 Boyle's law

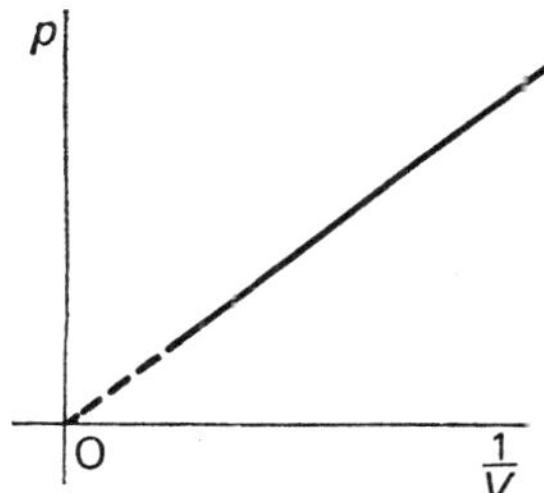

FIG. 4.8 Graph of pressure against reciprocal of volume (temperature constant)

Suppose the equation connecting x and y is $y = kx^n$, where k is a constant. If we put $z = x^n$ then $y = kz$. Thus a graph of y against z is a straight line, being a linear relationship. So plotting y against x^n produces a straight-line graph. For example if we observe the volume (v) of a gas under pressure (p) at constant temperature a graph of p against v produces a hyperbola because $p = k/v$ (Boyle's law).—Fig. 4.7. But if we plot p against $1/v$ a straight line is obtained passing through the origin.—Fig. 4.8.

As another example: the equation relating the periodic time of a helical spring executing vertical vibrations when carrying a load M is

$$T = 2\pi\sqrt{\frac{M + S/3}{kg}}$$

where T is the periodic time,
S is the mass of the spring,
k is the constant for the spring (i.e. the load in kg needed to stretch it 1 m)
and g is the acceleration of free fall.

Squaring both sides of this equation leads to

$$T^2 = 4\pi^2 \frac{M + S/3}{kg},$$

i.e

$$T^2 = \frac{4\pi^2}{kg} \cdot M + \frac{4\pi^2 S}{3kg}.$$

Thus a graph of T^2 against M produces a straight line, as shown in Fig. 4.9.

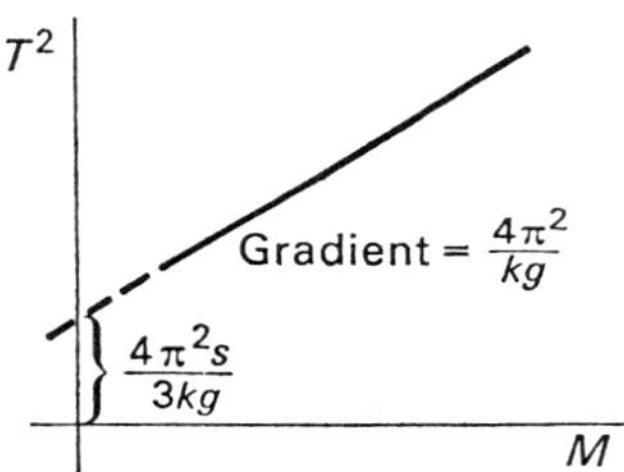

FIG. 4.9 Helical spring

If the last equation is compared with the general equation for the straight line, thus

$$T^2 = \frac{4\pi^2}{kg} \cdot M + \frac{4\pi^2 S}{3kg},$$

$$y = mx + c,$$

it is seen that the gradient of the graph of T^2 against M is $4\pi^2/kg$ and the intercept is $4\pi^2 S/3kg$.

From the graph these may be evaluated and hence if k is known a value for g can be found from the value of the gradient.

If the graph were plotted with the M-axis upright and the T^2-axis horizontal then the equation would be recast as follows:

$$T^2 \cdot \frac{kg}{4\pi^2} = M + \frac{S}{3},$$

i.e.

$$M = \frac{kg}{4\pi^2} T^2 - \frac{S}{3}$$

which compares with

$$y = mx + c$$

to show that the gradient of the second graph is $\frac{kg}{4\pi^2}$ and the intercept $-S/3$.

The Use of 'Log-plots'

To demonstrate relationships of the form $y = kx^n$, where n and k are constants, it is best first *to take logs of both sides*. Then

$$\log y = \log k + \log x^n = \log k + n \log x.$$

When $\log y$ is plotted against $\log x$, a straight line is therefore obtained whose slope is n. In this way the index n can be found. The intercept when $\log x$ is zero is $\log k$, and hence k can also be found. As an illustration, the current I through a diode valve is related to the p.d. V across it by the formula $I = kV^{3/2}$. Thus $\log I = \log k + \frac{3}{2} \log V$. The relationship can hence be tested by measuring I and V, and then plotting $\log I$ against $\log V$. A straight line whose slope is 3/2 should be obtained. The frequency f of the note from a given sonometer wire is given by $f = k\sqrt{T}$, where T is the tension; thus

$$\log f = \log k + \tfrac{1}{2} \log \mathrm{T}.$$

For a Helmholtz resonator, $f = k/\sqrt{V}$, where V is the volume of air; thus $\log f = \log k - \frac{1}{2} \log V$.

Two practical difficulties may be encountered when analysing physical processes by this method.

(i) If the number is a fraction the 'log' is a mixture of a *negative* characteristic and a *positive* mantissa (the mantissa is the part you look up in so-called 'log-tables'). Thus the log of 0.05 is $\bar{2}.3010$, which means $-2 + 0.3010$, i.e. -1.699.

When plotting such a log the simplest way to locate the correct point on the graph paper is to move the pencil from the origin, in the negative direction, by the number of units given by the characteristic, and then return in the *positive* direction by an amount equal to the mantissa. This is effectively doing the subtraction graphically. Thus to locate $x = \bar{2}.3010$, place the pencil point at the origin and move 2 units to the left and then return 0.3010 units to the right.

Similar considerations apply when evaluating the intercept of a log-plot. If the 'apparent intercept' were -1.699 this would be the point equivalent to a log of value $\bar{2}.3010$ and this quantity would then be transferred to 'antilog' tables.

(ii) In 'decay' graphs (see below) it is often the case that the logs should be to the base e (see p. 19), and it is worth remembering that $\log_e a = 2.3026 \log_{10} a$ (see p. 20). Thus it is sometimes easier to plot logs to the base 10 and to apply the correcting factor 2.3026 later, using this conversion formula.

Radioactivity

Radioactive materials decay (i.e. lose mass by disintegration of nuclei) at a rate which depends on (i) the amount of material present and (ii) the nature of the material. It follows that the rate of decay (the 'activity') decreases with time as there are decreasing amounts of material left behind. The relationship which applies in such cases is

$$\ln\left(\frac{m_0}{m}\right) = \lambda t,$$

where m_0 is the mass when $t = 0$, and m is the mass left after time t. λ, known as the 'decay constant', depends on the material and is constant for a given substance. From this equation it follows that

$$\ln m = -\lambda t + \ln m_0.$$

Thus a determination of any quantity, q, which is proportional to m can be used to obtain a log-plot, e.g. a graph of $\log_e q$ against t, the gradient of which will be $-\lambda$.

If a plot using logs to the base 10 is used the equation can be written

$$\frac{\ln m}{2.3026} = -\frac{\lambda t}{2.3026} + \frac{\ln m_0}{2.3026}.$$

Now $\ln m = 2.3026 \log_{10} m$ and $\ln m_0 = 2.3026 \ln m_0$ (see p. 20). Hence the equation may be written

$$\log_{10} m = -\frac{\lambda}{2.3026} \times t + \log_{10} m_0.$$

If $\log_{10} m$ is plotted against t a straight line should be obtained and the gradient of this line must be multiplied by 2.3026 to obtain the decay constant, λ.

The *half-life* is defined as the time required for half of the radioactive substance to disintegrate. If we let this be represented by $T_{\frac{1}{2}}$, then using the fundamental equation we obtain

$$\lambda T_{\frac{1}{2}} = \ln\left(\frac{m_0}{\frac{1}{2}m_0}\right) = \ln 2.$$

$$\therefore \quad T_{\frac{1}{2}} = \frac{1}{\lambda}\ln 2 = \frac{0.693}{\lambda},$$

which may be used to deduce $T_{\frac{1}{2}}$ from the value of λ already obtained from the graph.

EXERCISES 4

Linear Relationships

(1) The equation connecting the current in A (I), the p.d. in V (V) and the resistance in Ω (R) applying to a given resistor is $V = I \times R$.

Draw a graph of the set of observations given below and from it deduce the resistance of the specimen.

V (in V)	0.69	0.90	1.11	1.32	1.57	1.80	2.00	2.20
I (in mA)	30.5	40.0	50.1	59.5	70.3	80.0	90.0	99.0

(2) The coefficient of expansion of dry air (at constant pressure) was determined by measuring the length of a column of air, trapped in a uniform capillary tube, at various temperatures. The results were:

Temperature (°C)	23.3	32.0	41.0	53.0	62.0	71.2	87.0	99.0
Length of air column (cm)	7.1	7.3	7.5	7.8	8.0	8.2	8.6	8.9

Plot a graph of these observations and deduce a value for the expansivity of air (α) given that the equation connecting l_θ (the length at θ°C) and l_0 (the length at 0°C) is $l_\theta = l_0(1 + \alpha\theta)$.

(3) A spring was extended by loading with weights, and the reading of a pointer attached to the bottom of the spring was observed using a vertical scale. The following observations were recorded:

Load (g)	191.0	239.5	288.0	336.5	385.0	433.5
Mean reading of pointer (cm)	31.0	27.6	24.3	21.0	17.8	14.5

Find graphically the load in g needed to extend the spring 1 cm.

(4) An unknown resistance was included in the left-hand gap of a metre bridge and a dial resistance box, R, (0–9 Ω) connected across the right-hand gap. The following balance points for different values of R were recorded:

R (Ω)	1	2	3	4	5	6	7	8	9
Position of balance (l cm)	75.7	60.9	50.9	43.9	38.6	34.4	31.1	28.3	25.9

Draw a graph of $\frac{100 - l}{l}$ against R and from it obtain a value for the unknown resistance.

(5) The magnification (m) produced by a convex lens of focal length f is connected with the distance from the lens to the image (v) by the equation

$$m = \frac{v}{f} - 1.$$

In an experiment a circular hole 1.00 cm in diameter was used as an object so that the diameter of the image in cm was a measure of m. The following observations were recorded:

v (cm)	20.7	23.2	26.3	30.4	34.8	44.5	54
m	1.0	1.25	1.55	1.9	2.35	3.25	4.25

Plot a graph of m against v and deduce the focal length of the lens (i) from the gradient, (ii) from the intercept on the v-axis.

(6) A series of values of the current flowing through a tangent galvanometer and the deflection produced was obtained experimentally as follows:

Current in A (I)	0.45	0.72	0.95	1.27	1.60	1.82
Mean deflection (θ)	26° 30′	38° 30′	46° 45′	54° 30′	61°	63° 30′

The relationship between I and θ is $I = k \tan \theta$ where k is a constant known as the 'reduction factor'. Deduce a value for k from a suitable graph.

(7) How would you find the relation between resistance and temperature for a metal in the form of a wire? In an experiment the following values were obtained:

R (Ω)	1.48	1.60	1.72	1.83	1.94	2.06
t (°C)	0.0	20.0	40.0	60.0	80.0	100.0

Plot a graph from these data and use it to calculate the temperature coefficient of resistance of the material of the wire. (*L.*)

Non-linear Relationships

(8) Plot the graphs of resistance (in Ω) against voltage for the lamps for which the experimental data are given in Q. 27, p. 31, using the same axes for both graphs. Plot the resistances as ordinates and state the conclusions you draw from the graphs.

(9) Plot the graph of power against resistance from the data in Q. 28, p. 32, and deduce at what resistance the energy expended is a maximum.

(10) The periodic time (T) of a simple pendulum of length (l) is given by the formula

$$T = 2\pi\sqrt{\frac{l}{g}}.$$

How would you use experimental observations of values of l and T to construct a straight-line graph? What would be (i) the gradient, (ii) the intercept, of the graph? How would you obtain a value of g from the result?

(11) When a lath of thickness y and width z, supported horizontally and symmetrically by knife-edges distance x apart, is loaded at its centre by weight w, the depression D is given by

$$D = \frac{k \,.\, wx^3}{4zy^3}.$$

In an experiment a fixed weight w was applied and a series of values of D observed as x was varied. What graph would you plot to obtain a straight line and how would you proceed to evaluate k?

(12) The periodic time (T) of a rigid pendulum is given by the formula

$$T = 2\pi\sqrt{\frac{h^2 + k^2}{gh}},$$

where h is the distance from the centre of gravity to the point of suspension, k is a constant for the pendulum and g is the acceleration of free fall.

An experiment provides a series of corresponding values of T and h. How may these be used to obtain a straight-line graph? What will be the gradient of the graph? How may k be obtained?

(13) When a series of corresponding values of the object distance (u) and the image distance (v) are obtained with a spherical mirror, or a lens, the student is usually instructed to plot $\frac{1}{v}$ against $\frac{1}{u}$. The equation applying is $\frac{1}{v} + \frac{1}{u} = \frac{1}{f}$. By 'changing the variable' in this equation, and comparing the newly formed equation with $y = mx + c$, show how it is that the graph of $\frac{1}{v}$ against $\frac{1}{u}$ (i) is a straight line, (ii) why it slopes 'backwards', (iii) why it has equal intercepts, and (iv) how the focal length (f) is to be obtained.

(14) In the 'displacement method' of finding the focal length of a lens an object is set up, and the image formed by the lens located. The object is kept still and the lens moved until it produces an image in the same place as previously. If the lens is moved through a distance x when object and image are distance y apart, the focal length is given by

$$f = \frac{y^2 - x^2}{4y}.$$

The experimenter is usually instructed to observe a series of corresponding values of x and y and to obtain the focal length by a graphical method. What graph should be drawn and how is the value of f obtained from it?

(15) A resonance tube, with end-correction c, resonates to a tuning fork of frequency f when the length of the tube is l. The relationship is $l + c = \frac{V}{4f}$ where V is the velocity of sound in air. How would you analyse the results of an experiment in which a series of values of l corresponding to various values of f are recorded (both c and V are to be evaluated from the graph)?

(16) One method of verifying the inverse square law in magnetism consists in using a ball-ended magnet with one end vertically over a deflection magnetometer needle and the other to the Magnetic East (or West) of it; the deflection (θ) produced when the lower end is distance d from the needle is observed.

If m is a constant for the magnet and B_{hor} is the horizontal component of the earth's magnetic flux density,

$$\frac{m}{d^2} = B_{\text{hor}} \tan \theta$$

provided the inverse square law is true. How would you use a series of corresponding values of d and θ to verify the inverse square law?

(17) A cell of internal resistance r and e.m.f. E supplies current through a resistance of value R. The equation which applies is

$$r = R \,.\, \frac{E - V}{V}.$$

How would you use a series of corresponding values of V and R to obtain (graphically) a value for r?

(18) The table below gives corresponding values of the periodic time (T) and the load (M) for a helical spring executing vertical vibrations. The load (k) needed to extend the spring 1.00 cm is 14.8 g.

M (in g)	191.0	239.5	288.0	336.5	385.0	433.5
T (in s)	0.731	0.816	0.892	0.964	1.030	1.090

The equation connecting T and M is $T = 2\pi\sqrt{\frac{M + S/3}{100kg}}$

where S is the mass of the spring in g and g is the acceleration of free fall in m s^{-2}. Plot a suitable graph to obtain a straight line and from it obtain a value for g.

(19) In an experiment to verify Boyle's law the following observations of total pressure (p) applied to an air column enclosed in a uniform tube, and of the length of the air column (l), were obtained.

p (mm of mercury)	858	785	708	640	566	496	433	377
l (mm)	75	81	90	99	112	128	146	169

Plot graphs of (i) p against l and (ii) p against $\frac{1}{l}$. Discuss the results.

(20) The internal resistance of a battery (specially designed for the purpose) was determined by the usual potentiometer method. The relevant equation is

$$r = R\,.\left(\frac{l' - l}{l}\right),$$

where r is the required internal resistance, R is the value of the resistance box through which the battery is sending a current, l is the balance point on the potentiometer wire corresponding to value R, l' is the balance point when R is infinite (i.e. when the battery is on open circuit). The results were:

R (Ω)	∞	100	50	30	20	13	10	8	7	6	5
l (cm)	95.0	62.5	46.3	34.5	26.2	18.9	15.2	12.65	11.25	9.35	8.3

Plot a suitable graph and from it obtain a value for r.

(21) The object distance (u) and the image distance (v) for a concave mirror are connected by the equation $\frac{1}{v} + \frac{1}{u} = \frac{2}{r}$ where r is the radius of curvature. The following set of observations were obtained experimentally:

u (cm)	22.8	27.9	33.7	38.0	52
v (cm)	68	43.1	34.5	31.1	25.1

From a suitable graph obtain a value for r.

(22) The relationship between h and l is of the form $h = kl^p$, where k and p are constants. Use the values given in the table below to draw a graph and obtain values for k and p.

l	0.063	0.09	1.00	4.00	7.99
h	0.0024	0.003	0.010	0.020	0.028

(23) A metal bar was rigidly attached to a vertical wire clamped at its upper end. The bar was allowed to execute oscillations through a small angle in a horizontal plane. The periodic times for a range of different lengths of wire were determined and a summary of the results is given in the table:

Length of wire in cm (l)	20.3	35.9	51.0	79.0	98.0
Periodic time in s (T)	0.901	1.191	1.425	1.780	1.981

Given that the relationship between T and l is of the form

$$T = kl^m,$$

where k and m are constants, draw a graph from which k and m can be found and state the exact formula for T in terms of l.

(24) Newton's equation for a converging lens is

$$xy = f^2,$$

where x and y are the object and image distances from the first and second principal foci respectively, and f is the focal length. In an experiment the following values of x and y were found:

x (cm)	6.1	11.4	14.5	16.2	20.0
y (cm)	23.6	12.6	9.9	8.9	7.2

Plot a graph of log x against log y and from it deduce a value for f (make sure before starting to plot that both the intercepts will be on your graph paper—a preliminary rough sketch will help you here).

(25) The following readings were taken with a diode valve.

V_a (V)	20	40	60	80	100
I_a (mA)	0.6	1.6	3.3	4.9	6.5

If the law is $I_a = kV_a^n$ plot a suitable graph to demonstrate this relation and from it determine the value of n.

Answers

1. 22 Ω 2. 0.0036 K^{-1} 3. 14.6

4. 3.15 Ω 5. 10 cm 6. 0.9

7. 0.0039 K^{-1} 9. In the region of 53–54 Ω

10. Plot l (ordinates) against T^2; gradient $= g/4\pi^2$ and intercept is zero. Evaluate gradient and multiply by $4\pi^2$.

11. Plot D against x^3; gradient $= \dfrac{kw}{4zy^3}$; determine experimentally values for w, z and y and combine these with the value of the gradient to solve for k.

12. Plot h^2 against T^2h; gradient $= g/4\pi^2$; intercept $= k^2$.

13. Put $y = \dfrac{1}{v}$ and $x = \dfrac{1}{u}$; then $y + x = \dfrac{1}{f}$, i.e. $y = -1 \times x + \dfrac{1}{f}$; compare this with $y = mx + c$.

14. The equation transforms to $y = \dfrac{x^2}{y} + 4f$; plot y against $\dfrac{x^2}{y}$ and evaluate intercept on y-axis ($=4f$).

15. Plot l against $\dfrac{1}{f}$; gradient $= V/4$ and intercept on l-axis is $-c$.

16. The equation transforms to $d^2 = \dfrac{m \cot \theta}{B_{\text{hor}}}$. Plot d^2 against $\cot \theta$ and a linear result may be taken as verification of the law. Plotting d^2 against $\dfrac{1}{\tan \theta}$ is equally good but more work is involved.

17. Plot $\frac{1}{V}$ against $\frac{1}{R}$; intercept gives $-\frac{1}{r}$.

18. 9.87 m s^{-2}

19. The graph of p against l is a hyperbola and that of p against $\frac{1}{l}$ is a straight line if Boyle's Law is true.

20. Plot $\frac{1}{R}$ against $\frac{1}{l}$; intrecept on axis of $\frac{1}{R}$ gives $-\frac{1}{r}$. In this example r is approximately 54 Ω

21. 34 cm

22. $k = 0.01$, $p = 0.5$

23. $T = 0.2\sqrt{l}$

24. $f = 12$ cm

25. 1.5

5.
Basic Trigonometry

The Six Trigonometrical Ratios

Consider an angle θ, less than 90°. Draw $X\hat{A}Y = \theta$ (Fig. 5.1). Along AX choose *any* two points B_1 and B_2; draw B_1C_1 and B_2C_2 perpendicular to AY, as shown.

In triangles AB_1C_1, AB_2C_2

$$B_1\hat{C}_1A = B_2\hat{C}_2A \text{ (right angles, by construction),}$$

$$B_1\hat{A}C_1 = B_2\hat{A}C_2 \text{ (the common angle, } \theta\text{),}$$

$\therefore$ $\triangle AB_1C_1$ is similar to $\triangle AB_2C_2$.

$$\therefore \quad \frac{B_1C_1}{AB_1} = \frac{B_2C_2}{AB_2}.$$

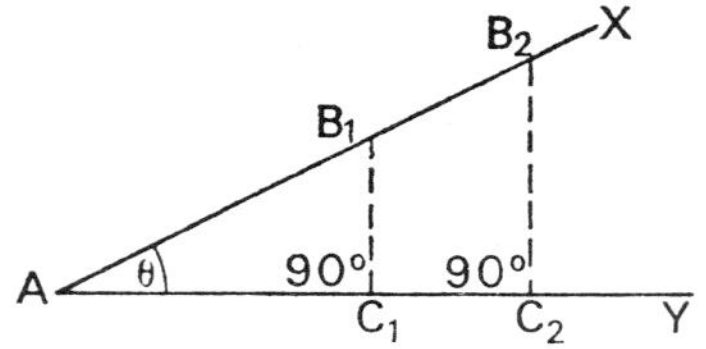

FIG. 5.1 Similar right-angled triangles

Now B_1 and B_2 were *any* two points AX and thus there is for each chosen value of θ a *fixed* value for the ratio—

$$\frac{\text{Perpendicular distance from AY of any point on AX}}{\text{Distance of that point from A}}.$$

Putting it another way, if a selected angle θ is included in a right-angled triangle ABC (see Fig. 5.2) the ratio $\frac{BC}{AB}$ is the same no matter what the *size* of the traingle may be.

This ratio is called the *sine of angle* θ and is usually written $\sin\theta$. The values of these ratios are to be found in sine tables which are printed in most collections of mathematical tables in common use.

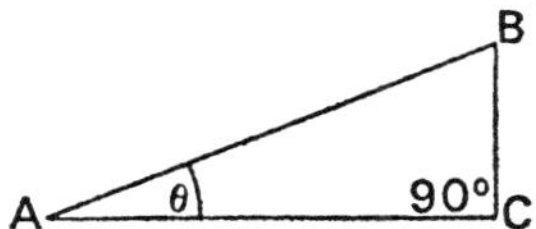

FIG. 5.2 Trigonometrical ratios for acute angles

A similar argument to that given above leads to the following five other trigonometrical ratios (the student should work through the argument for at least two of them):

Ratio $\frac{AC}{AB}$ is called cosine θ, abbreviated to $\cos\theta$, pronounced cŏz θ (short ŏ as in 'dot')

Ratio $\frac{BC}{AC}$ is called tangent θ, abbreviated to $\tan\theta$, pronounced tăn θ (short ă as in 'pat').

Ratio $\frac{AB}{BC}$ is called cosecant θ, abbreviated to cosec θ, pronounced cōsĕc θ (long ō as in 'bone', short ĕ as in 'pet').

Ratio $\frac{AB}{AC}$ is called secant θ, abbreviated to sec θ, pronounced sĕc θ.

Ratio $\frac{AC}{BC}$ is called cotangent θ, abbreviated to cot θ, pronounced cŏt θ.

Logarithms of Trigonometrical Ratios

Often the logarithm of a trigonometrical ratio is needed in a calculation without the actual value of the ratio being needed. For this purpose 'log-sine', 'log-cosine', 'log-tangent', 'log-cotangent', 'log-secant' and 'log-cosecant' tables are provided, though some books only give the first three because the last three are not essential—all calculations can be carried out using the first three.

To use such tables, look under the angle just as you do when looking up a sine or a cosine, etc., and the result will be the logarithm of the ratio. Thus if the logarithm of the sine of 35° 16′ is required, look under '35° 16′' in the log-sine-tables. Here is found $\bar{1}.7614$. This is much quicker than looking up sin 35° 16′ in sine tables (= 0.5771) and then looking up the logarithm of 0.5771 in log tables.

Thus to calculate the value of 1.518 sin 35° 16′ proceed as shown in the margin, using log-sine tables.

The answer is found to be 0.8764.

This sort of calculation is common when studying refraction, and here another hint to save labour can appropriately be included:

No.	Log
1.518	0.1813
sine 35° 16′	$\bar{1}.7614$
(sum)	$\bar{1}.9427$
Antilog $\bar{1}.9427$ =	0.8764

Suppose we were applying Snell's law in a problem to find the angle i in the equation

$$\frac{\sin i}{\sin 35^\circ\, 16'} = 1.518.$$

From the transformation $\sin i = 1.518 \times \sin 35^\circ\, 16'$ we proceed to the calculation just discussed, but we do *not* look up antilog $\bar{1}.9427$, and then find which angle has a sine of value 0.8764. Instead we find which angle has a log-sine $\bar{1}.9427$ using log-sine tables. This is found to be 61° 12′.

Trigonometrical Ratios of Angles 45°, 30° and 60°

The values of the trigonometrical ratios of the angles 45°, 30° and 60° can be deduced very quickly once the following two facts are memorized:

$$\sqrt{2} = 1.414 \quad \text{and} \quad \sqrt{3} = 1.732.$$

If you do not know these values learn them *now*.

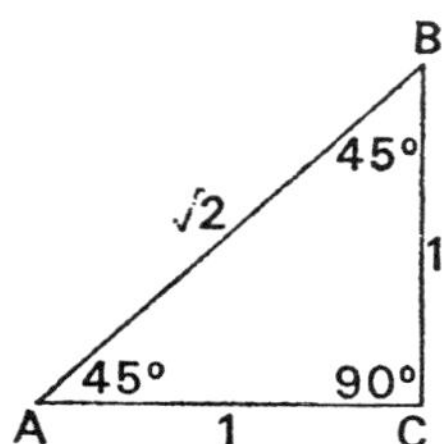

FIG. 5.3 Trigonometrical ratios for 45°

1. *The angle* 45°

Draw an isosceles right-angled triangle, ABC (see Fig. 5.3).

Let $\quad AC = BC = \text{unit length.}$

Then $\quad AB^2 = AC^2 + BC^2$ (Pythagoras' theorem)

$\therefore \quad AB^2 = 1^2 + 1^2 = 1 + 1 = 2$

$\therefore \quad AB = \sqrt{2}.$

Hence $\sin 45^\circ = \dfrac{1}{\sqrt{2}} = \dfrac{\sqrt{2}}{2}$ (see p. 12) $= \dfrac{1.414}{2} = 0.707.$

Similarly $\cos 45^\circ = \dfrac{1}{\sqrt{2}} = 0.707$

and $\tan 45^\circ = \dfrac{1}{1} = 1.$

The other ratios can be deduced just as easily. By making a mental picture of this triangle you will find that with very little practice you can write down any required ratio for 45°. (Refer also to p. 12 on the Rationalization of Surds.)

2. *The angles* 30° and 60°

The method here is similar to that used above for 45°, the triangle being the right-angled triangle formed by drawing one median of an equilateral traingle as shown in Fig. 5.4. The original triangle is ABD

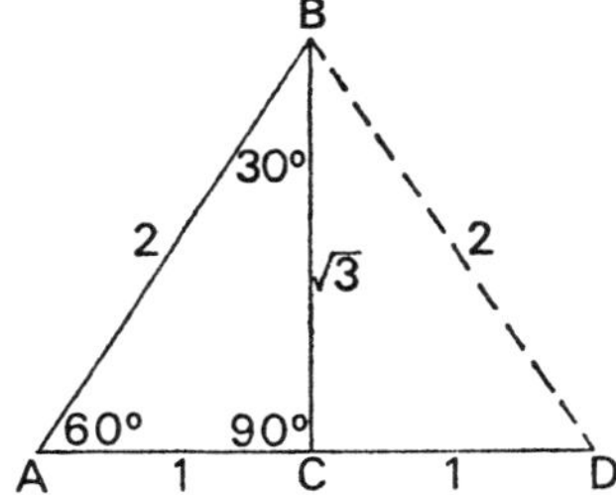

FIG. 5.4 Trigonometrical ratios for 30° and 60°

and is given a side of length 2 units, so that the triangle we use is ABC of sides AB = 2, AC = 1 and BC = $\sqrt{3}$ (obtained by applying Pythagoras' theorem to △ABC).

From this triangle any trigonometrical ratio for 30° or 60° can be found. For instance

$$\sin 60^\circ = \frac{\sqrt{3}}{2} = \frac{1.732}{2} = 0.866$$

and

$$\cot 30^\circ = \frac{BC}{AC} = \frac{\sqrt{3}}{1} = 1.732.$$

The student should now work out all six trigonometrical ratios for both 30° and 60°, and the results should be checked from trigonometrical tables. When dealing with these angles in problems the student should not eliminate the $\sqrt{\ }$ sign until necessary—following the excellent rule (in calculations) of never performing any unpleasant process until it cannot be avoided, as it may never become necessary. An example of this will be found on p. 78.

Solution of Right-angled Triangles

Now that the method of using tables is understood the application to right-angled triangles can be dealt with. The solution of other triangles is discussed later (p. 94). The following examples show the methods to be used:

EXAMPLE

A triangle PQR has $\hat{P} = 90°$, $\hat{Q} = 40° \, 17'$, QP = 6·38 cm. What are the values of PR and QR?

The triangle is shown in Fig. 5.5. By definition of tangent,

$$\frac{PR}{QP} = \tan \hat{Q}$$

$$\therefore \quad \frac{PR}{6{\cdot}38} = \tan 40° \, 17'$$

$$\therefore \quad PR = 6{\cdot}38 \tan 40° \, 17'.$$

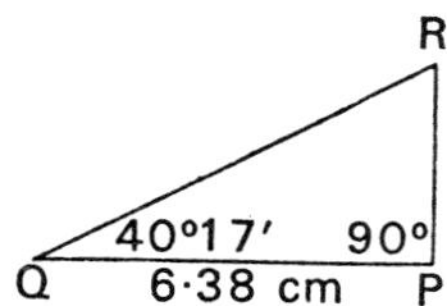

FIG. 5.5. Solution of triangle

Using log tables and log-tangent tables proceed as shown in the margin to obtain

$$PR = 5{\cdot}40 \text{ cm.}$$

No.	Log
6.38	0.8048
tan 40° 17′	$\bar{1}$.9272
Sum	0.7320
Antilog	5.395

To find QR:

$$\frac{QR}{QP} = \sec \hat{Q}$$

$$\therefore \quad \frac{QR}{6{\cdot}38} = \sec 40° \, 17'$$

$$\therefore \quad QR = 6{\cdot}38 \sec 40° \, 17'.$$

No.	Log
6.38	0.8048
sec 40° 17′	0.1175
Sum	0.9223
Antilog	8.362

Proceed as in the margin, remembering that:

(i) $\log_{10} 6{\cdot}38$ has already been used and therefore it can be copied down from the previous calculation;

(ii) if log-secant tables are not available use log-cosine tables.

$$\text{Log sec } 40° \ 17' = \log (1/\cos 40° \ 17') = -\log \cos 40° \ 17'.$$

Hence obtain the result:

$$QR = 8{\cdot}36 \text{ cm.}$$

Resolution of Forces

From the parallelogram of forces a single force called the 'resultant' can be found which has the same effect as two given forces. Obviously, two forces can be found which will have the same effect as one given force. The directions can be selected at will, their magnitudes then being determined by the parallelogram of forces relationship. In practice the chosen directions are nearly always at right angles to each other, and the components are then known as the 'resolved parts' of the force in the directions concerned.

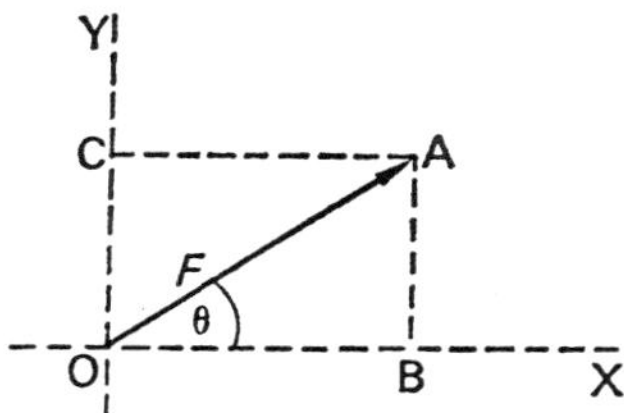

FIG. 5.6 Resolution of forces

In Fig. 5.6 let OA represent the force, *F*, which is to be resolved and OX, OY the directions along which the resolved parts are to act. Let $X\widehat{O}Y$ be 90° so that the process is the usual one of resolving 'in two directions at right angles'. Draw AB, AC perpendicular to OX and OY respectively, B and C lying in OX and OY respectively. OCAB may be regarded as a parallelogram of forces, and forces represented by OC and OB would have OA as their resultant. Thus OC and OB represent the required components in magnitude and direction.

If $A\widehat{O}X = \theta$, $OB = OA \cos \theta$ and $OC = BA = OA \sin \theta$.

Thus the required components are $F \cos \theta$ and $F \sin \theta$.

(Note that the component of a force in a direction which makes an angle θ with the force is Force $\times \cos \theta$.)

This process finds numerous applications in Statics and Dynamics. Very often the directions chosen are vertical and horizontal, but in problems involving inclined planes it is usually better to resolve parallel to and normal to the plane. It is worth remembering that the angle between the normal to the plane and the vertical is equal to the angle between the plane and the horizontal—the student should prove this for himself.

EXAMPLES

Use of Components in Statics

1. A weight of 10 N is supported by two strings, one making 30° with the vertical, the other 60° with the vertical. What is the tension in each string?

Method (i): The force diagram is shown in Fig. 5.7.

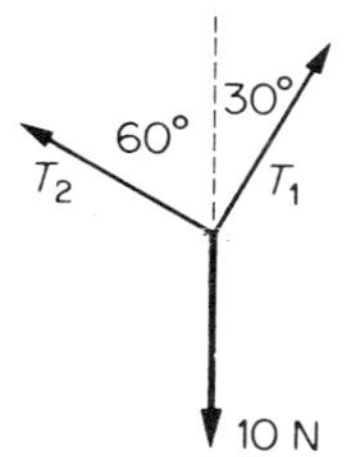

FIG. 5.7 Force diagram

Resolving vertically:

$$T_1 \cos 30° + T_2 \cos 60° = 10 \quad . \quad . \quad . \quad . \quad (1)$$

Resolving horizontally: $$T_1 \sin 30° = T_2 \sin 60° \quad . \quad . \quad . \quad (2)$$

These equations reduce to

$$\frac{\sqrt{3}}{2} . T_1 + \frac{T_2}{2} = 10 \quad . \quad . \quad . \quad . \quad . \quad (1)$$

and $$\frac{T_1}{2} = \frac{\sqrt{3}}{2} . T_2 \quad . \quad . \quad . \quad . \quad (2)$$

From (2), $$T_1 = \sqrt{3} T_2$$

and substituting this value in (1) we obtain

$$\frac{\sqrt{3}}{2} \times \sqrt{3} T_2 + \frac{T_2}{2} = 10$$

$$\therefore \quad T_2 \left(\frac{3}{2} + \frac{1}{2} \right) = 10$$

whence $$T_2 = 5 \text{ N}$$

$$\therefore \quad T_1 = 5\sqrt{3} = 5 \times 1.732 = 8.66 \text{ N}$$

Answer: 5 N and 8.7 N.

Method (ii): The angle between T_1 and T_2 is 30° + 60° = 90°.

Thus in this case we can resolve the 10 N in two directions at right angles—the directions of the strings.

Hence $T_1 = 10 \cos 30° = 10 \times \frac{\sqrt{3}}{2} = 8.7$ N

and $T_2 = 10 \cos 60° = 10 \times \frac{1}{2} = 5$ N.

2. A car of mass 1000 kg is held at rest by its brakes on a slope at an angle of 10° to the horizontal. What is the normal reaction of the road on the car and what is the magnitude of the force preventing the car from moving down the hill?

The car is held in equilibrium by the three forces W (its weight), R (the normal reaction) and B (the braking force) as shown in Fig. 5.8.

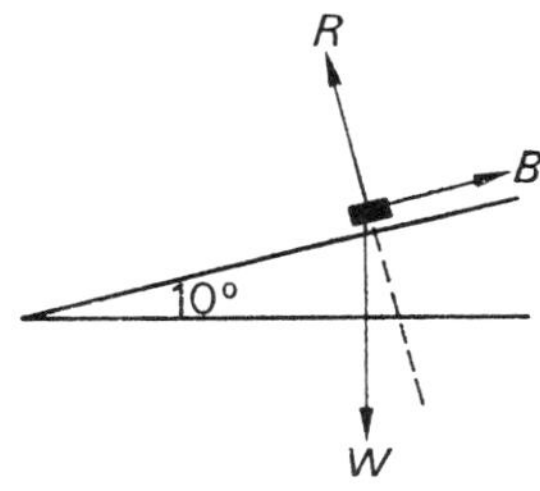

FIG. 5.8 Force diagram

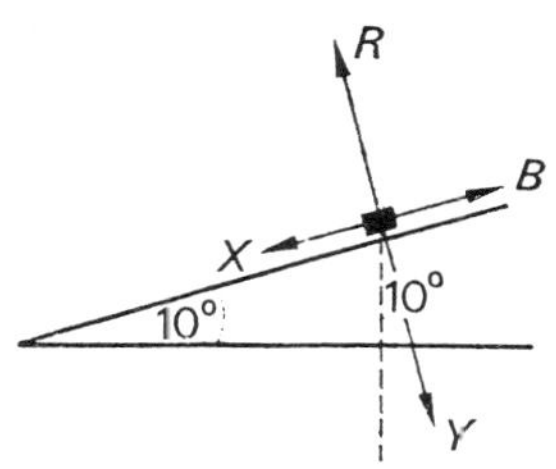

FIG. 5.9 Components of forces

If the components of W parallel to the plane and normal to the plane are X and Y respectively the force diagram becomes as shown in Fig. 5.9.

$$Y = W \cos 10° \quad \text{and} \quad X = W \sin 10° \text{ (see p. 76).}$$

Now $W = 1000\,g$ N = 9810 N, with $g = 9.81$ N kg^{-1}

$\therefore \quad Y = 9810 \cos 10° = 9663$ N

and $X = 9810 \sin 10° = 1700$ N

Answers: Normal reaction = 9660 N

Force preventing car from moving = 1700 N.

Use of Components in Dynamics

The acceleration of a given mass in a given direction can be found if the resultant force in that direction is known. It is thus necessary to resolve all the forces in the given direction in order to find their (algebraic) sum in this direction. A common case is that of a body moving on a slope.

EXAMPLES

1. What is the acceleration of a car rolling down a hill of gradient 1 in 10 if there is no friction?

If the mass of the car is M the weight will be Mg (p. 216). The component of this force parallel to the plane is $\frac{Mg}{10}$ and is the force responsible for motion down the plane. Substituting in the equation

Force in newton = (Mass in kg) × (Acceleration in m s^{-2}) we obtain

$$\frac{Mg}{10} = M \times \text{acceleration.}$$

$$\therefore \quad \text{Acceleration} = \frac{g}{10} = 0.98\ \text{m s}^{-2}$$

2. With what acceleration will a car of mass 1000 kg roll down a hill of 1 in 20 if the friction force is 100 N (assume that $g = 10$ N kg^{-1}).

Resolve the forces acting on the car in a direction *parallel* to the plane (Fig. 5.10).

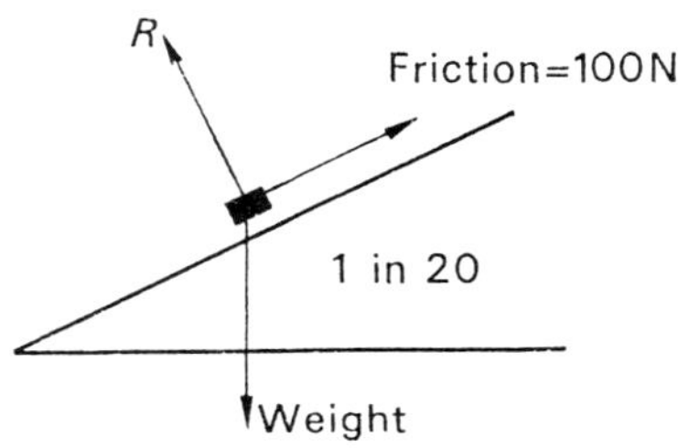

FIG. 5.10 Force diagram

R being normal to the plane has no component parallel to it. The friction force is already parallel to it and acts *up* the plane because it opposes motion down the plane. The component of the weight of the car is

$$\frac{1000g}{20} = 50g \text{ (in newton)}$$

The resultant force is therefore (500 − 100) N = 400 N.

Substituting in $F = ma$ we obtain:

$$400 = 1000 \times a$$

$$\therefore \quad a = 0.4\ \text{m s}^{-2}$$

3. A railway train of mass 500 tonne climbs a hill of gradient 1 in 100 at 9 km/h against a friction force of 50 newton per tonne. At what power is the engine working? (Take g as 10 N kg^{-1}.)

There are two forces acting against the train—the frictional force and the component of the weight of the train parallel to the plane.

(1) Friction force = 50 × 500 = 25 000 N = 2.5 × 10^4 N

(2) Component of weight parallel to plane $= 500 \times 1000 \times \frac{1}{100} \times g$ N
$= 5 \times 10^4$ N.

The engine is thus applying a force of $(5 + 2.5) \times 10^4$ N $= 7.5 \times 10^4$ N.

$$\text{Its speed} = 9\ \text{km/h} = \frac{9000}{3600}\ \text{m s}^{-1}$$

$$= 2.5\ \text{m s}^{-1}$$

So the engine applies the force of 7.5×10^4 N and moves the point of application 2.5 m in one second.

$$\therefore \quad \text{work done} = 7.5 \times 10^4 \times 2.5 \text{ joule in one second.}$$

This is the required power in J s^{-1}, i.e. in W.

$$\therefore \quad \text{Power} = \frac{7.5 \times 10^4 \times 2.5}{1000} \text{ kW} = 187.5 \text{ kW}$$

EXERCISES 5

Use of Trigonometrical Ratios

Using tables write down the values of the trigonometrical ratios in the following questions. If your answers are more than one out in the last place of decimals check your use of tables, especially making sure that you have *subtracted* 'differences' in those tables in which you are instructed to do so, i.e. when using cosine, cosecant and cotangent tables.

(1) Sin 30°; cos 30°; sec 30°; cosec 30°; tan 30°; cot 30°.

(2) Tan 45°; sin 45°; cos 45°; sec 45°; cosec 45°. [Explain the unusual features of this answer.]

(3) Sin 39° 12′; sec 39° 12′; cosec 39° 12′.

(4) Cos 58° 47′; cot 58° 47′; sec 58° 47′.

(5) Cot 30° 09′; sin 30° 09′; cos 30° 09′.

(6) Log-sin 26° 12′; log-cos 25° 14′; log-tan 58°; log-sec 71° 51′; log-cos 15° 05′; log-cot 13° 07′. [Be sure that you subtract 'differences' when using log-cosine, log-cosec, and log-cot tables. Be careful to record the characteristics—they are usually printed only at the beginning of each line in the tables.]

(7) Calculate the values of:

(i) $39.67 \sin 43° 18'$ (ii) $\dfrac{\cos 50° 17'}{1.89}$

(iii) $0.083 \tan 51°$ (iv) $6.800 \sin 30° + 0.900 \tan 81°$.

(8) Find the value of θ which satisfies the following equations:

(i) $\dfrac{\sin \theta}{\sin 20°} = 1.33$ (ii) $\dfrac{\sin 51° 28'}{\sin \theta} = 1.67$ (iii) $\dfrac{\tan \theta}{\cos 51°} = \dfrac{\cot 40°}{\sin 27°}$.

(9) Find the value for n from the prism equation (see p. 82)

$$n = \frac{\sin\left(\dfrac{A + D}{2}\right)}{\sin \dfrac{A}{2}} \text{ when } D = 38° 16' \text{ and } A = 60°.$$

[This is the equation applying to the position of minimum deviation for a prism of refractive index n and refracting angle A, D being the angle of minimum deviation.]

(10) Using the minimum deviation equation given in Q. 9, find the angle of minimum deviation for a prism of refracting angle 60° 05′ and refractive index 1.64.

(11) What are the angles of diffraction for the first and second order spectra of light of wavelength 5.896×10^{-7} m when a grating having 5.7×10^5 lines per metre is used?

The relevant formula is

$$\sin \theta = Nn\lambda$$

where θ is the angle of diffraction,
N is the grating spacing in lines per metre,
n is the order,
and λ is the wavelength in metre.

(12) Calculate the angle of minimum deviation for a prism of refracting angle 59° 54′ and made of glass having refractive index 1.70. The relevant formula is given in Q.9 above.

The Angles 30°, 45° and 60°

The following questions should be done *without using tables.*

$$\sqrt{2} = 1.414 \qquad \sqrt{3} = 1.732$$

(If necessary revise the rationalization of surds on p. 12).

(13) Without *drawing* a diagram—you should imagine it—and without using paper for the calculation, write down the values of the following: sin 60°; cos 60°; tan 45°; sec 30°; cot 60°; sin 45°; cot 30°; cos 45°; cot 45°; cosec 60°.

(14) Evaluate

$$\sqrt{3}\tan 30°;\ \sqrt{2}\sin 45°;\ \frac{2}{\sqrt{3}};\ \frac{\tan 30°}{\cos 45°};\ \frac{\tan 30°}{\sqrt{3}}.$$

(15) An aeroplane is flying in a direction N 30° E relative to the ground. The pilot is actually ‘pointing’ the aircraft due N and the airspeed indicator reads 173.2 knot. The speed of the aircraft relative to the ground is 200 knot. What is the speed and direction of the wind?

(16) In the tangent galvanometer the current (I) in ampere is found by multiplying the tangent of the deflection (θ) by the ‘reduction factor’ (k)—a constant for a given galvanometer in a given spot, i.e. $I = k \tan \theta$.

Experimentally k is deduced graphically by plotting a series of values of I against $\tan \theta$. Show that during the experiment the reading of the ammeter is equal to the reduction factor when the deflection of the tangent galvanometer needle is 45°. If $k = 0.80$, find I if $\theta = 30°$.

(17) If the horizontal component of the earth's magnetic flux density is 1.8×10^{-5} T at a place where the angle of dip is 60° find (i) the vertical component, (ii) the total flux density due to the earth, at the place.

(18) Light is incident on the surface of a refracting medium at 45° and the angle of refraction is 30°. What is (i) the refractive index, (ii) the critical angle for the medium?

Right-angled triangles

(19) Triangle PQR is right-angled at Q; PQ = 3.6 cm; QR = 4.8 cm. Find the values of the two acute angles and of the hypotenuse.

(20) The angle of elevation of the top of spire, the foot of which is 100 metre away, is 40° 33′. How tall is the spire?

(21) One of the guy-ropes of an aerial mast 50 m high is joined to the mast at a point half-way up it, and slopes at an angle of 44° to the vertical. How long is the guy-rope?

(22) An inclined plane slopes at 20° to the horizontal. Through what vertical height does a load move when dragged 100 metre up the plane?

(23) A cone has semi-vertical angle 40° and the radius of the base is 10.0 cm. What are its vertical and slant heights?

(24) A wheel of diameter 0.6 m and weight 200 N is scotched by a block. The spoke from the point of contact of the wheel with the block makes an angle of 40° with the vertical. What is the least turning moment needed to make the wheel mount the block?

(25) A uniform rod AB is hinged at A and is held horizontally by a string attached to B which makes an angle of 35° with the rod. If the rod weighs 6 N what is the tension in the string?

(26) A ship is travelling at 10 knot due E in a tide of 4 knot moving towards due N. If the tide were not running, but the ship was still steered as before, in what direction and with what speed would the ship move?

(27) A projectile is fired from a cliff 180 m above the sea and is given an initial horizontal velocity of 40 m s^{-1}. At what angle will it enter the sea? At what height above the sea will it have a velocity of 50 m s^{-1}? (Take the acceleration of free fall to be 10 m s^{-2} and neglect air resistance.)

(28) ABC is an isosceles triangle right-angled at B. At A and C are placed charges at 10 pC and −20 pC respectively. Calculate the direction of the resultant electric field at B.

Resolution of Forces

(29) Resolve the following forces horizontally and vertically:

(i) 100 N acting at 30° to the vertical.
(ii) 30 N acting at 45° to the horizontal.
(iii) 1.5 N acting at 35° to the horizontal.

(30) Resolve the following weights parallel to and normal to the given planes:

(i) 10 N on a plane making 30° with the horizontal.
(ii) 50 N on a plane making 45° with the horizontal.
(iii) 320 N on a plane making 70° with the horizontal.
(iv) W N on a plane making $\alpha°$ with the horizontal.

In the following questions assume that the acceleration of free fall g is 10 N kg^{-1}.

(31) A picture of mass 5 kg hangs symmetrically from a hook, the cord and the top of the picture making an equilateral triangle. What is the force on the hook? What is the tension in each part of the cord?

(32) Repeat Q 31 for the case when the parts of the cord at the hook form a right angle.

(33) A pendulum bob of mass 0.2 kg is pulled aside by a horizontal force so that the string makes an angle of 25° with the vertical. What is the increase in tension in the string so caused?

(34) A metal sphere of mass 150 g is suspended by a thread which will break under a tension of 2 N. If the sphere is slowly pulled aside by a force which is always acting horizontally at what angle to the vertical will the string break? What will be the value of the horizontal force when this happens?

(35) A car is parked with its brakes off on a hill of 1 in 40. If the friction force is 200 N what is the mass of the car?

(36) A block rests on a plane on which the friction force is 10% of the normal reaction. What is the maximum angle of slope to the horizontal at which the plane may be tilted for the block to remain at rest?

(37) With what acceleration (in m s^{-2}) will a body slide down smooth slopes of angle 20°; 30°; 45°; 60°?

(38) With what acceleration will a 10 kg mass move down a slope of gradient 1 in 20 if the friction force is 2 N?

(39) What force is needed to pull a car of mass 1 tonne up a hill of gradient 1 in 20 if the friction-force is equivalent to a pull of 100 N?

(40) Using the data of the previous question calculate the force which would be required to give the car an acceleration of 0.5 m s^{-2} up the hill.

(41) (i) A toboggan of mass 20 kg carrying a boy of mass 40 kg runs down a slope of 1 in 60 and of length 192 metre. At what speed will the boy be travelling at the foot of the slope, assuming the friction-force is negligible?

(ii) The boy hauls his toboggan back up the slope in 20 seconds. At what power does he work?

(42) A car of mass 900 kg reaches the top of a hill of gradient 1 in 30 when travelling at 60 km h^{-1} and coasts down it at constant speed. At the foot of the hill the road is level. How far from the bottom of the hill will the car come to rest?

(43) The car referred to in Q 42 is reversed and the driver approaches the hill along the level at 60 km h^{-1}. He climbs the hill at the same (steady) speed. At what power is the car working (i) on the level, (ii) on the hill?

(44) A ball rolls down a smooth slope of angle 45° for 2 second and then rolls up a slope of angle 30° and coefficient of friction 0.2. How far up the slope does the ball roll?

(45) A mass of 20 kg is pulled up a smooth plane which makes an angle of 30° with the horizontal by a force F acting on it. F is of value 200 N and always acts horizontally. Calculate the reaction of the plane on the mass and the acceleration of the body.

(46) A piece of elastic string 60 cm long is fixed horizontally to two supports 60 cm apart. A mass M is suspended at the centre of the string and causes a depression of 40 cm. If the string requires a force of 4 N to cause an extension of 1 metre, what is the mass of M?

Answers

1. 0.5000, 0.8660, 1.1547, 2.0000, 0.5774, 1.7321

2. 1.0000, 0.7071, 0.7071, 1.414, 1.414

3. 0.6320, 1.2904, 1.5822

4. 0.5183, 0.6060, 1.9294

5. 1.7216, 0.5023, 0.8648

6. $\bar{1}.6449$, $\bar{1}.9565$, 0.2042, 0.5065, $\bar{1}.9847$, 0.6326

7. (i) 27.20 (ii) 0.338 (iii) 0.103 (iv) 9.082

8. (i) 27° 04′ (ii) 27° 56′ (iii) 58° 49′

9. 1.512

10. 50° 17′

11. 19° 38′ and 42° 13′

12. 56° 16′

13. 0.866, 0.500, 1.000, 1.155, 0.577, 0.707, 1.732, 0.707, 1.000, 1.155

14. 1.000, 1.000, 1.155, 0.816, 0.333

15. 100 knot from W

16. 0.46

17. 3.1×10^{-5} T and 3.6×10^{-5} T

18. (i) 1.414 (ii) 45°

19. $\hat{R} = 36° 52'$, $\hat{P} = 53° 08'$

20. 85.56 m   21. 36 m   22. 34.2 m

23. 11.9 cm and 15.6 cm

24. 38.6 N m   25. 5.23 N

26. S 68° 12′ E at 10.77 knot

27. 56° 19′ to the horizontal; 135 m

28. 26° 34′ with BC (and on opposite side to A)

29. (i) 50 N and 87 N   (ii) 21.2 N and 21.2 N
(iii) 1.2 N and 0.9 N

30. (i) 5 N and 8.7 N   (ii) 35.4 N and 35.4 N
(iii) 301 N and 109 N   (iv) $W \sin \alpha$ and $W \cos \alpha$

31. 50 N, 29 N   32. 50 N, 35 N

33. 0.207 N   34. 41° 24′ and 1.32 N

35. 800 kg   36. Just over 5°

37. 3.42 m s^{-2}, 5.00 m s^{-2}, 7.07 m s^{-2}, 8.66 m s^{-2}

38. 0.3 m s^{-2} 39. 600 N   40. 1100 N

41. (i) 8 m s^{-1},   (ii) 96 W   42. 417 m

43. (i) 5 kW,   (ii) 10 kW   44. 14.9 m

45. 273 N and 3.7 m s^{-2} 46. 128 g

6. Further Trigonometry

Trigonometrical Ratios for Angles Exceeding a Right Angle

The definitions given earlier of the trigonometrical ratios depend on the angles concerned being included in a right-angled triangle. Obviously angles exceeding 90° cannot fulfil this condition and thus new definitions are needed for such angles. This is done by considering the angle swept out by an arm OP starting at position OP_0 and rotating anticlockwise about O (Fig. 6.1). The direction OP_0 is made the axis OX of the usual

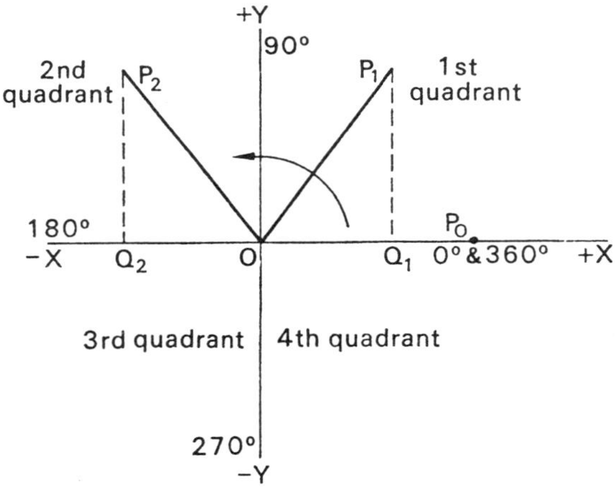

FIG. 6.1 Trigonometrical ratios for general angle

complete framework of four quadrants as shown, so that angles less than 90° lie in the first quadrant, those between 90° and 180° lie in the second quadrant, those between 180° and 270° lie in the third quadrant and those between 270° and 360° lie in the fourth quadrant.

The angle considered is always that swept out by OP moving from

OP_0 to its new position in an anticlockwise rotation. The position of P is dependent on this angle (since the length OP is fixed) and is thus another way of defining the angle.

For positions in the first quadrant (e.g. OP_1) the tangent of the angle P_0OP_1 is defined as

$$\frac{Q_1P_1}{OQ_1}, \text{ which is the same as } \frac{y\text{-co-ordinate of } P_1}{x\text{-co-ordinate of } P_1}.$$

This second definition is adopted when considering positions of P in other quadrants. Thus

$$\text{tangent of angle } P_0OP_2 = \frac{y\text{-co-ordinate of } P_2}{x\text{-co-ordinate of } P_2},$$

which will be negative because it is a positive quantity divided by a negative one.

Further it follows from this definition that the numerical value of tan $P_0\hat{O}P_2 = Q_2P_2/OQ_2$,

$$\text{i.e. } \tan P_0\hat{O}P_2 = \tan(180° - Q_2\hat{O}P_2) \text{ numerically.}$$

Thus we arrive at the result that if θ is an angle between 90° and 180°

$$\tan\theta = -\tan(180° - \theta).$$

The definitions for the other ratios are as follows:

$$\sin\theta = \frac{y\text{-co-ordinate of P}}{OP} \quad \text{and} \quad \cos\theta = \frac{x\text{-co-ordinate of P}}{OP},$$

the radius OP being positive no matter in which quadrant it lies. Thus

$$\sin P_0\hat{O}P_2 = +\sin(180° - Q_2\hat{O}P_2)$$

and

$$\cos P_0\hat{O}P_2 = -\cos(180° - Q_2\hat{O}P_2).$$

The same definitions apply to all quadrants and the signs are decided by considering the signs of the separate co-ordinates and of the (positive) radius OP. Study carefully the following nine examples which cover all common cases.

EXAMPLES

SECOND QUADRANT

1. Sin 150° = + sin (180° − 150°) = + sin 30° = + 0.5000 [y positive, OP positive].

2. Cos 150° = − cos (180° − 150°) = − cos 30° = − 0.8560 [x negative, OP positive].

3. Tan 150° = − tan (180° − 150°) = − tan 30° = − 0.5774 [y positive, x negative].

THIRD QUADRANT

4. Sin 220° = − sin (220° − 180°) = − sin 40° = − 0.6428 [y negative, OP positive].
5. Cos 220° = − cos (220° − 180°) = − cos 40° = − 0.7660 [x negative, OP positive].
6. Tan 220° = + tan (220° − 180°) = + tan 40° = + 0.8391 [y negative, x negative].

FOURTH QUADRANT

7. Sin 300° = − sin (360° − 300°) = − sin 60° = − 0.8660 [y negative, OP positive].
8. Cos 300° = + cos (360° − 300°) = + cos 60° = + 0.5000 [x positive, OP positive].
9. Tan 300° = − tan (360° − 300°) = − tan 60° = − 1.7321 [y negative, x positive].

The student should now prove for himself the following results:

Angle:	0°	90°	180°	270°	360°
Sine	0	1	0	−1	0
Cosine	1	0	−1	0	1
Tangent	0	∞	0	∞	0

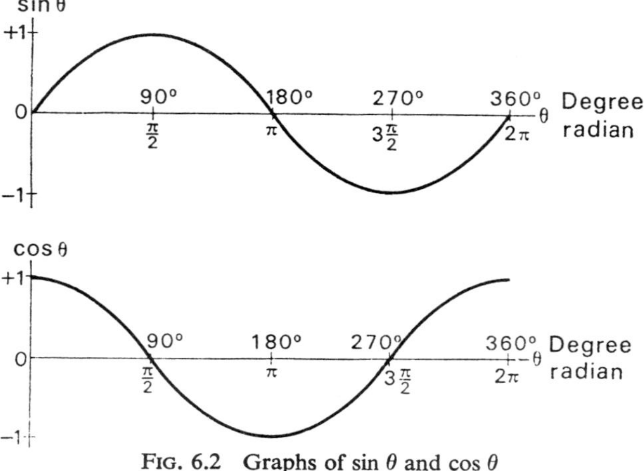

FIG. 6.2 Graphs of sin θ and cos θ

This table will form the skeleton of the curves showing how sin θ and cos θ vary with θ. To obtain the precise shapes of the curves some intermediate values are needed and the student who has never done so before should make a careful graph of sin θ against θ and of cos θ against θ.* The results will be like those in Fig. 6.2.

* A simple method of plotting the curves is described on pp. 253–4

Several points may be observed from these graphs:

1. They have a pattern which repeats indefinitely—the complete cycle being covered each 360° (or 2π radians). This is of course the period for one complete rotation of the arm sweeping out the angle (see Fig. 15.4, p. 254).

2. The graph of $\cos\theta$ is exactly like that of $\sin\theta$ but is 'moved' along by 90° $\left(\frac{\pi}{2}\text{ rad}\right)$. It is said to be '90° out of phase' with the other graph. Reference to p. 150 shows that the differential coefficient of $\sin\theta$ is $\cos\theta$. Thus the graph of $\cos\theta$ is the graph of the slope of the curve of $\sin\theta$. Examine the graphs to show that this is true.

The Use of Indices in Trigonometry

When a trigonometrical ratio is raised to a power, e.g. squared, care must be taken to make the intended meaning clear. Thus $\sin x^2$ could be taken to mean either $(\sin x)^2$ or $\sin (x^2)$ which are not identical. $(\sin x)^2$ is always written $\sin^2 x$. Sin (x^2) is written $\sin x^2$. Thus $\tan^3\theta$ means the cube of $\tan\theta$.

Negative indices are *not* used in this way and the symbol $\sin^{-1} x$ means 'the angle of which the sine is x'.*

Sin 30° = 0.5 and so we may write $\sin^{-1} 0.5 = 30°$. So the symbols $\sin^{-1} 0.5$, $\tan^{-1} x$, $\cos^{-1} 0.3$, etc., are *angles*—not trigonometrical ratios at all.

Some Important Identities

1. $\dfrac{\sin\theta}{\cos\theta} = \tan\theta.$

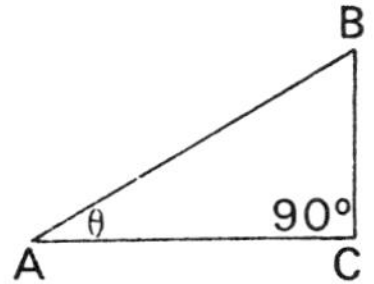

FIG. 6.3 Proof of identities

Proof: From Fig. 6.3 it is seen that

$$\sin\theta = \frac{BC}{AB} \quad\text{and}\quad \cos\theta = \frac{AC}{AB}.$$

$$\therefore \quad \frac{\sin\theta}{\cos\theta} = \frac{BC/AB}{AC/AB} = \frac{BC}{AC} = \tan\theta.$$

* The symbol 'arc sin x' is also used in place of '$\sin^{-1}x$'.

2. $\sin^2\theta + \cos^2\theta = 1$.

Proof: From Fig. 6.3

$$\sin^2\theta + \cos^2\theta = \frac{BC^2}{AB^2} + \frac{AC^2}{AB^2} = \frac{BC^2 + AC^2}{AB^2}.$$

But from Pythagoras' theorem

$$AC^2 + BC^2 = AB^2$$

$$\therefore \quad \frac{AC^2 + BC^2}{AB^2} = \frac{AB^2}{AB^2} = 1.$$

3.
$$\sin(A + B) = \sin A \cos B + \cos A \sin B \quad . \quad . \quad (1)$$
$$\sin(A - B) = \sin A \cos B - \cos A \sin B \quad . \quad . \quad (2)$$
$$\cos(A + B) = \cos A \cos B - \sin A \sin B \quad . \quad . \quad (3)$$
$$\cos(A - B) = \cos A \cos B + \sin A \sin B \quad . \quad . \quad (4)$$

These are quoted here for reference but they do not often find immediate application except in the special case when $A = B$. Substituting $B = A$ in (1) and (3) above, we obtain

$$\sin 2A = 2 \sin A \cos A \quad . \quad . \quad . \quad . \quad (5)$$

and
$$\cos 2A = \cos^2 A - \sin^2 A \quad . \quad . \quad . \quad . \quad (6)$$

Combining (6) with the identity $\sin^2 A + \cos^2 A = 1$, we obtain

$$\cos 2A = 1 - 2\sin^2 A \quad . \quad . \quad . \quad . \quad (7)$$

and
$$\cos 2A = 2\cos^2 A - 1 \quad . \quad . \quad . \quad . \quad (8)$$

These are important as aids to solution of problems (especially in integral calculus) when squares of trigonometrical ratios appear (p. 182).

Equation (7) transforms to $\sin^2 A = \dfrac{1 - \cos 2A}{2}$ . . . (9)

and (8) transforms to $\cos^2 A = \dfrac{1 + \cos 2A}{2}$ . . . (10)

(One important application will be found on p. 186.)

4.
$$\sin A + \sin B = 2 \sin \frac{A + B}{2} \cos \frac{A - B}{2} \quad . \quad . \quad (11)$$

$$\cos A + \cos B = 2 \cos \frac{A + B}{2} \cos \frac{A - B}{2} \quad . \quad . \quad (12)$$

$$\sin A - \sin B = 2 \cos \frac{A + B}{2} \sin \frac{A - B}{2} \quad . \quad . \quad (13)$$

$$\cos A - \cos B = -2 \sin \frac{A + B}{2} \sin \frac{A - B}{2} \quad . \quad . \quad (14)$$

The proof of equation (11) is as follows:
Adding (1) and (2), above $\sin(A + B) + \sin(A - B) = 2 \sin A \cos B$ (15)

Now let $x = A + B$ and $y = A - B$.
By adding, we obtain $x + y = 2A$

$$\therefore \quad A = \frac{x + y}{2}$$

By subtracting, we obtain $x - y = 2B$

$$\therefore \quad B = \frac{x - y}{2}$$

Hence, replacing all A's and B's in equation (15) by x and y, we obtain

$$\sin x + \sin y = 2 \sin \frac{x + y}{2} \cos \frac{x - y}{2},$$

which is of the same form as equation (11).

The student should apply this method to prove equations (12), (13) and (14) for himself.

One important application of such identities occurs in the analysis of adding together waves of equal amplitude (a) and frequency (f) travelling through a medium in opposite directions (p. 258). If their wavelength is denoted by λ, then the respective displacements y_1, y_2 at time t will be

$$y_1 = a \sin 2\pi \left(ft + \frac{x}{\lambda}\right) \quad . \quad . \quad . \quad . \quad (16)$$

and

$$y_2 = a \sin 2\pi \left(ft - \frac{x}{\lambda}\right) \quad . \quad . \quad . \quad . \quad (17)$$

(the change of sign in the second equation indicates the change in direction of travel).

The resultant amplitude (y) is $y_1 + y_2$.

$$\therefore \quad y = a\left[\sin 2\pi \left(ft + \frac{x}{\lambda}\right) + \sin 2\pi \left(ft - \frac{x}{\lambda}\right)\right]$$

Applying equation (11) above, we obtain

$$y = 2a \sin 2\pi ft \cos \frac{2\pi x}{\lambda}$$

This is a *stationary wave* of amplitude twice that of the separate components but of the same frequency.

If $x = (2n + 1)\frac{\lambda}{4}$, where $n = 0, 1, 2, \ldots$, then

$$\cos\frac{2\pi x}{\lambda} = \cos\left(N\frac{\pi}{2}\right),$$

where N is an odd number, $= 0.$

In these positions, then y is zero—and hence there is no displacement at any time. These are *nodes* of the wave. From above, it follows that the nodes are spaced at values of x which are separated by $\lambda/2$.

The maximum value of $\cos\frac{2\pi x}{\lambda}$ is 1. Hence in places where this occurs, we have

$$y = 2a \sin 2\pi ft.$$

These are the *antinodes* of the stationary wave. At these points the oscillation has an amplitude of $2a$.

EXAMPLES

1. Evaluate $\frac{\sin 25°}{\cos 25°}$.

$$\frac{\sin 25°}{\cos 25°} = \tan 25° = 0.4663 \text{ (using tangent tables).}$$

[This is much quicker than subtracting log-cos 25° from log-sin 25° and looking up the antilog.]

2. Prove that

$$1 + \tan^2\theta = \sec^2\theta.$$

$$1 + \tan^2\theta = 1 + \frac{\sin^2\theta}{\cos^2\theta} = \frac{\cos^2\theta + \sin^2\theta}{\cos^2\theta} = \frac{1}{\cos^2\theta} = \sec^2\theta.$$

[This is another identity worth memorizing as it is useful later on.]

3. Solve the equation $2\sin\theta = 3\cos\theta$.

Since $$2\sin\theta = 3\cos\theta$$

$$\frac{\sin\theta}{\cos\theta} = \frac{3}{2}, \text{ i.e. } \tan\theta = 1.5,$$

$$\therefore \quad \theta = 56°\ 19'.$$

SOLUTION OF TRIANGLES

By 'solution of triangles' is meant the determination of the values of the unknown sides and angles from data which are sufficient to define the triangle completely. For right-angled triangles the methods have already been discussed (see p. 76). If the triangle is not right-angled, one of the following two 'rules' must be used. The rules are stated without proof and should be memorized. (The proofs are omitted because they are of no direct importance to us—they may be found in any elementary trigonometry book intended for students of mathematics.)

It is usual to denote an angle in a triangle by a capital letter and the side opposite to it by the equivalent small letter. This is shown in Fig. 6.4, to which the rules given below refer.

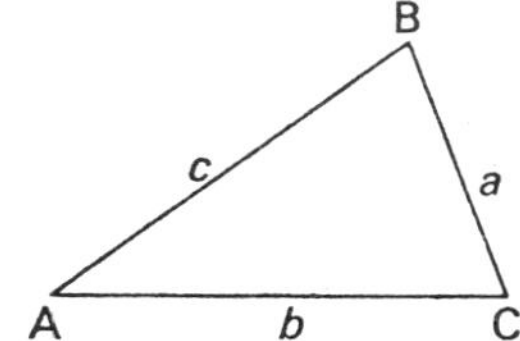

FIG. 6.4 The general triangle

Rule I: The Sine Rule

$$\frac{a}{\sin A} = \frac{b}{\sin B} = \frac{c}{\sin C}.$$

Rule II: The Cosine Rule

$$a^2 = b^2 + c^2 - 2bc \cos A.$$

$$\text{(Also it follows that } b^2 = c^2 + a^2 - 2ca \cos B$$

$$\text{and } c^2 = a^2 + b^2 - 2ab \cos C.)$$

Notes on the Use of the Rules

1. When two sides and the included angle are given, apply the cosine rule to find the third side. Then use the sine rule to evaluate a second angle. The third angle can then be found using the fact that the sum of the angles of a triangle is 180°.

2. If one side and two angles are given, use the sine rule to find the other two sides (after deducing the third angle).

3. If three sides are given, first use the cosine rule to find one angle, then the sine rule to find the next angle; deduce the third angle from the other two.

4. If, when applying the cosine rule, the angle substituted is greater than 90°, the sign of the last term will change because $\cos (180° - \theta)$ is $-\cos \theta$ (see second example, p. 96).

EXAMPLES

1. In triangle MPR, MP = 2.5 cm, MR = 3.4 cm, PMR = 50°. Find the length of PR and the value of angle RPM.

The triangle is shown in Fig. 6.5.

Applying the cosine rule:

$$\begin{aligned} PR^2 &= MP^2 + MR^2 - 2MP \cdot MR \cdot \cos P\hat{M}R \\ &= 2.5^2 + 3.4^2 - 2 \times 2.5 \times 3.4 \times \cos 50^\circ \\ &= 6.25 + 11.56 - 17.0 \cos 50^\circ \\ &= 17.81 - 10.93 \\ &= 6.88. \end{aligned}$$

$$\therefore \quad PR = \sqrt{6.88} = 2.6 \text{ cm. (Tables give 2.623.)}$$

Applying the sine rule:

$$\frac{PR}{\sin P\hat{M}R} = \frac{MR}{\sin R\hat{P}M} \qquad \therefore \frac{2.623}{\sin 50^\circ} = \frac{3.4}{\sin R\hat{P}M}$$

$$\therefore \quad \sin R\hat{P}M = \frac{3.4}{2.623} \times \sin 50^\circ. \qquad \therefore R\hat{P}M = 83^\circ\ 18'.$$

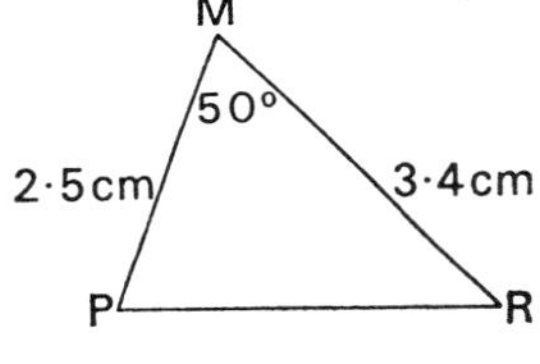

FIG. 6.5 Example

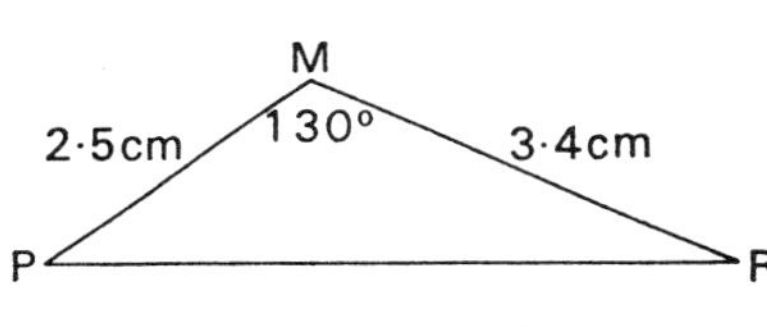

FIG. 6.6 Example

2. In triangle MPR, MP = 2.5 cm, MR = 3.4 cm, $P\hat{M}R = 130^\circ$ find the length of PR.

The triangle is shown in Fig. 6.6.

Applying the cosine rule:

$$\begin{aligned} PR^2 &= 2.5^2 + 3.4^2 - 2 \times 2.5 \times 3.4 \times \cos 130^\circ \\ &= 6.25 + 11.56 + 17.0 \cos 50^\circ \quad \text{[Note the sign change.]} \\ &= 17.81 + 10.93 \\ &= 28.74 \end{aligned}$$

$$\therefore \quad PR = \sqrt{28.74} = 5.4 \text{ cm.}$$

3. Find the magnitude and direction of the resultant of forces of 2 N and 3 N acting so that there is an angle of 60° between them.

The parallelogram of forces is shown in Fig. 6.7. Applying the cosine rule to triangle OBC we have

$$OC^2 = CB^2 + OB^2 - 2CB \times OB \times \cos O\hat{B}C.$$

By the geometry of the figure

$$O\hat{B}C = 180° - A\hat{O}B = 120°$$

$$\therefore \quad OC^2 = 2^2 + 3^2 - 2 \times 2 \times 3 \times \cos 120°$$
$$= 4 + 9 + 12 \cos 60°$$
$$= 13 + 12 \times \tfrac{1}{2}$$
$$= 19$$

$$\therefore \quad OC = \sqrt{19} = 4.359 \text{ units.}$$

i.e. the resultant has magnitude 4.4 N.

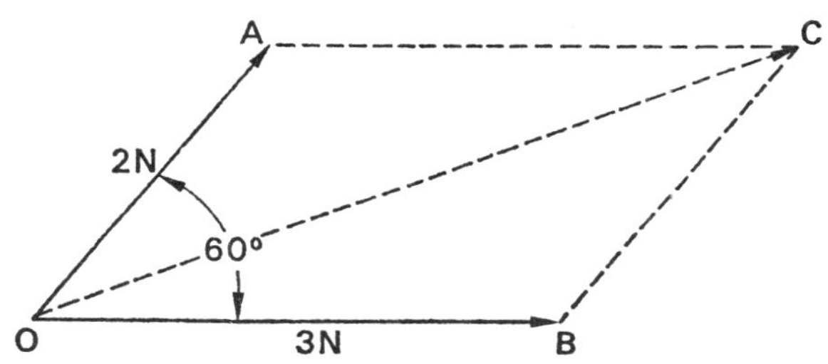

FIG. 6.7 Parallelogram of forces

To find $C\hat{O}B$ apply the sine rule to triangle COB:

$$\frac{2}{\sin C\hat{O}B} = \frac{4.359}{\sin 120°}$$

$$\therefore \quad \sin C\hat{O}B = \frac{2}{4.359} \sin 120° = \frac{2}{4.359} \sin 60°$$

$$\therefore \quad C\hat{O}B = 23° \, 24'$$

Answer: Resultant is 4.4 N acting in a direction which makes an angle of 23° with that of the 3 N.

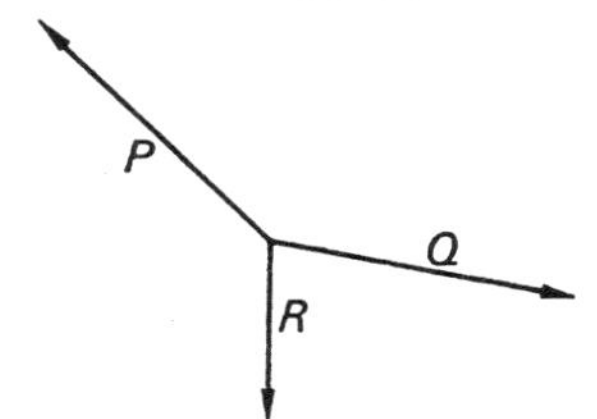

FIG. 6.8 Three forces acting at a point

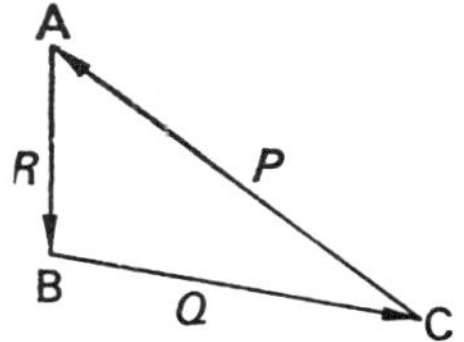

FIG. 6.9 Triangle of forces

The Triangle of Forces

Let P, Q, R be the three forces which are in equilibrium (see Fig. 6.8). If in Fig. 6.9 $\overrightarrow{AB}$ and $\overrightarrow{BC}$ be drawn to represent R and Q respectively in magnitude and direction, then $\overrightarrow{CA}$ represents P in magnitude and direction. This is a principle known as the 'triangle of forces'.

(The notation $\overrightarrow{AB}$ denotes that the force acts in a direction from A towards B. Were it in the opposite direction but of the same magnitude, it would be denoted by $\overrightarrow{BA}$ or by $\overleftarrow{AB}$.)

EXAMPLES

1. Example 3 on p. 96 can be solved alternatively thus: The triangle of forces is shown in Fig. 6.10. Application of the cosine rule to this figure leads to the solution along the same lines as on p. 97.

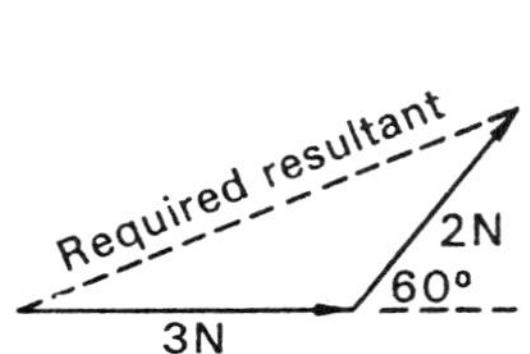

FIG. 6.10 Resultant of two forces

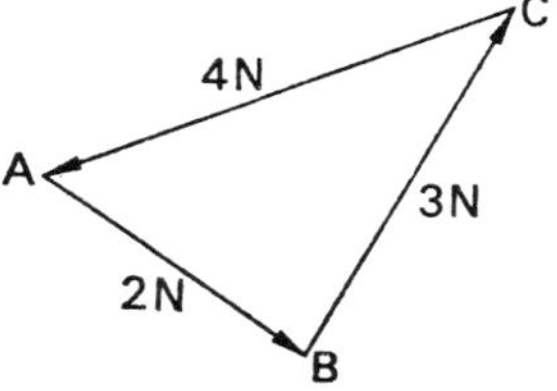

FIG. 6.11 Triangle of forces

2. Forces of 2 N, 3 N and 4 N are in equilibrium. Find the angle between the forces of 2 N and 3 N.

Fig. 6.11 shows the triangle of forces.

Solving this triangle for $\hat{B}$ by the cosine rule we have

$$4^2 = 2^2 + 3^2 - 2 \times 2 \times 3 \times \cos B$$

$$\therefore \quad \cos B = -\frac{16 - 13}{12} = -0.25.$$

Hence B must be obtuse (the sign being negative) and since $\cos^{-1} 0.25$ is $75° 31'$, $\hat{B} = 180° - 75° 31'$.

But the angle between the 2 N and the 3 N is actually $(180° - \hat{B})$, as can be seen from their directions in Fig. 6.11.

Hence the required angle is $75° 31'$.

EXERCISES 6

Angles Exceeding 90°

(1) Evaluate: sin 140°; cos 140°; tan 140°; cos 260°; tan 230°; cos 70°; tan 310°; sin 250°; cos 290°; sin 340°; sin 237°; tan 182°; tan 378°; cos 95°; sin 265°; tan 233°.

(2) Evaluate: tan 232° 17′; cos 120° 13′; tan 97° 06′; sin 295° 52′; sin 133° 17′; cos 193° 47′; tan 312° 47′; cos 283° 14′; sin 194° 53′.

(3) Evaluate without using tables: sec 120°; cot 240°; cosec 210°; cot 330°; tan 150°; cosec 150°; cos 225°; sec 60°; sin 135°; sec 315°.

Use of indices in combination with trigonometrical ratios.

(4) Evaluate: $\sin^2 30°$; $\cos^4 45°$; $\tan^2 27° 30'$; $\sec^2 58° 20'$; $1 + \tan^2 58° 20'$; $\sin^2 49° + \cos^2 49°$; $\sin^2 72° 31' + \cos^2 72° 31'$.

(5) Evaluate: $\sin^{-1}\left(\frac{1}{\sqrt{2}}\right)$; $\cos^{-1} 0.5$; $\tan^{-1} \sqrt{3}$; $\sec^{-1} 1.8361$; $\cos^{-1} 0.8000$; $\sin^{-1}\left(\frac{1}{n}\right)$ where $n = 1.5$.

(6) If $\frac{\sin i}{\sin r} = n$ show that when $i = 90°$, $r = \sin^{-1}\left(\frac{1}{n}\right)$. [This value of r is known as the critical angle of the medium of refractive index n.]

(7) Light is incident on a medium of refractive index n and is partially reflected and refracted. If the angle between the reflected and refracted rays is 90°, show that the angle of incidence is $\tan^{-1} n$. [This proof is associated with Brewster's law in the Polarization of Light.]

Identities

(8) Evaluate, using the simplest methods: $\frac{\sin 30°}{\cos 30°}$; $\frac{\sin 29° 28'}{\cos 29° 28'}$; $\frac{\cos 34°}{\sin 34°}$; $\sin^2 26° + \cos^2 26°$; $\frac{1}{\operatorname{cosec}^2 23°} + \frac{1}{\sec^2 23°}$; $1 + \tan^2 29°$.

(9) Find the values of θ between 0° and 90° which satisfy the following equations:

(i) $3 \sin \theta = 2 \cos \theta$ (ii) $\tan \theta = 2 \sin \theta$ (iii) $\sin^2 \theta = 3 \cos^2 \theta$
(iv) $\sin \theta = \cos \theta$ (v) $\sin \theta = 2 \cos \theta$ (vi) $\sin \theta = \cos 2\theta$

(10) Without referring to tables, evaluate the following (given that $\sqrt{2}$ is 1.414 and $\sqrt{3}$ is 1.732):

(i) sin 75° [regard it as sin (30° + 45°) and apply identity]
(ii) cos 75° (iii) $\sin^2 15°$ (iv) $\cos^2 15°$ (v) $\cos^2 22.5°$
(vi) sin 105° (vii) cos 105° (viii) tan 75°

(11) Find the values of θ (which lie between 0° and 90°) which satisfy the following equations:

(i) $\sin^2 \theta - \cos^2 \theta = 1$
(ii) $\sin \theta (0.3 - \sin \theta) = 0.02$
(iii) $\tan \theta (0.3 - \tan \theta) = 0.02$
(iv) $\sin^2 \theta + \cos \theta = \cos^2 \theta$
(v) $1.5 \tan^2 \theta = \sec^2 \theta$.

(12) Prove the following identities:

(i) $\cos(A + B) - \cos(A - B) + 2\sin A \sin B = 0$

(ii) $\sin(x + y) - \sin(x - y) = 2\cos x \sin y$

(iii) $\dfrac{\cos(P + Q)}{\sin P \sin Q} = \cot P \cot Q - 1$

(v) $\cot\theta + \cot\phi = \dfrac{\operatorname{cosec}\theta \operatorname{cosec}\phi}{\operatorname{cosec}(\theta + \phi)}$

Solution of Triangles; Problems on Forces

(13) Solve completely the following triangles:

(i) ABC, in which AB = 1 m, BC = 2 m and $A\hat{B}C$ = 45°

(ii) DEF, in which DE = EF = 10 cm and $D\hat{E}F$ = 100°

(iii) LMN, in which LM = 3 m, MN = 2.5 m and NL = 2 m

(iv) OPQ, in which OP = OQ, PQ = 3.5 cm and $P\hat{O}Q$ = 40°

(v) XYZ, in which XY = 43 cm, $X\hat{Y}Z$ = 130° and XZY = 20°

(vi) JKL, in which JK = 4.5 m, KL = 6.0 m, LJ = 7.5 m

(vii) RST, in which RS = 27.8 m, ST = 21.4 m, $R\hat{S}T$ = 47° 23′

(viii) GHI, in which GI = 4.8 m, $G\hat{H}I$ = 124° 40′, $H\hat{G}I = H\hat{I}G$

(14) Calculate the magnitude and direction of the resultants of the following pairs of forces, the angle given being in each case that between their lines of action.

(i) 5 N and 8 N at 120°

(ii) 200 N and 250 N at 45°

(iii) 17 N and 51 N at 60°

(iv) 40 N and 23 N at 72°

(v) 15 N and 20 N at 90°

(vi) 14.8 N and 29.6 N at 120°

(vii) 45 N and 75 N at 126° 52′

(viii) 12.7 N and 5.4 N at 180°

(15) In each of the following examples the three forces given are in equilibrium. Find in each case the angle between the lines of action of the two smallest forces:

(i) 1.6 N, 2.4 N and 3.2 N

(ii) 7 N, 5 N and 8 N

(iii) 13 N, 12 N and 5 N

(iv) 1.43 N, 2.72 N and 3.01 N

(v) 3.6 N, 6.0 N and 4.8 N

(16) A 20 kg mass is attached to a string which is drawn from the vertical by 30° by means of a horizontal force applied to the 20 kg mass. Find the value of this force and the tension in the string ($g = 10\ \text{N kg}^{-1}$).

(17) Forces of 30 N and 70 N are used to support a hanging weight of value 80 N. At which angle to the vertical does each of the two forces act?

(18) If point electrostatic charges of Q_1 units and Q_2 units are distance d cm apart they exert a force on each other of $k\dfrac{Q_1Q_2}{d^2}$ where k is a constant. Charges of +3 units are placed at each corner of an equilateral triangle of side 2 cm. Calculate (in terms of k) the force on each charge.

Answers

1. +0.6428, −0.7660, −0.8391, −0.1736, +1.1918, +0.3420, −1.1918, −0.9397, +0.3420, −0.3420, −0.8387, +0.0349, +0.3249, −0.0872, −0.9962, +1.3270

2. +1.2931, −0.5033, −8.0285, −0.8999, +0.7280, −0.9712, −1.0805, +0.2289, −0.2568

3. −2.000, +0.577, −2.000, −1.732, −0.577, +2.000, −0.707, +2.000, +0.707, +1.414

4. 0.25, 0.25, 0.271, 3.629, 3.629, 1.000, 1.000

5. 45° or 135°, 60° or 300°, 60° or 240°, 57° or 303°, 36° 52′ or 323° 08′, 41° 49′

8. 0.577, 0.5650, 1.4826, 1.000, 1.000, 1.308

9. (i) 33° 41′ (ii) 60° (iii) 60°
(iv) 45° (v) 63° 26′ (vi) 30°

10. (i) 0.9658 (ii) 0.2588 (iii) 0.0670
(iv) 0.9330 (v) 0.8535 (vi) 0.9658
(vii) −0.2588 (viii) 3.732

11. (i) 90°
(ii) 11° 32′ and 5° 44′
(iii) 11° 19′ and 5° 43′
(iv) 0° (the root $\cos\theta = -0.5$ gives $\theta = 120°$ etc.)
(v) 54° 44′

13. (i) AC = 1.47 m, $\hat{C}$ = 28° 40′, $\hat{A}$ = 106° 20′
(ii) DF = 15.3 cm, $\hat{D}$ = $\hat{F}$ = 40°
(iii) $\hat{L}$ = 55° 46′, $\hat{M}$ = 41° 25′, $\hat{N}$ = 82° 49′
(iv) OP = OQ = 5.1 cm, $\hat{P}$ = $\hat{Q}$ = 50°
(v) YZ = 62.9 cm, XZ = 96.3 cm, $\hat{X}$ = 30°
(vi) $\hat{J}$ = 53° 08′, $\hat{K}$ = 90°, $\hat{L}$ = 36° 52′
(vii) RT = 17.96 m, $\hat{R}$ = 50° 31′, $\hat{T}$ = 89° 06′
(viii) HG = HI = 2.71 m, $\hat{G}$ = $\hat{I}$ = 27° 40′

14. (i) 7 N making 38° with the 8 N force
(ii) 416 N making 20° with the 250 N force
(iii) 61 N making 14° with the 51 N force
(iv) 52 N making 47° with the 23 N force
(v) 25 N making 36° 52′ with the 20 N force
(vi) 25.6 N making 30° 00′ with the 29.6 N force
(vii) 60 N making 36° 52′ with the 75 N force
(viii) 7.3 N in the same direction as the 12.7 N force

15. (i) 75° 30′ (ii) 98° (iii) 90°
(iv) 92° 49′ (v) 90°

16. Force = 115 N and tension = 231 N

17. 60° 00′ and 21° 47′

18. 3.9 k

7. The Circle

If the radius of a circle is r its circumference is $2\pi r$ and its area πr^2.

If the radius of a sphere is r, its area is $4\pi r^2$ and its volume $\frac{4}{3}\pi r^3$.

If a cylinder is of length l and has a base of radius r, its volume is $\pi r^2 l$.

These facts should be memorized.

The value of π is 3.1416, but it is rarely employed as usually logarithms will be used or perhaps a calculator. On the latter the value of π is marked with a line labelled 'π' and for logarithmic work it is useful to know that $\log_{10} \pi = 0.4971$. There is a key for π on most calculators.

When performing calculations involving the formulae given above be very careful to substitute the value of the radius and not of the diameter—which is so often quoted in the data. Pay attention also to the units—watching especially for the use of millimetre when small diameters are quoted. In exercises on wires (such as in electrical resistance problems and in Young's modulus questions) it is common in students' work to find diameters in millimetre substituted instead of *radii* in *metre*.

EXAMPLE

What is the resistance of 1 metre of wire of diameter a tenth of a millimetre if the resistivity of the material is $49 \times 10^{-8}\ \Omega$ m.

The appropriate equation is $R = \rho \dfrac{l}{A}$.

where R = resistance in Ω, l = the length in m, A is the area of cross-section of the wire in m^2 and ρ is the resistivity in Ω m.

In this case $l = 1$ metre

The diameter $= 0.1$ mm $= 10^{-4}$ m

$\therefore$ radius $= 5 \times 10^{-5}$ m

$\therefore$ $A = \pi \times (5 \times 10^{-5})^2 = 25\pi \times 10^{-10}$ m^2

Substituting:

$$R = \frac{49 \times 10^{-8} \times 1}{25\pi \times 10^{-10}} = \frac{196}{\pi} = 62.5\ \Omega.$$

Circular Measure

In more advanced mathematical work, degrees are rarely used when measuring angles, radians being preferred.

Definition of a Radian

The angle subtended at the centre of a circle of radius r by an arc of length r is one radian (abbreviation is rad). The 'length of the arc' is the

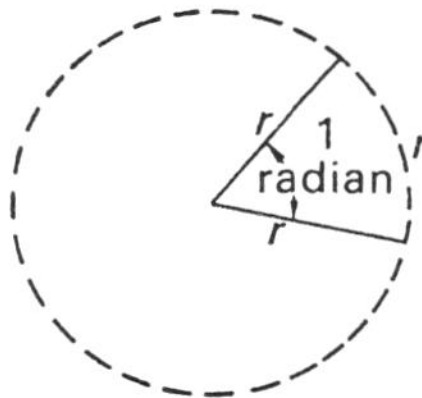

FIG. 7.1 Radian measure

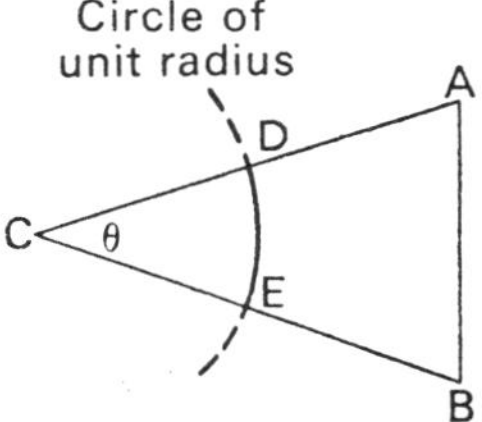

FIG. 7.2 Alternative definition of radian

'curved' length, i.e. measured round the arc (see Fig. 7.1). Since the whole circumference measures $2\pi r$ there must be 2π rad in one revolution, i.e.

$$2\pi \text{ rad} = 360°,$$

or

$$1 \text{ rad} = 360° \div 2\pi = 57°\ 18' \text{ approx.}$$

The following points should be noticed:

(1) The size of the radian is fixed, being independent of the radius of the circle used.

(2) The angle in degree can be expressed in radian by making use of the conversion table included in most collections of mathematical tables. The conversion from radian to degree is effected using the same table. Some calculators have conversion keys.

(3) From the definition of the radian it follows that the length of an arc which subtends an angle θ radians at the centre of a circle of radius r is $r\theta$. The same formula applies for any other units of length.

(4) It follows from (3) above that the angle θ subtended by a line AB at a point C is numerically equal to the length DE of the arc cut off by the lines AC, BC on a circle of unit radius described about C as centre. See Fig. 7.2.

Rotation

Speed of rotation could be measured in degree per second but in practice this is rarely used, the units chosen being commonly revolutions per minute (r.p.m.) or rad s^{-1}. The usual symbol for 'angular velocity' as it is called, in radian per second is ω, whereas rev min^{-1} (often still written 'r.p.m.') are usually denoted by n. The student should prove that, with this symbolism,

$$\omega = \frac{\pi n}{30}.$$

Angular acceleration (denoted by α) is commonly measured in rad s^{-2}. The calculus (see p. 124) shows that

$$\omega = \frac{d\theta}{dt} \quad \text{and} \quad \alpha = \frac{d\omega}{dt} = \frac{d^2\theta}{dt^2},$$

which should be compared with

$$v = \frac{ds}{dt} \quad \text{and} \quad a = \frac{dv}{dt} = \frac{d^2s}{dt^2}$$

for motion in a straight line, v and a being speed and acceleration respectively in a straight line.

If a disc of radius r is rotating with angular velocity ω a point on its circumference will move through a distance ωr in one second.

$\therefore$ The speed of this point is ωr.

If the disc is accelerating at α then a point on the circumference is accelerating by a where

$$a = \frac{d}{dt}(\omega r) = r \, . \frac{d\omega}{dt} = r\alpha.$$

Thus in general a point distant d from the axis of rotation of a body rotating with angular velocity ω is moving with a speed ωd. If the body is accelerating with angular acceleration α the actual acceleration of the point which is d from the axis of rotation is αd.

Comparison of Translation and Rotation

Motion in a straight line is referred to as 'translation'. In Chap. 13 the equations of uniformly accelerated translation are discussed. The letters u, v, a, s and t represent respectively initial velocity, final velocity, acceleration, distance and time. If for rotation these quantities are represented by ω_1, ω_2, α, θ and t, then similar equations apply, as shown below:

Translation	*Rotation*
$v = u + at$	$\omega_2 = \omega_1 + \alpha t$
$s = ut + \frac{1}{2}at^2$	$\theta = \omega_1 t + \frac{1}{2}\alpha t^2$
$v^2 = u^2 + 2as$	$\omega_2^2 = \omega_1^2 + 2\alpha\theta.$

Notice that it is not really necessary to learn the rotation equations once those for translation are known, provided the comparison is understood. The proofs for the equations applying to rotation are similar to those for translation, which are given on p. 214. A further discussion of the dynamics of rotation is given in Ch. 14.

EXAMPLES

1. A shaft of diameter 40 cm is rotating at 1000 r.p.m. What is the speed of a point on its surface?

$$\text{Radius of shaft} = 0.2 \text{ m}.$$

$\therefore$ In one minute the point moves $1000 \times 2 \times \pi \times 0.2$ m.

Hence its speed is $\dfrac{1000 \times 2\pi \times 0.2}{60}$ m s^{-1} = 21 m s^{-1}.

2. A body starting from rest reaches 600 r.p.m. in one minute. What was its angular velocity after 24 s?

Using symbols with customary significance

$$\omega_1 = 0$$

$$\omega_2 = \frac{600 \times 2\pi}{60} \text{ rad s}^{-1} = 20\pi \text{ rad s}^{-1}$$

$$t = 60 \text{ s}$$

α is required.

Substituting in $\omega_2 = \omega_1 + \alpha t$ we obtain

$$20\pi = 0 + 60\alpha$$

$$\therefore \qquad \alpha = \frac{\pi}{3} \text{ rad s}^{-2}.$$

To find angular velocity at 24 s,

$$\omega_1 = 0$$

ω_2 is required

$$\alpha = \frac{\pi}{3} \text{ rad s}^{-2}$$

$$t = 24 \text{ s}$$

$$\therefore \qquad \omega_2 = 0 + 24 \times \frac{\pi}{3} = 8\pi \text{ rad s}^{-1}.$$

APPROXIMATIONS APPLYING TO SMALL ANGLES

The table below records the values of θ measured as fractions of a radian, $\sin\theta$ and $\tan\theta$ for various values of θ given in degrees.

Angle θ		$\sin\theta$	$\tan\theta$
Degree	Radian		
1°	0.0175	0.0175	0.0175
3°	0.0524	0.0523	0.0524
5°	0.0873	0.0872	0.0875
10°	0.1745	0.1736	0.1763
20°	0.3491	0.3420	0.3640
30°	0.5236	0.5000	0.5774

It is apparent that for angles of 5° and below the difference between $\sin\theta$, $\tan\theta$ and θ in radian is negligible. Up to 10° it is very small. For higher values of θ the difference is significant. Thus we may generalize as follows:

If θ is less than 10°,

$$\sin\theta \simeq \tan\theta \simeq \theta \text{ (measured in radian).}$$

These are very important approximations. They are used in many proofs in Optics, and in deductions connected with simple harmonic motion. A series for $\sin x$ in terms of x is derived on p. 158.

Optics

The proofs in optics always involve 'narrow pencils of light'—i.e. small values of θ. Another way of putting this is that the 'aperture' of the optical device involved is small. In the case of a curved mirror or a lens, the 'aperture ratio' is defined as the diameter of the mirror (or lens) divided by the focal length. For the above approximations to apply, the aperture ratio must not exceed 0.17 approx., i.e. if the focal length is 20 cm the diameter should not exceed 3.4 cm if the familiar equations, such as $\frac{1}{v}+\frac{1}{u}=\frac{1}{f}$, are to be true.

The Application in Optics: Deviation by Prism of Small Angle

If light is incident at a small angle, i ($< 10°$), on a prism of small angle, θ ($< 10°$), the deviation, d, is given by $d = \theta(n - 1)$ where n is the refractive index. The proof is as follows:

Fig. 7.3 represents the passage of light through the prism but the angles are all drawn larger than they should be so that the geometry can more easily be followed.

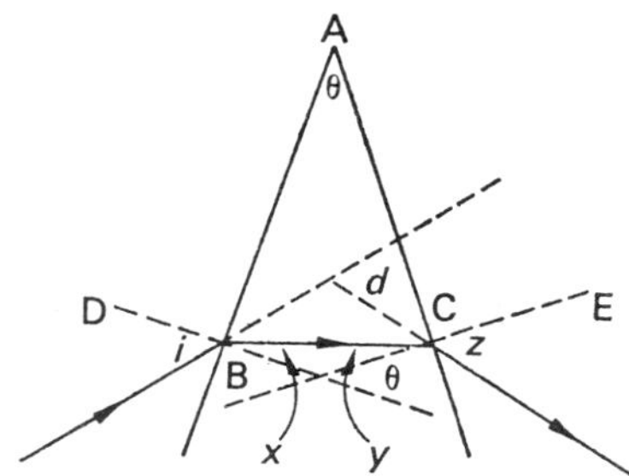

FIG. 7.3 Prism of small refracting angle

Let BD and CE be normals and the angles have the values marked. Then from geometry of the figure

$$d = (i - x) + (z - y) \quad . \quad . \quad . \quad . \quad (1)$$

Also

$$\theta = x + y \quad . \quad . \quad . \quad . \quad . \quad . \quad (2)$$

Now, by Snell's Law,

$$\frac{\sin i}{\sin x} = n \quad \text{and} \quad \frac{\sin z}{\sin y} = n.$$

But as i, x, y and z are all small angles, $\sin i = i$, etc.

$$\therefore \quad \frac{i}{x} = n \quad \text{and} \quad \frac{z}{y} = n,$$

or

$$i = nx \quad \text{and} \quad z = ny.$$

Substituting these values in (1) gives

$$\begin{aligned} d &= (nx - x) + (ny - y) \\ &= x(n - 1) + y(n - 1) \\ &= (x + y)(n - 1). \end{aligned}$$

But from (2) $\quad (x + y) = \theta$

$$\therefore \quad d = \theta(n - 1).$$

Focal Length of Lens

We may regard a lens as composed of small angled prisms and thin parallel-sided blocks, so that the deviation produced at a given distance from the axis is that due to a prism of angle equal to that between the

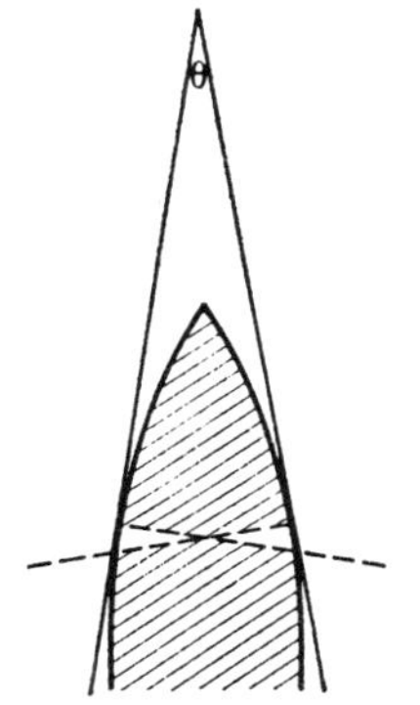

FIG. 7.4 Equivalence of lens and prism

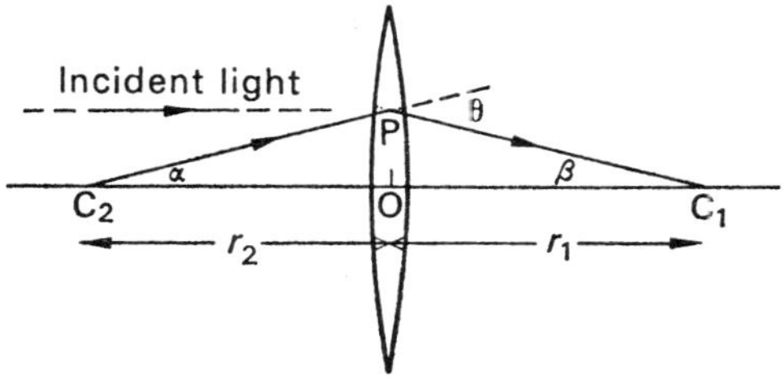

FIG. 7.5 Converging lens—radii of curvature

tangents to the faces of the lens (θ in Fig. 7.4). This is also the angle between the normals at these points. In Fig. 7.5 the connection between this angle and the centres of curvature of the faces may be traced, θ being the exterior angle of triangle PC_1C_2; thus

$$\theta = \alpha + \beta.$$

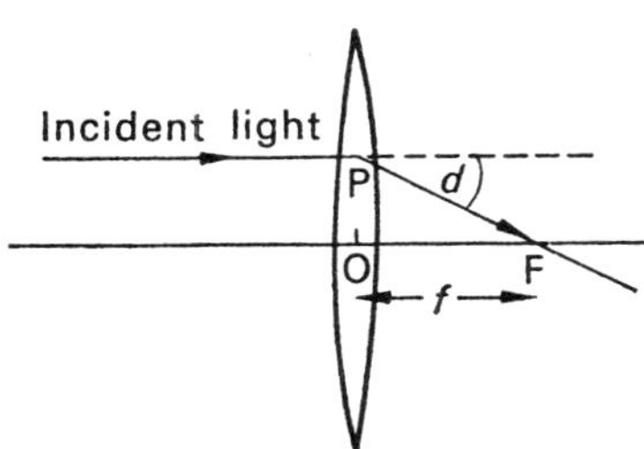

FIG. 7.6 Converging lens—focal length

In Fig. 7.6 the ray of light parallel to the axis and incident at P is shown deviated by angle d and subsequently intersecting the axis at F, the focus of the lens. (More strictly the 'second principal focus' of the lens.)

From geometry $\qquad d = \widehat{PFO}.$

Hence, using the result proved above,

$$d = \theta\,(n - 1)$$

$$\therefore \quad \widehat{PFO} = (\alpha + \beta)\,(n - 1) \quad . \quad . \quad . \quad . \quad . \quad (3)$$

Now *if all angles involved are small,*

$$\widehat{PFO} = \tan \widehat{PFO} = \frac{OP}{OF},$$

and

$$\alpha + \beta = \tan\alpha + \tan\beta = \frac{PO}{r_2} + \frac{PO}{r_1}.$$

Hence, substituting in (3), we obtain

$$\frac{PO}{OF} = \left(\frac{PO}{r_2} + \frac{PO}{r_1}\right)(n - 1)$$

or

$$\frac{1}{f} = (n - 1)\left(\frac{1}{r_1} + \frac{1}{r_2}\right).$$

Simple Harmonic Variations

In many deductions connected with s.h.m. the approximation $\theta = \sin\theta$ must be used before we can establish that the acceleration is proportional to displacement. In these cases, therefore, the motion will only be simple harmonic so long as the maximum angular displacement is less than 10°. The common cases met with in the laboratory where this applies are (i) the simple pendulum, (ii) the compound pendulum.

EXAMPLES

The scale of a reflecting galvanometer is 1 metre from the mirror attached to the suspension, and the angle through which the mirror is deflected is proportional to the current (this is usual in a moving-coil instrument). When 1 microampere is passed through the instrument the deflection of the spot on

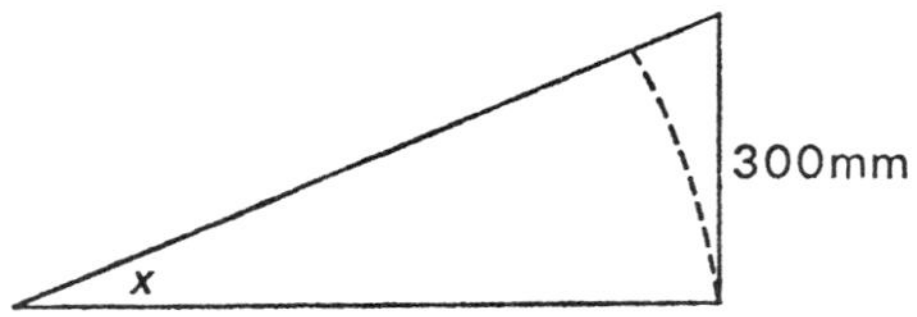

FIG. 7.7 Galvanometer scale

the scale is 50 mm. What percentage error is made by assuming that full-scale deflection (300 mm) is caused by 6 microampere?

Angular deflection per microampere is $\frac{5}{100}$ rad* = 0.05 rad.

---

* The angular deflection is actually $\tan^{-1}(5/100)$; this is 5/100 rad within 1 part in 500—see the table on p. 107.

For f.s.d. the deflection is x where $\tan x = \frac{300}{1000} = 0.3$ (see Fig. 7.7).

$$\therefore \quad x = 16^\circ\, 42' = 0.2915 \text{ rad}$$

$$\text{Hence current producing f.s.d.} = \frac{0.2915}{0.05} = 5.83\ \mu\text{A}.$$

Hence the error is 0.17 in 6.00, i.e. 17 in 600, i.e. about 3%.

2. A disc subtends an angle of 0.01° at the eye of a man. If he uses a microscope providing magnification of 50, what will be the diameter of the image when it is 25 cm away?

Since the magnification is 50, the angle subtended at the eye by the image is $50 \times 0.01^\circ = 0.5^\circ$.

Now $$0.5^\circ = 0.0088 \text{ rad}$$

The image is 25 cm from the eye and thus, if d is the diameter of the image,

$$\frac{d}{25} = 0.0088$$

$$\therefore \quad d = 0.22 \text{ cm}.$$

SOLID ANGLE

Consider a fixed point, P, at a given distance from a finite plane. Draw lines from P to all the points at the edge of the plane. These lines create 'an angle in three dimensions' subtended at P by the plane, and known as a 'solid angle'. As the plane moves farther from P this solid angle decreases.

In Physics the idea of solid angle is of importance when considering the space through which a point source of energy, such as a small electric-lamp filament, is emitting its effect, and it is necessary therefore

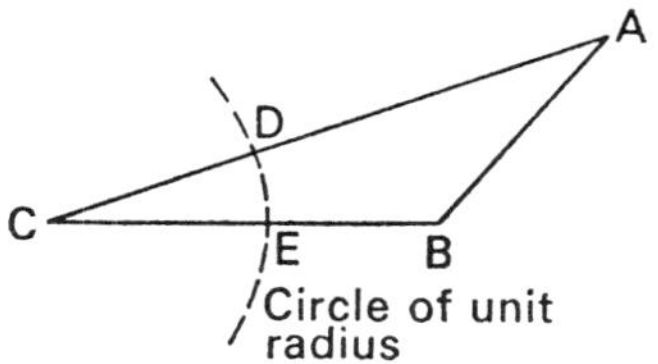

FIG. 7.8 Definition of radian

to give the idea quantitative significance. This is done in a way closely analogous to that used when defining the radian—the most useful unit for two-dimensional angles (see p. 104). There we observed that the angle in radian (θ), subtended by a line AB at a point C (Fig. 7.8), was numerically equal to the length of the *arc* DE cut off by AC and BC on a circle of unit radius drawn about C as centre. To define the solid angle subtended at a point P by a fine plane S, we describe a sphere of unit radius about P and regard the area on this sphere bounded by the lines joining P to all points on the perimeter of S as numerically equal to the solid angle. Fig. 7.9. The unit is sometimes known as a 'steradian' (the abbreviation is 'sr'). Generally, solid angle, ω, $= S/r^2$, where S is the area

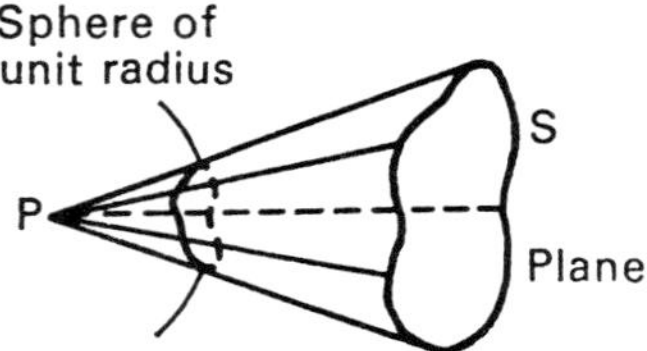

FIG. 7.9 Definition of solid angle

cut off on a sphere of radius r by the bounding lines of the solid angle. Thus all round a point, the solid angle $= 4\pi r^2/r^2 = 4\pi$.

Small Solid Angles

Consider a surface of area δS at distance r from a point P Fig. 7.10. Let δS be so small that the distance r may be regarded as the same for

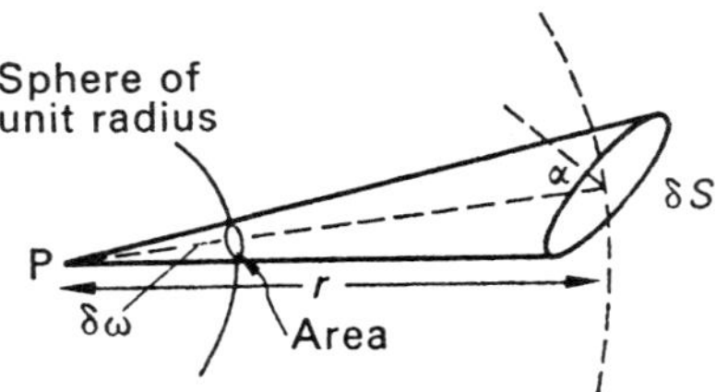

FIG. 7.10 Definition of steradian

all parts of the area. Let the solid angle subtended at P by δS be $\delta\omega$. Construct two spheres, one of unit radius and one of radius r about P. The area cut off on the latter by the bounding lines of δS is $\delta S \cos \alpha$, where α is the angle between the normal to δS and the line joining it to P. It follows from the geometry of the two spheres that

$$\frac{\delta S \cos \alpha}{r^2} = \frac{\delta\omega}{1^2}$$

$$\therefore \quad \delta\omega = \frac{\delta S \cos \alpha}{r^2}.$$

This equation is used in photometry and in electrical theory.

EXAMPLES

1. What is the solid angle subtended at the centre of a sphere of radius 10 m by (i) an area of 2 m^2 on its surface, (ii) an area of 100 m^2, (iii) half the surface area?

(i)
$$\text{Solid angle} = \frac{\text{area } S}{r^2}$$
$$= \frac{2}{10^2} = 0.02 \text{ sr.}$$

(ii)
$$\text{Solid angle} = \frac{100}{10^2}$$
$$= 1 \text{ sr.}$$

(iii)
$$\text{Solid angle} = \frac{\text{area of hemisphere}}{10^2}$$
$$= \frac{2\pi \,.\, 10^2}{10^2} = 2\pi \text{ sr.}$$

2. A rectangular screen measuring 3 cm by 4 cm is placed 5 m from an observer so that the plane of the screen makes an angle of 30° with the line joining the observer to the screen. What is the solid angle subtended by the screen at the observer's eye?

$$\text{Area of screen} = 3 \times 4 = 12 \text{ cm}^2 = 12 \times 10^{-4} \text{ m}^2.$$

Angle between normal to screen and direction of observer

$$= 90° - 30° = 60°.$$

Hence, substituting in

$$\delta\omega = \frac{\delta S \,.\, \cos\alpha}{r^2},$$

$$\delta\omega = \frac{12 \times 10^{-4} \times \cos 60°}{5^2} = 2.4 \times 10^{-5} \text{ sr.}$$

Use of Solid Angle in Photometry

A lamp emits energy of different kinds, much of it not in the visible spectrum. In photometry we are concerned with that energy which does lie within the visible spectrum and we therefore use the term 'luminous flux' to mean the amount of luminous energy emitted in each second. The unit used is the 'lumen', which is defined as the luminous flux emitted within unit solid angle by a source of intensity one candela (see p. 2). Hence a lumen is the product of candela and steradian.

It may help the reader if he visualizes a cone of light starting at the light source. If the intensity of the light sources is I, then through every steradian the flux passing will be I, and through solid angle ω the flux will be $I\omega$. From this it also follows that the *total* flux emitted all round a source of intensity I is $4\pi I$ (in lumen).

If the source is at the centre of a sphere of radius r (in metre) the flux will be uniformly distributed over an area of $4\pi r^2$. Thus the illumination at the surface of the sphere

$$\frac{4\pi I}{4\pi r^2} = \frac{I}{r^2}.$$

The unit of E will be 'lumen per square metre', which is therefore the SI unit of illumination known as a 'lux' (abbreviated to lx). Since this is the illumination at 1 metre from a source of intensity one candela, it follows that a lux is also one candela-metre.

The illumination due to bright sunshine in Britain is about 50 klx and this rises to about twice that value around noon in the tropics. For reading the required illumination is 50—100 lx, which is the order of illumination at about 1 metre from a 50—100 watt filament lamp, since the efficiency of filament lamps (from the lighting aspect) is about 4π lm W^{-1}.

EXERCISES 7

Circles, Spheres and Cylinders

(1) Find the mass of 2000 lead shot each of diameter 1.0 mm (density of lead = 1.14×10^4 kg m^{-3}).

(2) A spool consists of 454 g of copper wire of s.w.g. 16. How many metres of wire are there on the spool? (Density of copper = 8.9×10^3 kg m^{-3}; s.w.g. 16 = diameter 1.63 mm.)

(3) A horizontal metal ring of radius 10 cm is slowly withdrawn from the surface of water of surface tension 0.07 N m^{-1}. What is the force due to surface tension acting on the ring just before it leaves the surface?

(4) The mean diameter of a set of steel balls was determined by weighing a number of them and assuming the density of steel to be 7.7×10^3 kg m^{-3}. The mass of 12 was found to be 122.65 g. What was the mean diameter?

5. A hollow glass sphere of radius 4 cm is loaded with lead shot so that it will sink in water. What will be the difference between its apparent weight in water and in a liquid of density 800 kg m^{-3}?

(6) In order to determine the diameter of a capillary tube a thread of mercury was introduced and its length measured by means of a vernier microscope. The mass of the mercury was determined so that its volume could be deduced, assuming that the density of mercury in kg m^{-3} was

1.36×10^4. The microscope readings were 10.926 cm and 4.758 cm. The empty crucible weighed 6.610 g and when the mercury was added it weighed 6.884 g. What was the diameter of the bore of the tube?

(7) What is the resistance of 25 metre of copper wire of diameter 0.274 mm if the resistivity of copper is $1.78 \times 10^{-8}\ \Omega$ m?

(8) The resistance of 59.0 cm of constantan wire of diameter 0.044 cm is found to be 1.83 Ω. What value does this experiment give for the resistivity of constantan?

(9) The brass cylinder of a 'cylinder and bucket' apparatus is of diameter 2 cm and length 3 cm. The bucket is also of brass and is 1 mm thick (sides and base). The handle and hook weigh (together) 2 g. How much sand is needed for counterpoising initially? What weight of liquid, of density 1200 kg m^{-3}, will the bucket hold? [Density of brass = 8.4×10^3 kg m^{-3}.]

(10) How long is the line of latitude 52° N? (Radius of earth may be taken as 6370 km.)

(11) The bulb of a mercury-in-glass thermometer has a volume of 0.5 cm^3 up to the 0°C mark. If the distance apart of the marks for 0°C and 100°C is 20 cm what is the diameter of the capillary tube? [Apparent expansivity of mercury in glass = 0.000 174 K^{-1}.]

(12) A rectangular lawn measures 25 m by 32 m. A circular rose bed is to be made in the middle so that the area of the rose garden is equal to half the original area of the grass. Can this be done?

If the plan was altered so that the diameter of the rose garden was 15 m what fraction of the original area would be preserved as lawn?

(13) Tennis balls are sometimes packed in rectangular boxes and sometimes in cylindrical boxes. In each case the minimum space is wasted. Calculate the percentage of space wasted in each case.

(14) A hollow sphere of outside diameter 50 cm is made of material of thickness 10 cm and density 6000 kg m^{-3}. What is the mass of the sphere?

(15) A hollow cylinder of outside diameter 20.0 cm is made of metal of thickness 4 mm. It is open at both ends. A student calculates the volume by multiplying the area of the outside surface by the thickness of the metal. What is the percentage error in his answer and is it too great or too small?

Radians and Degrees; Rotation

(16) Express the following angles in radian:
20°; 27° 36′; 60°; 10° 14′; 90°; 135°; 180°; 17° 39′; 75° 55′.

(17) Express the following angles in degrees and minutes:
0.3142 rad; π rad; 0.2 rad; $\pi/4$ rad; 0.8761 rad; 5 rad.

(18) Express 12 000 rev/min in rad s^{-1}.

(19) A wheel accelerates uniformly from rest to a speed of 60 rad s^{-1} in 10 s. What was its angular acceleration? How many revolutions has it done in this time? If its axle is 4 cm in diameter at what speed is a point on the axle moving after 5 second, in cm s^{-1}?

(20) A motor engine slows down from 4240 rev/min to 1000 rev/min in $\frac{1}{2}$ minute. What was the angular deceleration of the crankshaft?

(21) An engine increases its speed from 500 rev/min to 2646 rev/min in 10 s. How many revolutions did it make in that time?

(22) (i) What is the angular velocity of the earth about its axis?
(ii) If the radius of the earth is 6370 km, what is the speed in km h^{-1}, due to the earth's rotation, of a place at latitude 60° N?

(23) A lorry accelerates uniformly from rest to 48 km h^{-1} in 12 s. What is the angular acceleration of the wheels if the tyres have an effective diameter of 0.72 m? What will be the final engine speed in rev/min if the gear then in use has an overall ratio of 10:1?

(24) What is the angular velocity of the label on an LP record rotating at 33 rev/min? If the playing time is 20 min how far does a point 10 cm from the centre of the disc travel whilst the record is being played?

(25) A car is brought to rest in 200 m from an initial speed of 144 km h^{-1}. What is the angular deceleration of the road wheels if the tyres have an effective diameter of 0.60 m?

(26) Through what angle will the minute hand of a clock turn between noon and when the hands are next together?

(27) Communications satellites remain stationary with respect to the earth. Such a satellite is put 'into orbit' over the equator. Calculate the height at which it will have an orbital period of 24 hours (i.e. achieve the object) given that for any earth satellite $\omega^2 r^3 = GM$ where $\omega =$ the angular velocity of the satellite in rad s^{-1}, $r =$ the distance from the centre of the earth, $G = 6.67 \times 10^{-11}$ (in SI), $M = 5.97 \times 10^{24}$ (in SI units). The radius of the earth is 6371 km; 1 day = 86 400 s.

(28) A triangular lamina ABC is rotated about an axis through A and perpendicular to ABC. It is found that C travels 1.2 times as far as B in a given time. When a similar axis through B is used C has a linear velocity of 0.8 of that of A. Calculate the ratio of the linear speed of A to that of B when the rotation occurs about C.

(29) A metal sphere is rolled down a slope at a constant speed of 8 cm s^{-1} in a straight line. One second after it has started another sphere of diameter

8 mm rolls along the same line from the same starting point and has a constant angular velocity of 25 rad s^{-1}. How far from the starting point will they collide?

(30) The weight in a grandfather's clock falls 2 m in each 24 h period and causes rotation of a shaft (s) which has diameter 6 cm. What is the overall gear ratio between s and the shaft to which the hour hand is fixed?

Small Angle Approximation

(31) Write down, using tables: sin 6°; tan 6°; 6° as radian.

(32) Calculate, mentally, the angle in radian subtended by a line 1 mm long at a point 1 m away.

(33) A pin 2 cm high is 4 m from an observer. What angle does it subtend at his eye?

(34) A galvanometer has a pointer 4 cm long and has a sensitivity of 20 μA/division. The scale divisions are 1 mm apart. Through what angle does the coil turn when 3.8 μA is passed through the instrument?

(35) A slide containing a small object is placed 20 cm below the eye in a microscope of magnifying power 300. The image is formed 25 cm from the eye and measures 1 mm in length. What is the size of the object?

(36) The legs of an optical lever form an equilateral triangle of side 2 cm, the front pair being mounted on a rigid support. The scale is a metre from the mirror. Through what distance is the rear leg moved when the spot moves 1 cm on the scale?

(37) A track is stated as having a gradient of 1 in 100 and a calculation is made of the total rise per km assuming that the track rises 1 m for every 100 m of *track*. It is later discovered that in fact the track rises 1 m for every 100 m moved *horizontally*. What percentage error is made as a result of the wrong interpretation?

(38) Explain the terms *dispersion, dispersive power*. Describe briefly the determination of the dispersive power of the material of a glass prism by a spectrometer method.

A narrow parallel beam consisting of red light and blue light is incident on a thin converging lens at a point 1 cm from its centre, the beam travelling parallel to the principal axis of the lens. Calculate the angle between the emerging red and blue rays being given that the focal length of the lens for red light is 15 cm and the refractive indices of glass for red and blue light are 1.641 and 1.664 respectively. (*L.*)

(39) A body travelling at 2 m s^{-1} changes direction by 3° in 0.4 s. What is the acceleration in this interval?

(40) Two thin lines 2 mm apart were drawn on a piece of paper and viewed by a student who found he could only 'separate' the lines (i.e. be sure there were two and not one only) when nearer than 5 m. If the effective distance of the lens of the eye from the retina is 2 cm what is the resolving power of his eye and what is the separation of the images of the lines on the retina?

Solid Angles

(41) Assuming that the diameter of the sun is 13.9×10^5 km and its distance from the earth is 1.5×10^8 km calculate the solid angle subtended by the sun at the earth.

(42) The mean distance to the moon is 3.84×10^5 km and its diameter is 3460 km. What solid angle does its illuminated surface subtend at an observer on the earth at the time of half-moon?

(43) A point source of light is emitted through 0.2 sr. What area will it illuminate at 20 m? (Assume that the area is normal to the incident light.)

(44) Water from a hose pipe nozzle (which may be regarded as a point source) is directed vertically downwards from a height of 2 m and sprays an area of 80 cm^2. What solid angle does this represent?

(45) Good quality filament lamps rated at 100 W may, to a reasonable approximation, be looked on as 100 cd sources. What value for lm W^{-1} is required for this assumption to be accurate?

(46) The illumination due to bright sunshine at the equator is about 100 klx when the sun is overhead. Assuming that there is no absorption by the atmosphere and that the sun may be regarded as a point source of light estimate the power of the sun in cd, given that the distance of the earth from the sun is 1.5×10^{11} m.

(47) A 3 cd lamp is used to illuminate a plane surface 4 m away and normal to the incident light. What is the illumination of this surface in mlx?

(48) Adequate illumination for 'close' work is about 200 lx. If a desk lamp of 100 W (producing 12.5 lm W^{-1}) is used for the purpose, how near to the surface being inspected must the lamp be placed?

Answers

1. 11.9 g
2. 24.5
3. 0.088 N
4. 13.6 mm
5. 0.054 kgf
6. 0.65 mm
7. 7.56 Ω
8. 4.7×10^{-7} Ω m
9. 101 g and 11.3 g
10. 2.46×10^{4} km
11. 0.24 mm
12. Yes, leaving 1.25 m on each side; 0.78
13. 48% and 33%
14. 364 kg
15. Student's value is 2% too great
16. 0.349, 0.482, 1.047, 0.179, $\frac{\pi}{2}$ (=1.571), $\frac{3\pi}{4}$ (=2.356), π (=3.142), 0.308, 1.325
17. 18° 00′, 180°, 11° 27′, 45°, 50° 12′, 286° 28′
18. 1257 rad s^{-1}
19. 6 rad s^{-2}, 48 rev, 60 cm s^{-1}
20. 11.3 rad s^{-2}
21. 262 rev
22. (i) 7.27×10^{-5} rad s^{-1}, (ii) 834 km h^{-1}
23. 3.09 rad s^{-2}; 3550 rev min^{-1}
24. 3.46 rad s^{-1}; 415 m

25. 13.3 rad s^{-2}

26. 6.85 rad

27. 35.9×10^6 m

28. 1.5

29. 40 cm

30. 0.188

31. 0.1045, 0.1051, 0.1047

32. 0.001

33. 5×10^{-3} rad

34. 4.75×10^{-3} rad

35. 2.7×10^{-3} mm

36. 0.087 mm

37. 0.005%

38. 9′

39. 0.262 m s^{-2}

40. 4×10^{-4} rad; 8×10^{-3} mm

41. 6.7×10^{-5} sr

42. 3.2×10^{-5} sr

43. 80 m^2

44. 2×10^{-3} sr

45. 4π

46. 2.25×10^{27} cd

47. 188 mlx

48. 0.7 m

8.
Principles of Differential Calculus

Velocity and Small Quantities

Calculus is a subject which deals with small quantities, and was invented by Newton and Leibnitz in the seventeenth century. We can illustrate the need for a technique of dealing with small quantities if we consider the velocity of a stone dropped from rest at a point O above the ground (Fig. 8.1). The distance s fallen in a time t is given approximately by

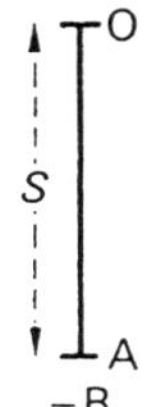

FIG. 8.1 Motion under gravity

the formula $s = 5t^2$, where s is in metre (m) and t in second (s). After 2 s, then, the stone has fallen a distance OA or s_1 given by

$$s_1 = 5 \times 2^2 = 20 \text{ m}.$$

Suppose the velocity *at* 2 s is required. After 2.1 s, the distance OB fallen, s_2, is given by

$$s_2 = 5 \times 2.1^2 = 22.05 \text{ m}$$

Thus

$$\text{average velocity from A to B} = \frac{\text{distance AB}}{\text{time}}$$

$$= \frac{22.05 - 20}{0.1}$$

$$= 20.5 \text{ m s}^{-1}$$

We can get nearer to 2 s by finding the distance travelled in 2.01 s from O, which is given by

$$s = 5 \times 2.01^2 = 20.2005.$$

Consequently, during a time from 2.00 to 2.01 s,

$$\text{average velocity} = \frac{20.2005 - 20}{0.01}$$
$$= 20.05 \text{ m s}^{-1}$$

If we proceed to diminish the time interval from 2.000 to 2.001 s and less, we get nearer and nearer to the velocity *at* 2 s. The calculus provides a technique of finding this limit or velocity.

Calculus Notation

A small increase in time t, like that just considered, is written as δt; 'δA' means 'a small increase in A', 'δx' means a small increase in x. The square and cube of the small increase in x is written $(\delta x)^2$, $(\delta x)^3$ respectively. The student should take special note that δx is a *single* quantity; it does not imply the product of δ and x.

Consider a square brass plate of side x. The area A is then x^2. If the metal is heated so that each side expands by a length δx, the new area $= (x + \delta x)^2$. The increased area is written as $(A + \delta A)$, i.e. the original area plus the small increase in area. Thus

$$A = x^2$$
$$\therefore \quad A + \delta A = (x + \delta x)^2$$
$$\therefore \quad \delta A = (x + \delta x)^2 - x^2 = 2x \, . \, \delta x + (\delta x)^2$$
$$\therefore \quad \frac{\delta A}{\delta x} = 2x + \delta x.$$

If $x = 1$ m, and the small increase in length δx is 0.01 m, then

$$\frac{\delta A}{\delta x} = 2 \times 1 + 0.01 = 2.01$$

Thus the ratio of the small increase in area to the small increase in length is 2.01.

Suppose we wish to find the ratio of the consequent small increase in volume, δV, of a metal cube to the small increase in length, δx, of one side. If V is the volume and x is the length, then

$$V = x^3$$
$$\therefore \quad V + \delta V = (x + \delta x)^3$$
$$\therefore \quad \delta V = (x + \delta x)^3 - x^3 = 3x^2 \, . \, \delta x + 3x \, . \, (\delta x)^2 + (\delta x)^3$$
$$\therefore \quad \frac{\delta V}{\delta x} = 3x^2 + 3x \, . \, \delta x + (\delta x)^2.$$

When $x = 1$ m and $\delta x = 0.01$ m,

$$\frac{\delta V}{\delta x} = 3 \times 1^2 + 3 \times 1 \times 0.01 + 0.01^2$$
$$= 3 + 0.03 + 0.0001 = 3.0301,$$

It should be carefully noted that the terms with δx and $(\delta x)^2$ contribute very little to the ratio $\delta V/\delta x$ when δx is very small, and this is also true for higher powers of δx such as $(\delta x)^3$, $(\delta x)^4$.

Differentiation

Consider again the problem of finding the velocity of a stone exactly 2 second after it is dropped from rest under gravity. The distance s travelled in a time t is given by

$$s = 5t^2 \quad \text{(p. 121)}$$
$$\therefore \quad s + \delta s = 5(t + \delta t)^2 = 5t^2 + 10t \times \delta t + 5(\delta t)^2$$
$$\therefore \quad \delta s = 10t \times \delta t + 5(\delta t)^2$$
$$\therefore \quad \frac{\delta s}{\delta t} = 10t + 5 \times \delta t \quad . \quad . \quad . \quad . \quad . \quad . \quad \text{(i)}$$

When $t = 2$ s, and $\delta t = 0.1$ s, i.e. 0.1 s after 2 s,

$$\frac{\delta s}{\delta t} = 10 \times 2 + 5 \times 0.1 = 20.5 \text{ m s}^{-1}.$$

Now δs is the small distance travelled after 2 s in a further small time δt. Thus $\delta s/\delta t$ is the *average velocity* in this time. If $\delta t = 0.001$ s,

$$\frac{\delta s}{\delta t} = 10 \times 2 + 5 \times 0.001 = 20.005 \text{ m s}^{-1}.$$

From (i) it follows that, as δt gets smaller and smaller, the value of $\delta s/\delta t$ approaches the value $10t$, or 20 when $t = 2$. We write $\frac{\mathrm{d}s}{\mathrm{d}t}$ for the *limiting value* of $\frac{\delta s}{\delta t}$ as δt tends to zero; and hence

$$\frac{\mathrm{d}s}{\mathrm{d}t} = 10t.$$

Similarly, on p. 122 we obtained

$$\frac{\delta A}{\delta x} = 2x + \delta x,$$

and as δx tends to zero, the limiting value of $\frac{\delta A}{\delta x}$ is given by

$$\frac{\mathrm{d}A}{\mathrm{d}x} = 2x.$$

Also since, on p. 122,

$$\frac{\delta V}{\delta x} = 3x^2 + 3x \,.\, \delta x + (\delta x)^2,$$

the limiting value of $\delta V/\delta x$ as δx tends to zero is given by

$$\frac{\mathrm{d}V}{\mathrm{d}x} = 3x^2.$$

The limiting values $\mathrm{d}s/\mathrm{d}t$, $\mathrm{d}A/\mathrm{d}x$ and $\mathrm{d}V/\mathrm{d}x$ are called *differential coefficients* (or first derivatives), and the process of finding the differential coefficients is called *differentiation.*

In general, it can be seen that the differential coefficient is the *limiting value of a function as* $\delta x \to 0$. In mathematical notation, if $y = f(x)$, where $f(x)$ is any function of x, then

$$\frac{\mathrm{d}y}{\mathrm{d}x} = \underset{\delta x \to 0}{\mathrm{Lt}} \frac{f(x + \delta x) - f(x)}{\delta x}.$$

Physical Quantities as Differential Coefficients

From our previous discussion, it follows that '$\mathrm{d}s/\mathrm{d}t$' represents the *velocity*, v, at an instant t if s is the distance travelled, or the 'rate of change' of s with respect to t. Thus the kinetic energy of a moving object $= \frac{1}{2}mv^2 = \frac{1}{2}m\left(\frac{\mathrm{d}s}{\mathrm{d}t}\right)^2$. The rate of change of velocity, v, with respect to time t is represented by $\mathrm{d}v/\mathrm{d}t$, which is therefore the *acceleration.* If θ is the angle of rotation of an object and t is the time, then $\mathrm{d}\theta/\mathrm{d}t$ represents the *angular velocity*, ω. The *angular acceleration* is $\mathrm{d}\omega/\mathrm{d}t$. In an alternating current circuit, $\mathrm{d}I/\mathrm{d}t$ represents the rate of change of the current where I is the current. Also, $I = \mathrm{d}Q/\mathrm{d}t$, the rate of change of Q, the quantity of electricity.

If $\mathrm{d}s/\mathrm{d}t$ is differentiated again with respect to t, the result is expressed as $\mathrm{d}^2s/\mathrm{d}t^2$. Now the velocity v is represented by $\mathrm{d}s/\mathrm{d}t$, and thus the acceleration $= \mathrm{d}v/\mathrm{d}t = \mathrm{d}^2s/\mathrm{d}t^2$. Similarly, for motion in a curve, $\mathrm{d}^2\theta/\mathrm{d}t^2$ represents the angular acceleration, since the angular velocity $= \mathrm{d}\theta/\mathrm{d}t$. If $\mathrm{d}y/\mathrm{d}x$ is differentiated again with respect to x, it is written as $\mathrm{d}^2y/\mathrm{d}x^2$.

In 'dot' notation, $\mathrm{d}x/\mathrm{d}t$ is expressed as $\dot{x}$ and $\mathrm{d}^2x/\mathrm{d}t^2$ as $\ddot{x}$ (see p. 154).

General Rule for Differentiating Power of x

If $y = x^n$, where n is a number, it can be shown that the differential coefficient is always given by

$$\frac{\mathbf{d}y}{\mathbf{d}x} = nx^{n-1} \quad . \quad . \quad . \quad . \quad . \quad \text{(i)}$$

or, writing this in an alternative way,

$$\frac{\mathrm{d}}{\mathrm{d}x}(x^n) = nx^{n-1} \quad . \quad . \quad . \quad . \quad \text{(ii)}$$

EXAMPLES

1. If $$V = x^3,$$
$$\frac{\mathrm{d}V}{\mathrm{d}x} = 3x^{3-1} = 3x^2.$$

2. If $$y = 2x^2,$$
$$\frac{\mathrm{d}y}{\mathrm{d}x} = 2 \times 2x^{2-1} = 4x.$$

3. If $$y = 6,$$
$$\frac{\mathrm{d}y}{\mathrm{d}x} = 0,$$

since 6 is a constant; this result is true for any number.

4. If $$y = \frac{1}{x} = x^{-1},$$
$$\frac{\mathrm{d}y}{\mathrm{d}x} = -1x^{-1-1} = -x^{-2} = -1 \times x^{-2} = -\frac{1}{x^2}.$$

5. If $$y = \frac{1}{x^2} = x^{-2},$$
$$\frac{\mathrm{d}y}{\mathrm{d}x} = -2x^{-2-1} = -2 \times x^{-3} = -2 \times \frac{1}{x^3} = -\frac{2}{x^3}.$$

6. If $$y = 2x^3 - 3x^2 + 6x - 2,$$

the differential coefficient is obtained by differentiating each term separately. Thus

$$\frac{\mathrm{d}y}{\mathrm{d}x} = 6x^2 - 6x + 6.$$

Differentiating again, $$\frac{\mathrm{d}^2y}{\mathrm{d}x^2} = 12x - 6.$$

7. If $$y = \sqrt{x} = x^{\frac{1}{2}},$$
$$\frac{\mathrm{d}y}{\mathrm{d}x} = \frac{1}{2}x^{\frac{1}{2}-1} = \frac{1}{2}x^{-\frac{1}{2}} = \frac{1}{2} \times \frac{1}{\sqrt{x}} = \frac{1}{2\sqrt{x}}.$$

8. If $$y = \frac{1}{\sqrt{x}} = x^{-\frac{1}{2}},$$
$$\frac{\mathrm{d}y}{\mathrm{d}x} = -\frac{1}{2}x^{-\frac{1}{2}-1} = -\frac{1}{2}x^{-\frac{3}{2}} = -\frac{1}{2} \times \frac{1}{\sqrt{x^3}} = -\frac{1}{2\sqrt{x^3}}.$$

Isothermal Bulk Modulus of a Gas

When a gas expands or contracts isothermally, i.e. at constant temperature, the pressure p and volume V obey the relation $pV = k$, where k is a constant. This is Boyle's law.

$$\therefore \quad p = \frac{k}{V} = kV^{-1}.$$

Differentiating both sides with respect to V,

$$\frac{\mathrm{d}p}{\mathrm{d}V} = -kV^{-1-1} = -kV^{-2} = -k \times \frac{1}{V^2}$$

Substituting $k = pV$,

$$\frac{\mathrm{d}p}{\mathrm{d}V} = -\frac{pV}{V^2} = -\frac{p}{V}$$

$$\therefore \quad -V\frac{\mathrm{d}p}{\mathrm{d}V} = p \quad . \quad . \quad . \quad . \quad . \quad . \quad . \quad \text{(i)}$$

Suppose a gas is subjected to an increase in pressure δp, and the resulting change in volume is $-\delta V$, where V is the original volume. Then, by definition,

$$\textit{bulk stress} \text{ on gas} = \text{force per unit area} = \delta p$$

and

$$\textit{bulk strain} = -\delta V/V.$$

$$\therefore \quad \text{bulk modulus} = \frac{\text{stress}}{\text{strain}} = \frac{\delta p}{-\delta V/V} = -V\frac{\delta p}{\delta V}.$$

In the limit,

$$\text{bulk modulus} = -V\frac{dp}{\mathrm{d}V} \quad . \quad . \quad . \quad \text{(ii)}$$

But, from (i),

$$-V\frac{\mathrm{d}p}{\mathrm{d}V} = p,$$

the pressure, when isothermal changes are made.

$$\therefore \quad \textit{isothermal bulk modulus} = p. \quad . \quad . \quad . \quad . \quad . \quad . \quad \text{(iii)}$$

Adiabatic Bulk Modulus

When air undergoes an *adiabatic* change it obeys the relation $pV^{1.4} = c$, where c is a constant.

$$\therefore \quad p = \frac{c}{V^{1.4}} = cV^{-1.4}$$

$$\therefore \quad \frac{\mathrm{d}p}{\mathrm{d}V} = -1.4cV^{-1.4-1} = -1.4cV^{-2.4} = \frac{-1.4c}{V^{2.4}}.$$

Substituting $pV^{1.4}$ for c,

$$\therefore \quad \frac{dp}{dV} = -\frac{1.4pV^{1.4}}{V^{2.4}} = -\frac{1.4p}{V}$$

$$\therefore \quad -V\frac{dp}{dV} = 1.4p.$$

Hence, from (ii) above, the adiabatic bulk modulus for air $= 1.4p$.

Generally, adiabatic changes obey the relation $pV^{\gamma} = c$, where γ is the ratio of the principal specific heat capacities of the gas concerned.

$$\therefore \quad p = \frac{c}{V^{\gamma}} = cV^{-\gamma}$$

$$\therefore \quad \frac{dp}{dV} = -\gamma cV^{-\gamma-1} = -\gamma c \times V^{-(\gamma+1)} = -\frac{\gamma c}{V^{\gamma+1}}.$$

Substituting $c = pV^{\gamma}$,

$$\therefore \quad \frac{dp}{dV} = -\frac{\gamma pV^{\gamma}}{V^{\gamma+1}} = -\frac{\gamma p}{V}$$

$$\therefore \quad -V\frac{dp}{dV} = \gamma p.$$

Hence, from (ii),

adiabatic bulk modulus $= \gamma p.$

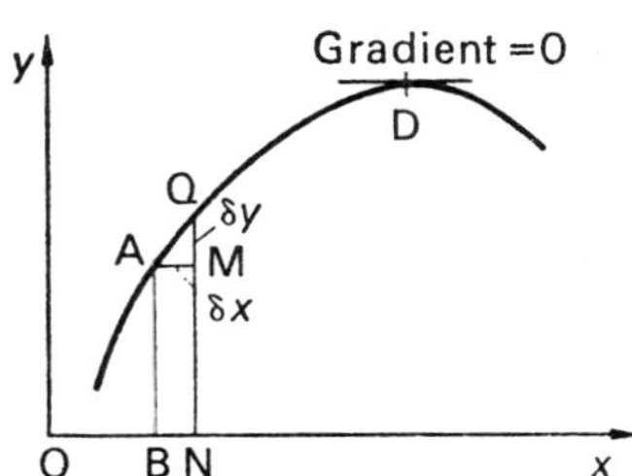

FIG. 8.2 Differential coefficient and gradient

Gradients of Curves

Suppose the relation between two quantities, y and x, is represented by the curve in Fig. 8.2. If A is a point on the curve such that OB $= x$, BA $= y$, and Q is a point close to A so that ON $= x + \delta x$ and NQ $= y + \delta y$, then the *gradient* of the chord AQ is defined as the ratio QM/AM. Thus the gradient $= \delta y/\delta x$.

As Q approaches A, δx and δy both become smaller. In the limit, as δx tends to zero, $\delta y/\delta x$ has a value equal to $\mathrm{d}y/\mathrm{d}x$, the differential coefficient of y with respect to x; at the same time the chord AQ becomes the *tangent at A* to the curve. Consequently $\mathrm{d}y/\mathrm{d}x$ *represents the gradient of the tangent* at a point on the curve. Similarly, $\mathrm{d}\theta/\mathrm{d}t$ represents the gradient of the tangent at a point on the temperature (θ)-time (t) curve.

Potential Gradient and Electric Intensity

If V represents the electric potential in an electric field, and r is the distance of points in the field from a fixed point or origin, $\mathrm{d}V/\mathrm{d}r$ represents the *potential gradient* round a point. Thus if the variation of V with r is known, the potential gradient at a point is obtained by finding the gradient of the tangent to the curve. The potential gradient is numerically equal to the electric intensity, E, at the point concerned, and as V diminishes when r increases, a minus sign is introduced into the expression for E (see p. 274). Thus

$$E = -\frac{\mathrm{d}V}{\mathrm{d}r}.$$

Rate of Cooling

If θ represents the temperature of a cooling body and t the time, then $-\mathrm{d}\theta/\mathrm{d}t$ represents the rate of *fall* of temperature. The rate of loss of heat of the body = mass × specific heat capacity × rate of fall of temperature

$$= -mc\frac{\mathrm{d}\theta}{\mathrm{d}t}.$$

If θ_0 is the temperature of the surroundings, $(\theta - \theta_0)$ is the excess temperature over the surroundings. Now by Newton's law of cooling, the rate of loss of heat of a body is proportional to the excess temperature over the surroundings under conditions of forced convection.

$$\therefore \quad -mc\frac{\mathrm{d}\theta}{\mathrm{d}t} = k(\theta - \theta_0),$$

where k is a constant.

$$\therefore \quad -\frac{\mathrm{d}\theta}{\mathrm{d}t} \propto (\theta - \theta_0).$$

$\mathrm{d}\theta/\mathrm{d}t$ is the gradient of the tangent to the temperature (θ)-time (t) curve at the temperature concerned, and can be measured from the graph. On plotting the gradients against the corresponding excess temperature a straight line passing through the origin is obtained, thus verifying Newton's law.

Conduction of Heat

When a lagged bar is heated at one end the various sections attain a constant temperature after a time, and the bar is then said to be in a 'steady' state. The temperature, θ, decreases with the distance x from the hot end, and the *temperature gradient* at a section is thus represented by $-\mathrm{d}\theta/\mathrm{d}x$. The *quantity of energy per second* through a section is represented by $\mathrm{d}Q/\mathrm{d}t$, where Q is the quantity and t is the time. In the steady state, the quantity of energy per second is proportional to the area, A, of the section and to the temperature gradient there, or

$$\text{quantity of energy per second} = kA \times \text{temperature gradient},$$

where k is the thermal conductivity.

$$\therefore \quad \frac{\mathrm{d}Q}{\mathrm{d}t} = -kA\frac{\mathrm{d}\theta}{\mathrm{d}x}.$$

This is the fundamental equation in conduction. When the bar is lagged, the quantity of energy per second flowing through each section is constant. Hence, from above,

$$\frac{\mathrm{d}\theta}{\mathrm{d}x} = \text{constant},$$

and thus the temperature gradient is the same at all sections. This means that the temperature falls *linearly* with distance along the bar. If the bar is not lagged, some energy is lost from the sides and the temperature gradient diminishes along the bar away from the hot end.

Inductance of a Coil

When a current changes in a coil, an induced e.m.f. E is set up which opposes the rate of change of the current, $\mathrm{d}I/\mathrm{d}t$. The *inductance*, L, of the coil is defined by the relation

$$E = -L\frac{\mathrm{d}I}{\mathrm{d}t}. \qquad (1)$$

In this relation E is in volts when L is in henrys and $\mathrm{d}I/\mathrm{d}t$ is in ampere per second.

If the coil has N turns of area A, and a uniform flux density B due to the current I links all the turns normally at an instant, then

$$\text{total flux linkage } \Phi = NAB$$

$$= \frac{NA \times \mu NI}{l} = \frac{\mu N^2 AI}{l}, \qquad (2)$$

since $B = \mu NI/l$ for a solenoid, where μ is the permeability of the medium and l is the length of the solenoid. Here we assume no flux leakage. But, from Faraday's law of electromagnetic induction,

$$E = -\frac{d\Phi}{dt} = -\frac{\mu N^2 A}{l} \cdot \frac{dI}{dt}. \quad . \quad . \quad . \quad (3)$$

From (1) and (3) it follows that, for a solenoid with no flux leakage,

$$L = \frac{\mu N^2 A}{l}. \quad . \quad . \quad . \quad . \quad (4)$$

Suppose the relative permeability μ_r of the soft-iron in the solenoid $= 1000$, $N = 500$, $l = 50$ cm $= 0.5$ m, $A = 40$ cm^2 $= 40 \times 10^{-4}$ m^2. Then, from (4), since $\mu = \mu_r\mu_0 = 1000 \times 4\pi \times 10^{-7}$,

$$L = \frac{1000 \times 4\pi \times 10^{-7} \times 500^2 \times 40 \times 10^{-4}}{0.5}$$

$$= 2.5 \text{ H (approx.)}.$$

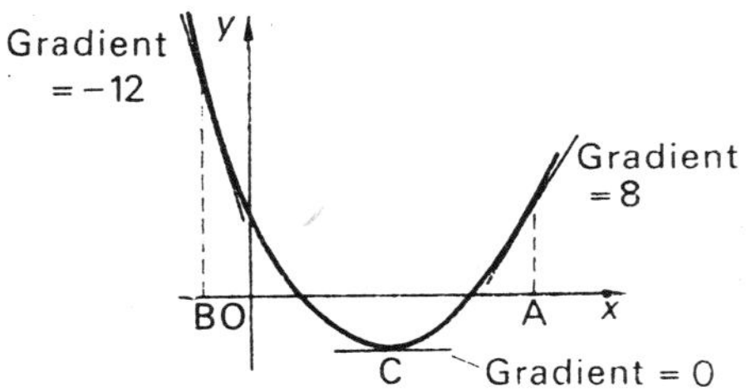

FIG. 8.3 Gradient values

Gradient Values, Maxima and Minima

Suppose $y = 2x^2 - 8x + 2$ represents the curve shown in Fig. 8.3. Then

$$\frac{dy}{dx} = 4x - 8.$$

Thus at A, where $x = 4$,

$$\frac{dy}{dx} = 16 - 8 = 8;$$

at B, where $x = -1$,

$$\frac{dy}{dx} = -4 - 8 = -12,$$

the negative gradient implying that the curve slopes downward in this case.

At the minimum value, C, in Fig. 8.3, the gradient is zero. At a maximum value, a, in Fig. 8.4 (i), the gradient is also zero. These results are true generally. Thus

$$\frac{dy}{dx} = 0 \textit{ at maximum or minimum values of } y.$$

Suppose the maximum and minimum values of

$$y = x^3 - 3x^2 - 9x + 1$$

are required. Then

$$\frac{dy}{dx} = 3x^2 - 6x - 9.$$

Hence, at a maximum and minimum value,

$$3x^2 - 6x - 9 = 0$$

or

$$x^2 - 2x - 3 = 0$$

$$\therefore \quad (x - 3)(x + 1) = 0$$

$$\therefore \quad x = 3 \text{ or } -1.$$

Thus at $x = 3$ or -1, a maximum or minimum value occurs.

Distinguishing between Maximum and Minimum Values

We can tell whether $x = 3$ corresponds to a maximum or minimum value by studying the gradient just before and just after this point. If it is a maximum, then, as shown in Fig. 8.4 (i), the gradient is +ve before

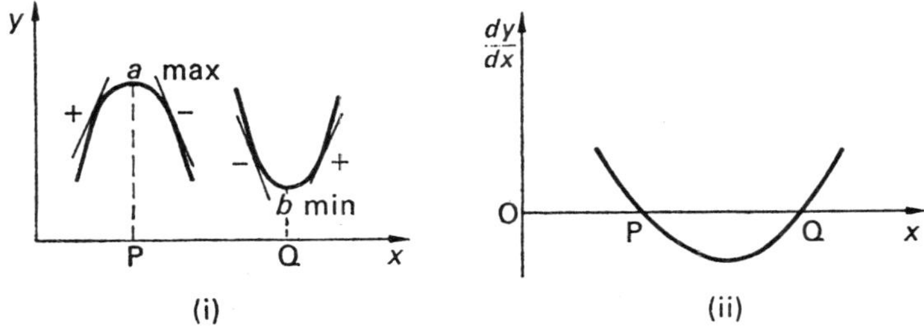

FIG. 8.4 Maximum and minimum

$x = 3$, for example at $x = 2\frac{1}{2}$, and −ve after $x = 3$, for example at $x = 3\frac{1}{2}$. If it is a minimum value at $x = 3$, as at Q, the reverse is true. Now if $x = 3\frac{1}{2}$, then from above

$$dy/dx = 3x^2 - 6x - 9 = 3(x - 3)(x + 1) = 6\tfrac{3}{4},$$

that is, dy/dx is +ve; if $x = 2\frac{1}{2}$, then dy/dx is −ve. Thus $x = 3$ corresponds to a *minimum* value, as at b in Fig. 8.4 (i).

To find whether $x = -1$ corresponds to a maximum or minimum value, substitute $x = -1\frac{1}{2}$ in

$$dy/dx = 3(x - 3)(x + 1);$$

then dy/dx is +ve. Now substitute $x = -\frac{1}{2}$; then dy/dx is −ve. Thus $x = -1$ corresponds to a maximum value, as at *a* in Fig. 8.4 (i).

A more convenient way of distinguishing maximum and minimum values is shown in Fig. 8.4 (ii), which illustrates the variation of dy/dx as one proceeds through a maximum point such as that in Fig. 8.4 (i). dy/dx then goes from a positive to a negative value through the zero value of dy/dx at P. At P the curve slopes downwards, and hence the differential coefficient at P is −ve. Now the differential coefficient of dy/dx is d^2y/dx^2.

$$\therefore \quad \frac{d^2y}{dx^2} \textit{ is } -ve \textit{ at a maximum value.}$$

From Q in Fig. 8.4 (ii), it also follows that

$$\frac{d^2y}{dx^2} \textit{ is } +ve \textit{ at a minimum value.}$$

EXAMPLES

1. Find whether $2x^2 + 4x - 1$ has a maximum or minimum value and state the magnitude of the latter.

$$y = 2x^2 + 4x - 1$$

$$\therefore \quad \frac{dy}{dx} = 4x + 4 \quad \text{(i)}$$

For max or min, $$\frac{dy}{dx} = 0$$

$$\therefore \quad 4x + 4 = 0$$

$$\therefore \quad x = -1.$$

From (i), $$\frac{d^2y}{dx^2} = 4, \text{ which is } + ve.$$

$$\therefore \quad x = -1 \text{ gives a } \textit{minimum} \text{ value}$$

$$\therefore \quad \text{minimum value of } y = 2x^2 + 4x - 1 = 2 - 4 - 1 = -3.$$

2. Find the values of x which make $y = x^3 + 3x^2 - 9x + 5$ a maximum or minimum.

$$y = x^3 + 3x^2 - 9x + 5$$

$$\therefore \quad \frac{dy}{dx} = 3x^2 + 6x - 9 \quad \text{(i)}$$

and $$\frac{d^2y}{dx^2} = 6x + 6 \quad \text{(ii)}$$

From (i), if $\dfrac{dy}{dx} = 0,$

$$3x^2 + 6x - 9 = 0,$$

or $$3(x + 3)(x - 1) = 0$$

$$\therefore \quad x = -3 \quad \text{or} \quad +1.$$

From (ii), when $x = -3$,

$$\frac{d^2y}{dx^2} = 6x + 6 = -12, \text{ which is } -\text{ve.}$$

$$\therefore \quad x = -3 \text{ gives a maximum value.}$$

From (ii), when $x = 1$,

$$\frac{d^2y}{dx^2} = 6x + 6 = 12, \text{ which is } +\text{ve.}$$

$$\therefore \quad x = 1 \text{ gives a minimum value.}$$

3. The perimeter of a rectangular field is 400 m. Calculate the maximum area possible with this perimeter.

Let x = length of one side; then $(200 - x)$ = length of other side, both lengths being in metre.

$$\therefore \quad \text{area, } A, = x(200 - x) = 200x - x^2$$

$$\therefore \quad \frac{dA}{dx} = 200 - 2x$$

$$\therefore \quad \frac{d^2A}{dx^2} = -2 = -\text{ve quantity, indicating a } \textit{maximum} \text{ value.}$$

The maximum value is given by $\dfrac{dA}{dx} = 0$

$$\therefore \quad 200 - 2x = 0 \quad \text{or} \quad x = 100$$

$$\therefore \quad \text{length of other side} = 200 - x = 100$$

$$\therefore \quad \text{maximum area} = 100 \times 100 = 10\,000 \text{ m}^2.$$

Point of Inflexion

In Fig. 8.5 (i), the S-shaped curve shown has a gradient (dy/dx) which increases from zero at the minimum H to a *maximum* at the point P, and then decreases to zero at K. Since the gradient at P is a maximum when the gradient, dy/dx, is plotted against x, it follows that the differential coefficient of dy/dx at P = 0. *Hence* $d^2y/dx^2 = 0$ *at P.*

The turning point P on the curve is called a *point of inflexion.* Although $d^2y/dx^2 = 0$ at P, note that dy/dx at P has a +ve value; this value is equal to the gradient of the tangent AB to the curve at P, Fig. 8.5 (i). In Fig. 8.5 (ii), however, the curve shown has a point of inflexion at Q, so $d^2y/dx^2 = 0$ at Q, but the gradient of the tangent CD at Q is also zero. Thus, in this special case, $d^2y/dx^2 = 0$ and $dy/dx = 0$.

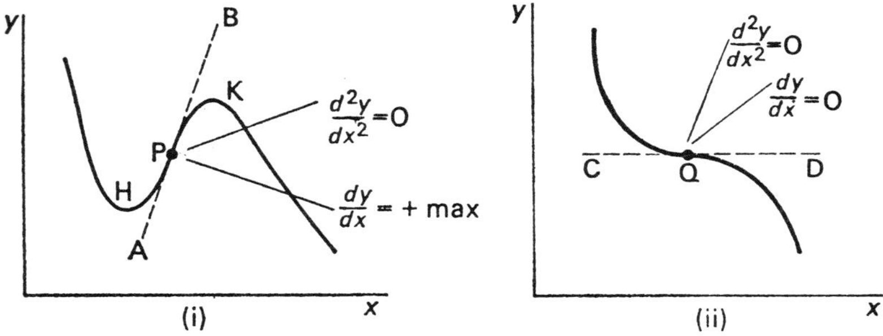

FIG. 8.5 Points of inflexion

As an illustration, consider the cubic curve

$$y = x^3 - x^2 - 5x + 1.$$

Then
$$\frac{dy}{dx} = 3x^2 - 2x - 5$$

and
$$\frac{d^2y}{dx^2} = 6x - 2.$$

The maximum and minimum values of x are given by

$$3x^2 - 2x - 5 = 0 = (3x - 5)(x + 1).$$

Thus $x = \frac{5}{3}$(min) and -1(max). The point of inflexion is given by $6x - 2 = 0$, so $x = \frac{1}{3}$. The point of inflexion lies between the min and max values.

Intermolecular Potential and Force

The potential energy V between two molecules is a function of their separation r. Fig. 8.6 (i) shows roughly the variation of V with r. The *intermolecular force* $F = -dV/dr$ (also p. 274). Hence, from the values of the gradients of the V against r curve, the F against r curve is roughly that shown in Fig. 8.6 (ii).

Some special points can now be noted.

(1) At $r = r_0$, V has a minimum value V_0. Fig. 8.6 (i). Thus r_0 is the *equilibrium separation* of the two molecules. This is approximately 3×10^{-10} to 5×10^{-10} m for solids.

(2) When $r > r_0$, the force F is an attraction. Thus over large distances of separation, F is attractive.

When $r < r_0$, the force F is a repulsion. Thus when the molecules come very close to each other, a short-range repulsive force is predominant. At $r = r_0$, the repulsive and attractive forces balance each other.

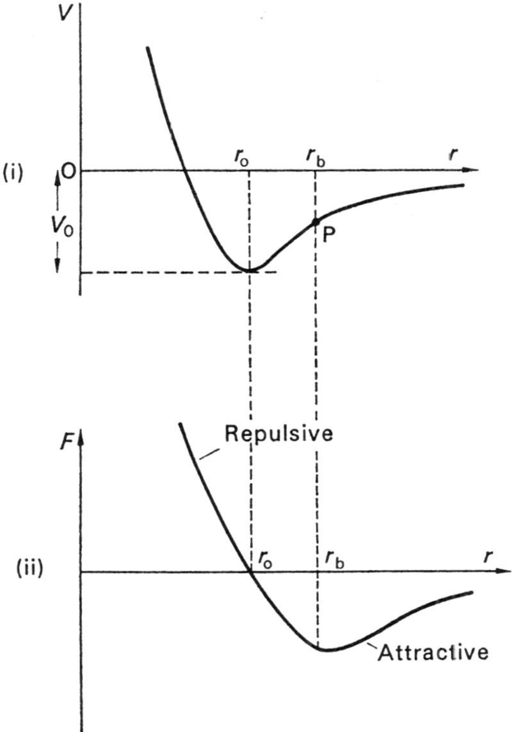

FIG. 8.6 Intermolecular potential V and force F

(3) The $V - r$ curve has a point of inflexion at P, where $r = r_b$. Thus $d^2V/dr^2 = 0$ or $dF/dr = 0$ at $r = r_b$. Since F *decreases* when $r > r_b$, it follows that r_b is the separation of the molecules in say a chain of molecules when the chain breaks.

Breaking Strain

Suppose that the intermolecular potential energy V between two molecules is given by

$$V = V_0\left[-2\left(\frac{r_0}{r}\right)^6 + \left(\frac{r_0}{r}\right)^{12}\right], \quad . \quad . \quad . \quad (1)$$

where V_0 and r_0 are constants. The intermolecular force F is given by

$$F = -\frac{\mathrm{d}V}{\mathrm{d}r} = -12V_0\left[\left(\frac{r_0}{r}\right)^7 - \left(\frac{r_0}{r}\right)^{13}\right]. \quad . \quad . \quad (2)$$

Now at $r = r_b$, the point of inflexion, $\mathrm{d}F/\mathrm{d}r = 0$. Hence, from (2),

$$\frac{\mathrm{d}F}{\mathrm{d}r} = -12V_0\left[-7\left(\frac{r_0}{r}\right)^8 + 13\left(\frac{r_0}{r}\right)^{14}\right] = 0$$

$$\therefore \quad 7\left(\frac{r_0}{r}\right)^8 = 13\left(\frac{r_0}{r}\right)^{14}$$

$$\therefore \quad \left(\frac{r_0}{r}\right)^6 = \frac{7}{13}$$

$$\therefore \quad r = \left(\frac{13}{7}\right)^{1/6} r_0 = r_b$$

$$\therefore \quad \text{breaking strain} = \frac{r_b - r_0}{r_0} = \left(\frac{13}{7}\right)^{1/6} - 1$$

$$= 11\% \text{ (approx.)}.$$

This is approximately the observed value in many materials.

EXERCISES 8

Differentiate the following with respect to x:

(1) $3x^2$.

(2) x^3.

(3) $x + 2$.

(4) $\frac{1}{x} + 2x$.

(5) $\frac{1}{x^2} + \frac{1}{x}$.

(6) $x^2 - 2x + 1$.

(7) $3x^3 - x^2 + x - 3$.

(8) $\frac{3}{x} - \frac{2}{x^2} + x$.

(9) If s represents distance and t time, write down an expression in terms of the calculus for (i) velocity, (ii) acceleration. If the distance s in metre fallen by an object in a time t in second is given by $s = 5t^2$, calculate its velocity after (*a*) 1 s, (*b*) 3 s, and find the acceleration.

(10) An object moves upwards through a distance s given by $s = 40t - 5t^2$, where t is the time. Calculate (i) the velocity after 2 s, (ii) the time the particle takes to come to rest, (iii) the retardation, (iv) the distance travelled when the velocity is 10 m s^{-1}.

Differentiate the following with respect to the variable concerned:

(11) θ^2.

(12) $\sqrt{2x}$.

(13) $\dfrac{1}{\sqrt{l}}$.

(14) $t^{2.4}$.

(15) $V^{0.4}$.

(16) $\sqrt{a} + \dfrac{1}{\sqrt{a}}$.

(17) $V^{1.4}$.

(18) $\dfrac{1}{m}$.

(19) The period T of a simple pendulum is given by $T = 2\pi\sqrt{\dfrac{l}{g}}$ where l is the length in m and $g = 9.81$ m s^{-2}. Calculate the rate of change of T with respect to l, dT/dl, when $l = 1$ m.

(20) The potential V at a point due to a small charge q is given by $V = 9 \times 10^9\, q/r$, where r is the distance from the charge to the point. When q is in coulomb and r in metre, then V is in volt. Find the potential gradient, dV/dr, where (i) $r = 0.5$ m, (ii) $r = 0.05$ m, if q is 10^{-8}C.

(21) The potential V between two molecules is given by $a/r^{12} - b/r^6$, where a, b are constants and r is the separation of the molecules. Find the separation when $dV/dr = 0$ in terms of a and b.

Gradients. Max and Min.

(22) Find (i) the gradient at $x = 3$, (ii) the gradient at $x = -1$, (iii) the minimum value, of $y = 2x^2 - 8x - 3$.

(23) Draw the graph of $y = 3 - 2x - x^2$ from $x = -4$ to $+4$. Find (i) the gradient at $x = 0$, (ii) the gradient at $x = 1$, (iii) the maximum value of y from your drawing, and verify each answer by calculation.

(24) Find the gradient at $V = 2$ for (i) $p = \frac{10}{V}$, (ii) $p = \frac{10}{V^{1\cdot 4}}$.

Find the maximum and/or minimum values of the following:

(25) $y = x^3 - 3x$.

(26) $2x^2 - 6x + 2$.

(27) $x^3 - 3x^2 - 9x$.

(28) $x + \frac{1}{x}$.

(29) A rectangle has a perimeter of 40 m. Calculate the maximum possible area.

(30) A ball thrown vertically upwards travels a distance s given by $s = 20t - 5t^2$. Calculate the greatest height attained.

(31) The sag s of a beam is given by $s = \frac{1}{200}(9l^2 - l^3)$, where l is the distance from one end. Calculate the maximum sag.

(32) The sum of the length of a parcel and its perimeter round the base must not exceed 2 m. If the base is square, calculate the maximum volume of the parcel.

(33) The potential V between two ions separated a distance x in a solid is given by $V = -a/x + b/x^9$. Find the value of x in terms of a and b when V is a minimum.

Show that your result gives a minimum and not a maximum.

(34) The total energy W of a liquid drop is given by $W = ar^2 - br^3$, where a, b are constants and r is the radius. For growth of the drop, the critical size occurs when W is a maximum. Calculate the critical radius in terms of a and b, and the corresponding value of W.

(35) The equation of a curve is $y = x^3 - 2x^2 - 7x + 2$. Calculate the value of x at the maximum, minimum and point of inflexion. Draw a rough sketch of the curve.

(36) Find the point of inflexion of the curve $y = x(x - 2)^2$.

(37) Find the maximum and minimum points, and the point of inflexion, of the curve

$$y = x^3 - 3x^2 - 9x - 5$$

(38) What is the volume of the largest cylinder which can be inscribed inside a sphere of radius a?

(39) A ladder makes an angle θ with the horizontal ground and rests against a vertical wall. If the top slides down with a vertical speed v, show that the bottom slides with horizontal speed $v \tan \theta$.

(40) A rectangular box with square base and open at the top is to be made out of a given area of material. Ignoring the thickness of the material, show that the largest volume will be obtained when the box has its base of side equal to twice the length of a vertical edge.

(41) Find the values of x for which $y = \frac{(x-1)(x-2)}{x}$ has stationary values and determine which of them gives a maximum and which a minimum value of y.

Sketch the graph of $y = \frac{(x-1)(x-2)}{x}$. (*O.*)

(42) A wine glass in the form of an inverted cone has a height of 5 cm and the diameter of its circular top is 6 cm. Show that when the height of the wine in the glass is x cm, the volume of wine is $3\pi x^3/25$ cm^3.

If the wine is being poured in at a rate of 6 cm^3 per second, find the rate at which the height of the wine is increasing at the instant when the height of wine in the glass is 4 cm. (*O.*)

Answers

1. $6x$
2. $3x^2$
3. 1
4. $-\frac{1}{x^2}+2$
5. $-\frac{2}{x^3}-\frac{1}{x^2}$
6. $2x-2$
7. $9x^2-2x+1$
8. $-\frac{3}{x^2}+\frac{4}{x^3}+1$
9. (*a*) 10 (*b*) 30 m s^{-1}; accn. = 10 m s^{-2}
10. (i) 20 m s^{-1} (ii) 4 s (iii) 10 m s^{-2} (iv) 75 m
11. 2θ
12. $\frac{1}{\sqrt{2x}}$
13. $-\frac{1}{2\sqrt{l^3}}$
14. $2.4t^{1.4}$
15. $0.4V^{-0.6}$
16. $\frac{1}{2\sqrt{a}}-\frac{1}{2\sqrt{a^3}}$
17. $1.4V^{0.4}$
18. $-\frac{1}{m^2}$
19. 1.0 s m^{-1}
20. (i) 360 (ii) 36 000 V m^{-1}
21. $(2a/b)^{1/6}$
22. (i) 4 (ii) −12 (iii) −11
23. (i) −2 (ii) −4 (iii) 4
24. (i) −2.5 (ii) −2.7
25. Max 2, min −2
26. Min. −2.5
27. Max 5, min −27
28. Max −2, min 2
29. 100 m^2
30. 20 m
31. 0.54
32. 2/27 m^3

33. $(9b/a)^{1/8}$

34. $2a/3b$; $W = 4a^3/27b^2$

35. $\frac{7}{3}$ (min), -1 (max), $\frac{2}{3}$ (inflexion)

36. $x = \frac{4}{3}$, $y = \frac{16}{27}$

37. Max: $-1, 0$; min: $3, -32$; inflexion: $1, -16$

38. $4\sqrt{3}\pi a^3/9$

41. $-\sqrt{2}$ (max), $+\sqrt{2}$ (min)

42. $25/24\pi$ cm s^{-1}

9. Further Differential Calculus

Differentiation of Function of a Function

To find the differential coefficient of

$$y = (3x - 2)^6,$$

let $$z = 3x - 2. \qquad \text{(i)}$$

Then $$y = z^6. \qquad \text{(ii)}$$

Now $$\frac{\delta y}{\delta x} = \frac{\delta y}{\delta z} \times \frac{\delta z}{\delta x},$$

and hence, in the limit, $$\frac{dy}{dx} = \frac{dy}{dz} \times \frac{dz}{dx}.$$

But, from (ii), $$\frac{dy}{dz} = 6z^5;$$

and from (i), $$\frac{dz}{dx} = 3.$$

$$\therefore \quad \frac{dy}{dx} = 6z^5 \times 3 = 18z^5$$

$$= 18(3x - 2)^5.$$

Since $$\frac{dy}{dx} = \frac{dy}{dz} \times \frac{dz}{dx},$$

we can always write down the differential coefficient, dy/dx, (i) by differentiating y with respect to z, the quantity in the bracket, (ii) then multiplying the result by the differential coefficient of z itself. Thus if

$$y = (x^2 - 4)^5,$$

i.e. $$z = x^2 - 4,$$

$$\frac{dy}{dx} = 5(x^2 - 4)^4 \times 2x = 10x(x^2 - 4)^4.$$

Similarly, if $y = (2x^2 - 3x + 1)^3$,

$$\frac{dy}{dx} = 3(2x^2 - 3x + 1)^2 \times (4x - 3)$$
$$= 3(4x - 3)(2x^2 - 3x + 1)^2.$$

Rate of Growth

The rate of growth of the volume V of a sphere is dV/dt; the rate of growth of its radius r is dr/dt. Since

$$V = \tfrac{4}{3}\pi r^3$$

$$\therefore \quad \frac{dV}{dt} = 4\pi r^2 \frac{dr}{dt}. \quad . \quad . \quad . \quad . \quad (1)$$

Thus if the radius grows steadily at a rate of 0.1 millimetre per second, the rate at which the volume increases when $r = 10$ mm is given, from (1), by

$$\frac{dV}{dt} = 4\pi \times 10^2 \times 0.1 = 126 \text{ mm}^3 \text{ s}^{-1} \text{ (approx.)}.$$

Differentiation of Products

On occasions we may need to differentiate a product of functions of x, such as $(x^2 - 4x + 2)(x^5 - 3x^2 + 1)$. Suppose $y = u \times v$, where u, v are functions of x. In this case $u = x^2 - 4x + 2$, $v = x^5 - 3x^2 + 1$. Then

$$y + \delta y = (u + \delta u)(v + \delta v)$$
$$\therefore \quad \delta y = (u + \delta u)(v + \delta v) - uv$$
$$= v\delta u + u\delta v + \delta u\delta v$$
$$\therefore \quad \frac{\delta y}{\delta x} = v\frac{\delta u}{\delta x} + u\frac{\delta v}{\delta x} + \frac{\delta u\delta v}{\delta x}.$$

Now as δx tends to zero,

$$\delta y/\delta x \to dy/dx,$$
$$v\,\delta u/\delta x \to v\,du/dx,$$
$$u\,\delta v/\delta x \to u\,dv/dx,$$

and
$$\delta u\,.\,\delta v/\delta x \to 0,$$

since δu and δv each contains δx and higher powers of δx. Thus, in the limit,

$$\frac{dy}{dx} = v\frac{du}{dx} + u\frac{dv}{dx}.$$

Thus if

$$y = (2x^2 - x + 3)(x^2 - 2x + 1),$$

then
$$\frac{dy}{dx} = (x^2 - 2x + 1)\frac{d}{dx}(2x^2 - x + 3) + (2x^2 - x + 3)\frac{d}{dx}(x^2 - 2x + 1)$$

$$= (x^2 - 2x + 1)(4x - 1) + (2x^2 - x + 3)(2x - 2)$$

$$= 8x^3 - 15x^2 + 14x - 7.$$

Differentiation of Quotients

Suppose $y = u/v$, where u, v are functions of x. Then

$$y = u\,v^{-1}.$$

$$\therefore \quad \frac{dy}{dx} = u \times \frac{d}{dx}(v^{-1}) + v^{-1}\frac{d}{dx}(u)$$

$$= u \times \left(-v^{-2}\frac{dv}{dx}\right) + v^{-1}\frac{du}{dx}$$

$$= -\frac{u}{v^2}\cdot\frac{dv}{dx} + \frac{1}{v}\cdot\frac{du}{dx}$$

$$\therefore \quad \frac{dy}{dx} = \frac{v\dfrac{du}{dx} - u\dfrac{dv}{dx}}{v^2}.$$

Thus if
$$y = \frac{3x + 4}{2x - 2},$$

$$u = 3x + 4,$$

$$v = 2x - 2.$$

Hence, from the formula,

$$\therefore \quad \frac{dy}{dx} = \frac{(2x - 2) \times 3 - (3x + 4) \times 2}{(2x - 2)^2}$$

$$= \frac{6x - 6 - 6x - 8}{(2x - 2)^2} = -\frac{14}{(2x - 2)^2}.$$

Again, if
$$y = \frac{x}{(x + 5)^2},$$

$$u = x,$$

$$v = (x + 5)^2$$

$$\therefore \quad \frac{du}{dx} = 1,$$

$$\frac{dv}{dx} = 2(x + 5)$$

$$\therefore \quad \frac{dy}{dx} = \frac{(x + 5)^2 \,.\, 1 - x \,.\, 2(x + 5)}{(x + 5)^4}$$

$$= \frac{x^2 + 10x + 25 - 2x^2 - 10x}{(x + 5)^4}$$

$$= \frac{25 - x^2}{(x + 5)^4} = \frac{(5 - x)(5 + x)}{(x + 5)^4} = \frac{5 - x}{(x + 5)^3}.$$

Minimum Distance between Object and Screen for Real Image

If a screen is less than a certain distance from an object, a converging lens will not produce an image on the screen. To find the minimum distance between object and screen, suppose x is the image distance, y is the distance from the object to the screen, and the focal length of the converging lens is 20 cm. Then

$$\text{object distance, } u, = y - x,$$

and substituting in the lens equation ('real is positive' sign convention)

$$\frac{1}{v} + \frac{1}{u} = \frac{1}{f},$$

we obtain
$$\frac{1}{(+x)} + \frac{1}{+(y - x)} = \frac{1}{+20}$$

$$\therefore \quad \frac{y - x + x}{x(y - x)} = \frac{1}{20}$$

$$\therefore \quad 20y = xy - x^2$$

$$\therefore \quad y = \frac{x^2}{x - 20}. \qquad \text{(i)}$$

To find the minimum value of y, we must find $\frac{dy}{dx}$ and equate to zero.

If $u = x^2$, $v = x - 20$, then

$$\frac{du}{dx} = 2x,$$

$$\frac{dv}{dx} = 1$$

$$\therefore \quad \frac{dy}{dx} = \frac{v\frac{du}{dx} - u\frac{dv}{dx}}{v^2}$$

$$= \frac{(x - 20)2x - x^2 . 1}{(x - 20)^2}$$

$$= \frac{x^2 - 40x}{(x - 20)^2} . \qquad \text{(ii)}$$

$$\therefore \quad \frac{dy}{dx} = 0$$

when $x^2 - 40x = 0,$

or $x = 40 \quad \text{or} \quad 0.$

When x is less than 40, $\frac{dy}{dx}$ is negative from (ii); when x is greater than 40, $\frac{dy}{dx}$ is positive from (ii). Thus $x = 40$ corresponds to a minimum value. (See p. 131.) Substituting for x in (i),

$$\therefore \quad y = \frac{40^2}{40 - 20} = 80.$$

Thus object and screen must be 80 cm apart. As the student can verify, the minimum distance between object and screen is always $4f$, where f is the focal length of the converging lens.

Maximum Power from Battery

Consider a battery of constant e.m.f. E and internal resistance r connected to an external resistance R. The current flowing is then

$$I = \frac{E}{R + r}$$

$\therefore$ power in R, $$P = I^2R = \frac{E^2R}{(R + r)^2}.$$

On plotting P against R, a curve having a maximum value is obtained. (See Ex. 4, No. 9, p. 65.) The maximum occurs when $dP/dR = 0$. Now if

$$y = \frac{R}{(R + r)^2} = \frac{u}{v},$$

then $$\frac{dy}{dR} = \frac{v\frac{du}{dR} - u\frac{dv}{dR}}{v^2} = \frac{(R + r)^2 \times 1 - R(2R + 2r)}{(R + r)^4}$$

[the differential coefficient with respect to R of R is 1, and of $(R + r)^2$, or $R^2 + 2Rr + r^2$, it is $2R + 2r$]. Simplifying,

$$\frac{dy}{dR} = \frac{r^2 - R^2}{(R + r)^4} = \frac{(r - R)(r + R)}{(R + r)^4} = \frac{r - R}{(R + r)^3}.$$

Thus if $$P = \frac{E^2R}{(R + r)^2}$$

$$\frac{dP}{dR} = \frac{E^2(r - R)}{(R + r)^3}$$

$$\therefore \quad \frac{dP}{dR} = 0$$

when $$r - R = 0,$$

or $$R = r.$$

When $R > r$, from above dP/dr is $-$ve; when $R < r$, dP/dr is $+$ve. Hence $R = r$ is a maximum value of P. Thus a battery delivers maximum power to an external resistance when the latter is equal to the internal resistance.

Van der Waals' Equation. Critical Temperature

Van der Waals' equation for the relation between the pressure p, volume V and kelvin temperature T of unit amount of a *real* gas is

$$\left(p + \frac{a}{V^2}\right)(V - b) = RT. \quad . \quad . \quad . \quad (1)$$

As explained on p. 134, a is a constant concerned with the intermolecular attractions; b is a constant proportional to the volume occupied by the molecules. The graph is a cubic relation between p and V since, on expansion, a V^3 term is obtained.

At low temperatures such as T_1 in Fig. 9.1, the $p - V$ curve is S-shaped as shown. As the temperature is raised to the particular value of T_c, the *critical temperature* of the gas, the shape of the graph changes and a point of inflexion Q is obtained. Above T_c the gas cannot be liquified by pressure alone; below T_c it can be liquified by pressure alone.

To illustrate how the calculus can be applied to van der Waals' curves, we write the equation (1) in the form

$$p = \frac{RT}{V - b} - \frac{a}{V^2}. \quad . \quad . \quad . \quad . \quad (2)$$

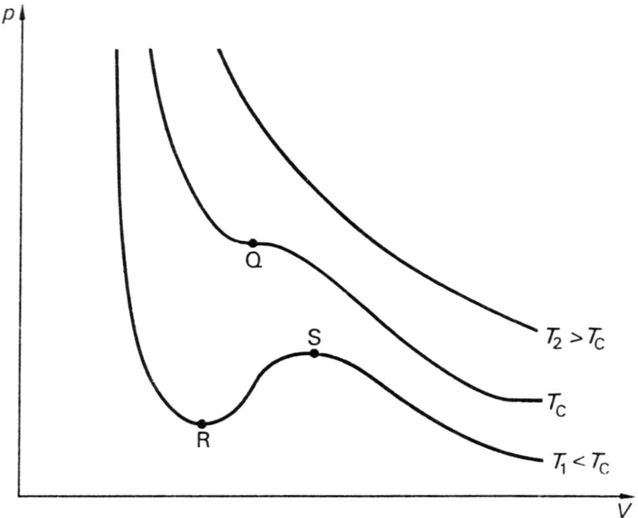

FIG. 9.1 Point of inflexion—van der Waals equation

At constant temperature T, and with a, b and R constants, differentiating (2),

$$\therefore \quad \frac{dp}{dV} = -\frac{RT}{(V-b)^2} + \frac{2a}{V^3} \quad . \quad . \quad . \quad (3)$$

$$\therefore \quad \frac{d^2p}{dV^2} = \frac{2RT}{(V-b)^3} - \frac{6a}{V^4}. \quad . \quad . \quad . \quad (4)$$

At points such as R and S, $dp/dV = 0$. At Q, $dp/dV = 0$ and $d^2p/dV^2 = 0$. Hence, from (3) and (4),

$$\frac{2a}{V^3} = \frac{RT}{(V-b)^2} \quad \text{and} \quad \frac{6a}{V^4} = \frac{2RT}{(V-b)^3}.$$

By division of the two equations,

$$\therefore \quad \frac{V}{3} = \frac{V-b}{2}$$

$$\therefore \quad V = 3b = V_c, \quad . \quad . \quad . \quad . \quad . \quad (5)$$

where V_c is the volume at Q or *critical volume*. Using the relation

$$2a/V_c^3 = RT_c/(V_c - b)^2$$

from above, we find

$$T_c = \frac{2a \times (2b)^2}{R \times (3b)^3} = \frac{8a}{27Rb}. \quad . \quad . \quad . \quad (6)$$

The *critical pressure*, p_c, is given, from (2), by

$$p_c = \frac{RT_c}{2b} - \frac{a}{9b^2}.$$

From (6), $RT_c = 8a/27b$.

$$\therefore \quad p_c = \frac{4a}{27b^2} - \frac{a}{9b^2} = \frac{a}{27b^2}. \quad . \quad . \quad . \quad (7)$$

From (5), (6) and (7), it follows that

$$\frac{RT_c}{p_c V_c} = \frac{8a}{27b} \times \frac{27b^2}{a} \times \frac{1}{3b} = \frac{8}{3}.$$

In practice, RT_c/p_cV_c is *not* a constant value equal to $\frac{8}{3}$ for all gases, as the van der Waals' equation predicts. Other predictions from the equation are also only approximately true.

EXAMPLE

Twelve cells of e.m.f. 2 V and of internal resistance $\frac{1}{2}$ Ω are arranged in a battery of *n* rows and an external resistance of $\frac{3}{8}$ Ω is connected to the poles of the battery. Determine the current flowing through the resistance in terms of *n*. Obtain numerical values of the current for the possible values which *n* may take and draw a graph of current against *n* by drawing a smooth curve through the points. Give the value of the current corresponding to the maximum of the curve and find the internal resistance of the battery when the maximum current is obtained. (*L.*)

Since there are *n* rows, number of cells in each row $= \frac{12}{n}$,

$\therefore$ total e.m.f. of battery = e.m.f. of $\frac{12}{n}$ cells in series $= \frac{24}{n}$ V.

The total internal resistance in each row $= \frac{12}{n} \times \frac{1}{2} = \frac{6}{n}$; and hence internal resistance, *r*, of battery is given by

$$\frac{1}{r} = \frac{n}{6} + \frac{n}{6} + \ldots \text{ to } n \text{ terms} = \frac{n^2}{6},$$

or

$$r = \frac{6}{n^2}.$$

$$\therefore \quad \text{current, } I = \frac{\text{e.m.f.}}{\text{total resistance}} = \frac{24/n}{\frac{6}{n^2} + \frac{3}{8}}$$

$$\therefore \quad I = \frac{64n}{16 + n^2}.$$

We now find the maximum value of I by means of the calculus. If

$$u = 64n, \qquad v = 16 + n^2,$$

then
$$\frac{du}{dn} = 64, \qquad \frac{dv}{dn} = 2n.$$

$$\therefore \quad \frac{dI}{dn} = \frac{v\frac{du}{dn} - u\frac{dv}{dn}}{v^2} = \frac{(16 + n^2)64 - 64n(2n)}{(16 + n^2)^2}.$$

For maximum or minimum, $\frac{dI}{dn} = 0$

$$\therefore \quad (16 + n^2)64 - 64n(2n) = 0$$

$$\therefore \quad 16 + n^2 - n(2n) = 0$$

$$\therefore \quad n = \pm 4.$$

On testing (p. 134), it will be found that $n = 4$ is a maximum value of I.

$$\therefore \quad \text{maximum value of } I = \frac{64n}{16 + n^2} = \frac{64 \times 4}{16 + 16} = 8 \text{ A}$$

Since the internal resistance of the battery, from above, $= \frac{6}{n^2}$,

$$\therefore \quad \text{internal resistance in this case} = \frac{6}{4^2} = \frac{3}{8}\,\Omega.$$

Differential Coefficient of Trigonometric Functions

In Physics we often meet varying trigonometrical functions. An alternating current, for example, is represented by $I = I_0 \sin \omega t$, where I_0 is the maximum current, ω is a constant, and t is the time. We shall therefore require the differential coefficients of the sine, cosine and tangent functions.

Suppose
$$y = \sin \theta$$

Then
$$y + \delta y = \sin(\theta + \delta\theta)$$

$$\therefore \quad \delta y = \sin(\theta + \delta\theta) - \sin\theta$$

$$= 2\cos\left(\theta + \frac{\delta\theta}{2}\right) \times \sin\frac{\delta\theta}{2}$$ (see p. 92)

$$\therefore \quad \frac{\delta y}{\delta\theta} = \cos\left(\theta + \frac{\delta\theta}{2}\right) \times \frac{\sin(\delta\theta/2)}{\delta\theta/2} \quad . \quad . \quad . \quad (1)$$

When θ is in radians and $\delta\theta \to 0$, then, in the limit,

$$\frac{\delta y}{\delta \theta} \to \frac{dy}{d\theta}, \quad \cos\left(\theta + \frac{\delta\theta}{2}\right) \to \cos\theta, \quad \text{and} \quad \sin(\delta\theta/2)/(\delta\theta/2) \to 1.$$

Hence, from (1),

$$\frac{dy}{d\theta} = \cos\theta. \qquad . \quad . \quad . \quad . \qquad (2)$$

By a similar proof, if $y = \cos\theta$,

$$\frac{dy}{d\theta} = -\sin\theta. \qquad . \quad . \quad . \quad . \quad . \qquad (3)$$

Graphs of Differential Coefficients

We can verify the results in (2) and (3) from graphs of $\sin\theta$ and $\cos\theta$ respectively.

In Fig. 9.2 (i), the curve A represents a sine curve, $y = \sin x$; thus at O, $\sin x = 0$, and at P, $\sin x = \sin 90° = 1$. Fig. 9.2 (ii) represents a cosine curve C, $y = \cos x$; at O, $\cos 0° = 1$, and at 90°, Q, $\cos 90° = 0$. Now on p. 128 we learned that the differential coefficient at a point on a curve is equal to the gradient of the tangent at that point. In Fig. 9.2 (i), the gradient at O is a maximum, and the gradient diminishes to

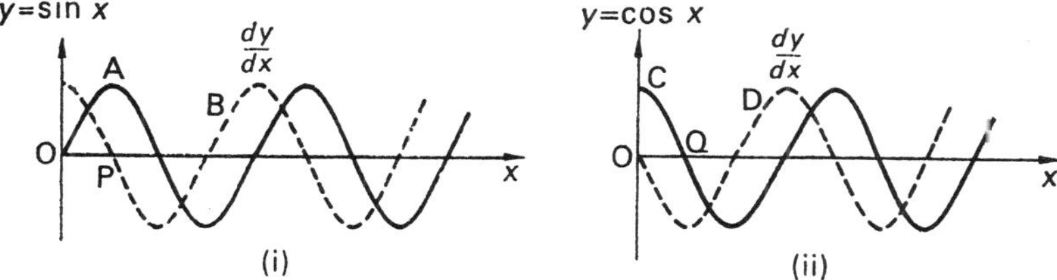

FIG. 9.2 Sine and cosine functions

zero at P; on the other side of the maximum the gradient is negative. On plotting the magnitude of the gradient at points on the $y = \sin x$ curve, the curve B is obtained. By comparing B with C, Fig. 9.2 (ii), we see that a *cosine* curve is obtained. Thus if

$$\mathbf{y = \sin x,}$$

$$\mathbf{\frac{dy}{dx} = \cos x.}$$

Fig. 9.2 (ii) shows a cosine curve, C, $y = \cos x$, and the curve D, which is the variation of the gradient of the tangents at points on the curve. By comparing D with curve A in Fig. 9.2 (i), it can be seen that D is the curve $-\sin x$. Thus if

$$y = \cos x,$$

$$\frac{dy}{dx} = -\sin x.$$

Differentiation of More Complicated Trigonometrical Quantities

Suppose now we require to differentiate $y = \sin 3x$ with respect to x. Let $\theta = 3x$, i.e. $y = \sin \theta$. Now

$$\frac{dy}{dx} = \frac{dy}{d\theta} \times \frac{d\theta}{dx}.$$

From above, $$\frac{dy}{d\theta} = \cos \theta,$$

and $$\frac{d\theta}{dx} = 3.$$

$\therefore$ $$\frac{dy}{dx} = 3 \cos \theta = 3 \cos 3x.$$

Again, suppose $y = \cos (4x - \alpha)$, where α is a constant. Let $\theta = 4x - \alpha$. Then $y = \cos \theta$. Now

$$\frac{dy}{dx} = \frac{dy}{d\theta} \times \frac{d\theta}{dx}.$$

Hence, from above,

$$\frac{dy}{dx} = (-\sin \theta) \times 4 = -4 \sin \theta = -4 \sin (4x - \alpha).$$

We can now formulate a rule for differentiating trigonmetrical functions:

(1) *Differentiate the sine or cosine*, (2) *then multiply by the differential coefficient of the function 'next to' the sine or cosine.*

Thus suppose $y = \sin 5x$. Then (1) 'cosine' is the differential coefficient of sine, (2) 5 is the differential coefficient of $5x$. Hence

$$\frac{dy}{dx} = 5 \cos 5x.$$

Again, suppose $y = \cos (3x - \alpha)$ where α is a constant; then

$$dy/dx = -3 \sin (3x - \alpha).$$

Similarly, if $y = \cos \omega t$ where ω is a constant, then

$$dy/dt = (-\sin \omega t) \times \omega = -\omega \sin \omega t.$$

The differential coefficient of $y = \sin(\omega t - \alpha)$, where ω, α are constants is given by

$$dy/dt = [\cos(\omega t - \alpha)] \times \omega = \omega \cos(\omega t - \alpha).$$

E.M.F. in Simple Dynamo

A simple dynamo consists of a coil of N turns and area A, rotating with a constant angular velocity ω radians per second about an axis perpendicular to a uniform field of flux density B. Suppose the plane PQ of the coil makes an angle θ with B at some instant t measured from

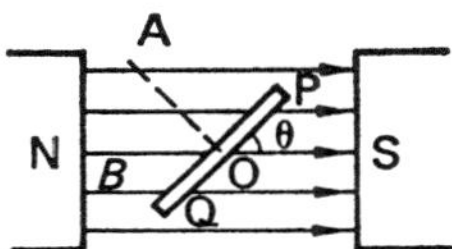

FIG. 9.3 Simple dynamo

the time the coil was parallel to the field (Fig. 9.3). Then the component of B along AO normal to PQ

$$= B\cos(90° - \theta) = B\sin\theta.$$

$$\therefore \quad \text{flux linking the coil, } \Phi, = NAB\sin\theta.$$

But $\theta = \omega t$, by definition of ω.

$$\therefore \quad \Phi = NAB\sin\omega t.$$

From Faraday's law, the induced e.m.f., E, in volts is given numerically by

$$E = \frac{d\Phi}{dt}.$$

The differential coefficient of $\sin\omega t$ with respect to time t is $\cos\omega t \times \omega$ or $\omega\cos\omega t$.

$$\therefore \quad E = \omega NAB\cos\omega t.$$

Since ω, N, A, B are constants, we can write this as

$$E = E_0\cos\omega t,$$

where $E_0 = \omega NAB$. Thus the variation of E with time t follows a cosine curve and it is an *alternating e.m.f.* Since the maximum value of a cosine is 1, E_0 is the maximum value of the e.m.f.

Simple Harmonic Motion

The bob of a simple pendulum moving through a small angle executes simple harmonic motion (s.h.m.). The vibrations of particles of air due to a sounding tuning-fork are also simple harmonic. The simplest equation representing s.h.m. is

$$x = a \sin \omega t, \qquad \text{(i)}$$

where x is the distance or displacement from the mean (undisturbed) position at a time t measured from the moment the mean position was passed, ω is a constant, and a is the amplitude of the motion, i.e. maximum displacement. The velocity at an instant, v, is given by $\mathrm{d}x/\mathrm{d}t$ or by $\dot{x}$ (p. 124).

$$\therefore \quad v = \dot{x} = \omega a \cos \omega t. \qquad \text{(ii)}$$

Now $\cos^2 \theta = 1 - \sin^2 \theta$ (p. 91).

Thus $\cos^2 \omega t = 1 - \sin^2 \omega t.$

$$\therefore \quad (\dot{x})^2 = \omega^2 a^2 (1 - \sin^2 \omega t)$$

$$= \omega^2 (a^2 - a^2 \sin^2 \omega t).$$

But $x = a \sin \omega t.$

$$\therefore \quad (\dot{x})^2 = \omega^2 (a^2 - x^2). \qquad \text{(iii)}$$

The acceleration, $\ddot{x} = \mathrm{d}v/\mathrm{d}t.$

Hence, from (ii), $\ddot{x} = -\omega^2 a \sin \omega t = -\omega^2 x,$

and thus the acceleration is proportional to the displacement x.

Simple harmonic motion is discussed fully on p. 248.

Diffraction Grating

A *diffraction grating*, illuminated normally by light of various wavelengths λ, produces strong diffraction images for these wavelengths in directions θ given by

$$d \sin \theta = m\lambda, \qquad (1)$$

where d is the grating spacing and $m = 0, 1, 2, \ldots$. Differentiating

$$\therefore \quad d \cos \theta \frac{\mathrm{d}\theta}{\mathrm{d}\lambda} = m$$

$$\therefore \quad \frac{\mathrm{d}\theta}{\mathrm{d}\lambda} = \frac{m}{d \cos \theta}. \qquad (2)$$

$\mathrm{d}\theta/\mathrm{d}\lambda$ is the *dispersion* produced by the grating. From (2), the dispersion is proportional to m, the order of the spectrum. Hence the angular separation of two close wavelengths in the second order is twice that in the first order. The dispersion is also proportional to $1/d$, the number of lines per millimetre, from (2).

EXAMPLE

A varying current I is given by $I = 10 \sin 100t + 20 \cos 100t$, where t is the time. Calculate (i) the instant when the maximum current is obtained, (ii) the maximum current.

Since $\qquad I = 10 \sin 100t + 20 \cos 100t,$

$$\frac{dI}{dt} = 10 \times 100 \cos 100t - 20 \times 100 \sin 100t.$$

For a maximum, $\dfrac{dI}{dt} = 0.$

$$\therefore \quad 1000 \cos 100t - 2000 \sin 100t = 0$$

$$\therefore \quad \frac{\sin 100t}{\cos 100t} = \frac{1000}{2000} = \frac{1}{2}$$

$$\therefore \quad \tan 100t = \frac{1}{2}$$

$$\therefore \quad 100t = 26° \, 34' = \frac{26.6\pi}{180} \text{ (radian)}$$

$$\therefore \quad t = \frac{26.6\pi}{100 \times 180} = 0.005 \text{ s (approx.)}.$$

The maximum current is obtained when $100t = 26° \, 34'$.

$$\therefore \quad I = 10 \sin 26° \, 34' + 20 \cos 26° \, 34'$$
$$= 22.$$

Differentiation of cosec θ, sec θ, cot θ, tan θ

1. Suppose

$$y = \operatorname{cosec} \theta = \frac{1}{\sin \theta} = \frac{u}{v} \text{ say.}$$

Then $u = 1$ and $v = \sin \theta$, that is,

$$\frac{du}{d\theta} = 0,$$

$$\frac{dv}{d\theta} = \cos \theta.$$

$$\therefore \quad \frac{dy}{d\theta} = \frac{v\dfrac{du}{d\theta} - u\dfrac{dv}{d\theta}}{v^2} = -\frac{\cos \theta}{\sin^2 \theta} = -\cot \theta \, . \operatorname{cosec} \theta.$$

2. If

$$y = \sec \theta = \frac{1}{\cos \theta} = \frac{u}{v} \text{ say,}$$

then $u = 1$ and $v = \cos\theta$, that is,

$$\frac{du}{d\theta} = 0,$$

$$\frac{dv}{d\theta} = -\sin\theta.$$

$$\therefore \quad \frac{dy}{d\theta} = \frac{v\dfrac{du}{d\theta} - u\dfrac{dv}{d\theta}}{v^2} = +\frac{\sin\theta}{\cos^2\theta} = \tan\theta \,.\, \sec\theta.$$

3. If

$$y = \cot\theta = \frac{\cos\theta}{\sin\theta} = \frac{u}{v},$$

then $u = \cos\theta$ and $v = \sin\theta$, that is,

$$\frac{du}{d\theta} = -\sin\theta,$$

$$\frac{dv}{d\theta} = \cos\theta.$$

$$\therefore \quad \frac{dy}{d\theta} = \frac{-\sin^2\theta - \cos^2\theta}{\sin^2\theta} = -\frac{1}{\sin^2\theta} = -\text{cosec}^2\,\theta,$$

since $\sin^2\theta + \cos^2\theta = 1$. See p. 92.

4. If

$$y = \tan\theta = \frac{\sin\theta}{\cos\theta},$$

then $u = \sin\theta$, $v = \cos\theta$, that is,

$$\frac{du}{d\theta} = \cos\theta,$$

$$\frac{dv}{d\theta} = -\sin\theta.$$

$$\therefore \quad \frac{dy}{d\theta} = \frac{\cos^2\theta + \sin^2\theta}{\cos^2\theta} = \frac{1}{\cos^2\theta} = \sec^2\theta.$$

Differentiation of e^x and ln x

The quantity e was defined on p. 19. The series e^x is given by

$$e^x = 1 + x + \frac{x^2}{1\,.\,2} + \frac{x^3}{1\,.\,2\,.\,3} + \ldots \text{ to infinity.}$$

$$\therefore \quad \frac{d}{dx}(e^x) = 1 + x + \frac{x^2}{1.2} + \ldots \text{ to infinity}$$

$$= e^x.$$

Hence if $y = e^x$,

$$\frac{dy}{dx} = e^x. \quad \ldots \quad \text{(i)}$$

Suppose $y = e^{3x}$. If $u = 3x$, $y = e^u$.

$$\therefore \quad \frac{dy}{dx} = \frac{dy}{du} \times \frac{du}{dx} = e^u \times 3 = 3e^u = 3e^{3x}.$$

Similarly, if $y = e^{mx}$,

$$\frac{dy}{dx} = me^{mx}. \quad \ldots \quad \text{(ii)}$$

Suppose $y = \ln x$. Then $e^y = x$. (See p. 20.) Differentiating with respect to y,

$$\therefore \quad \frac{d}{dy}(e^y) = \frac{dx}{dy}$$

$$\therefore \quad e^y = \frac{dx}{dy}$$

$$\therefore \quad \frac{1}{e^y} = \frac{dy}{dx}$$

$$\therefore \quad \frac{dy}{dx} = \frac{1}{x}. \quad \ldots \quad \text{(iii)}$$

Similarly, if $y = \ln(2x - 3)$,

$$\frac{dy}{dx} = \frac{1}{2x - 3} \times \frac{d}{dx}(2x - 3)$$

$$= \frac{2}{2x - 3}.$$

Also, if $y = \ln(x - a)$,

where a is a constant,

$$\frac{dy}{dx} = \frac{1}{x - a}. \quad \ldots \quad \text{(iv)}$$

Binomial Theorem. Series for sine, cosine

Binomial theorem. We can obtain the series for $(1 + x)^n$ by writing

$$(1 + x)^n = a_0 + a_1x + a_2x^2 + a_3x^3 + \dots, \qquad (1)$$

where a_0, a_1, a_2 . . . are constants. Differentiating both sides with respect to x,

$$\therefore \quad n(1 + x)^{n-1} = a_1 + 2a_2x + 3a_3x^2 + \dots \qquad (2)$$

when $x = 0$, $\qquad n = a_1.$

Differentiating (2),

$$\therefore \quad n(n - 1)(1 + x)^{n-2} = 2a_2 + 2 \times 3a_3x + \dots. \qquad (3)$$

When $x = 0$, $\qquad n(n - 1) = 2a_2,$

$$\therefore \quad a_2 = \frac{n(n - 1)}{2}.$$

By differentiating (3) and putting $x = 0$, we find

$$a_3 = n(n - 1)(n - 2)/2.3.$$

Further, putting $x = 0$ in (1), then $a_0 = 1$. Hence, from (1),

$$(1 + x)^n = 1 + nx + \frac{n(n - 1)}{1 \cdot 2}x^2 + \frac{n(n - 1)(n - 2)}{1 \cdot 2 \cdot 3}x^3 + \dots. \qquad (4)$$

Sine, cosine series. A series for $\sin x$ in terms of x can be found in a similar way. Suppose

$$\sin x = a_0 + a_1x + a_2x^2 + a_3x^3 + \dots \qquad (1)$$

$$\therefore \quad \cos x = a_1 + 2a_2x + 3a_3x^2 + \dots. \qquad (2)$$

When $x = 0$, $\cos x = 1$. Hence $a_1 = 1$. Differentiating (2),

$$\therefore \quad -\sin x = 2a_2 + 3.2a_3x + \dots.$$

When $x = 0$, $-\sin x = 0$. Hence $a_3 = 0$. Further, substituting $x = 0$ in (1), then $a_0 = 0$. In this way the coefficients of x are found to be given by

$$a_0 = 0,$$

$$a_1 = 1,$$

$$a_2 = 0,$$

$$a_3 = -\frac{1}{3 \cdot 2} = -\frac{1}{3!}.$$ (see p. 301)

Hence $$\sin x = x - \frac{x^3}{3!} + \frac{x^5}{5!} - \dots.$$

Similarly, $$\cos x = 1 - \frac{x^2}{2!} + \frac{x^4}{4!} - \dots.$$

e^x, ln(1 + x)

By expressing e^x and ln $(1 + x)$ in the form of a series as in (1), and then differentiating and putting $x = 0$, *the coefficients* a_0, a_1, a_2, . . . can be found as before for $-1 < x < 1$. Then

$$e^x = 1 + x + \frac{x^2}{1 . 2} + \frac{x^3}{1 . 2 . 3} + \dots \quad (5)$$

and $$\ln (1 + x) = x - \frac{x^2}{2} + \frac{x^3}{3} - \dots \quad (6)$$

Errors

The calculus enables *errors* to be calculated in estimates or measurements. As a simple example, suppose an error of 2% was made in measuring the height h and radius r of a cylindrical block and that the consequent error in the volume V is required. Now

$$V = \pi r^2 h.$$

Taking logs to the base e, a procedure which has advantages in calculating errors as seen shortly,

$$\therefore \quad \ln V = \ln \pi + 2 \ln r + \ln h. \quad (1)$$

The small changes in the variable quantities V, r, h in equation (1) are given respectively by

$$\delta(\ln V) = \frac{1}{V} \times \delta V = \frac{\delta V}{V},$$

$$\delta(2 \ln r) = \frac{2}{r} \times \delta r = \frac{2 \times \delta r}{r},$$

and $$\delta(\ln h) = \frac{1}{h} \times \delta h = \frac{\delta h}{h}.$$

These relations follow because, if

$$y = f(x),$$

$$\delta y = (\mathrm{d}y/\mathrm{d}x) \times \delta x$$

to a good approximation when δx is small.

Also, $$\delta(\ln \pi) = 0,$$

since $\ln \pi$ is a constant quantity. Hence, from (1),

$$\delta(\ln V) = \delta(2 \ln r) + \delta(\ln h)$$

$$\therefore \quad \frac{\delta V}{V} = 2\frac{\delta r}{r} + \frac{\delta h}{h}. \qquad . \quad . \quad . \quad . \quad . \quad (2)$$

But $\delta r/r$ = fractional change in $r = \pm 2\%$, the percentage error in r (see above), and likewise $\delta h/h = \pm 2\%$. Thus, from (2),

$$\frac{\delta V}{V} = \pm 4\% \pm 2\%.$$

The maximum fractional error in V, which is $\delta V/V$, is equal to the sum of 4% and 2%

$$\therefore \quad \frac{\delta V}{V} = \text{maximum fractional error in } V = 6\%. \quad . \quad . \quad (3)$$

Suppose the actual measurement of r was 50 ± 1 mm (2% error in r), and the actual measurement of h was 10.0 ± 0.2 mm (2% error in h). Using $r = 50$ mm, $h = 10$ mm, the volume V is given by

$$V = \pi r^2 h = \pi \times 50^2 \times 10 = 78\,500 \text{ mm}^3.$$

From (3), error in V = 6% of 78 500 = 5000 mm^3

$$\therefore \quad V = 78\,500 \pm 5000 \text{ mm}^3.$$

Viscosity of Liquid

For uniform or laminar flow of liquid through a pipe, Poiseuille's formula states that the volume per second V is given by

$$V = \frac{\pi p a^4}{8 \eta l},$$

where p is the excess pressure between the ends of the pipe, a its radius, l its length, and η is the coefficient of viscosity of the liquid. If errors are made in the measurements of a, p, l and V, we can proceed as before to find the resulting error in the calculated value of η. Thus, from above,

$$\eta = \frac{\pi p a^4}{8 V l}$$

$$\therefore \quad \ln \eta = \ln(\pi/8) + \ln p + 4 \ln a - \ln V - \ln l.$$

Taking small changes

$$\therefore \quad \delta(\ln \eta) = \delta(\ln p) + 4\delta(\ln a) - \delta(\ln V) - \delta(\ln l). \qquad (1)$$

The change in $\ln(\pi/8)$ is zero since this is a constant quantity.

As on p. 159, equation (1) becomes

$$\frac{\delta\eta}{\eta} = \frac{\delta p}{p} + \frac{4\delta a}{a} - \frac{\delta V}{V} - \frac{\delta l}{l}. \qquad (2)$$

Suppose the percentage errors in the measurements are

$$\frac{\delta p}{p} = \pm 1\%, \quad \frac{\delta a}{a} = \pm 2\%, \quad \frac{\delta V}{V} = \pm 3\%, \quad \frac{\delta l}{l} = \pm 1\%.$$

Then, taking the *maximum* possible error in η, from (2) we have

$$\frac{\delta\eta}{\eta} = +1\% + 4 \times 2\% + 3\% + 1\% = 13\%.$$

Note that the large percentage error in η is due to the 'a^4' term. This produces a percentage error 4 times that of a, thus introducing an error in a^4 of 8%. If the error in a were only 1%, the error in a^4 would drop to 4%, and the error $\delta\eta/\eta$ would then be 9%. In experiments, therefore, particular care should be taken to measure as accurately as possible quantities such as a which are raised to high powers.

Summary of Differential Calculus

We can now summarize our main results:

1. If $y = x^n$, $\quad \frac{dy}{dx} = nx^{n-1}$.

If $y = (ax + b)^n$, $\quad \frac{dy}{dx} = n(ax + b)^{n-1} \times a$.

If $y = uv$, $\quad \frac{dy}{dx} = v\frac{du}{dx} + u\frac{dv}{dx}$.

If $y = \frac{u}{v}$, $\quad \frac{dy}{dx} = \left(v\frac{du}{dx} - u\frac{dv}{dx}\right)\Big/ v^2$.

If $y =$ constant, $\quad \frac{dy}{dx} = 0$.

If $y = \sin x$, $\quad \frac{dy}{dx} = \cos x$.

If $y = \cos x$, $\quad \frac{dy}{dx} = -\sin x$.

If $y = \sin \omega t$, $\quad \frac{dy}{dt} = \omega \cos \omega t$.

If $y = \cos \omega t$, $\dfrac{dy}{dt} = -\omega \sin \omega t.$

If $y = \tan x$, $\dfrac{dy}{dx} = \sec^2 x.$

If $y = \cot x$ $\dfrac{dy}{dx} = -\mathrm{cosec}^2 x.$

If $y = \mathrm{cosec}\, x$, $\dfrac{dy}{dx} = -\cot x \,.\, \mathrm{cosec}\, x.$

If $y = \sec x$, $\dfrac{dy}{dx} = \tan x \,.\, \sec x.$

If $y = \ln x$, $\dfrac{dy}{dx} = \dfrac{1}{x}.$

If $y = e^{mx}$, $\dfrac{dy}{dx} = me^{mx}.$

2. dx/dt is the rate of change of x with respect to t. If x represents distance and t the time, then dx/dt represents the *velocity* of a moving object. dv/dt, or d^2x/dt^2, represents the acceleration.

3. If θ represents temperature, t the time, and x the distance, then $d\theta/dt$ represents the rate of temperature change and $d\theta/dx$ represents the temperature gradient. Electric current, $I = dQ/dt$.

4. If y is plotted against x, dy/dx at a given point represents the *gradient of the tangent* to the curve.

At a maximum value,

$$\frac{dy}{dx} = 0 \quad \text{and} \quad \frac{d^2y}{dx^2} \text{ is } -ve.$$

At a minimum value,

$$\frac{dy}{dx} = 0 \quad \text{and} \quad \frac{d^2y}{dx^2} \text{ is } +ve.$$

At a point of inflexion,

$$\frac{d^2y}{dx^2} = 0.$$

EXERCISES 9

Function of function. Product, Quotient

Differentiate the following with respect to the variable concerned:

(1) $(4x + 3)^5$.

(2) $(3a^2 - 2a)^3$.

(3) $(x^2 + 1)(x^3 - 2x)$.

(4) $(x + 4)^5(x + 2)^6$.

(5) $\dfrac{3x + 2}{x - 1}$.

(6) $\dfrac{t - 2}{2t + 1}$.

(7) $\dfrac{R}{(R - 4)^2}$.

(8) $(3a^2 - 4)^4$.

(9) $(4b^3 - 2b^2)(2b^2 - 1)$.

(10) $\dfrac{x - 5}{x^2 - 2x + 1}$.

(11) An object and screen are fixed y cm apart. Calculate the minimum value of y in order that a converging lens of focal length 10 cm should produce an image on the screen.

(12) Repeat Question 11 for a converging lens of focal length 15 cm.

(13) A battery of e.m.f. 2 V and internal resistance 4 Ω is connected to a resistance R Ω. Calculate the power developed in R. Find by differentiation the magnitude of R for maximum power.

(14) Repeat Question 13 for a battery of e.m.f. 4 V, internal resistance 10 Ω, connected to a resistance R Ω.

(15) The magnetic flux density B at a point A along the axis of a narrow circular coil of N turns and radius a carrying a current I is given by

$$B = \frac{\mu_0 N I a^2}{2(a^2 + x^2)^{3/2}}$$

where x is the distance of A from the coil. By successive differentiation, prove that $\mathrm{d}^2B/\mathrm{d}x^2 = 0$ when $x = a/2$.

Trigonometrical Functions

Differentiate the following with respect to the variable concerned:

(16) $\cos x$.

(17) $\sin x$.

(18) $\cos 2x$.

(19) $\sin 4x - \cos 2x$.

(20) $\sin 2\omega t$.

(21) $\sin \theta + \cos \theta$.

(22) $\sin\left(2t - \frac{\pi}{4}\right)$.

(23) $\cos\left(3t + \frac{\pi}{4}\right)$.

(24) The displacement x in metre of a vibrating object is related to the time t by $x = 10 \sin 50\pi t$. Find (i) the velocity, (ii) the acceleration at $t = 0.005$ s.

(25) Repeat Question 9 when $x = 8 \cos 25\pi t$.

(26) The flux Φ linking a coil rotating in a magnetic field is given by $\Phi = 0.2 \cos 100\pi t$. Calculate the numerical value of the rate of change of the flux at (i) $t = 0.0025$ s, (ii) $t = 0$, (iii) $t = 0.005$ s.

Differentiate the following with respect to x:

(27) $x \sin x$ (product of functions).

(28) $\frac{x}{\cos x}$ (division of functions).

(29) $x^2 \sin 2x$.

(30) $\frac{\sin x}{2x}$.

(31) $2x \cos 3x$.

(32) $\frac{\sin x}{1 - \cos x}$.

(33) Find the maximum value of $(\sin x + \cos x)$.

(34) Find the maximum value of $(4 \cos x + 3 \sin x)$.

(35) The flux Φ linking a rotating coil in a magnetic field is given by $\Phi = 0.1 \sin 100t$, where t is the time. If the induced e.m.f. E in volts is given by $-\dfrac{d\Phi}{dt}$, calculate (i) the maximum e.m.f., (ii) the e.m.f. when $t = \pi/300$.

(36) If $E = -5\, dI/dt$ and $I = \frac{1}{200} \sin 400\pi t$, calculate E when (i) $t = 0$, (ii) $t = 1/800$, (iii) $t = 1/1200$. For what value of t is E a maximum?

Further Functions

Differentiate the following with respect to x:

(37) $\tan x$.

(38) $\operatorname{cosec} x$.

(39) $\cot x + \sec x$.

(40) $\tan (3x + 2)$.

(41) $\cot (2x - 4)$.

(42) $\tan x - \cot x$.

(43) e^{2x}.

(44) e^{3x}.

(45) $\ln 2x$.

(46) $\ln 3x$.

(47) $\ln (x + 2)$.

(48) $\ln (4x - 2)$.

(49) $\ln (3 - x)$.

(50) e^{-2x+1}.

(51) $\ln (6 - 3x)$.

(52) $\ln (ax + b)$.

(53) e^{x^2}.

Harder Examples

(54) If the radius of a circle increases at the rate of 2.0 cm s^{-1}, find the rate at which its area is increasing when the radius is 12 cm.

(55) If the area of a circle increases at the rate of 5.0 $m^2\, s^{-1}$, find the rate at which the radius is increasing when the circumference is 10.0 m.

(56) Water is poured into an inverted hollow cone which has a semi-vertical angle of 30°. If the depth of water increases at a steady rate of 2.0 cm s^{-1} what is the quantity of water being supplied per second when the depth of water in the cone is 24 cm?

(57) A solution is poured into a conical filter funnel at the rate of 3.0 $cm^3\, s^{-1}$ and it runs out at the rate of 1.0 $cm^3\, s^{-1}$ The radius of the top of the funnel is 10.0 cm and the vertical height is 30.0 cm. At what rate is the level of the liquid in the funnel rising when it is a third of the way up the funnel?

(58) An air bubble below the surface of water of surface tension 0.07 N m^{-1} has a radius of 1.0 mm at a particular instant and the excess pressure maintaining it is then changing at 10^4 Pa s^{-1}. What is the rate of change of the volume of the bubble at this instant? (The excess pressure required to maintain a bubble in a liquid is twice the surface tension divided by the radius of the bubble when all quantities are expressed in SI.)

Answers

1. $20(4x+3)^4$
2. $(18a-6)(3a^2-2a)^2$
3. $5x^4-3x^2-2$
4. $(11x+34)(x+2)^5(x+4)^4$
5. $-5/(x-1)^2$
6. $5/(2t+1)^2$
7. $-(4+R)/(R-4)^3$
8. $24a(3a^2-4)^3$
9. $40b^4-16b^3-12b^2+4b$
10. $(9-x)/(x-1)^3$
11. 40 cm
12. 60 cm
13. $4R/(R+4)^2$; 4 Ω
14. $16R/(R+10)^2$; 10 Ω
16. $-\sin x$
17. $\cos x$
18. $-2\sin 2x$
19. $4\cos 4x+2\sin 2x$
20. $2\omega\cos 2\omega t$
21. $\cos\theta-\sin\theta$
22. $2\cos(2t-\pi/4)$
23. $-3\sin(3t+\pi/4)$
24. (i) 1110 (ii) $-174\,500$
25. (i) -240 (ii) 45 600
26. (i) 44.4 (ii) 0 (iii) 62.8
27. $x\cos x+\sin x$
28. $(\cos x+x\sin x)/\cos^2 x$
29. $2x^2\cos 2x+2x\sin 2x$
30. $(x\cos x-\sin x)/2x^2$
31. $-6x\sin 3x+2\cos 3x$
32. $-1/(1-\cos x)$

33. $\sqrt{2}$

34. 5

35. (i) 10 V (ii) 5 V

36. (i) -10π (ii) 0 (iii) -5π; $t = 0$

37. $\sec^2 x$

38. $-\cot x \operatorname{cosec} x$

39. $-\operatorname{cosec}^2 x + \tan x \,.\, \sec x$

40. $3 \sec^2 (3x + 2)$

41. $-2 \operatorname{cosec}^2 (2x - 4)$

42. $\sec^2 x + \operatorname{cosec}^2 x$

43. $2e^{2x}$

44. $3e^{3x}$

45. $1/x$

46. $1/x$

47. $1/(x + 2)$

48. $4/(4x - 2)$

49. $-1/(3 - x)$

50. $-2e^{-2x+1}$

51. $-1/(2 - x)$

52. $a/(ax + b)$

53. $2xe^{x^2}$

54. 151 $\text{cm}^2\ \text{s}^{-1}$

55. 0.5 m s^{-1}

56. 1206 cm^3 (per second)

57. 0.06 cm s^{-1}

58. 898 $\text{mm}^3\ \text{s}^{-1}$

10. Principles of Integral Calculus

Integration can be considered as the reverse of differentiation; that is, we are given the differential coefficient and are required to find the function originally differentiated, or *integral* of the differential coefficient.

Integration of Functions

We have already seen that if

$$y = x^2 + 2 \quad \text{or} \quad y = x^2 - 6,$$

then $$\mathrm{d}y/\mathrm{d}x = 2x;$$

given $$\mathrm{d}y/\mathrm{d}x = 2x,$$

it therefore follows that

$$y = x^2 + c,$$

where c is some unknown constant. Similarly, if

$$\frac{\mathrm{d}y}{\mathrm{d}x} = x^2,$$

then $$y = \tfrac{1}{3}x^3 + c,$$

as we can test by differentiating

$$y = \tfrac{1}{3}x^3 + c.$$

A general rule for integration can thus be stated, excluding $n = -1$: If

$$\frac{\mathrm{d}y}{\mathrm{d}x} = x^n,$$

$$\therefore \quad y = \frac{x^{n+1}}{n+1} + c, \quad \text{or} \quad y = \frac{1}{n+1}x^{n+1} + c. \qquad \text{(i)}$$

Thus if $$\frac{dy}{dx} = \frac{1}{x^2} = x^{-2},$$

$$y = \frac{x^{-2+1}}{-2+1} + c = \frac{x^{-1}}{-1} + c$$

$$= -x^{-1} + c = -\frac{1}{x} + c.$$

If $$\frac{dy}{dx} = 2x^2 - x + 2,$$

then, integrating, $y = \frac{2}{3}x^3 - \frac{1}{2}x^2 + 2x + c.$
Each term is integrated separately; and we can consider 2 as $2x^0$, so that its integral is $2x^1/1$ or $2x$. (For $dy/dx = 1/x$, see p. 188.)

Integral Notation

If $$\frac{dy}{dx} = 2x,$$

$$dy = 2x \,.\, dx.$$

$\therefore$ integral of dy = integral of $2x \,.\, dx$.

An elongated S is written to denote the process of integration, and thus

$$\int dy = \int 2x \,.\, dx.$$

'$\int dy$' is called the 'integral of dy', and is obviously y.

$\int 2x \,.\, dx$ is called the 'integral of $2x \,.\, dx$'.

Thus $$y = \int 2x \,.\, dx.$$

To integrate $2x \,.\, dx$, the integration rule is applied to $2x$; this gives

$$\frac{2x^{1+1}}{1+1} + c = x^2 + c$$

$$\therefore \quad y = x^2 + c.$$

Similarly, $$\int (x^2 - 3x + 1) \,.\, dx = \tfrac{1}{3}x^3 - \tfrac{3}{2}x^2 + x + c,$$

integrating each term separately, and

$$\int (2x^3 - 3x^2 - x - 5) \,.\, dx = \tfrac{1}{2}x^4 - x^3 - \tfrac{1}{2}x^2 - 5x + c.$$

It should be noted that the inclusion of 'dx' under the integral sign is essential, and that it disappears on integration.

Definite Integrals. Limits

We have seen that if $dy/dx = 2x$, the most general answer for y is $y = x^2 + c$, where c is a constant. If we are given the additional information that $y = 10$ when $x = 3$, then, substituting,

$$10 = 3^2 + c, \quad \text{or} \quad c = 1.$$

In this case we have the definite result that

$$y = x^2 + 1.$$

If we were given that $y = 1$ when $x = 2$, then, substituting in $y = x^2 + c$, $c = -3$. In this case

$$y = x^2 - 3.$$

On numerous occasions we wish to integrate a quantity between certain defined values or *limits*. Thus suppose the value of $\int(x - 3)\,dx$ is required from $x = 4$ to $x = 6$. This is written

$$\int_4^6 (x - 3)\,dx.$$

Now generally

$$\int (x - 3)\,dx = \tfrac{1}{2}x^2 - 3x + c.$$

If $x = 6$ is substituted, we obtain a value I_1 given by

$$I_1 = \tfrac{1}{2} \cdot 6^2 - 3 \cdot 6 + c;$$

if $x = 4$ is substituted, a value I_2 is obtained given by

$$I_2 = \tfrac{1}{2} \cdot 4^2 - 3 \cdot 4 + c.$$

The value from $x = 4$ to $x = 6$ is $(I_1 - I_2)$. By subtraction, c is eliminated, whatever its value may be. This is generally true, and *hence there is no need to insert c on integrating between definite limits.* We express a definite integral thus:

$$\int_4^6 (x - 3)\,dx = \Big[\tfrac{1}{2}x^2 - 3x\Big]_4^6$$
$$= (\tfrac{1}{2} \cdot 6^2 - 3 \cdot 6) - (\tfrac{1}{2} \cdot 4^2 - 3 \cdot 4) = 4.$$

Similarly,

$$\int_1^3 (3x^2 - 2x + 1)\,dx = \Big[x^3 - x^2 + x\Big]_1^3$$
$$= (3^3 - 3^2 + 3) - (1^3 - 1^2 + 1) = 20.$$

Electric Potential

The electric potential at a point due to a charge Q is defined as numerically equal to the work done in moving a unit positive charge from infinity to that point. Suppose, in its movement from infinity, that the charge reaches a distance x from the charge Q. If the latter is a point charge, the force on the unit charge in free space in $\frac{Q}{4\pi\varepsilon_0 x^2}$ where ε_0 is a constant, the 'permittivity of free space'. When x is measured outwards from the charge Q, a displacement δx towards the charge is negative. Thus if the unit charge is moved through a small distance δx.

work done on charge = force × distance

$$= \frac{Q}{4\pi\varepsilon_0 x^2} \times (-\delta x) = -\frac{Q}{4\pi\varepsilon_0 x^2} \cdot \delta x.$$

The total work done, V, from infinity to a distance r from the charge, is hence given by

$$V = -\int_\infty^r \frac{Q}{4\pi\varepsilon_0 x^2} \cdot \mathrm{d}x = -Q\int_\infty^r \frac{1}{4\pi\varepsilon_0 x^2} \cdot \mathrm{d}x.$$

But $$\int \frac{1}{x^2} \cdot \mathrm{d}x = \int x^{-2} \cdot \mathrm{d}x = x^{-2+1}/(-2+1)$$

$$= -x^{-1} = -1/x.$$

$$\therefore \quad V = \frac{Q}{4\pi\varepsilon_0}\left[\frac{1}{x}\right]_\infty^r = \frac{Q}{4\pi\varepsilon_0}\left[\frac{1}{r} - \frac{1}{\infty}\right] = \frac{Q}{4\pi\varepsilon_0 r}$$

as $1/\infty = 0$.

Energy in Capacitor and in Stretched Wire

When a capacitor of capacitance C is charged by a battery of e.m.f. V, the p.d. across the capacitor rises from zero to V. Suppose, at an instant, that the p.d. across the capacitor reaches a value v, and that the charge on it is q, where $q = Cv$. When a further charge δq flows from one plate to the other, the small, additional amount of energy stored in the capacitor $= v \cdot \delta q$, because v is the work done in taking *unit* charge from one plate to the other.

Therefore total amount of energy,

$$W = \int_0^V v \cdot \mathrm{d}q.$$

Since $$q = Cv,$$

$$\frac{\mathrm{d}q}{\mathrm{d}v} = C,$$

i.e. $$\mathrm{d}q = C \cdot \mathrm{d}v,$$

$$\therefore \quad W = \int_0^V Cv \cdot \mathrm{d}v = C\left[\tfrac{1}{2}v^2\right]_0^V = \tfrac{1}{2}CV^2.$$

Suppose a *wire* is extended by a length e from its natural length l by placing a load on it less than the elastic limit of the wire. When the extension is x, the force F in the wire is given by $F = EAx/l$, where A is the cross-sectional area of the wire, from the definition of Young's modulus, E. The work done in stretching the wire a further distance δx

$$= \text{force} \times \text{distance} = F \, . \, \delta x.$$

$$\therefore \quad \text{total work done} = \text{energy in wire} = \int_0^e \frac{EAx}{l} \, . \, dx$$

$$= \frac{EA}{l} \int_0^e x \, . \, dx = \frac{EA}{l} \left[\frac{x^2}{2} \right]_0^e = \frac{EAe^2}{2l}.$$

If the extension of the wire is from a to b, within the elastic limit of the wire, we alter the limits accordingly. Thus

$$\text{energy in wire} = \int_a^b \frac{EAx}{l} \, . \, dx = \frac{EA}{l} \int_a^b x \, . \, dx = \frac{EA}{l} \left[\frac{x^2}{2} \right]_a^b$$

$$= \frac{EA}{l} \left[\frac{b^2}{2} - \frac{a^2}{2} \right].$$

Areas and Integrals

Consider a graph LS such as $y = x^2 - 2x + 3$ (Fig. 10.1). Suppose M is a point on the graph corresponding to $x = \text{OA}$, $y = \text{AM}$, and N a point very close to M corresponding to $x + \delta x = \text{OB}$, $y + \delta y = \text{BN}$.

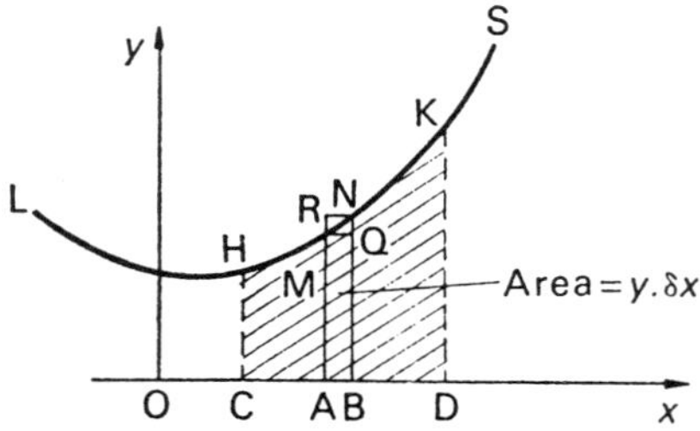

FIG. 10.1 Area by integration

If we draw perpendiculars from N to AM produced, meeting it in R, and from M to NB, meeting it in Q, it can be seen that the area MNBA is less than the area of the rectangle ARNB and greater than the area of the rectangle AMQB. The former area $= \text{AR} \times \text{AB} = (y + \delta y) \, . \, \delta x$; the latter area $= \text{AM} \times \text{AB} = y \, . \, \delta x$. As N approaches M the areas of the rectangles approach each other, and at the same time each approaches the area MNAB between the curve and the x-axis. Since

$(y + \delta y)\delta x$ and $y \,.\, \delta x$ both approach the value $y \,.\, \delta x$ as δx and δy become smaller, it follows, in the limit, that

$$\textit{area between curve and x-axis} = \int y \,.\, \mathrm{d}x,$$

the limits of the integral corresponding to the boundaries of that part of the curve under discussion. Thus area between HK and the x-axis

$$= \int_c^d y \,.\, \mathrm{d}x,$$

where OC $= c$, OD $= d$. The lower limit c is placed below the integral sign, the upper limit d is placed above the integral sign.

Suppose $c = 1$, $d = 4$. Then, since $y = x^2 - 2x + 3$

$$\begin{aligned}\text{area CDKH} &= \int_1^4 y \,.\, \mathrm{d}x = \int_1^4 (x^2 - 2x + 3) \,.\, \mathrm{d}x \\ &= \left[\frac{x^3}{3} - x^2 + 3x\right]_1^4 \\ &= \left(\frac{64}{3} - 16 + 12\right) - \left(\frac{1}{3} - 1 + 3\right) \\ &= 21 - 15 + 9 = 15.\end{aligned}$$

EXAMPLE

(i) Find the area enclosed by the curve $y = \dfrac{1}{x^2}$ and the x-axis, from $x = 2$ to $x = 5$. (ii) Find the area enclosed by the curve $y = x^2 - 3x + 4$ and the x-axis, from $x = 1$ to $x = 4$.

$$\begin{aligned}\text{(i) Area} &= \int_2^5 y \,.\, \mathrm{d}x = \int_2^5 \frac{1}{x^2} \,.\, \mathrm{d}x = \int_2 x^{-2} \,.\, \mathrm{d}x = \left[\frac{x^{-2+1}}{-2+1}\right]_2^5 \\ &= \left[-x^{-1}\right]_2^5 = \left[-\frac{1}{x}\right]_2^5 = \left(-\frac{1}{5}\right) - \left(-\frac{1}{2}\right) \\ &= \frac{3}{10}.\end{aligned}$$

$$\begin{aligned}\text{(ii) Area} &= \int_1^4 y \,.\, \mathrm{d}x = \int_1^4 (x^2 - 3x + 4)\mathrm{d}x \\ &= \left[\frac{x^3}{3} - \frac{3}{2}x^2 + 4x\right]_1^4 \\ &= \left(\frac{4^3}{3} - \frac{3}{2} \,.\, 4^2 + 4 \,.\, 4\right) - \left(\frac{1^3}{3} - \frac{3}{2} \,.\, 1^2 + 4 \,.\, 1\right) \\ &= 10.5.\end{aligned}$$

Energy in Capacitor. Gravitational Potential

Fig. 10.2 (i) illustrates how the p.d. v across a capacitor C varies with the charge q as C is charged by a battery of e.m.f. V. Since $q \propto v$, a *straight-line* graph OH is obtained. When the charge on C is q and the p.d. is v, the point B on the line OH is reached. If a further charge δq(AR) then flows, the small amount of *energy* stored $= v \,.\, \delta q =$ area ABSR. The total energy stored is thus the area OTD, where OD $= Q$ $=$ final charge and DT $= V =$ final p.d. $=$ e.m.f. of battery. Since OTD is a triangle,

$$\text{total energy stored} = \tfrac{1}{2}\text{OD} \times \text{DT} = \tfrac{1}{2}QV.$$

This relation was also derived on p. 171 since $\frac{1}{2}QV = \frac{1}{2}CV^2$.

Fig. 10.2 (ii) illustrates how the gravitational intensity E *outside* the earth varies with the distance r from the centre of the earth. E is the 'force per unit mass' and is measured in 'newton per kilogramme' (p. 233). At a point distance r where the intensity is E, a small movement

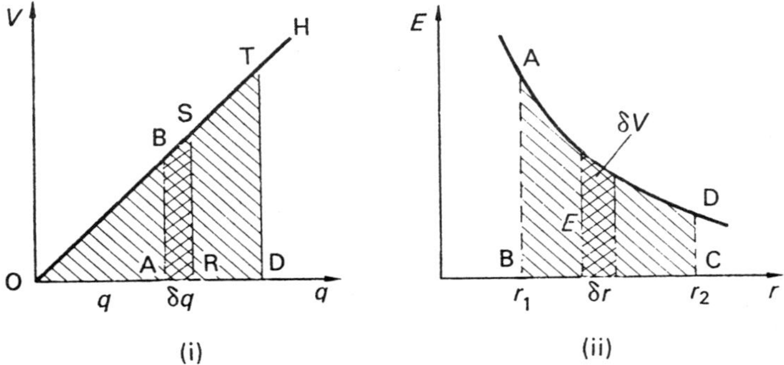

FIG. 10.2 Areas: (i) capacitor energy, (ii) potential difference

to a distance $(r + \delta r)$ will require an amount of work δW per unit mass given by $E \times \delta r$, which is the strip of area shown in Fig. 10.2 (ii). Thus the total work done per unit mass in moving a mass from a distance r_1 to a distance r_2 is equal to the area ABCD.

The 'work per unit mass' in moving a mass between two points in the earth's gravitational field is called the gravitational potential V between the two points. Thus the strip of area $E \,.\, \delta r$ represents the small change in potential δV, and the area ABCD represents the change in potential V from a distance r_1 to a distance r_2.

Solids of Revolution

The calculus also enables the volumes of solids to be calculated. Suppose, for example, that the curve $y = x^2$ is rotated about the x-axis,

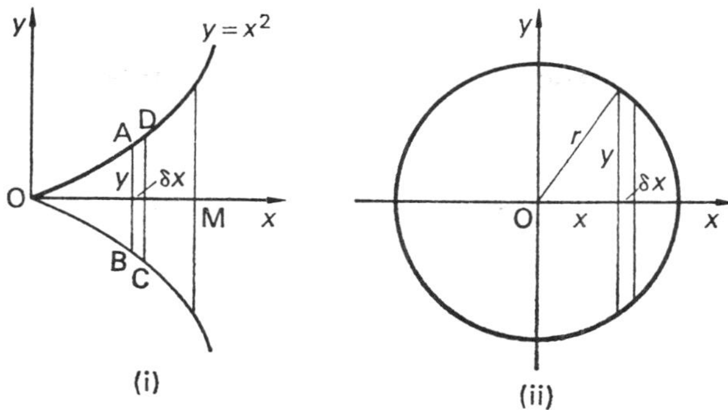

FIG. 10.3 Volumes by integrals

thus forming a solid (Fig. 10.3 (i)). A small element of the solid is a *disc* of thickness δx and surface area πy^2, between AB and DC; and thus, adding all the small volumes, i.e. integrating,

$$\text{volume of solid from O } (x = 0) \text{ to M } (x = 5) = \int_0^5 \pi y^2 \, . \, \mathrm{d}x.$$

Now $y = x^2$.

$$\therefore \quad \text{volume} = \int_0^5 \pi x^4 \, . \, \mathrm{d}x = \pi \left[\frac{x^5}{5}\right]_0^5 = 625\pi.$$

We can now find the *volume of a sphere*. A small element has a volume $\pi y^2 \, . \, \delta x$, as above (Fig. 10.3 (ii)). Thus if r is the radius of the sphere,

$$\text{volume of sphere} = 2\int_0^r \pi y^2 \, . \, \mathrm{d}x.$$

But $$x^2 + y^2 = r^2,$$

or $$y^2 = r^2 - x^2.$$

$$\begin{aligned}
\therefore \quad \text{volume} &= 2\int_0^r \pi(r^2 - x^2) \, . \, \mathrm{d}x \\
&= 2\int_0^r \pi r^2 \, . \, \mathrm{d}x - 2\pi\int_0^r x^2 \, . \, \mathrm{d}x \\
&= 2\pi r^2 \Big[x\Big]_0^r - 2\pi\left[\frac{x^3}{3}\right]_0^r \\
&= 2\pi r^3 - \tfrac{2}{3}\pi r^3 \\
&= \tfrac{4}{3}\pi r^3.
\end{aligned}$$

Moments of Inertia

The concept of moment of inertia is used in dealing with the mechanics of rotating rigid objects (see also Chapter 14, p. 237).

By definition, moment of inertia about an axis $= \Sigma mr^2$, where m is the mass of a particle, r is its distance from the axis, and Σ denotes that the values of mr^2 are summed or integrated over the whole of the object. As an example consider the moment of inertia of a uniform rod of length l and mass M about an axis O at one end perpendicular to its length (Fig. 10.4 (i)). A small element δx of the rod has a mass $\left(\frac{\delta x}{l} M\right)$.

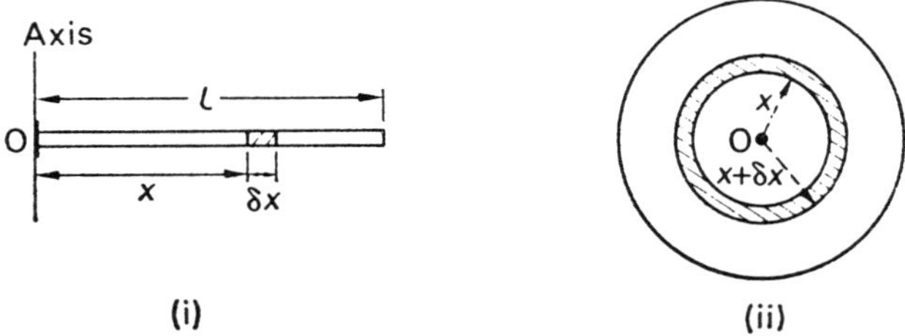

FIG. 10.4 Moments of inertia

The moment of inertia, I, about O

$$= \Sigma \left(\frac{\delta x}{l} M\right) \times x^2 = \int_0^l \frac{M}{l} \,.\, x^2 \,.\, \mathrm{d}x,$$

as the limits of x are from $x = 0$ to $x = l$. Now M/l are constants.

$$\therefore \quad I = \frac{M}{l} \int_0^l x^2 \,.\, \mathrm{d}x$$

$$= \frac{M}{l} \cdot \left[\frac{x^3}{3}\right]_0^l = \frac{Ml^2}{3}.$$

Again, suppose the moment of inertia of a circular disc of radius a is required about an axis perpendicular to the plane of the disc passing through the centre O (Fig. 10.4 (ii)). A small circular element of the disc between radii x and $(x + \delta x)$ has a length $2\pi x$ and a width δx. Thus the area is $2\pi x \,.\, \delta x$. If the mass of the whole disc is M, which corresponds to an area πa^2, the mass of the small element

$$= \frac{2\pi x \,.\, \delta x}{\pi a^2} \,.\, M = \frac{2x \,.\, \delta x}{a^2} \,.\, M.$$

Each portion of the ring is distant x from O. Hence the moment of inertia, I, about O is given by

$$I = \sum \left(\frac{2x \,.\, \delta x}{a^2} M \right) \times x^2$$

$$= \int_0^a \frac{2M}{a^2} \,.\, x^3 \,.\, \mathrm{d}x = \frac{2M}{a^2} \int_0^a x^3 \,.\, \mathrm{d}x$$

$$= \frac{2M}{a^2} \left[\frac{x^4}{4} \right]_0^a = \frac{2M}{a^2} \times \frac{a^4}{4}$$

$$= \frac{Ma^2}{2}.$$

EXERCISES 10

Integrate the following with respect to x:

(1) x^2.

(2) $2x - 3$.

(3) $\sqrt{x}$.

(4) $\dfrac{1}{x^2} + \dfrac{1}{x^3}$.

(5) $2x^2 - 2x - 1$.

(6) $2x^3 - 5 + \dfrac{1}{x^2}$.

(7) $\dfrac{5}{x^3}$.

(8) $x^2 + \dfrac{1}{x^2}$.

(9) $2x^{3/2}$.

(10) $x^2 + 4x + 2$.

(11) $x^{-1.4} + x^{1.4}$.

Evaluate the following:

(12) $\int_1^3 (x - 4)\mathrm{d}x$.

(13) $\displaystyle\int_{-2}^{4}(3x^2 - 2x + 1)\mathrm{d}x.$

(14) $\displaystyle\int_{-1}^{2}\frac{\mathrm{d}x}{x^3}.$

(15) $\displaystyle\int_{0}^{3}(3x + 4)\mathrm{d}x.$

(16) The velocity of an object after t seconds is given by $v = 4 + 7t$ where v is in m s^{-1} and t in s. By integration, find the distance travelled in the period from $t = 1$ to $t = 5$ s.

(17) The gradient of a curve is given generally by $\mathrm{d}y/\mathrm{d}x = 2x - 1$. If $x = 2$ when $y = 0$, find the equation to the curve.

(18) The velocity of an object after a time t is given by $v = 12 + 8t + 3t^2$. Find the distance travelled when $t = 10$, given $s = 20$ when $t = 0$.

(19) The tension in a string is given by $T = 80x$, where x is the extension. Calculate, by integration, the work done when the string is stretched (i) from $x = 0$ to $x = 2$, (ii) from $x = 3$ to $x = 5$.

(20) Prove that the electric potential at a point distant r from a charge is given by $Q/4\pi\varepsilon_0 r$.

(21) The force in a wire is given by $F = kx$, where x is the extension and $k = 10^8$ N m^{-1}. Find (i) energy stored in the wire when $x = 8$ mm, (ii) the extra energy required to increase the extension from 8 to 10 mm.

(22) The gravitational intensity E outside the earth $= -4 \times 10^{14}/r^2$, where r is the distance from the earth's centre in metre and E is in N kg^{-1}. Find the potential difference between the earth's surface and infinity if the radius of the earth is 6.4×10^6 m.

(23) The intensity E outside a charged sphere is given by $E = 100/r^2$, where r is the distance from the centre in metre and E is in V m^{-1}. Find the potential of the sphere if its radius is (i) 1 m, (ii) 1 mm.

Areas, Volumes. Moments of Inertia

(24) Find the area bounded by the curve $y = x^3$, the x-axis, and the ordinates $x = 1$ and $x = 4$.

(25) Find the area bounded by the curve $y = x^2 + 2x + 1$, the x-axis and the ordinates $x = 2$ and $x = 5$.

(26) A curve passes through the origin, and its gradient is given generally by $\mathrm{d}y/\mathrm{d}x = 2x - 1$. Find the area bounded by the curve, the x-axis and the ordinates $x = -1$, $x = -2$.

(27) Find the area enclosed by the graph $y = 4x - x^2$ and the x-axis.

(28) Find the area enclosed by the graph $y = (x - 2)(x - 4)$ and the x-axis.

(29) The line $y = 2x$ is rotated about the x-axis. Find the volume of the solid generated between $x = 0$ and $x = 6$.

(30) The curve $y^2 = 6x$ is rotated about the x-axis. Find the volume of the solid generated between $x = 2$ and $x = 5$.

(31) The curve $y^2 = 4x - 2$ is rotated about the x-axis. Find the volume of the solid generated between $x = 1$ and $x = 3$.

(32) Prove that the volume of a sphere is given by $4\pi r^3/3$, where r is the radius.

(33) Find the volume generated between $x = 2$ and $x = 4$ when the line $y = 2x + 1$ is rotated about the x-axis.

(34) A uniform rod has a mass of 4 kg and a length of 3 m. Calculate from first principles its moment of inertia about an axis perpendicular to its length (i) at one end, (ii) at its mid-point.

(35) A uniform circular disc has a mass of 0.1 kg and a radius of 0.08 m. Calculate from first principles its moment of inertia about an axis through its centre perpendicular to its plane.

(36) Prove that the moment of inertia of a sphere about a diameter is $2mr^2/5$, where m is the mass and r is the radius. (*Hint*. Take a disc of radius x and thickness dy; apply 'moment of inertia = mass of disc $\times$ $x^2/2$'; and integrate after using $x^2 + y^2 = r^2$.)

Answers

1. $\frac{1}{3}x^3 + c$

2. $x^2 - 3x + c$

3. $\frac{2}{3}x^{3/2} + c$

4. $-\dfrac{1}{x} - \dfrac{1}{2x^2} + c$

5. $\frac{2}{3}x^3 - x^2 - x + c$

6. $\frac{1}{2}x^4 - 5x - \dfrac{1}{x} + c$

7. $-\dfrac{5}{2x^2} + c$

8. $\frac{1}{3}x^3 - \dfrac{1}{x} + c$

9. $\frac{4}{5}x^{5/2} + c$

10. $\frac{1}{3}x^3 + 2x^2 + 2x + c$

11. $-\dfrac{1}{0.4x^{0.4}} + \dfrac{x^{2.4}}{2.4} + c$

12. -4

13. 66

14. 3/8

15. $25\frac{1}{2}$

16. 100 m

17. $y = x^2 - x - 2$

18. 1540

19. (i) 160 (ii) 640

21. (i) 32 000 J (ii) 1800 J

22. 6.25×10^7 J kg^{-1}

23. (i) 100 V (ii) 10^5 V

24. $63\frac{3}{4}$

25. 63

26. $3\frac{5}{6}$

27. $10\frac{2}{3}$

28. $1\frac{1}{3}$

29. 288π

30. 63π

31. 12π

33. $100\frac{2}{3}\pi$

34. (i) 12 (ii) 3 kg m^2

35. 3.2×10^{-4} kg m^2

11. Further Integral Calculus

Integrals of Trigonometrical Functions

We have now to consider the integrals of sines and cosines, that is,

$$\int \sin x \,.\, dx \quad \text{and} \quad \int \cos x \,.\, dx.$$

On p. 151, we showed that if $y = \sin x$, $dy/dx = \cos x$. Thus if c is a constant,

$$\therefore \quad \int \cos x \,.\, dx = \sin x + c. \qquad . \quad . \quad . \quad \text{(i)}$$

Similarly, it was shown on p. 151 that if $y = \cos x$, $dy/dx = -\sin x$.

$$\therefore \quad \int \sin x \,.\, dx = -\cos x + c. \qquad . \quad . \quad . \quad \text{(ii)}$$

Suppose that $\int \cos 2x \,.\, dx$ is required. Let $2x = y$; then

$$2\frac{dx}{dy} = 1$$

or

$$dx = \frac{dy}{2}$$

$$\therefore \quad \int \cos 2x \,.\, dx = \int \cos y \,.\, \frac{dy}{2} = \tfrac{1}{2}\int \cos y \,.\, dy$$

$$= \tfrac{1}{2}\sin y + c,$$

from (i),

$$\therefore \quad \int \cos 2x \,.\, dx = \tfrac{1}{2}\sin 2x + c.$$

Similarly, it can be shown that

$$\int \sin 3x \,.\, dx = -\tfrac{1}{3}\cos 3x + c,$$

a result which can be checked by differentiation. Generally, if ω is a constant,

$$\int \sin \omega t \,.\, dt = -\frac{1}{\omega}\cos \omega t + c,$$

and

$$\int \cos \omega t \,.\, dt = \frac{1}{\omega}\sin \omega t + c.$$

Integrals of $\sin^2 x$ and $\cos^2 x$

When the integrals of $\sin^2 x$ or $\cos^2 x$ are required, we substitute for $\sin^2 x$ and $\cos^2 x$ in terms of $\cos 2x$. Thus, since

$$\cos 2x = 2\cos^2 x - 1 \quad (\text{p. } 92),$$

$$\cos^2 x = \tfrac{1}{2}(1 + \cos 2x).$$

$$\therefore \quad \int \cos^2 x \,.\, dx = \int \tfrac{1}{2}(1 + \cos 2x) \,.\, dx$$

$$= \int \tfrac{1}{2} \,.\, dx + \tfrac{1}{2}\int \cos 2x . dx.$$

$$= \tfrac{1}{2}x + \tfrac{1}{4}\sin 2x + c.$$

Also, since

$$\cos 2x = 1 - 2\sin^2 x,$$

$$\therefore \quad \sin^2 x = \tfrac{1}{2}(1 - \cos 2x)$$

$$\therefore \quad \int \sin^2 x \,.\, dx = \int \tfrac{1}{2}(1 - \cos 2x) \,.\, dx$$

$$= \int \tfrac{1}{2} \,.\, dx - \int \tfrac{1}{2} \,.\, \cos 2x \,.\, dx$$

$$= \tfrac{1}{2}x - \tfrac{1}{4}\sin 2x + c.$$

Magnetic Flux Density B Due to Current

The magnetic flux density δB due to a small current-carrying element δl of a wire at a point P is normal to the plane containing P and the wire. Fig. 11.1 (i). From the Biot–Savart law, the magnitude of δB is given by

$$\delta B = \frac{\mu_0 I \delta l \sin \theta}{4\pi r^2}, \quad . \quad . \quad . \quad . \quad (1)$$

where I is the current in ampere, δl and the distance r of P from the element are in metre, θ is the angle between the element and the line joining the element to P, and δB is in tesla (T).

Circular Coil. Consider a narrow circular coil C of radius r carrying a current I (Fig. 11.1 (ii)). A small element δl of the wire always makes an angle of 90° with the line joining it to the centre. Hence the total field value B at the centre O is given by

$$B = \int \frac{\mu_0 I \sin 90° \,.\, dl}{4\pi r^2} = \frac{\mu_0 I}{4\pi r^2} \int_0^l dl,$$

since i and r are constants. Now

$$\int_0^l dl = \text{total length of coil} = 2\pi N r$$

if the coil has N turns.

$$\therefore \quad B = \frac{\mu_0 I \times 2\pi r N}{4\pi r^2} = \frac{\mu_0 N I}{2r}.$$

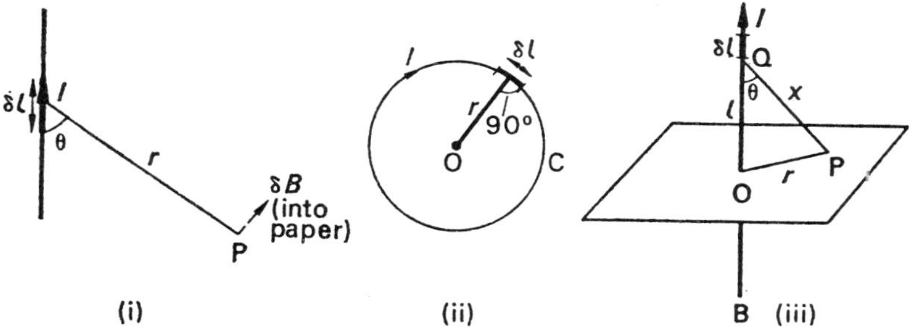

FIG. 11.1 Values of B due to currents

Integration by Substitution

In a number of cases, integration is assisted by substituting a different variable from that given. As a simple illustration, consider the integral $\int(2x + 1)^4 \,.\, dx$. In this case, let

$$z = 2x + 1.$$

Then $$\frac{dz}{dx} = 2$$

and $$(2x + 1)^4 = z^4$$

$$\therefore \quad \int (2x + 1)^4 \,.\, dx = \int z^4 \times \tfrac{1}{2}\, dz = \tfrac{1}{2} \int z^4 \,.\, dz$$

$$= \tfrac{1}{10} z^5 + c = \tfrac{1}{10}(2x + 1)^5 + c.$$

As another example, consider the integral

$$\int_0^{1/2} \frac{dx}{(1 - x^2)^{3/2}}.$$

In this case let $x = \sin\theta$. Then the limits change from 1/2 and 0 to $\pi/6$ and 0. Also,

$$\frac{dx}{d\theta} = \cos\theta$$

and $$(1 - x^2)^{3/2} = (\cos^2\theta)^{3/2} = \cos^3\theta$$

$$\therefore \quad \int_0^{1/2} \frac{dx}{(1-x^2)^{3/2}} = \int_0^{\pi/6} \frac{\cos\theta \,.\, d\theta}{\cos^3\theta} = \int_0^{\pi/6} \sec^2\theta \,.\, d\theta$$

$$= \Big[\tan\theta\Big]_0^{\pi/6} = \tan\pi/6 = \frac{1}{\sqrt{3}}.$$

Straight Wire

Consider the field B at a point P distant r from a very long straight vertical wire carrying a current I [Fig. 11.1 (iii)]. The field due to a small element δl of the wire, where l is the length from O to the element, is given by

$$\delta B = \frac{\mu_0 I \delta l \sin\theta}{4\pi x^2},$$

where x is the distance from P to the element.

$$\therefore \quad \text{total field, } B, = \int \frac{\mu_0 I \sin\theta \,.\, dl}{4\pi x^2}.$$

At the point O, $\theta = \pi/2(90°)$; if the wire is infinitely long, the upper end of the wire corresponds to $\theta = 0$. The total field B is twice that due to half the wire. Hence

$$B = 2\int_{\pi/2}^{0} \frac{\mu_0 I \sin\theta \,.\, dl}{4\pi x^2}. \qquad \text{(i)}$$

In this expression x and l vary, but r (=OP) is constant; we therefore obtain x and l in terms of r. From the right-angled triangle OPQ

$$x = r\,\text{cosec}\,\theta,$$
$$l = r\cot\theta.$$

Differentiating,

$$\therefore \quad dl = -r\,\text{cosec}^2\,\theta \,.\, d\theta$$ (see p. 156).

Substituting for x and dl in (i),

$$\therefore \quad B = 2\int_{\pi/2}^{0} \frac{-\mu_0 I\, r\,\text{cosec}^2\,\theta \,.\, \sin\theta \,.\, d\theta}{4\pi r^2\,\text{cosec}^2\,\theta}$$

$$= \frac{\mu_0 I}{2\pi r}\int_{\pi/2}^{0} -\sin\theta\, d\theta.$$

Now $\int \sin\theta \,.\, d\theta = -\cos\theta$ (p. 181),

$$\therefore \quad B = \frac{\mu_0 I}{2\pi r}\Big[\cos\theta\Big]_{\pi/2}^{0} = \frac{\mu_0 I}{2\pi r}$$

since $\cos 0 = 1$

and $\cos \pi/2 = 0.$

EXAMPLE

A current of 2 A flows in a wire in the shape of a square of side 10 cm. Calculate the magnetic field value B in the centre of the square. ($\mu_0 = 4\pi \times 10^{-7}$ H m^{-1}.)

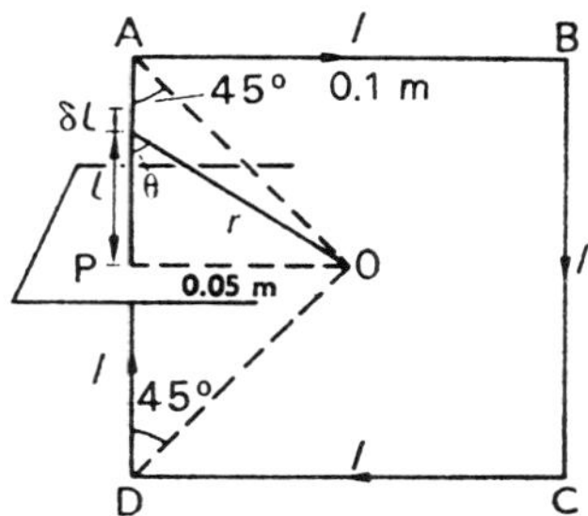

FIG. 11.2 B due to rectangular conductor

Suppose O is the centre of the square ABCD (Fig. 11.2). A small element δl of the side AD then has a field value δB at O given, from Ampere's law, by

$$\delta B = \frac{\mu_0 I\,\delta l \sin\theta}{4\pi r^2}$$

where $I = 2$ A and r is the distance from O to the element in metre.

$$\therefore \quad \text{total field } B \text{ due to AD} = \frac{2\mu_0 I}{4\pi}\int_{\theta=\pi/2}^{\theta=\pi/4} \frac{\sin\theta \,.\, dl}{r^2},$$

as $\theta = \pi/2 (90°)$ corresponds to P, the middle of AD, and $\theta = \pi/4 (45°)$ corresponds to A.

Now $l = 0.05 \cot\theta$; hence $dl = -0.05 \operatorname{cosec}^2\theta \,.\, d\theta$ (p. 156).

Also, $r = 0.05 \operatorname{cosec}\theta$.

Substituting, $\therefore\ B = \dfrac{2\mu_0 I}{4\pi}\displaystyle\int_{\theta=\pi/2}^{\theta=\pi/4} \frac{-0.05 \operatorname{cosec}^2\theta \,.\, \sin\theta \,.\, d\theta}{0.0025 \operatorname{cosec}^2\theta}$

$$= \frac{10\mu_0 I}{\pi}\int_{\theta=\pi/2}^{\theta=\pi/4} -\sin\theta \,.\, d\theta$$

$$= \frac{10\mu_0 I}{\pi}\Big[\cos\theta\Big]_{\theta=\pi/2}^{\theta=\pi/4} = \frac{10\mu_0 I}{\pi}\Big[\cos 45^\circ - \cos 90^\circ\Big]$$

$$= \frac{10\mu_0 I \cos 45^\circ}{\pi} = \frac{4\pi \times 10^{-7} \times 20 \times \cos 45^\circ}{\pi}$$

$$= 5.7 \times 10^{-6}\ \text{T}$$

$\therefore$ Magnitude of the field B due to 4 sides of ABCD $= 4 \times 5.7 \times 10^{-6} = 2.3 \times 10^{-5}$ T.

Root-mean-square Value of A.C.

The alternating current I from the mains varies with time t according to the relation

$$I = I_0 \sin \omega t,$$

where I_0 is the maximum current and ω is the constant angular velocity ($\omega = 2\pi f$, where f is the number of cycles per second).

The root-mean-square (r.m.s.) of an alternating current may be defined as the square root of the average value of I^2 during one cycle. The average value of I^2 during the time of one period, T, can thus be found by finding $\int I^2 \,.\, dt$ in this time, and dividing by the total time T, which is $\int_0^T dt$:

$$\therefore \quad \text{average value of } I^2 = \frac{\int_0^T I_0^2 \sin^2 \omega t \,.\, dt}{\int_0^T dt} \quad . \quad . \quad \text{(i)}$$

Since $\sin^2\theta = \frac{1}{2}(1 - \cos 2\theta)$, p. 92,

$$\therefore \quad \sin^2 \omega t = \tfrac{1}{2}(1 - \cos 2\omega t).$$

$$\therefore \quad \int_0^T I_0^2 \sin^2 \omega t \,.\, dt = \tfrac{1}{2}I_0^2 \int_0^T (1 - \cos 2\omega t) \,.\, dt$$

$$= \tfrac{1}{2}I_0^2 \left[\int_0^T dt - \int_0^T \cos 2\omega t \,.\, dt.\right]$$

Now the integral

$$\int_0^T \cos 2\omega t \,.\, dt$$

represents the total area enclosed by the graph of cos $2\omega t$ and the time axis (p. 173). This is *zero*, since the cosine curve is symmetrical about the time-axis for a complete period T (p. 90).

$$\therefore \quad \int_0^T I_0^2 \sin^2 \omega t \, . \, \mathrm{d}t = \tfrac{1}{2} I_0^2 T.$$

Hence, from (i),

$$\text{average value of } I^2 = \frac{\tfrac{1}{2} I_0^2 T}{T} = \tfrac{1}{2} I_0^2$$

$$\therefore \quad \text{r.m.s. value} = \sqrt{\tfrac{1}{2} I_0^2} = \frac{1}{\sqrt{2}} I_0$$

$$= 0.71 I_0 \text{ (approx.).}$$

Average Output of D.C. Dynamo

When a simple dynamo has a split-ring commutator, double half-waves in the same direction are obtained. Thus a varying direct current is obtained. The average value, I_A, is the average value over half a period, $T/2$.

$$\therefore \quad I_A = \frac{\int_0^{T/2} I_0 \sin \omega t \, . \, \mathrm{d}t}{\int_0^{T/2} \mathrm{d}t}. \quad . \quad . \quad . \quad . \quad \text{(i)}$$

Now $$\int_0^{T/2} \sin \omega t \, . \, \mathrm{d}t = -\frac{1}{\omega} \Big[\cos \omega t \Big]_0^{T/2}$$

$$= -\frac{1}{\omega} \left(\cos \frac{\omega T}{2} - \cos 0^\circ \right).$$

But $$T = \frac{2\pi}{\omega},$$

or $$\frac{\omega T}{2} = \pi = 180^\circ.$$

$$\therefore \quad \cos \frac{\omega T}{2} = \cos 180^\circ = -1.$$

Also, $$\cos 0^\circ = 1.$$

$$\therefore \quad \int_0^{T/2} \sin \omega t \, . \, \mathrm{d}t = -\frac{1}{\omega}(-1 - 1) = \frac{2}{\omega}.$$

Thus, from (i), $$I_A = \frac{2 I_0/\omega}{T/2} = \frac{4 I_0}{\omega T}.$$

But, from $$T = 2\pi/\omega,$$

$$\omega T = 2\pi.$$

$$\therefore \qquad I_A = \frac{4I_0}{2\pi} = \frac{2}{\pi} I_0 = 0.64 I_0 \text{ (approx.)}.$$

Integration of 1/*x*

On p. 157 we showed that if $y = \ln x$, then

$$\frac{dy}{dx} = \frac{1}{x}.$$

It therefore follows that, if c is a constant,

$$\int \frac{dx}{x} = \ln x + c. \qquad \text{(i)}$$

It was stated on p. 157 that if

$$y = \ln (x - a),$$

$$\frac{dy}{dx} = \frac{1}{x - a}.$$

Thus $$\int \frac{dx}{x - a} = \ln (x - a) + c. \qquad \text{(ii)}$$

From (i), $$\int_2^4 \frac{dx}{x} = \Big[\ln x\Big]_2^4 = \ln 4 - \ln 2$$

$$= \ln \left(\frac{4}{2}\right) = \ln 2 = 0.7.$$

Also, from (ii),

$$\int_4^6 \frac{dx}{(x - 1)} = \Big[\ln (x - 1)\Big]_4^6$$

$$= \ln (6 - 1) - \ln (4 - 1)$$

$$= \ln 5 - \ln 3 = \ln \left(\frac{5}{3}\right) = 0.5.$$

Radioactivity. Decay Constant and Half-life Period

In radioactivity, the nuclei of heavy atoms such as uranium disintegrate, forming new nuclei. These in turn disintegrate and form other new nuclei. The number of nuclei per second which are disintegrating appears to follow the law of probability, that is, the number per second disintegrating is directly proportional to the number of nuclei present.

Suppose N is the number of atoms present at a time t. The rate at which nuclei are disintegrating at this time is thus represented by $\mathrm{d}N/\mathrm{d}t$.

$$\therefore \quad \frac{\mathrm{d}N}{\mathrm{d}t} = -\lambda N,$$

where λ is a constant known as the *decay constant* or *transformation constant* or *radioactive constant.*

$$\therefore \quad \int \frac{\mathrm{d}N}{N} = -\lambda \int \mathrm{d}t$$

$$\therefore \quad \ln N = -\lambda t + c \qquad \text{(i)}$$

where c is a constant. At $t = 0$, suppose the number of atoms present is N_0. Then

$$\ln N_0 = c.$$

From (i) $\quad \therefore \quad \ln N - \ln N_0 = -\lambda t$

$$\therefore \quad \ln\left(\frac{N}{N_0}\right) = -\lambda t$$

$$\therefore \quad N = N_0 e^{-\lambda t} \qquad \text{(ii)}$$

Thus the number N of radioactive atoms diminishes exponentially with time t. At some time T, known as the *half-life period*, the number of atoms disintegrate to one-half of their original number. From (ii),

$$\therefore \quad \frac{N_0}{2} = N_0 e^{-\lambda T}$$

$$\therefore \quad e^{\lambda T} = 2, \quad \text{or} \quad \lambda T = \ln 2$$

$$\therefore \quad T = \frac{1}{\lambda} \ln 2 = \frac{0.693}{\lambda} \qquad \text{(iii)}$$

Since at a time T the radioactive activity I diminishes to one-half, measurements of I enable the half-life period to be found (see p. 62).

Thermal Conduction

In a steady state, the quantity of energy per second, $\mathrm{d}Q/\mathrm{d}t$, through a material is related to the thermal conductivity k, the area A, and the temperature gradient, $\mathrm{d}\theta/\mathrm{d}x$, by the formula (p. 129)

$$\frac{\mathrm{d}Q}{\mathrm{d}t} = -kA\,\frac{\mathrm{d}\theta}{\mathrm{d}x}.$$

In the case of a lagged bar heated at one end, as in Searle's apparatus to find the thermal conductivity of a good conductor, *linear flow* of heat occurs and $\mathrm{d}Q/\mathrm{d}t$ is constant in the steady state. Suppose the constant is g. Then, from above,

$$-kA\frac{\mathrm{d}\theta}{\mathrm{d}x} = g.$$

$$\therefore \quad \frac{\mathrm{d}\theta}{\mathrm{d}x} = -\frac{g}{kA} = -m, \text{ another constant.}$$

Integrating, $\therefore \quad \theta = -mx + c,$

where c is a constant. When $x = 0$, θ = temperature of hot end = θ_0 say.

Substituting, $\therefore \quad \theta_0 = c$

$$\therefore \quad \theta = -mx + \theta_0.$$

This is a straight-line relation between θ and x, with θ diminishing as x increases.

Radial Flow

In the experiment to find the thermal conductivity of glass in the form of a pipe, or a rubber tube, heat flows from the inside to the outside through the circular cross-section and hence this is termed *radial flow* of heat. In the steady state we can apply

$$\frac{\mathrm{d}Q}{\mathrm{d}t} = -kA\frac{\mathrm{d}\theta}{\mathrm{d}x}.$$

Here $A = 2\pi rl$, where r is the radius of a cylindrical section and l is the length; writing r for x, $\mathrm{d}\theta/\mathrm{d}r$ is the temperature gradient at this section. Thus if $\mathrm{d}Q/\mathrm{d}t = g$, a constant, we have, from above,

$$g = -k\,.\,2\pi rl\frac{\mathrm{d}\theta}{\mathrm{d}r}.$$

$$\therefore \quad \int_{r_1}^{r_2}\frac{\mathrm{d}r}{r} = -\frac{2\pi l\,.\,k}{g}\int_{\theta_0}^{\theta_1}\mathrm{d}\theta,$$

where r_1, r_2 are the radii of the inner and outer surfaces of the pipe, and θ_0, θ_1 are their corresponding temperatures.

$$\therefore \quad \Big[\ln r\Big]_{r_1}^{r_2} = -\frac{2\pi l\,.\,k}{g}\Big[\theta\Big]_{\theta_0}^{\theta_1}$$

$$\therefore \quad \ln r_2 - \ln r_1 = -\frac{2\pi l\,.\,k}{g}(\theta_1 - \theta_0)$$

$$\therefore \quad \ln\left(\frac{r_2}{r_1}\right) = -\frac{2\pi l\,.\,k}{g}(\theta_1 - \theta_0) = \frac{2\pi l\,.\,k}{g}(\theta_0 - \theta_1)$$

$$\therefore \quad k = \frac{g}{2\pi l(\theta_0 - \theta_1)}\ln\left(\frac{r_2}{r_1}\right).$$

Work Done by or on a Gas

When a gas expands by a small volume δV at a pressure p, then, from work done = force × distance, we find

$$\text{work done} = \text{pressure} \times \text{volume change}$$
$$= p \,.\, \delta V.$$

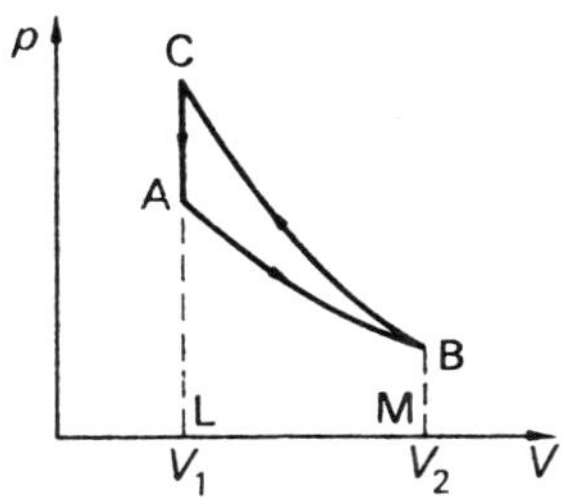

FIG. 11.3 Work done on gas

Suppose the gas expands *isothermally* from a volume V_1 (A) to a volume V_2 (B) (Fig. 11.3). Then

$$\text{total work done, } W, = \int_{V_1}^{V_2} p \,.\, \mathrm{d}V,$$

which is represented by the area ABML between AB and the volume-axis, as explained previously. For an isothermal change of 1 mole of gas, $pV = k$, a constant, where $k = RT$ in the usual notation and R is the molar gas constant. Thus $p = k/V$. Substituting for p,

$$W = \int_{V_1}^{V_2} \frac{k}{V} \,.\, \mathrm{d}V = k \int_{V_1}^{V_2} \frac{1}{V} \,.\, \mathrm{d}V$$

$$= k \Big[\ln V\Big]_{V_1}^{V_2} = k[\ln V_2 - \ln V_1]$$

$$= k \ln \left(\frac{V_2}{V_1}\right) = RT \ln \left(\frac{V_2}{V_1}\right) \quad . \quad . \quad . \quad \text{(i)}$$

Suppose the gas at B is compressed *adiabatically* along BC until the volume V_1 is again reached (Fig. 11.3). The adiabatic curve at B is steeper than the isothermal through this point and hence the graph moves to C, above A. The work done on the gas, W, is given by

$$W = \int_{V_2}^{V_1} p \,.\, \mathrm{d}V.$$

But $pV^{\gamma} = c$, a constant, for an adiabatic change, where γ is the ratio of the principal specific heats of the gas, i.e. $p = c/V^{\gamma}$. Substituting for p,

$$\therefore \quad W = \int_{V_2}^{V_1} \frac{c \,.\, \mathrm{d}V}{V^{\gamma}} = c \int_{V_2}^{V_1} V^{-\gamma} \,.\, \mathrm{d}V$$

$$= c \left[\frac{V^{-\gamma+1}}{-\gamma+1}\right]_{V_2}^{V_1} = -\frac{c}{\gamma-1}\left[\frac{1}{V^{\gamma-1}}\right]_{V_2}^{V_1}$$

$$= -\frac{c}{\gamma-1}\left[\frac{1}{V_1^{\gamma-1}} - \frac{1}{V_2^{\gamma-1}}\right]$$

$$= -\frac{1}{\gamma-1}\left[\frac{c}{V_1^{\gamma-1}} - \frac{c}{V_2^{\gamma-1}}\right].$$

Now $c = p_1 V_1^{\gamma} = p_2 V_2^{\gamma}$.

$$\therefore \quad W = -\frac{1}{\gamma-1}\left[\frac{p_1 V_1^{\gamma}}{V_1^{\gamma-1}} - \frac{p_2 V_2^{\gamma}}{V_2^{\gamma-1}}\right]$$

$$= -\frac{1}{\gamma-1}[p_1 V_1 - p_2 V_2] \qquad . \quad . \quad . \quad \text{(ii)}$$

This work is represented by the area between BC and the volume-axis in Fig. 11.3. If the cycle of operations is completed by moving from C to A, when the volume of the gas is constant,

net work done on gas in cycle = area CBML − area ABML
= area CBA.

EXAMPLE

A gas expands (i) isothermally, (ii) adiabatically from a volume of 0.1 m^3 to 0.3 m^3. In (i) the gas obeys the relation $pV = 10^4$; in (ii) the gas obeys the relation $pV^{1.4} = 10^5$ where p is in N m^{-2} and V in m^3. Calculate the work done by the gas in each case.

(i) Since $\quad pV = 10^4, \quad p = \dfrac{10^4}{V}$

$$\therefore \quad \text{work done} = \int_{0.1}^{0.3} p \,.\, \mathrm{d}V = \int_{0.1}^{0.3} \frac{10^4 \,.\, \mathrm{d}V}{V} = 10^4 \int_{0.1}^{0.3} \frac{\mathrm{d}V}{V}$$

$$= 10^4 \Big[\ln V\Big]_{0.1}^{0.3}$$

$$= 10^4(\ln 0.3 - \ln 0.1) = 10^4 \ln\left(\frac{0.3}{0.1}\right)$$

$$= 10^4 \ln 3 = 1.1 \times 10^4 \text{ J}$$

(ii) Adiabatically,

$$pV^{1.4} = 10^5, \text{ hence } p = \frac{10^5}{V^{1.4}}$$

$$\therefore \quad \text{work done} = \int_{0.1}^{0.3} p\,.\,\mathrm{d}V = \int_{0.1}^{0.3} \frac{10^5\,.\,\mathrm{d}V}{V^{1.4}} = 10^5 \int_{0.1}^{0.3} V^{-1.4}\,.\,\mathrm{d}V$$

$$= 10^5 \left[\frac{V^{-1.4+1}}{-1.4+1}\right]_{0.1}^{0.3} = 10^5 \left[\frac{V^{-0.4}}{-0.4}\right]_{0.1}^{0.3}$$

$$= -\frac{10^5}{0.4}\left[\frac{1}{V^{0.4}}\right]_{0.1}^{0.3} = -\frac{10^5}{0.4}\left[\frac{1}{0.3^{0.4}} - \frac{1}{0.1^{0.4}}\right]$$

$$= 2.2 \times 10^5 \text{ J}$$

Summary of Integral Calculus

1. If $\dfrac{\mathrm{d}y}{\mathrm{d}x} = x^n$, $\quad y = \dfrac{1}{n+1}\,x^{n+1} + c$, where c is a constant;

   or $\displaystyle\int x^n\,.\,\mathrm{d}x = \frac{1}{n+1}\,x^{n+1} + c.$

2. If $\dfrac{\mathrm{d}y}{\mathrm{d}x} = \sin x$, $\quad y = -\cos x + c.$

   If $\dfrac{\mathrm{d}y}{\mathrm{d}x} = \cos x$, $\quad y = \sin x + c.$

   $\displaystyle\int \cos \omega t\,.\,\mathrm{d}t = \frac{1}{\omega}\sin \omega t + c.$

   $\displaystyle\int \sin \omega t\,.\,\mathrm{d}t = -\frac{1}{\omega}\cos \omega t + c.$

3. If $\dfrac{\mathrm{d}y}{\mathrm{d}x} = \dfrac{1}{x}$, $\quad y = \ln x + c;$

   or $\displaystyle\int \frac{1}{x}\,.\,\mathrm{d}x = \ln x + c.$

   $\displaystyle\int \frac{\mathrm{d}x}{x-a} = \ln (x-a) + c.$

4. For sine waves of period T,

   $\displaystyle\int_0^T \sin^2 \omega t\,.\,\mathrm{d}t = \frac{T}{2},$

   $\displaystyle\int_0^{T/2} \sin \omega t\,.\,\mathrm{d}t = \frac{T}{\pi}.$

EXERCISES 11

Integrate the following with respect to the variable concerned:

(1) $\cos x$.

(2) $\sin 3t$.

(3) $\sin \omega t$.

(4) $\cos 4t$.

(5) $\sin^2 \theta$.

(6) $\cos \omega t - \sin \omega t$.

(7) $\sin (3t - \pi/4)$.

(8) $\cos (2x + \pi/4)$.

(9) $\cos^2 \omega x$.

(10) $\sin \theta - \cos \theta$.

(11) $2 \sin 4t + \cos 2t$.

Evaluate the following:

(12) $\int_0^{\pi/2} -\sin \theta \, . \, d\theta$.

(13) $\int_0^{\pi/2} \cos \theta \, . \, d\theta$.

(14) $\int_0^{\pi/2} \sin 2\theta \, . \, d\theta$.

(15) (i) $\int_{-\pi/2}^{\pi/2} \cos \theta \, . \, d\theta$. (ii) $\int_0^{\pi/2} \sin^2 t \, . \, dt$.

(16) Each half-wave of a rectified alternating current obeys the relation $I = 80 \sin 100t$. If double half-waves in one direction are obtained, deduce the average value of the current from first principles.

(17) Find the area bounded by the curve $y = \sin x$, the x-axis, and the ordinates $x = \pi/6$ and $x = \pi/2$.

(18) Starting from the Biot-Savart law, $\delta B = \mu_0 I \, . \, \delta l \, . \sin \theta / 4\pi r^2$, derive the value for the field B due to an infinitely long straight wire carrying a current of 4 A at a point 5 cm from the wire. How is the result for B affected by a finite length of wire? ($\mu_0 = 4\pi \times 10^{-7}$ H m^{-1})

(19) Prove from first principles that the root-mean-square value of an alternating current represented by $I = 5 \cos 100\, t$ is given by $5/\sqrt{2}$.

(20) Derive from first principles the average value of a rectified (double half-wave) alternating current represented by $I = 10 \sin 400\, t$.

(21) Derive from first principles the root-mean-square value of an alternating current represented by $I = 8 \sin 200\, t$.

(22) A single flat coil, consisting of 100 turns of mean area 200 cm² and resistance 4 Ω, is fitted with a commutator and rotates at 1500 r.p.m. about a diameter at right angles to a uniform magnetic field of 6×10^{-3} T. The brushes bearing on the commutator are connected to a resistance of 16 Ω. Determine (*a*) the mean e.m.f. generated, (*b*) the mean current flowing, (*c*) the mean potential difference across the brushes. (*C.*)

(23) The electric field E emerging from a Polaroid is given by $E = E_0 \cos \theta$, where θ is the angle between the 'allowed' direction and E_0. If the Polaroid spins in its own plane about an axis parallel to the incident field E_0 with a constant angular velocity, find the mean intensity I of the emerging light if the intensity $I = kE^2$ where k is a constant.

Log Functions

Integrate the following with respect to x:

(24) $\dfrac{4}{x}$.

(25) $\dfrac{3}{2x}$.

(26) $-\dfrac{2}{x}$.

(27) $\dfrac{1}{x+4}$.

(28) $\dfrac{2}{x-1}$.

(29) $\dfrac{3}{2x+1}$.

(30) $\dfrac{1}{3-2x}$.

(31) $\dfrac{1}{ax-b}$.

(32) $\frac{1}{3 - x}$.

(33) $\frac{1}{7 - 5x}$.

Evaluate the following:

(34) $\int_2^8 \frac{dV}{V}$.

(35) $\int_0^2 \frac{dx}{3 - x}$.

(36) $\int_2^6 \frac{dx}{4 + x}$.

(37) $\int_0^{10} \frac{40dx}{4x + 2}$.

(38) A gas expands isothermally according to the relation $pV = 200$. Calculate the work done from $V = 20$ to $V = 100\ \text{cm}^3$ if p is in N m^{-2} and V in m^3.

(39) Calculate the work done when a gas expands isothermally from a volume of $80\ \text{cm}^3$ to $160\ \text{cm}^3$ if $pV = 40$ and p is in N m^{-2} and V in m^3.

(40) Write down the formula for Newton's law of cooling in terms of the calculus. If a hot body cools from 40°C to 30°C in 5 minutes, calculate the time taken to cool from 30°C to 20°C assuming Newton's law. Assume the room temperature is 15°C.

(41) The temperature of a liquid decreases from 50°C to 30°C in 10 minutes, the temperature of the room being 10°C. How long will the liquid take to cool from 30°C to 20°C, assuming Newton's law of cooling?

(42) Assuming that the gradient at a point on an adiabatic curve is γ times the gradient of the isothermal curve ($pV =$ constant) at the point of intersection, prove that the equation of the adiabatic curve is $pV^\gamma =$ constant.

(43) A current in a circuit diminishes according to the relation $dI/dt = -10I$. If $I = 10$ A when $t = 0$, calculate the current magnitude when $t = \frac{1}{5}$ s.

(44) A current in a circuit diminishes according to the relation $dI/dt = 8 - 2I$. If $I = 2$ A when $t = 0$, determine the magnitude of I when $t = \frac{1}{2}$ s.

(45) From first principles, derive a formula for the thermal conductivity of a cylindrical glass tube with radial flow of heat.

Calculate the heat per second in the steady state passing through a cylindrical glass tube in radial flow, given that $k = 3 \times 10^{-4}$ W m^{-1} K^{-1}, the inside temperature is 100°C, the outside temperature is 20°C, the length of the tube is 1 metre, and the internal and external radii are 4 and 6 mm respectively.

(46) A gas expands adiabatically according to the relation $pV^{1.4} = 800$, where p is in N m^{-2} and V in m^3. Calculate the work done when the volume of the gas increases from 100 to 400 cm^3. What work would be done if the gas were to expand isothermally according to the relation $pV = 800$ (p in N m^{-2} and V in m^3) from $V = 100$ to 400 cm^3?

Integration by Substitution

(47) $\displaystyle\int \frac{dx}{(3x-1)^4}$ (let $z = 3x - 1$).

(48) $\displaystyle\int_0^{\pi/2} \cos^3 x \,.\, \sin x \,.\, dx$ (let $z = \cos x$).

(49) $\displaystyle\int \frac{dx}{(a^2 - x^2)^{3/2}}$.

(50) $\displaystyle\int \frac{x \,.\, dx}{(1 + x^2)^{3/2}}$.

(51) $\displaystyle\int_0^1 \frac{e^x \,.\, dx}{1 + e^x}$.

(52) $\displaystyle\int_0^1 \sqrt{4 - x^2} \,.\, dx$.

Answers

1. $\sin x + c$

2. $-\frac{1}{3}\cos 3t + c$

3. $-\dfrac{1}{\omega}\cos \omega t + c$

4. $\frac{1}{4}\sin 4t + c$

5. $\frac{1}{2}\theta - \frac{1}{4}\sin 2\theta + c$

6. $\dfrac{1}{\omega}(\sin \omega t + \cos \omega t) + c$

7. $-\frac{1}{3}\cos\left(3t - \dfrac{\pi}{4}\right) + c$

8. $\frac{1}{2}\sin\left(2x + \dfrac{\pi}{4}\right) + c$

9. $\frac{1}{2}x + \dfrac{1}{4\omega}\sin 2\omega x + c$

10. $-(\sin\theta + \cos\theta) + c$

11. $\frac{1}{2}(\sin 2t - \cos 4t) + c$

12. -1

13. 1

14. 1

15. (i) 2, (ii) $\pi/4$

16. $160/\pi$

17. $\sqrt{3}/2$

18. 1.6×10^{-5} T

20. $20/\pi$

21. $4\sqrt{2}$

22. (i) 1.2 V, (ii) 0.06 A, (iii) 0.96 V

23. $kE_0^2/2$

24. $4\ln x + c$

25. $\frac{3}{2}\ln x + c$

26. $-2\ln x + c$

27. $\ln(x + 4) + c$

28. $2\ln(x - 1) + c$

29. $\frac{3}{2} \ln (2x + 1) + c$

30. $-\frac{1}{2} \ln (3 - 2x) + c$

31. $\dfrac{1}{a} \ln (ax - b) + c$

32. $- \ln (3 - x) + c$

33. $-\frac{1}{5} \ln (7 - 5x)$

34. $\ln 4$

35. $\ln 3$

36. $\ln (5/3)$

37. $10 \ln 21$

38. 322 J

39. 28 J

40. 10.8 min

41. 10 min

43. 1.35 A

44. 3.26 A

45. 0.37 W

46. 3.4×10^4 J, 1109 J

47. $-1/9(3x - 1)^3 + c$

48. $1/4$

49. $x/a^2(a^2 - x^2)^{1/2} + c$

50. $-1/(1 + x^2)^{1/2} + c$

51. $\ln [(1 + e)/2]$

52. $(\pi/3) + (\sqrt{3}/2)$

12. Introduction to Differential Equations

To conclude integration, we discuss the solutions to some simple *differential equations* met in Physics and Chemistry. A 'first order' differential equation is one which contains only the first differential coefficient, for example, dx/dt. A 'second order' differential equation is one which contains a second differential coefficient, for example, d^2x/dt^2.

Discharge of Capacitor (C) through Resistor (R)

In certain radio or computer circuits, charged capacitors discharge through resistors. Suppose a capacitor C has been charged to an initial

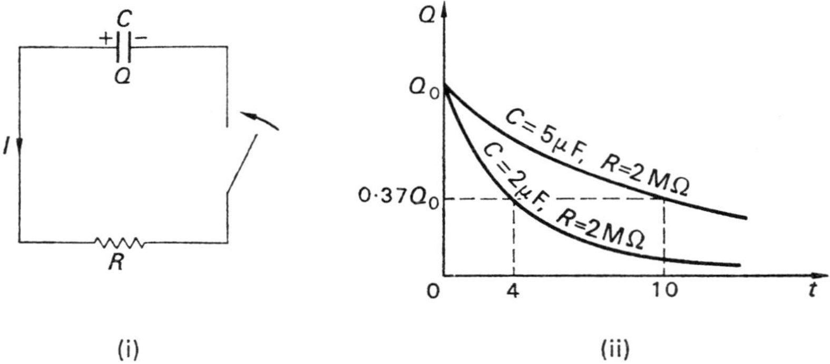

FIG. 12.1 Discharge of C through R

quantity Q_0 and then discharges through a resistance R. Fig. 12.1 (i). After a time t, the charge falls to an amount say Q, and suppose the current flowing at this instant is I. Then

$$\text{p.d. across } R = IR = \frac{Q}{C}.$$

But $I = -\mathrm{d}Q/\mathrm{d}t$, the minus showing that the charge Q *diminishes* with time t.

$$\therefore \quad -R\frac{\mathrm{d}Q}{\mathrm{d}t} = \frac{Q}{C} \quad . \quad . \quad . \quad . \quad (1)$$

Equation (1) is a *first order* differential equation, since $\mathrm{d}Q/\mathrm{d}t$ is a first order differential coefficient. To solve it, we simply separate, or transpose, the two variables, Q and t. We then have

$$\int_{Q_0}^{Q} \frac{\mathrm{d}Q}{Q} = -\frac{1}{CR}\int_0^t \mathrm{d}t.$$

the lower limit Q_0 corresponding to $t = 0$. Integrating,

$$\therefore \quad \ln Q - \ln Q_0 = -\frac{t}{CR}$$

$$\therefore \quad \ln\frac{Q}{Q_0} = -\frac{t}{CR}$$

$$\therefore \quad Q = Q_0 \mathrm{e}^{-t/CR} \quad . \quad . \quad . \quad . \quad . \quad (2)$$

Q thus diminishes exponentially with time t. The curve relating Q and t is an *exponential decay* curve. Fig. 12.1 (ii) shows two curves, for $C = 2\mu$F and $R = 2$ MΩ and for $C = 5$ μF and $R = 2$ MΩ.

In a time $t = CR$, from (2) we have $Q = Q_0\,\mathrm{e}^{-1} = Q_0/2.72 = 0.37\,Q_0$. Thus in $t = CR$, the charge diminishes to about 37% of its initial value. This is true for all values of Q_0 and 'CR' is called the *time-constant* of the circuit. CR is in second when C is in farad and R in ohm. Thus with a circuit of $C = 2$ μF and $R = 2$ MΩ, $CR = 2 \times 10^{-6} \times 2 \times 10^6 = 4$ second.

In general, the greater the CR value, the *slower* is the discharge. Although in theory $Q = 0$ when $t = \infty$ from (2), the capacitor is practically (99%) discharged in a time of about $5CR$.

Charging *C* through *R*

The *charging* of a capacitor C through a resistor R also leads to an exponential relationship.

Suppose a battery of e.m.f. E and negligible resistance is connected to C and R in series. Fig. 12.2 (i). At some instant t, the charge Q then on C produces a p.d. V *in opposition* to the e.m.f. E. Thus if I is the instantaneous current,

$$I = \frac{E - V}{R}.$$

$$\therefore \quad IR = E - V$$

$$\therefore \quad R\frac{\mathrm{d}Q}{\mathrm{d}t} = E - \frac{Q}{C}$$

$$\therefore \quad CR\frac{\mathrm{d}Q}{\mathrm{d}t} = EC - Q \quad . \quad . \quad . \quad . \quad (1)$$

$$\therefore \quad \int_0^Q \frac{\mathrm{d}Q}{EC - Q} = \frac{1}{CR}\int_0^t \mathrm{d}t$$

$$\therefore \quad \Big[-\ln (EC - Q)\Big]_0^Q = \frac{t}{CR}$$

$$\therefore \quad \ln\left(\frac{EC - Q}{EC}\right) = -\frac{t}{CR}$$

$$\therefore \quad Q = EC(1 - \mathrm{e}^{-t/CR})$$

$$\therefore \quad Q = Q_0(1 - \mathrm{e}^{-t/CR}), \quad . \quad . \quad (2)$$

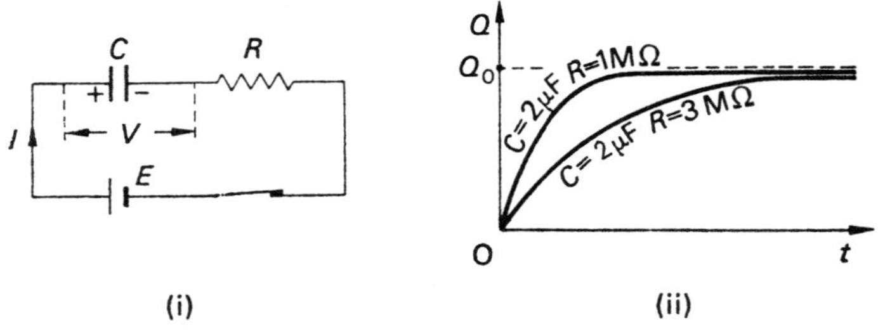

FIG. 12.2 Charging C through R

where $Q_0 = EC$ = maximum or final charge on C. The growth of charge Q with time t, from (2), is shown in Fig. 12.2 (ii). In a time $t = CR$, $Q = Q_0(1 - \mathrm{e}^{-1}) = 0.63Q_0$. The time CR is the 'time-constant' of the circuit.

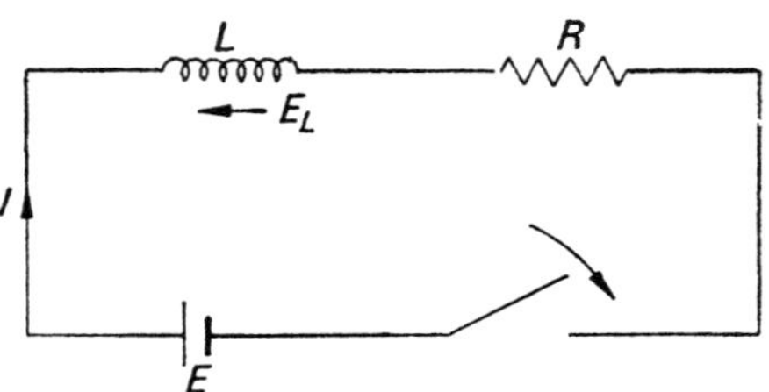

FIG. 12.3 Charging L through R

Current Growth in L and R Series Circuit

An *inductor*, such as a coil of wire, *opposes* the growth of current in a circuit. Its *inductance* L can be defined by the ratio $E_L/(\mathrm{d}I/\mathrm{d}t)$, where E_L is the induced or opposing e.m.f. in the coil and $\mathrm{d}I/\mathrm{d}t$ is the rate of change of current at this instant. Thus $E_L = L\,dI/dt$. L is in henry (H) when E_L is in volt and dI/dt is in ampere per second.

Consider the growth of current I in the circuit shown in Fig. 12.3, which consists of a battery of e.m.f. E connected to L and R in series. At a time t after the circuit is made, the current I flowing is given by

$$I = \frac{E - E_L}{R}$$

$$\therefore \quad E_L = E - IR$$

$$\therefore \quad L\frac{dI}{dt} = E - IR \quad . \quad . \quad . \quad . \quad (1)$$

$$\therefore \quad \int_0^I \frac{dI}{E - IR} = \frac{1}{L}\int_0^t dt,$$

since at $t = 0$, the current $I_0 = 0$.

$$\therefore \quad \left[-\frac{1}{R}\ln(E - IR)\right]_0^I = \frac{t}{L}$$

$$\therefore \quad \ln\left(\frac{E - IR}{E}\right) = -\frac{R}{L}t$$

$$\therefore \quad I = \frac{E}{R}(1 - e^{-Rt/L})$$

$$\therefore \quad I = I_0(1 - e^{-Rt/L}) \quad . \quad . \quad (2)$$

where $I_0 = E/R$ = final current flowing. The current thus increases with time according to the relation (2).

When $t = L/R$, the current $I = I_0(1 - e^{-1}) = 0.63I_0$. The time $t = L/R$ is called the *time-constant* of the circuit and is in second when L is in henry and R is in ohm. Generally, the larger L and the smaller R, the longer will the current take to reach its final value I_0.

EXAMPLES

1. A battery of e.m.f. 40 V and negligible internal resistance is connected to a 20 H coil of negligible resistance in series with a 10 Ω resistor. Calculate (i) the steady current flowing, (ii) the rate of growth of current at the instant of making the circuit, (iii) the rate of growth of current when the current is 3 A, (iv) the current flowing 2 second after the circuit is made.

(i) Steady current $I = E/R = 40/10 = 4$ A.

(ii) At the instant of making the circuit, there is no p.d. across the resistor. The whole of the applied e.m.f. is then equal to the back e.m.f. across the coil.

$$\therefore \quad 40 = \text{back e.m.f.} = L\frac{dI}{dt} = 20\frac{dI}{dt}$$

$$\therefore \quad \frac{dI}{dt} = 2\ \text{A s}^{-1}$$

(iii) At $I = 3$ A, p.d. across $R = IR = 30$ V.
∴ back e.m.f. across coil $= 40 - 30 = 10$ V

$$\therefore \quad L\frac{\mathrm{d}I}{\mathrm{d}t} = 20\frac{\mathrm{d}I}{\mathrm{d}t} = 10$$

$$\therefore \quad \frac{\mathrm{d}I}{\mathrm{d}t} = \tfrac{1}{2}\ \mathrm{A\ s^{-1}}$$

(iv) The time-constant $= L/R = 20/10 = 2$ s.

$$\therefore \quad \text{current } I = I_0(1 - \mathrm{e}^{-Rt/L}) = I_0(1 - e^{-1})$$
$$= 0.63I_0 = 0.63 \times 4\ \mathrm{A} = 2.52\ \mathrm{A}$$

2. A capacitor C of 5 μF is charged by a 200 V battery and then discharged through a resistor R of 2 MΩ. Calculate (i) the initial charge, (ii) the charge after 10 s, (iii) the time taken for the current to decrease to 25 μA.

(i) Initial charge $Q_0 = 5 \times 10^{-6} \times 200 = 10^3$ C.
(ii) Time constant, $CR = 5 \times 10^{-6} \times 2 \times 10^6 = 10$ s

$$\therefore \quad Q = Q_0\mathrm{e}^{-t/CR}$$
$$= 10^{-3} \times \mathrm{e}^{-10/10} = 10^{-3} \times \mathrm{e}^{-1}$$
$$= 3.7 \times 10^{-4}\ \mathrm{C}$$

(iii) Since $\quad Q = Q_0\,\mathrm{e}^{-t/CR}$,

$$\therefore \quad I = \frac{\mathrm{d}Q}{\mathrm{d}t} = -\frac{Q_0}{CR}\mathrm{e}^{-t/CR}$$

At $t = 0$, $\quad I = I_0 = -\dfrac{V}{R} = \dfrac{200}{2 \times 10^6} = 100$ μA.

$$\therefore \quad I = I_0\,\mathrm{e}^{-t/CR} = 100\,\mathrm{e}^{-t/CR}\ \mu\mathrm{A}$$

When $I = 25$ μA, $\quad \therefore \quad 25 = 100\,\mathrm{e}^{-t/10}$

$$\therefore \quad \tfrac{1}{4} = 4^{-1} = \mathrm{e}^{-t/10}$$

$$\therefore \quad \ln 4 = \frac{t}{10}$$

$$\therefore \quad t = 10 \ln 4$$
$$= 13.9\ \mathrm{s}.$$

3. The count rate or activity I of a radioactive sample decreases from 1000 min^{-1} to 200 min^{-1} in 3 minutes. Calculate the half life T.

$$I = I_0\,\mathrm{e}^{-\lambda t}, \qquad . \quad . \quad . \quad . \quad . \quad . \quad (1)$$

since $I \propto N$ and $N = N_0\,\mathrm{e}^{-\lambda t}$ (see p. 189).

The half life T is the time for I_0 to decrease to $I_0/2$.

$$\therefore \quad \frac{I_0}{2} = I_0\,\mathrm{e}^{-\lambda T}$$

Simplifying, $\quad \therefore \quad T = \dfrac{1}{\lambda}\ln 2 \qquad . \quad . \quad . \quad . \quad . \quad . \quad (2)$

In $t = 3$ min $= 180$ s, $$I = \frac{200}{1000} I_0 = \frac{1}{5} I_0$$

From (1) $$\therefore \quad e^{-180\lambda} = \frac{1}{5}$$

Taking logs to base e, $$\therefore \lambda = \frac{\ln 5}{180} \quad . \quad . \quad . \quad . \quad . \quad (3)$$

Hence, from (2) $$T = \frac{180 \ln 2}{\ln 5} = \frac{180 \times 0.693}{1.6096}$$
$$= 77.5 \text{ s.}$$

Second Order Differential Equations. Simple Harmonic Variation

The equation

$$\frac{d^2x}{dt^2} = -n^2x, \quad \text{or} \quad \frac{d^2x}{dt^2} + n^2x = 0, \quad . \quad . \quad (1)$$

is an example of a *second order* differential equation. Here d^2x/dt^2 represents an acceleration which is proportional to the displacement x of the particle concerned from a fixed point.

We can verify by direct differentiation that a solution to (1) is given by

$$x = A \sin (nt + \phi), \quad . \quad . \quad . \quad (2)$$

where A and ϕ are constants. Thus, from (2),

$$\frac{dx}{dt} = n A \cos (nt + \phi),$$

and hence $$\frac{d^2x}{dt^2} = -n^2A \sin (nt + \phi) = -n^2x,$$

which is equation (1).

Resistive Forces. Damping of Harmonic Motion

An object such as a pendulum bob, moving with simple harmonic motion, is also subject to an *opposing* or *resistive force* due to air friction. This force is roughly proportional to the velocity of the object, which is dx/dt. The equation of motion of the mass m is then given by:

$$m \frac{d^2x}{dt^2} = -n^2x - k \frac{dx}{dt},$$

so that $$m \frac{d^2x}{dt^2} + k \frac{dx}{dt} + n^2x = 0 \quad . \quad . \quad . \quad (1)$$

This is another second order differential equation.

The general solution of this equation is beyond the scope of the book. If the system is not 'over-damped' by the resistive force, the solution is of the form $x = Ae^{-at} \sin (nt + \phi)$. This represents a simple harmonic oscillation whose amplitude Ae^{-at} decays exponentially with time. Fig. 12.4. The magnitude of the decay constant a depends largely on the magnitude of k in the value of the opposing force.

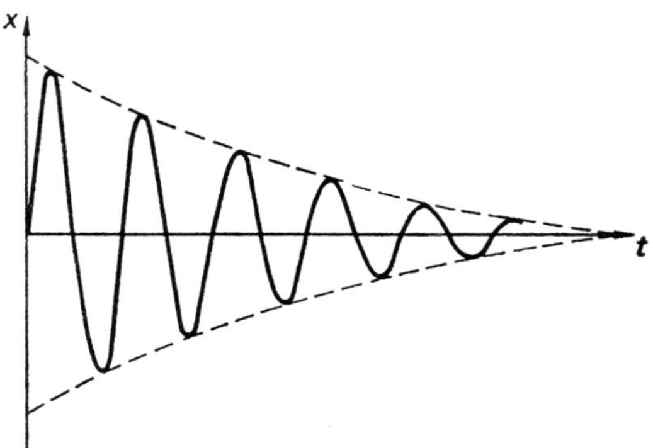

FIG. 12.4 Damped oscillations

If k is large, the system may be over-damped. In this case the solution is of the form $x = Ae^{at} + Be^{bt}$, where a and b are constants which depend on the values of m, k and n in equation (1). No oscillation is now obtained; the displacement x decays exponentially with time t.

Rates of Chemical Reaction

According to the *law of mass action*, the rate at which a chemical reaction proceeds is directly proportional to the 'active mass' or *concentration* of the reacting substances A, B. This can be expressed as *rate* $= k[A][B]$, where $[A]$ and $[B]$ represent the respective concentrations of A and B.

As a simple example, suppose we first consider only one reactant A say, which has a concentration x at a time t and produces a particular product in the reaction. Then, from the law of mass action, the rate at which A *disappears*, which is $-\mathrm{d}x/\mathrm{d}t$, is proportional to x. Thus if k is the rate constant of the reaction,

$$\frac{\mathrm{d}x}{\mathrm{d}t} = -kx \quad . \quad . \quad . \quad . \quad . \quad (1)$$

$$\therefore \quad \int_a^x \frac{\mathrm{d}x}{x} = -k \int_0^t \mathrm{d}t,$$

where a is the initial concentration of A.

$$\therefore \quad \ln x - \ln a = -kt$$

$$\therefore \quad \ln x = \ln a - kt$$

If logarithms to the base 10 are used, then, since $\ln x = 2.3 \log x$ (approx) and $\ln a = 2.3 \log a$ (approx), we have

$$2.3 \log x = 2.3 \log a - kt \qquad . \quad . \quad . \quad (2)$$

Hence the rate constant k is given by

$$k = \frac{1}{t} 2.3 \log \left(\frac{a}{x}\right) \qquad . \quad . \quad . \quad . \quad (3)$$

Rate of Product

Suppose the *product* in the above reaction has a concentration y at a time t and a final concentration a at the end of the reaction equal to the initial concentration of the reactant. The rate at which the product grows is $\mathrm{d}y/\mathrm{d}t$. This is proportional to the concentration x of the reactant at the time t concerned, which is $(a - y)$. Hence, from the law of mass action,

$$\frac{\mathrm{d}y}{\mathrm{d}t} = k(a - y) \quad . \quad . \quad . \quad . \quad (1)$$

$$\therefore \quad \int_0^y \frac{\mathrm{d}y}{a - y} = k \int_0^t \mathrm{d}t.$$

(Note that $y = 0$ at $t = 0$).

$$\therefore \quad \Big[-\ln (a - y)\Big]_0^y = kt$$

$$\therefore \quad -\ln (a - y) + \ln a = kt$$

Using logs to the base 10,

$$\therefore \quad 2.3 \log (a - y) = 2.3 \log a - kt \quad . \quad . \quad . \quad (2)$$

and

$$k = \frac{2.3}{t} \log \left(\frac{a}{a - y}\right) \quad . \quad . \quad (3)$$

Second Order Reactions

If two reactants are present, the products of the concentrations may lead to a differential equation of the form

$$\frac{\mathrm{d}x}{\mathrm{d}t} = -kx^2 \quad . \quad . \quad . \quad . \quad . \quad (1)$$

or

$$\frac{\mathrm{d}y}{\mathrm{d}t} = k(a - y)^2 \quad . \quad . \quad . \quad . \quad (2)$$

From (1),

$$\int_a^x - \frac{\mathrm{d}x}{x^2} = k \int_0^t \mathrm{d}t,$$

$$\therefore \quad \frac{1}{x} - \frac{1}{a} = kt \quad . \quad . \quad . \quad . \quad . \quad (3)$$

From (2), by similar integration,

$$\frac{1}{a-y} - \frac{1}{a} = kt \quad . \quad . \quad . \quad . \quad . \quad (4)$$

If the initial concentrations are different and equal to a and b respectively, then the equation for the rate at which the product is formed becomes

$$\frac{\mathrm{d}y}{\mathrm{d}t} = k(a-y)(b-y) \quad . \quad . \quad (5)$$

$$\therefore \quad \int_0^y \frac{\mathrm{d}y}{(a-y)(b-y)} = k\int_0^t \mathrm{d}t \quad . \quad . \quad . \quad . \quad (6)$$

If we write

$$\frac{1}{(a-y)(b-y)} = \frac{X}{a-y} + \frac{Y}{b-y} = \frac{X(b-y) + Y(a-y)}{(a-y)(b-y)},$$

where X and Y are constants, we must have the numerators identically equal.

$$\therefore \quad 1 \equiv X(b-y) + Y(a-y).$$

When $y = b$, $1 = Y(a-b)$; so $Y = 1/(a-b)$.
When $y = a$, $1 = X(b-a)$; so $X = 1/(b-a)$.

$$\therefore \quad \int_0^y \frac{\mathrm{d}y}{(a-y)(b-y)} = \frac{1}{b-a}\int_0^y \frac{\mathrm{d}y}{(a-y)} - \frac{1}{b-a}\int_0^y \frac{\mathrm{d}y}{b-y}$$

$$= \frac{1}{b-a}\ln\left[\frac{a(b-y)}{b(a-y)}\right]$$

Hence, from (6), using logs to the base 10,

$$\frac{2.3}{b-a}\log\left(\frac{b-y}{a-y}\right) + \frac{2.3}{b-a}\log\left(\frac{a}{b}\right) = kt \quad . \quad . \quad (7)$$

EXERCISES 12

Solve the following differential equations:

(1) $\mathrm{d}y/\mathrm{d}x = -4x$, if $x = 0$ when $y = 2$.

(2) $\mathrm{d}x/\mathrm{d}t = -kx$, if $x = A$ when $t = 0$.

(3) $\mathrm{d}y/\mathrm{d}t = -ky^2$, if $y = a$ when $t = 0$.

(4) $\mathrm{d}x/\mathrm{d}t = 4(x - 10)$, if $x = 20$ when $t = 0$.

(5) $\mathrm{d}x/\mathrm{d}t = 5(a - x)^2$, if $x = a/2$ when $t = 0$.

(6) $\mathrm{d}^2x/\mathrm{d}t^2 = -4x$, if $x = 0$ when $t = 0$.

(7) $dx/dt = -(3 - x)(4 - x)$, if $x = 0$ when $t = 0$.

(8) Show that $x = 2 \sin 3t$ is a solution to the differential equation

$$\frac{d^2x}{dt^2} + 9x = 0$$

(9) A 2 μF capacitor C is in series with a 3 MΩ resistor R, and a 150 V battery of negligible resistance is connected across them. Calculate (i) the final charge on C, (ii) the time constant, (iii) the charge on C after 6 s, (iv) the charge after 12 s, (v) the p.d. across R at the instant the circuit is made, (vi) the p.d. across R after 6 s.

(10) An unknown resistor R is placed in series with a capacitor C of 4 μF, and a 100 V battery of negligible internal resistance is connected across them. When the current is switched on, the charge on C rises to 200 μC in 8 s. Calculate (i) R, (ii) the time taken for the charge to reach 300 μC, (iii) the initial current value, (iv) the time taken for the current to decrease to 30 μA.

(11) Show that, when a p.d. is applied to a series arrangement of $C = 2$ μF and $R = 4$ MΩ, the charge Q on C at a time t is given by

$$Q = Q_0(1 - e^{-t/8})$$

If the initial current I_0 is 200 μA, find, by differentiating the above expression for Q, the current 6 s after switching on.

(12) A capacitor C is charged by a battery of e.m.f. E and negligible internal resistance through a resistor R. Show that, after a time t, the p.d. V across the resistor rises to $V = E(1 - e^{-t/CR})$.

A 1 μF capacitor C is charged through a 2 MΩ resistor by a battery of e.m.f. E and negligible internal resistance. After 1 second the p.d. across C is 0.5 V. Calculate E.

(13) A capacitor C of 3 μF is charged by a 200 V battery and then discharged through a resistor R of 2 MΩ. Calculate (i) the charge on C after 6 s, (ii) the charge after 12 s, (iii) the time taken for the p.d. across C to fall to 50 V.

(14) A capacitor C, charged initially by a battery, is discharged through a resistor R of 4 MΩ. After 2 s, the current decreases to 20 μA from an initial current of 25 μA. Calculate (i) the magnitude of C, (ii) the p.d. across C after 4 s.

(15) A radioactive element, initially with a mass 10.0 mg of undecayed atoms, has a decay constant λ of $10^{-2}\ s^{-1}$. Calculate (i) the half life, (ii) the time taken for 2.5 mg to remain undecayed, (iii) the time taken for 1.0 mg to remain undecayed.

(16) If n is the number of radioactive atoms which remain undecayed after a time t and n_0 is the initial number, the rate of decay is governed by

$\mathrm{d}n/\mathrm{d}t = -\lambda n$, where λ is the decay constant. Find (i) n in terms of n_0, t and λ, (ii) the half life T in terms of λ.

For a particular radioactive substance, $\lambda = 10^{-6}\ \mathrm{s}^{-1}$. How long does it take for 255/256th of the substance to decay?

(17) In an experiment with a radioactive substance of half life 60 s, the initial count rate (activity) is $1000\ \mathrm{min}^{-1}$. Calculate the count rate after (i) 30 s, (ii) 240 s. In what time will the count rate fall to $100\ \mathrm{min}^{-1}$?

(18) A radioactive substance has initially a mass of 50 mg of undecayed atoms. The radioactive decay is governed by the relation $n = n_0\,\mathrm{e}^{-\lambda t}$, where n_0 is the initial number of undecayed atoms, n is the number after a time t, and $\lambda = 0.01\ \mathrm{s}^{-1}$. If the molar mass is 200 g and the Avogadro constant is assumed to be $6 \times 10^{23}\ \mathrm{mol}^{-1}$, calculate (i) the initial number of undecayed atoms, (ii) the time taken for 3×10^{19} atoms to remain undecayed, (iii) the rate of decay in a time t of 50 s.

(19) The velocity, $\mathrm{d}x/\mathrm{d}t$, of an elastic used in a catapult is given in $\mathrm{mm\ s}^{-1}$ by $\mathrm{d}x/\mathrm{d}t = 5(10 - x)^2$, where x is the distance from a fixed point. If $x = 0$ when $t = 0$, calculate (i) the distance x travelled in a time of $\frac{1}{20}$ s, (ii) the time t taken to reach a distance of 4 mm.

(20) In a certain chemical reaction, the concentration x of a new product at a time t is governed by $\mathrm{d}x/\mathrm{d}t = 10^{-2}(a - x)^2$, where a is the initial concentration of a reactant. If x reaches the value $a/2$ in 2 seconds, find the magnitude of the constant a.

(21) The growth of a chemical substance in a reaction is governed by the relation $\mathrm{d}x/\mathrm{d}t = 0.02(a - x)$, where x is the concentration at a time t and a is a constant. If the concentration is initially zero, how long does it take for the concentration to reach (i) 50%, (ii) 90%, (iii) 99.99% of the value a?

(22) The motion of a mass m is represented by the differential equation

$$m\frac{\mathrm{d}^2x}{\mathrm{d}t^2} + a\frac{\mathrm{d}x}{\mathrm{d}t} + bx = 0.$$

Give the physical meaning of the three terms which appear in the equation. Draw a sketch showing roughly how x may vary with t for one possible solution to the equation.

(23) The acceleration a in $\mathrm{m\ s}^{-2}$ of a car which starts from rest is given at time t seconds by

$$a = \frac{1}{20}t^2 \quad \text{for} \quad 0 \leqslant t \leqslant 10$$

and

$$a = \frac{1}{2}t \quad \text{for} \quad 10 \leqslant t \leqslant 15$$

Find the speed of the car after 5 seconds and after 15 seconds from rest. (*O.*)

Answers

1. $y = -2x^2 + 2$

2. $x = A\,e^{-kt}$

3. $1/y = kt + 1/a$

4. $x = 10(e^{4t} + 1)$

5. $1/(a - x) - 2/a = 5t$

6. $x = A \sin 2t$

7. $\ln [4(3 - x)/3(4 - x)] = t$

9. (i) 300 μC (ii) 6 s (iii) 190 μC
   (iv) 259 μC (v) 150 V (vi) 55 V

10. (i) 2.9 MΩ (ii) 16 s (iii) 35 μA
    (iv) 1.7 s

11. 94.5 μA

12. 1.3 V

13. (i) 221 μC (ii) 81 μC (iii) 8.3 s

14. (i) 2.24 μF (ii) 64 V

15. (i) 69.3 s (ii) 138.6 s (iii) 230.3 s

16. (i) $n = n_0\,e^{-\lambda t}$ (ii) $T = \dfrac{1}{\lambda} \ln 2$ (iii) 5.5×10^6 s

17. (i) 707 min^{-1} (ii) 62.5 min^{-1}; 199 s

18. (i) 1.5×10^{20} (ii) 161 s (iii) -9×10^{17} s^{-1}

19. (i) $7\frac{1}{7}$ mm (ii) $\frac{1}{75}$ s

20. $a = 50$

21. (i) 35 s (ii) 115 s (iii) 461 s

23. 2.1, 47.9 m s^{-1}

13.
Linear Motion

Motion and forces occur in all branches of Physics. In electricity, for example, moving electrons are deflected by forces in cathode-ray tubes. Satellites are kept in circular orbits by gravitational forces. Inside a combustion engine, the pressure due to an expanding vapour drives the pistons. Sound is produced by forces due to vibrating particles of air. And the forces between the numerous particles inside a normal atom keep the atom stable.

We begin with motion and proceed to forces later.

Velocity

If a car is moving in a constant direction, its *velocity* is defined as the *distance moved per second* in that direction or the *displacement per second.* Thus

$$\text{average velocity} = \frac{\text{displacement}}{\text{time taken}}.$$

If the velocity of the car is constant, it is said to be travelling with a *uniform* velocity. Velocity may be measured in metre per second (m s^{-1}), or kilometre per hour (km h^{-1}). Note that

$$36\ \text{km h}^{-1} = 10\ \text{m s}^{-1}.$$

Vectors and Scalars. Speed

When a quantity has direction as well as magnitude, it is called a *vector* quantity. 'Velocity' is an example of a vector because it is defined as the distance travelled per second in a particular direction. Later we shall come across many other examples of vectors.

A quantity which has magnitude only is called a *scalar* quantity. The 'density' of an object, for example, is a scalar quantity, because no direction is associated with density. *Speed* is a scalar quantity because it is not associated with a specific direction. Thus a racing car moving round a circular track has an average *speed* given by *track distance/time taken*.

If we imagine the motion 'frozen' at some instant, the car will point along the *tangent* to the circular track where it is positioned. This is the direction of the velocity at this instant. A car moving once round the circular track at constant speed will thus have velocities pointing in opposite directions at the ends of a diameter and equal in magnitude. Hence the 'average velocity' round the track is zero.

The table below shows some of the more common vectors and scalars encountered in Mechanics.

Vector	Scalar
Velocity	Mass
Acceleration	Speed
Force	Density
Momentum	Energy
Weight	Work

Acceleration

When the velocity of a car is increasing, it is said to be accelerating. The magnitude a of the average *acceleration* is given by

$$a = \frac{\text{velocity change}}{\text{time taken}}.$$

Thus if a car increases its velocity by 2 m s^{-1} every second, it is said to be moving with a uniform (constant) acceleration of 2 m s^{-2}, as the time element is repeated. Objects which fall freely under gravity have a uniform acceleration of about 9.8 m s^{-2}, or 10 m s^{-2} in round figures, which is commonly denoted by the symbol g.

If a car has a velocity u, and accelerates uniformly to a velocity v in a time t, then

$$a = \frac{\text{change in velocity}}{\text{time}} = \frac{v - u}{t}$$

$$\therefore \quad v = u + at \quad . \quad . \quad . \quad . \quad (1)$$

When brakes are applied to a train its velocity decreases. The train is said to undergo 'negative acceleration' or *retardation* as it slows down. The magnitude of the retardation is the change in velocity per second. When a ball is thrown vertically upwards its velocity diminishes, and its acceleration = -10 m s^{-2} (approx.)

Distance Travelled under Constant Acceleration

When an object accelerates uniformly from a velocity u to a velocity v in a time t, the distance travelled, s, is given by

$$s = \text{average velocity} \times t = \left(\frac{u+v}{2}\right)t.$$

But $$v = u + at$$

$$\therefore \quad s = \left(\frac{u+u+at}{2}\right)t$$

$$\therefore \quad s = ut + \tfrac{1}{2}at^2 \qquad . \quad . \quad . \quad . \quad . \quad . \quad (2)$$

To find the relation between v, u and s, we substitute $t = (v - u)/a$ in

$$s = \text{average velocity} \times t.$$

Then $$s = \frac{v+u}{2} \,.\, t = \frac{v+u}{2} \,.\, \frac{v-u}{a},$$

from which, by simplification,

$$v^2 = u^2 + 2as \qquad . \quad . \quad . \quad . \quad (3)$$

EXAMPLES

1. A car travelling at 20 m s^{-1} undergoes a uniform acceleration of 0.6 m s^{-2} for 10 s. Calculate the velocity at the end of the time and the distance travelled.

Here u = 20 m s^{-1}, a = 0.6 m s^{-2}, t = 10 s

$$\therefore \quad v = u + at = 20 + 0.6 \times 10 = 26 \text{ m s}^{-1} \qquad . \quad . \quad (i)$$

Also, $$s = ut + \tfrac{1}{2}at^2$$

$$\therefore \quad s = 20 \times 10 + \tfrac{1}{2} \times 0.6 \times 10^2 = 230 \text{ m} \quad . \quad . \quad . \quad (ii)$$

2. A train travelling at 108 km h^{-1} undergoes a constant retardation and is then brought to rest in a distance of 100 m. Calculate the retardation.

Here

$$u = 108 \text{ km h}^{-1} = 30 \text{ m s}^{-1},\ s = 100 \text{ m, and } v = \text{final velocity} = 0.$$

Substituting in $$v^2 = u^2 + 2as$$

$$\therefore \quad 0 = 30^2 + 2 \times a \times 100$$

$$\therefore \quad a = -\frac{900}{200} = -4.5 \text{ m s}^{-2}$$

Note. The minus sign indicates a retardation.

3. An object is thrown vertically upwards and reaches the top, X, of its flight in 2 second. What was the velocity of throw, the distance to X, and the velocity half-way? (Assume g = 10 m s^{-2}.)

(i) At the top of the flight the velocity $v = 0$. Also, $t = 2$ s and $a = -g = -10$ m s^{-2}. Thus, since $v = u + at$, the initial velocity u is given by

$$0 = u - 10 \times 2, \quad \text{i.e.} \quad u = 20 \text{ m s}^{-1}.$$

(ii) The distance travelled, $s = ut + \frac{1}{2}at^2$

$$= 20 \times 2 - \tfrac{1}{2} \times 10 \times 2^2 = 20 \text{ m}.$$

(iii) When $s = 10$ m, the velocity v is given by

$$v^2 = u^2 + 2as = 20^2 - 2 \times 10 \times 10$$

$$\therefore \quad v = \sqrt{200} = 14 \text{ m s}^{-1} \text{ (approx.)}$$

Momentum and Force

Newton has stated three Laws of Motion, which follow from experience and experiment.

Law I. *Objects will continue to move in a straight line with uniform motion, or remain at rest, unless acted upon by a force.*

Law II. *Force is proportional to the rate of change of momentum.*

Law III. *To every Action there is an equal and opposite Reaction.*

The first law recognises that objects have an amount of *inertia*, which has to be overcome before a change can be made in the velocity or state of rest. From this law it also follows that a force acts on a car or any other object moving in a curve (p. 230).

The second law shows how force can be measured. 'Momentum' is defined as 'mv', the product of the mass and velocity of the object. Since mass is a scalar and velocity is a vector, momentum is a vector quantity. According to the second law, the magnitude of the force acting on an object is proportional to the change in momentum per second it produces.

Suppose water, issuing from a horizontal hose-pipe with velocity of 4 m s^{-1}, impinges on a vertical plate. In one second a column of water 4 m long emerges. Thus if the area of cross-section of the hose is 6×10^{-4} m^2, 2.4 kg of water strike the plate every second. If the velocity is reduced to zero, the momentum change per second $= 2.4 \times 4 = 9.6$ kg m s^{-1}. This is a measure of the force on the plate. As we soon see, the force $= 9.6$ N.

Acceleration and Force

If an object has a mass m and a velocity u, and increases its velocity to v in a time t, then

$$\text{change of momentum per second} = \frac{mv - mu}{t} = \frac{m(v - u)}{t},$$

assuming the mass is constant. But the acceleration, $a = (v - u)/t$ (p. 213).

$$\therefore \quad \text{force, } F, \propto ma$$

$$\therefore \quad F = kma \quad . \quad . \quad . \quad . \quad . \quad \text{(i)}$$

where k is a constant. Thus *the force is proportional to the acceleration produced.*

We can now define a unit of force. The SI unit is the *newton* (N); this is the force which gives a mass of 1 kg an acceleration of 1 m s^{-2}. From this definition, $F = 1$ when $m = 1$ and $a = 1$, and hence, on substitution in (i), $k = 1$. Thus $F = ma$ is the relation between a force F acting on a mass of m which produces an acceleration a, where F is in newtons when m is in kilograms and a is in metres per second^2. A mass of 2 kg, given an acceleration of 4 m s^{-2}, was hence subjected to a force $F = ma = 8$ N.

Gravitational intensity and *g*

The force due to gravity acting on an object is called its *weight*. 'Mass' is constant all over the universe. 'Weight' varies; for example, the weight of an object at the poles of the earth is slightly greater than at the equator, because the poles are nearer the centre of the earth than the equator.

On the surface of the earth, the gravitational force produces an acceleration of about 9.8 m s^{-2} or 10 m s^{-2} in round figures. From $F = ma$, it follows that the force due to gravity on a mass of 1 kg $=$ $1 \times 9.8 = 9.8$ N. The force due to gravity on a mass of 1 kg at a particular place on the earth is called the *intensity* of the earth's gravitational field. So g can also be expressed as '10 N kg^{-1}', 10 newtons per kilogram. As we see later, the intensity of an electric field is measured in newtons per coulomb.

On the surface of the moon, the gravitational acceleration is only about $g/6$, or about $1\frac{2}{3}$ N kg^{-1}. Thus the downward pull due to gravity is six times less than on the earth, which accounts for the 'floating' appearance of astronauts seen walking over the moon's surface.

EXAMPLES

1. The engine force on a truck of 500 kg is 1000 N. The motion is opposed by a constant frictional force of 0.1 N per kg. Find the acceleration of the truck.

Frictional force $= 0.1 \times 500 = 50$ N.

$$\therefore \quad \text{net force on truck, } F = 1000 - 50 = 950 \text{ N}$$

$$\therefore \quad \text{acceleration, } a = \frac{F}{m} = \frac{950 \text{ N}}{500 \text{ kg}} = 1.9 \text{ m s}^{-2}$$

2. A balloon and contents of total mass 1000 kg are falling freely with an acceleration of 2 m s^{-2}. Find the change in the vertical motion after 200 kg of ballast has been thrown out, neglecting air friction. (Assume $g = 10$ N kg^{-1}.)

Suppose U is the upward force in newtons due to the buoyancy of the air. Then, since weight of 1000 kg is 10 000 N,

$$\therefore \quad 1000 \times 10 - U = 1000 \times 2$$

$$\therefore \quad U = 8000 \text{ N}$$

If 200 kg of ballast is thrown out, then, in a downward direction,

resultant force = weight − upthrust = 8000 − 8000 = 0

∴ balloon now falls with uniform velocity.

3. 10^{23} molecules of a gas are contained in a cube of side 10 cm. The velocity of all the molecules, each of mass 10^{-26} kg, can be taken as 200 m s^{-1}. Estimate the average gas pressure (force per unit area on sides of cube).

If a molecule strikes one side normally and rebounds with an equal speed, then

momentum change $= 10^{-26} \times 200 - (-10^{-26} \times 200) = 4 \times 10^{-24}$ kg m s^{-1}

Time taken by molecule to cross cube = 0.1 m/200 m s^{-1} = 1/2000 s.

$$\therefore \quad \text{momentum change per second at face} = 4 \times 10^{-24} \div 1/2000$$

$$= \text{force} = 8 \times 10^{-21} \text{ N} \quad . \quad . \quad . \quad . \quad (1)$$

We can imagine that one-third of the molecules move *to-and-from* this cube face, and hence that 1/6th move *towards* it. Thus, from (1),

$$\text{total force on face} = (\tfrac{1}{6} \times 10^{23}) \times 8 \times 10^{-21} = 133 \text{ N}$$

But area of face = 0.1 × 0.1 m^2 = 0.01 m^2.

$$\therefore \quad \text{average pressure} = \text{force per unit area} = 133 \text{ N}/0.01 \text{ m}^2$$

$$= 13\,300 \text{ N m}^{-2}.$$

Pressure of Gas. Gas Law

The calculation for the gas pressure just discussed can be made in more general terms using the simple *kinetic theory of gases*.

Suppose the molecules inside the cube of length l each have a mass m and a velocity u_x in the x-direction normal to one face of the cube. If the molecules are perfectly elastic, they rebound with an equal momentum after striking the face of the cube.

$$\therefore \quad \text{momentum change in } x\text{-direction} = mu_x - (-mu_x) = 2mu_x.$$

The time taken by the molecule to rebound across the cube and back towards the face $= \dfrac{2l}{u_x}$

$$\therefore \text{momentum change per second} = \text{force on face} = \frac{2mu_x}{2l/u_x} = \frac{mu_x^2}{l} \quad (1)$$

Taking account of the components in the x-direction of all the various molecular speeds, we write $\overline{u_x^2}$ for their mean-square value. Further, if $\overline{u_y^2}$, $\overline{u_z^2}$ are the respective mean-square values of the components in the y- and z-directions and $\overline{c^2}$ is the mean-square value of all the speeds,

$$\overline{u_x^2} + \overline{u_y^2} + \overline{u_z^2} = \overline{c^2}.$$

Further, $\overline{u_x^2} = \overline{u_y^2} = \overline{u_z^2}$, and hence $\overline{u_x^2} = \frac{1}{3}\overline{c^2}$.

Thus, from (1), if N is the number of all the molecules

$$\text{force on face} = N \times \frac{1}{3}\frac{m\overline{c^2}}{l} = \frac{1}{3}\frac{Nm\overline{c^2}}{l}$$

$$\therefore \qquad \text{pressure, } p = \frac{\text{force}}{\text{area}} = \frac{1}{3}\frac{Nm\overline{c^2}}{l \times l^2} = \frac{1}{3}\frac{Nm\overline{c^2}}{V}, \qquad (2)$$

where $V = l^3$ = the volume of the gas. Now Nm = mass M of gas, so $Nm/V = \rho$, the density. Hence, from (2),

$$p = \tfrac{1}{3}\rho\overline{c^2} \qquad (3)$$

$$\therefore \qquad \sqrt{\overline{c^2}} = \text{r.m.s. value of speed} = \sqrt{\frac{3p}{\rho}} \qquad (4)$$

In this expression, the r.m.s. value will be in m s^{-1} when p is in N m^{-2} and ρ in kg m^{-3}. The density of hydrogen at s.t.p. (0°C and 1.013×10^5 N m^{-2} pressure) is about 0.09 kg m^{-3}. Thus the r.m.s. value of the speed of hydrogen molecules is given by

$$\sqrt{\frac{3 \times 1.013 \times 10^5}{0.09}} = 1840 \text{ m s}^{-1} \text{ (approx)}$$

From (2), it also follows that

$$pV = \tfrac{1}{3}M\overline{c^2},$$

where M is the mass of the gas. For a monatomic gas, the *translational kinetic energy* $= \frac{1}{2}M\overline{c^2}$. Hence

$$pV = \tfrac{2}{3} \times \textit{translational kinetic energy} \qquad (5)$$

If we assume that the translational kinetic energy is directly proportional to the kelvin temperature T, then, from (5),

$$pV \propto T, \quad \text{or} \quad pV = RT,$$

where R is the gas constant per mole, assuming this is the amount of gas used.

Action and Reaction

When a person leans with an elbow on a table, he exerts a force which may be termed the 'action' on the table. At the same time the table exerts an *equal and opposite* force on the elbow, which may be termed the 'reaction' of the table. In the jet aeroplane, gases are burned and ejected from the tail of the machine; the force of reaction urges the plane in a forward direction. Newton stated in his third law of motion that *action and reaction are equal and opposite* (p. 215).

When a force occurs in a system of bodies, an equal and opposite force, the reaction, automatically comes into existence. If a nail is struck by a hammer, the force F on the nail drives it forward considerably because the resistance to the motion is small. The reaction on the hammer is equal in magnitude to F. As we see later, forces of action and reaction occur in electric and magnetic fields.

Reaction in Lift

Another example of action and reaction is shown in Fig. 13.1; R is the reaction of the floor X on a man standing in a lift. The weight W of the man acts downwards, and if the lift does not move, $W = R$. If the lift moves down with an acceleration, however, there must now be a net force, F, downwards on the man; in this case, therefore, W is greater than R, and $F = W - R$.

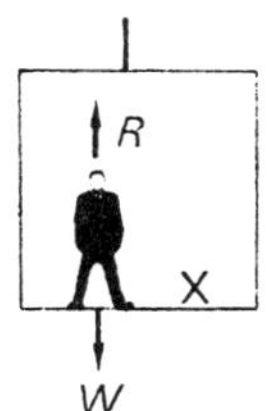

FIG. 13.1 Reaction at ground

Suppose the mass of the man is 70 kg. His weight W is then $70 \times 10 = 700$ N, assuming $g = 10 \text{ m s}^{-2}$. If the lift moves *down* with an acceleration of 2 m s^{-2}, then, from $F = ma$,

$$700 - R = 70 \times 2$$

$$\therefore \quad R = 560 \text{ N}.$$

If the lift, due to a break in the cable, falls freely, then $a = g = 10 \text{ m s}^{-2}$

$$\therefore \quad F = 700 - R = 70 \times 10$$

$$\therefore \quad R = 0.$$

Thus in free-fall a person experiences no reaction due to contact with his surroundings.

If the lift moves *up* with an acceleration of 2 m s^{-2}, then, from $F = ma$,

$$R - 700 = 70 \times 2$$

$$\therefore \quad R = 840 \text{ N}.$$

The reaction at the floor is now greater than the weight of the man.

Surface Tension and Rise in Capillary Tube

An example of action and reaction occurs in consideration of the rise of liquid in a capillary tube dipping into a beaker of the liquid. Fig. 13.2 (i). The column of liquid then stands in equilibrium at a particular height h above the external level. h depends on the surface tension γ of the liquid, its density ρ, and the radius r of the capillary tube.

Consider first the equilibrium of the *whole column* of liquid. Its weight W, acting downwards, must be equal to the upward force F_G at the meniscus due to surface tension—all other forces between the liquid and the glass are radial and cancel each other out.

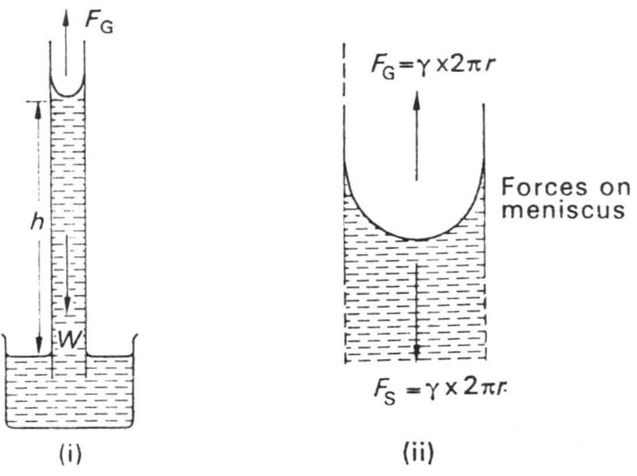

FIG. 13.2 Rise of liquid in capillary tube

Now consider the equilibrium of the meniscus itself, which is the line of liquid at the top of the column. The *upward* force on it is F_G, the force due to the glass on the meniscus. Fig. 13.2 (ii). The *downward* force is the force F_S due to the surface tension of the liquid, which acts downwards round the meniscus. Now F_S is equal to $2\pi r \times \gamma$.

$$\therefore \quad F_G = 2\pi r\gamma$$

But, from above, F_G = weight W of column of liquid $= \pi r^2 h\rho g$.

$$\therefore \quad 2\pi r\gamma = \pi r^2 h\rho g$$

$$\therefore \quad \gamma = \frac{rh\rho g}{2}$$

Force on Conductor in a Magnetic Field

In 1820 Oersted discovered that a current-carrying wire AD deflected a magnet NS when AD was close and parallel to NS. From the Law of Action and Reaction, it follows that a force, the reaction, is exerted on the current-carrying wire. To find how a current-carrying wire moves when a magnet is near it, imagine a north pole N just above the centre of a circular current-carrying wire A (Fig. 13.3). If the current is

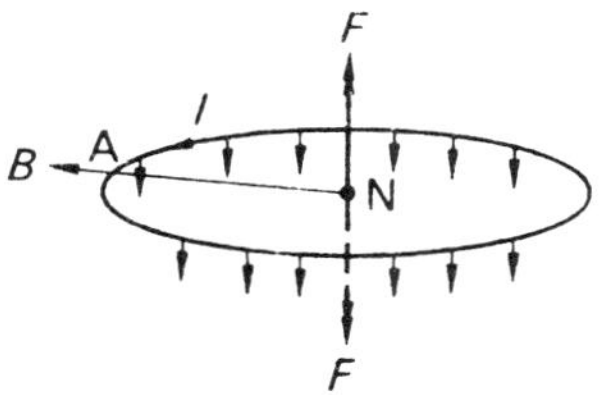

FIG. 13.3 Reaction—force on conductor

anticlockwise when viewed from above, this face of the coil acts like a north pole. Hence N is urged upwards. By the Law of Action and Reaction, an equal downward force F acts on the coil. The forces on every part of element of the coil together total F, and they are shown in Fig. 13.3.

The magnetic field B at an element such as A is in the direction NA, since a north pole at A is urged by N in this direction. Thus the force F on A is perpendicular to both the current I and the field B. Its direction is given by Fleming's left-hand rule, as the reader should verify, which is downward.

In an electric motor, the coil rotates in a magnetic field. Here the force of reaction spins the coil round.

Work and Energy. Potential Energy

If a force moves an object in its own direction through a certain distance, the force is said to do an amount of *work*, W, defined by

$$W = force \times distance.$$

The SI unit of work is the *joule*, symbol J. Thus the work done in pulling an object 5 m with a force of 20 N in the direction of motion = 20 × 5 = 100 J.

If an object of mass 4 kg is raised vertically and steadily to a height of 10 m, then the force overcome = weight of mass 4 kg = 40 N, assuming $g = 10\ \text{m s}^{-2}$. Thus the work done in raising the mass to this height = 40 × 10 = 400 J.

At the height of 10 m above the ground, the object is said to have an amount of gravitational *potential energy* equal to 400 J. If it fell to the ground, it would lose potential energy of 400 J and gain an equal amount of heat energy due to collision with the ground. 'Potential energy' may be defined as 'the energy due to level or position', in this case above the ground. Sea-level is often taken as the 'zero' of gravitational potential energy.

The potential energy of an object due to its height above the ground is the result of work done against gravitational forces. A coiled spring has potential energy due to the work done against molecular forces; its molecules are displaced from their original position when the spring is wound up.

Kinetic Energy

When an object of mass m is moving with a velocity u it is said to have 'kinetic energy'. The amount of energy can be calculated by supposing the object is brought to rest by a constant force F in a distance s. Then, since the work done $= F \times s$, the kinetic energy is $F \times s$. But, from

$$v^2 = u^2 + 2as \text{ (p. 214)},$$

$$0 = u^2 - 2as,$$

where a is the retardation. Thus $as = u^2/2$. Also, $F = ma$ (p. 216).

$$\therefore \quad \text{kinetic energy} = F \times s = ma \times s = \tfrac{1}{2}mu^2 \qquad \text{(i)}$$

When m is in kg and u in m s^{-1}, then the kinetic energy is in J. Thus a boy of mass 50 kg running with a velocity of 4 m s^{-1} has kinetic energy given by

$$\text{k.e.} = \tfrac{1}{2}mu^2 = \tfrac{1}{2} \times 50 \times 4^2 = 400 \text{ J}.$$

An electron, mass 9.1×10^{-31} kg, moving with a velocity of 10^6 m s^{-1} in a television tube has a kinetic energy given by

$$\text{k.e.} = \tfrac{1}{2}mu^2 = \tfrac{1}{2} \times 9.1 \times 10^{-31} \times (10^6)^2 = 4.6 \times 10^{-19} \text{ J}$$

The Conservation of Energy

The concept of energy grew from the results of countless experiments over the past two centuries. We associate energy with the ability to move things, that is, to do 'work'. Energy can exist in many forms, such as heat, light, sound, electrical energy, mechanical energy, chemical energy and nuclear energy. By means of machines, we can convert one form of energy into another. Thus an electric motor changes electrical to mechanical energy, and a dynamo does the reverse; a microphone changes sound to electrical energy, and the telephone earpiece does the reverse; a steam engine converts heat to mechanical energy; a television camera converts light to electrical energy, and a television receiver does the reverse; a battery converts chemical to electrical energy, and the reverse process occurs in a silver voltameter when current is passed. Einstein showed that mass is a form of energy, and in nuclear energy the relation $W = mc^2$ is used, where W is the energy in joule produced when the nucleus diminishes by a mass m kg and c is 3×10^8, the velocity of light in metre per second.

Although energy can be changed from one form to another, the total energy produced is equal to the original energy. Thus if 100 J of electrical energy is supplied to a motor, we may get 80 J of mechanical energy, 19.8 J of heat, and 0.2 J of sound energy. We can never lose energy, nor can we gain more energy than originally supplied—the aim of 'perpetual motion' machines, which are foredoomed to failure. This is expressed in a law of science which has stood the test of experiment for centuries. It is known as the *Principle of the Conservation of Energy*, and states: the total energy in a closed system is constant, no matter how the energy is transformed from one kind to another.

EXAMPLES

1. An object suspended from a rope swings in an arc of a circle so that it just rises a vertical height of 1.0 metre. Calculate the velocity at the bottom of the swing ($g = 10$ N kg^{-1}).

From the Principle of the Conservation of Energy,

kinetic energy at bottom = potential energy at height of 1 metre.

Thus if m is the mass of the object and v its velocity at the bottom,

$$\tfrac{1}{2}mv^2 = mgh = mg \times 1$$

$$\therefore \quad v^2 = 2g \times 1 = 2 \times 10 \times 1$$

$$\therefore \quad v = 4.5 \text{ m s}^{-1}.$$

2. In passing through a wood block 8 cm thick the velocity of a bullet is reduced from 700 m s^{-1} to 300 m s^{-1}. If the mass of the bullet is 10 g, find the average resistance to penetration.

Let F = the average resistance in newton.

Then

$$F \times 0.08 = \text{work done in joules in penetration}$$
$$= \text{loss in kinetic energy of bullet in joule}$$
$$= \tfrac{1}{2} \times 0.01 \times 700^2 - \tfrac{1}{2} \times 0.01 \times 300^2$$
$$= 2000$$

$$\therefore \quad F = \frac{2000}{0.08} = 25\,000 \text{ N}$$

Power

Power is defined as the *rate of doing work*, or work done per second. An engine working at 5000 J s^{-1} has twice the power of another working at 2500 J s^{-1}. In general, if W is the work done or energy expended by a machine in a time t, then

$$\text{average power, } P = \frac{W}{t}$$

The SI unit of power is the *watt*, symbol W. 1 watt = 1 joule per second. Larger units of power, used in industry, are the *kilowatt*, kW (= 1000 W) and the megawatt, MW (= 10^6 W).

Suppose an engine exerts a force of 1500 N on a car moving steadily at 15 m s^{-1}. Then work done per second = 1500 × 15 = 22 500 W = 22.5 kW = power of engine.

If the *resistive force*, F, on the car is proportional to its velocity v, then $F = kv$. The power needed to overcome the resistive force = $F \times v = kv^2$.

The blades of a helicopter sweep the air downward with a velocity v say. If A is the area per second described by the rotating blades, the mass of air per second moving down = ρAv, where ρ is the density of air. The force of the engine, F = momentum change per second = mass per second × velocity = $\rho Av \times v = \rho Av^2$. The average *power* of the engine = $F \times v = \rho Av^3$.

Conservation of Linear Momentum

Consider two spheres A, B moving towards each other in the same straight line. When they collide, a force F is exerted by B on A which lasts for the time of contact between A and B. Now a force is equal to the change in momentum per second it produces (p. 215)

$$\therefore \quad F = \frac{\text{momentum change in A}}{t}$$

$$\therefore \quad Ft = \text{momentum change in A} \quad . \quad . \quad . \quad \text{(i)}$$

Newton's third law says that action and reaction are equal and opposite (p. 215). Thus F is also the magnitude of the force exerted by A on B. Since t is the same for B, we have, from the above argument,

$$Ft = \text{momentum change in B} \quad . \quad . \quad . \quad \text{(ii)}$$

Now the forces F in (i) and (ii) are opposite. It can therefore be seen that the momentum change of A on collision is equal and opposite to that of B. Consequently the total momentum of A and B before collision must equal their total momentum after collision. This conclusion is true for any number of colliding objects, and it is known generally as the *Principle of the Conservation of Linear Momentum.*

Usually, some of the kinetic energy is transformed into internal energy when two moving bodies collide, that is, the kinetic energy of their molecules increases. This is called an *inelastic collision.* In this case the total linear momentum is conserved but not the total kinetic energy due to motion.

An *elastic collision* is one in which the total kinetic energy is conserved. It represents an ideal case in collisions between large objects, but elastic collisions can occur between electrons or molecules. Suppose

m_1, m_2 are the respective masses of an electron and an atom moving in the same direction with velocities u_1 and u_2 respectively. If an elastic collision occurs and the respective velocities after collision in the same direction are v_1 and v_2, then

$$m_1u_1 + m_2u_2 = m_1v_1 + m_2v_2 \text{ (conservation of momentum)}$$

and $\frac{1}{2}m_1u_1^2 + \frac{1}{2}m_2u_2^2 = \frac{1}{2}m_1v_1^2 + \frac{1}{2}m_2v_2^2$ (conservation of energy).

EXAMPLES

1. A rocket of total mass 10 000 kg is fired with an *initial* velocity of 10 m s^{-1}. Calculate the recoil velocity v of the earth of mass 6×10^{24} kg.

From the principle of conservation of linear momentum,

$$6 \times 10^{24} \times v = 10\,000 \times 10$$

$$\therefore \quad v = 1.7 \times 10^{-20} \text{ m s}^{-1}$$

(This extremely small velocity shows that the effect on the earth is negligible.)

2. An object X of mass 1 kg moving with a velocity of 5 m s^{-1} collides with a stationary object Y of equal mass. If X rebounds with a velocity of 3 m s^{-1} making an acute angle of α with its initial direction, and Y rebounds with a velocity of 4 m s^{-1}, making an angle β with the initial direction, Fig. 13.4 (i), show that the collision is an *elastic* one and find α and β.

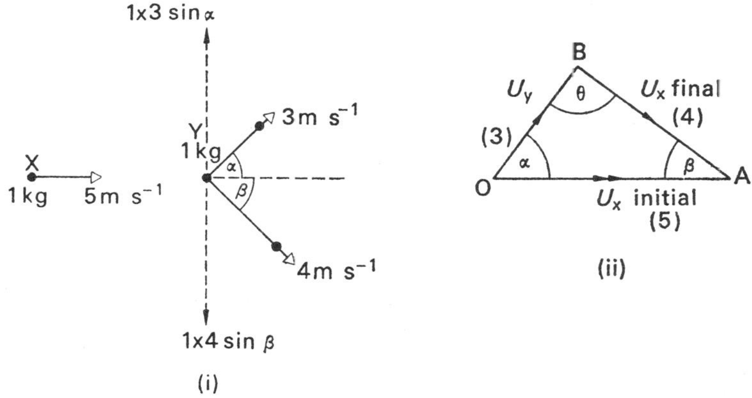

FIG. 13.4 Conservation of linear momentum

Fig. 13.4 (i) shows the masses X and Y, and their initial and final velocities. Fig. 13.4 (ii) shows the *momentum* diagram; this is a vector diagram since momentum, U, is a vector. Now OA = U_X initially = $1 \times 5 = 5$ kg m s^{-1}, OB = $1 \times 3 = 3$ kg m s^{-1} and BA = $1 \times 4 = 4$ kg m s^{-1}. Since $5^2 = 4^2 + 3^2$, it follows, from Pythagoras, *that angle θ in Fig.* 13.4 (*ii*) is 90°.

Further, kinetic energy = $\frac{1}{2}mu^2$. Since $5^2 = 4^2 + 3^2$, it follows that

$$\tfrac{1}{2} \times 1 \times 5^2 = \tfrac{1}{2} \times 1 \times 4^2 + \tfrac{1}{2} \times 1 \times 3^2,$$

or initial k.e. of X = k.e. of Y + k.e. of X after collision

$\therefore$ collision is elastic

We can now find α or β. Since $\alpha + \beta = 90°$, $\beta = 90° - \alpha$. In a direction *perpendicular* to the initial direction ($5\ \text{m s}^{-1}$) of X in Fig. 13.4 (i), there is no force and hence no momentum change occurs in this direction. The initial momentum in this direction is zero. Hence the final momentum is zero.

$$\therefore \quad 1 \times 3 \sin \alpha - 1 \times 4 \sin \beta = 0$$

$$\therefore \quad 3 \sin \alpha = 4 \sin \beta = 4 \sin (90° - \alpha) = 4 \cos \alpha$$

$$\therefore \quad \tan \alpha = \tfrac{4}{3}$$

$$\therefore \quad \alpha = 53° \quad \text{and} \quad \beta = 37°$$

EXERCISES 13

(*Assume* $g = 10\ m\ s^{-2}$ *or* $10\ N\ kg^{-1}$.)

(1) A car with an initial velocity of $10\ \text{m s}^{-1}$ accelerates for 2 s at $2\ \text{m s}^{-2}$. Calculate (i) the velocity, (ii) the distance travelled at the end of 2 s.

(2) A ball is thrown vertically upwards with an initial velocity of $20\ \text{m s}^{-1}$. Find the time to reach the top of its flight and the maximum height.

(3) Define the newton. Calculate the force on a mass of 2 kg which gives it an acceleration of $0.4\ \text{m s}^{-2}$.

(4) A car of mass 1000 kg has (i) a constant velocity of $20\ \text{m s}^{-1}$, (ii) an acceleration of $2\ \text{m s}^{-2}$. Determine the net force on the car in each case.

(5) An object of mass 10 kg is attached to a spring balance suspended from the roof of a lift. What is the reading on the spring balance if the lift is (i) descending with an acceleration of $2\ \text{m s}^{-2}$, (ii) ascending with a velocity of $1.5\ \text{m s}^{-1}$, (iii) ascending with an acceleration of $3\ \text{m s}^{-2}$.

(6) Calculate the energy of (i) a projectile of mass 0.2 kg moving with a velocity of $30\ \text{m s}^{-1}$, (ii) an object of mass 0.08 kg held 2 m above the ground.

(7) An object of mass 50 kg is held stationary 80 m above the ground at a point A. It is then released and passes a point B 20 m above the ground. Calculate the potential energy of the object at A, the kinetic energy at B, the kinetic energy just before the object strikes the ground.

(8) A ball of mass 10 kg moving with a velocity of $20\ \text{m s}^{-1}$ strikes a stationary ball of mass 40 kg. If the balls coalesce and move together in the same direction as the striking ball, calculate their common velocity. State the principle used in the calculation and the reason for its truth.

(9) A ball X of mass 5 kg moving with a velocity of 20 m s^{-1} strikes another ball Y of mass 15 kg moving in the same direction with a velocity of 4 m s^{-1}. If the balls coalesce, calculate (i) their common velocity, (ii) the energy lost on impact.

(10) What is (*a*) the principle of the *conservation of energy*, (*b*) the principle of the *conservation of linear momentum*?

A bullet of mass 20 g, travelling horizontally at 100 m s^{-1}, imbeds itself in the centre of a block of wood of mass 1 kg which is suspended by light vertical strings 1 metre in length. Calculate the maximum inclination of the strings to the vertical.

(11) A man of mass 70 kg stands in a lift. Calculate the force which the floor of the lift exerts on his feet when the lift has an acceleration of 2 m s^{-2}, (*a*) upwards, (*b*) downwards. In what circumstances is the force equal to 700 N? (*L.*)

(12) State Newton's second law of motion and use it to calculate:

(*a*) The force exerted on a vertical wall by a horizontal jet of water of diameter 2 cm, the rate of flow being 1 litre per second. (Assume that the water strikes the wall normally and does not rebound.)

(*b*) The reaction exerted by the floor of a lift on a mass of 80 kg resting on it when the lift has an upward acceleration of 4 m s^{-2}. (*L.*)

(13) A string which passes over a light frictionless pulley supports at its ends masses of 10 g and 12 g. What will be the velocity of the system when the string has moved 2.2 m from rest?

(14) Explain the terms *potential energy*, *kinetic energy*.

A mass of 1 kg is hung from one end of a light string 1 metre long fixed at the other end. The string is held taut horizontally and the mass is then released. Calculate its velocity when the string (*a*) makes an angle of 30° with the vertical, (*b*) is vertical. At the bottom of its swing the kilogramme mass strikes another equal mass and both move on together. Through what height will they rise? (*L.*)

(15) Obtain a value for the height in metres from which a hailstone at 0°C and at rest must fall in order that when its strikes the ground one-fiftieth part of it shall melt. Neglect air resistance and assume the temperature of the surroundings to be everywhere 0°C and that one quarter of the energy possessed by the hailstone when it strikes the ground is converted into heat within the hailstone. (Assume specific latent heat of fusion of ice = 336 000 J kg^{-1}.)

(16) A tractor of mass 2000 kg is towing a loaded trailer of total mass 1500 kg along a level road, the total resistance being 3000 N.

(*a*) Find the total force exerted by the tractor when accelerating with its load at 2 m s^{-2}. (*b*) What will be the tension in the coupling at this time if one-quarter of the resistance acts on the trailer? (*c*) Find also the rate of working of the tractor when it is towing the trailer against the same resistance at a steady speed of 8 m s^{-1}. (*O.*)

(17) A truck of mass 500 kg when empty is moving freely along level rails against a negligible resistance. Initially the velocity of the truck is 4 m s^{-1}. Every 5 seconds, starting after 5 seconds, a bag of cement of mass 100 kg is dropped vertically into the truck.

(*a*) Calculate the velocity of the truck after one, two and three bags are dropped into the truck. (*b*) Plot a graph of the velocity against time for the first 20 seconds of the motion. Indicate on a rough sketch how this graph would continue as further bags were dropped. (*O*.)

(18) A man of mass 70 kg is standing on the flat top of a truck of mass 210 kg which is moving freely on a horizontal rail at 5 m s^{-1}. The man suddenly runs at 5 m s^{-1} relative to the truck for 2 seconds in a direction opposite to that in which the truck is moving, and then stops.

What will be the velocity of the truck just after the man has stopped? How far will the truck travel while the man is running? (*O*.)

(19) A man of mass 60 kg is skiing on level snow at a speed of 20 m s^{-1}. He turns so that 2 seconds later he is moving at 15 m s^{-1} at an angle of 60° to his original direction. What is the mean force, in magnitude and direction, exerted on the man by the snow to cause this change of direction and speed? (A graphical solution is recommended.) (*O*.)

Answers

1. (i) 14 m s^{-1}, (ii) 24 m
2. 2 s, 20 m
3. 0.8 N
4. (i) 0, (ii) 2000 N
5. (i) 80 N, (ii) 100 N, (iii) 130 N
6. (i) 90 J, (ii) 1.6 J
7. 40 000 J; 30 000 J; 40 000 J
8. 4 m s^{-1}
9. (i) 8 m s^{-1}, (ii) 480 J
10. 36.5°
11. (*a*) 840 N, (*b*) 560 N; uniform velocity or stationary
12. (*a*) 3.2 N, (*b*) 1120 N
13. 2 m s^{-1}
14. (*a*) 4.2, (*b*) 4.5 m s^{-1}; 0.25 m
15. 2688 m
16. (*a*) 10 000 N, (*b*) 3750 N, (*c*) 24 kW
17. (*a*) $3\frac{1}{3}$, $2\frac{6}{7}$, $2\frac{1}{2}$ m s^{-1}
18. 5 m s^{-1}, $12\frac{1}{2}$ m
19. 541 N at 134° to original direction

14. Motion in Circle. Gravitation. Rotation

Circular Motion. Acceleration Towards Centre

If a stone is whirled round in a vertical circle by a string, the tension in the string keeps it moving in the curved path. Hence the force on the stone acts towards the centre of the circle. When a racing-car moves round a circular track the force towards the centre is provided by the forces at the ground acting on the wheels. The force acting towards the centre is called the *centripetal force.* On account of this force, an object moving in a circle has an acceleration towards the centre, as we shall now show.

Suppose an object moves from A to B through an angle θ while travelling in a circle with uniform speed v Fig. 14.1 (i). At A it has a

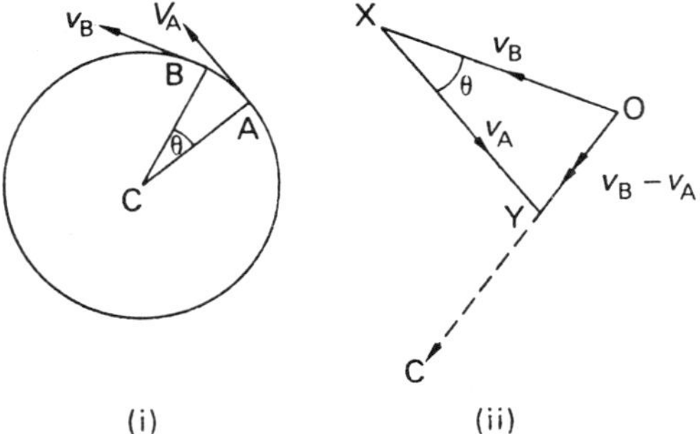

FIG. 14.1 Acceleration in circular motion

velocity v (or v_A) in a direction along the tangent at A; at B it has a velocity v (or v_B) in a direction along the tangent at B. The tangents are inclined at an angle θ. The change in the velocity $= \vec{v}_B - \vec{v}_A$. The vector diagram is shown in Fig. 14.1 (ii), where XY represents $-\vec{v}_A$ and OX represents $\vec{v}_B$. Then OY represents the vector difference (p. 213).

Now OY, the base of isosceles triangle OXY,

$$= 2v \sin(\theta/2) = 2v \times \theta/2 = v\theta,$$

when θ is small, as $\sin \theta = \theta$ in radian (p. 107).

Since OY is directed towards the centre C of the circle, there is a change in velocity, and hence an acceleration a, towards the centre. The magnitude of a is given by

$$a = \frac{\text{change in velocity}}{\text{time}} = \frac{v\theta}{t}.$$

$$\therefore \quad a = v\frac{\theta}{t} = v\omega,$$

where ω = angular velocity = θ/t. But $\omega = v/r$.

$$\therefore \quad a = v^2/r = r\omega^2$$

$$\therefore \quad \text{centripetal force} = \frac{mv^2}{r} = mr\omega^2$$

EXAMPLE

A bucket containing 2 kg of water is whirled in a vertical circle of radius 0.8 m with a constant speed of 4 m s^{-1}. Calculate the reaction of the bucket on the water when the bucket is vertically overhead. If the speed is reduced slowly, at what speed will the water begin to pour out of the bucket when it is overhead?

The downward reaction R of the bucket on the water when overhead, plus the weight W of water, provide the necessary centripetal force F. Now

$$F = \frac{mv^2}{r} = \frac{2 \times 4^2}{0.8} = 40 \text{ N},$$

and $W = mg = 2 \times 10 = 20$ N, assuming $g = 10$ m s^{-2}.

$$\therefore \quad R + 20 = F = 40$$

$$\therefore \quad R = 20 \text{ N} \quad . \quad . \quad . \quad . \quad . \quad (1)$$

The water just begins to pour out of the bucket vertically overhead when $R = 0$. In this case

$$\text{weight } W = mg = \frac{mv^2}{r}$$

$$\therefore \quad v = \sqrt{rg} = \sqrt{0.8 \times 10} = 2.8 \text{ m s}^{-1}.$$

Law of Gravitation

The force of attraction F between two small masses m_1, m_2 distance r apart is given by

$$F = G\frac{m_1 m_2}{r^2}, \quad . \quad . \quad . \quad . \quad . \quad (1)$$

where G is a universal constant known as the *constant of gravitation.* This is called *Newton's law of gravitation.* The magnitude of G is about 6.67×10^{-11} N m^2 kg^{-2}.

The gravitational force of attraction between a planet in the solar system and the sun provides the centripetal force necessary to maintain the planet in its orbit round the sun. The gravitational force of attraction between the moon and the earth keeps the moon in its orbit round the earth.

We can show evidence of the truth of Newton's law by considering the case of the moon moving round the earth with a constant angular velocity ω in a circular orbit of radius R. Suppose m is the mass of the moon and M_E that of the earth. Then, since the gravitational force provides the centripetal force,

$$G\frac{M_E m}{R^2} = mR\omega^2$$

$$\therefore \quad GM_E = R^3\omega^2 \qquad . \quad . \quad . \quad . \quad (1)$$

Now for a mass m_1 on the earth's surface,

$$\frac{GM_E m_1}{R_E{}^2} = m_1 g,$$

where R_E is the radius of the earth.

$$\therefore \quad GM_E = gR_E{}^2 \qquad . \quad . \quad . \quad . \quad (2)$$

From (1) and (2),

$$\therefore \quad gR_E{}^2 = R^3\omega^2$$

$$\therefore \quad g = \frac{R^3\omega^2}{R_E{}^2} \qquad . \quad . \quad . \quad . \quad (3)$$

Observations show that $R_E = 6.4 \times 10^6$ m, $R = 60.1\ R_E = 60.1 \times 6.4 \times 10^6$ m; and $\omega = 2\pi/T = 2\pi/(24 \times 3600)$ rad s^{-1}, since the period of the moon round the earth is roughly 28 days. Substituting in (3), we find a value for g approximately equal to the expected value.

The mass M_E of the earth can be found from equation (2). We have

$$M_E = \frac{gR_E{}^2}{G} = \frac{9.8 \times (6.4 \times 10^6)^2}{6.67 \times 10^{-11}} = 6.0 \times 10^{24} \text{ kg}$$

Communications Satellites

Consider a satellite of mass m, launched from the earth, which circles the earth in a radius R in the plane of the equator with a velocity v. For motion in the circle,

$$\frac{mv^2}{R} = \frac{GM_E m}{R^2}, \qquad . \quad . \quad . \quad . \quad (1)$$

where M_E is the mass of the earth. But $GM_E = gR_E{}^2$ from above.

From (1),

$$\therefore \quad v^2 = \frac{gR_E^{\,2}}{R}.$$

If T is the period of the satellite in orbit, then $T = 2\pi R/v$. Substituting for v,

$$\therefore \quad \frac{4\pi^2 R^2}{T^2} = \frac{gR_E^{\,2}}{R}$$

$$\therefore \quad T^2 = \frac{4\pi^2 R^3}{gR_E^{\,2}} \quad . \quad . \quad . \quad . \quad . \quad (2)$$

If the period T of the satellite is the same as the period of the earth as it turns about its axis, i.e. 24 h, the satellite will stay over the same place on the earth. It is then said to be in a 'parking or synchronous orbit'. The satellite can now be used to relay television programmes continuously from one part of the world to another, or to relay pictures from another satellite orbiting low over particular regions of the earth.

The height above the earth for a parking orbit can be found from (2). We have $T = 24 \times 3600$ s, $R_E = 6.4 \times 10^6$ m, $g = 9.8$ m s^{-2}

$$\therefore \quad R = \sqrt[3]{\frac{(24 \times 3600)^2 \times 9.8 \times (6.4 \times 10^6)^2}{4\pi^2}}$$

$$= 4.24 \times 10^7 \text{ m} = 42\,400 \text{ km}.$$

$$\therefore \quad \text{height} = R - R_E = 42\,400 - 6400 \text{ km} = 36\,000 \text{ km}.$$

Variation of Gravitational Intensity

(1) *Outside the earth.* For calculating the force on a mass outside the earth, the mass M_E of the earth can be considered concentrated at its centre.

The force on a mass m at a distance R from the centre is then given by $F = GM_E m/R^2$. The name *gravitational intensity* is given to the *force per unit mass*, F/m. Thus

$$\text{gravitational intensity} = \frac{GM_E}{R^2} \quad . \quad . \quad . \quad (1)$$

If g' is the particular value of the acceleration due to gravity distance R from the centre, then $F = mg'$. Thus

$$g' = \text{gravitational intensity} = \frac{GM_E}{R^2}$$

If g is the value at the earth's surface, then, from p. 232, $GM_E = gR_E^{\,2}$.

$$\therefore \quad g' = \frac{R_E^{\,2}}{R^2}g \quad . \quad . \quad . \quad . \quad . \quad (2)$$

Hence, from (2), $g' \propto 1/R^2$. This inverse-square relationship can also be seen from (1). Fig. 14.2.

(2) *Inside the earth.* At a point inside the earth distant r from the centre, the effective attracting mass m of the earth is a sphere *of radius* r. The mass outside r can be shown to have no resultant force at the point. If the earth had a constant density throughout, then, since mass $\propto$ radius^3,

$$m = \frac{r^3}{R_E{}^3} M_E \quad . \quad . \quad . \quad . \quad (3)$$

Now at the point distance r from the centre, from (2),

$$\text{gravitational intensity } g'' = \frac{Gm}{r^2} = \frac{GM_E}{R_E{}^3} \cdot r$$

$$\therefore \quad g'' \propto r \quad . \quad . \quad . \quad . \quad . \quad (4)$$

Fig. 14.2 shows the variation of the gravitational intensity. OA is a straight line if the earth density is assumed constant; AB is a curve which follows an inverse-square law.

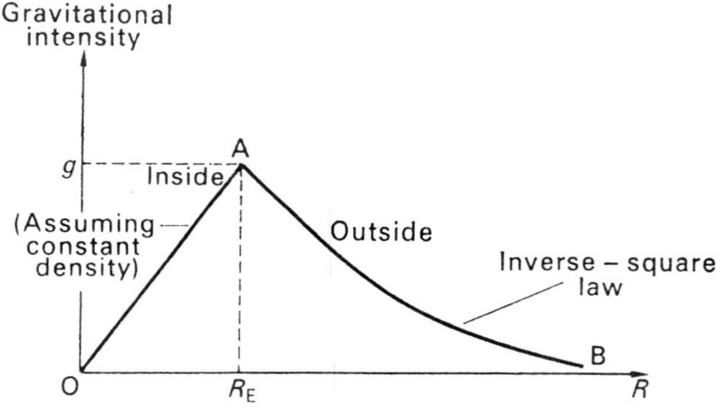

FIG. 14.2 Gravitational intensity due to Earth

In fact, the earth's density depends on depth, so the result is not as simple as above.

Gravitational Potential

In a field of force, the *potential* V at a point is defined as 'the work done per unit mass in taking a mass from infinity to that point'.

At infinity, the force per unit mass is zero. Thus 'infinity' is chosen as the zero of potential. For attraction on a mass outside the earth, the mass of the earth M_E can be considered concentrated at its centre. The force per unit mass at a distance r from the centre is then GM_E/r^2; and the work done per unit mass by the gravitational field from infinity to a point distant R from the centre, where $R > R_E$, is given by

$$V_R = \int_{\infty}^{R} \frac{GM_E}{r^2} \cdot dr = -\frac{GM_E}{R} \quad . \quad . \quad . \quad (1)$$

The negative sign shows that the potential at infinity, zero by convention, is *greater* than the potential at a point near the earth. From (1), it follows that, at the earth's surface,

$$V_E = -\frac{GM_E}{R_E} \quad . \quad . \quad . \quad . \quad (2)$$

Relation between Gravitational Intensity and Potential Difference

Consider two points P and Q outside the earth and distance r and $r + \delta r$ respectively from the centre. If the gravitational intensity is E between the points, then the work per unit mass by the field $= E \,.\, \delta r$ when a mass is moved steadily from Q to P.

But the work done per unit mass is the difference in potential between the points distance r and $(r + \delta r)$ from the centre. Further, the difference of potential = final value − initial value $= -\delta V$, the minus indicating that the potential diminishes nearer the earth as r decreases.

$$\therefore \quad E \,.\, \delta r = -\delta V$$

$$\therefore \quad E = -\frac{\delta V}{\delta r} = -\frac{dV}{dr} \quad . \quad . \quad (1)$$

in the limit when $\delta r \to 0$. Hence the intensity at a point is numerically equal to the *potential gradient* at that point.

We can check this relationship. From equation (1) above at a point distance R from the centre,

$$V = -\frac{GM_E}{R}$$

$$\therefore \quad E = -\frac{dV}{dR} = -\frac{GM_E}{R^2}.$$

The minus sign indicates that E is attractive; note that the direction of E is opposite to the direction of the distance R measured outwards from the centre of the earth.

The total energy of an object moving under gravitational forces is constant. The gravitational field is hence said to be an example of a *conservative field.* The potential energy of a mass in the field depends only on the magnitude of R, its distance from the centre. Thus the potential energy change from one point to another is *independent* of the direction moved between the two points. 'Potential' is thus a *scalar*. In contrast, 'intensity' E is a *vector* since it has direction as well as magnitude.

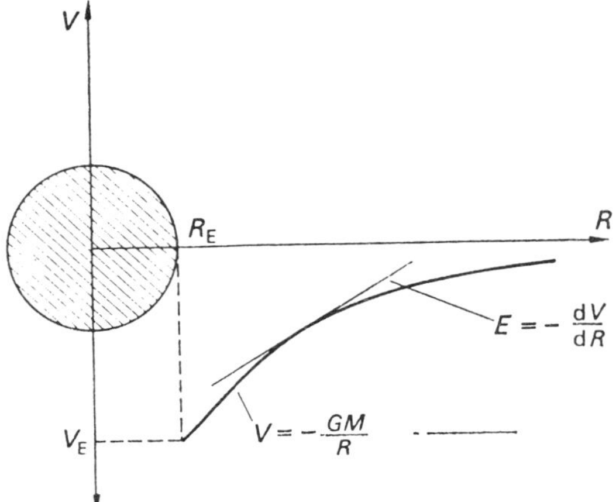

FIG. 14.3 Potential (V) and intensity (E) outside earth

Velocity of Escape

If a rocket is fired from the earth's surface so that it just escapes completely from the earth's gravitational field, then the initial kinetic energy of the rocket must equal the work done in moving it from the earth's surface to infinity.

Suppose the rocket has a mass m. Then, with the usual notation,

potential energy change from earth's surface to infinity $= \dfrac{GM_E m}{R_E}$

$$\therefore \quad \tfrac{1}{2}mv^2 = \frac{GM_E m}{R_E}$$

$$\therefore \quad v = \sqrt{\frac{2GM_E}{R_E}}$$

But $GM_E = gR_E{}^2$ (p. 232).

$$\therefore \quad v = \sqrt{2gR_E} \quad . \quad . \quad . \quad . \quad . \quad (1)$$

Substituting $g = 9.8 \text{ m s}^{-2}$ and $R_E = 6.4 \times 10^6 \text{ m s}^{-1}$, we find $v = 11\,000 \text{ m s}^{-1}$ (approx.). Thus the escape velocity is about 11 km s^{-1}.

At normal temperatures, air molecules have an average velocity of about 0.5 km s^{-1}, which is much less than the escape velocity. The value for hydrogen molecules at normal temperatures, however, is about 2 km s^{-1}. This accounts for the lack of hydrogen in the atmosphere. The escape velocity for the moon is much less than that for the earth, which accounts for the absence of atmosphere round the moon.

Rotation. Couples. Energy of Rotation. Moment of Inertia

The equations of uniformly accelerated rotation were discussed on p. 105 but no treatment of the cause of the rotational acceleration was given. Linear acceleration is produced by a resultant *force*, whereas rotational or angular acceleration is caused by a resultant *couple*. A couple is a pair of equal and opposite forces which do not act through the same point, as shown in Fig. 14.4. The moment of a couple about

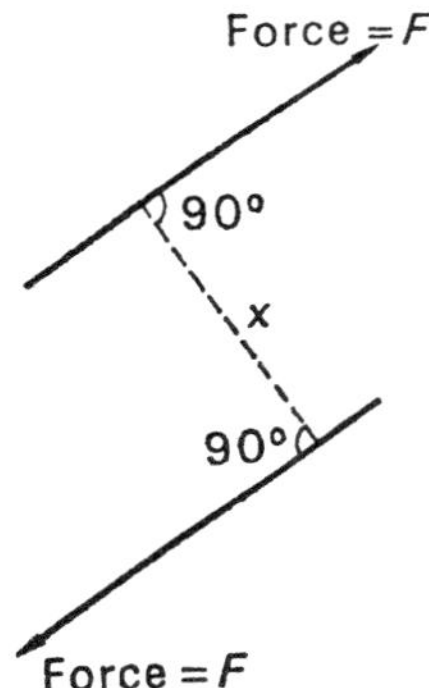

FIG. 14.4 Moment (Torque) of couple

any point is $F \times x$. The student should prove this for himself by choosing a general point, taking the moments of the two forces separately, and then finding the value of their resultant moment or turning effect.

The angular acceleration produced by a given couple is determined partly by the mass of the body *and* by its shape. The equation relating the quantities is

$$T = I\alpha$$

where T is the moment or torque of the resultant couple,
α is the angular acceleration,
and I is a property of the body known as the 'moment of inertia' about the axis for which rotation is occuring (p. 176). The evaluation of the moment of inertia is discussed below, and on p. 176.

Note particularly that one cannot speak of the 'moment of inertia of a body', but only of the 'moment of inertia of a body about a stated axis'. The minimum value of I occurs about an axis through the centre of gravity.

To evaluate the rotational kinetic energy of the body about any axis we proceed as follows:

Suppose a rigid body rotates about an axis through O and perpendicular to the plane of the diagram (Fig. 14.5). Let the angular velocity at a chosen instant be ω. If a particle P of the object has a mass m_1 and is r_1 from O, the velocity v_1 of $P = r_1\omega$ (p. 105).

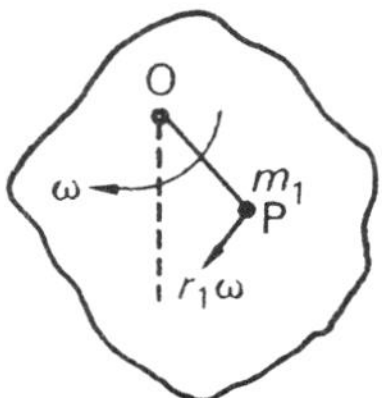

FIG. 14.5 Kinetic energy of rotation

$\therefore$ kinetic energy of particle $= \frac{1}{2}m_1v_1^2 = \frac{1}{2}m_1r_1^2\omega^2$. Since ω is the same for all particles, the kinetic energy W of the whole body is given by

$$W = \tfrac{1}{2}m_1r_1^2\omega^2 + \tfrac{1}{2}m_2r_2^2\omega^2 + \ldots$$
$$= \tfrac{1}{2}\omega^2(m_1r_1^2 + m_2r_2^2 + \ldots)$$
$$= \tfrac{1}{2}I\omega^2,$$

where $I = m_1r_1^2 + m_2r_2^2 + \ldots = \Sigma mr^2$, the sum of all the values of 'mr^2' for every particle of the body. I is known as the *moment of inertia* of the body. Thus for movement from place to place the *translational kinetic energy* of a particle $= \frac{1}{2}mv^2$, whereas the *rotational kinetic energy* of a rigid object $= \frac{1}{2}I\omega^2$.

Moment of Inertia Values

From the calculus method illustrated on p. 176, the following moment of inertia values can be obtained:

(1) *Uniform rod* about axis through centre perpendicular to length, $I = ml^2/12$, where m is the mass and l is the length.

(2) *Uniform rod* about axis at one end perpendicular to length, $I = ml^2/3$.

(3) *Circular ring* about axis through centre perpendicular to plane, $I = ma^2$, where a is the radius.

(4) *Circular ring* about diameter, $I = ma^2/2$.

(5) *Circular disc* about axis through centre perpendicular to plane, $I = ma^2/2$.

(6) *Circular disc* about diameter, $I = ma^2/4$.

(7) *Circular disc* about tangent to disc in the plane, $I = 5ma^2/4$.

(8) *Sphere* about diameter, $I = 2ma^2/5$.

(9) *Rectangular bar* about axis through centre perpendicular to its length and breadth, $I = m(l^2 + b^2)/12$, where l is the length and b the breadth.

(10) *Cylindrical bar* about axis through centre perpendicular to its length, $I = m\left(\frac{l^2}{12} + \frac{r^2}{4}\right)$, where r is the radius and l is the length.

Routh's Rule

Routh has given a useful rule for memorizing moment of inertia values. It states:

Take three mutually perpendicular axes of symmetry through the centre of gravity. Then the moment of inertia (I) about any one of the axes is equal to the *mass* (m) × *sum of square of the other two semi-axes divided by*

3 *for a rectangle, cube, or cuboid,*
4 *for a circle or ellipse,*
5 *for a sphere or spheroid.*

Thus for a uniform rod about an axis through its middle perpendicular to its length l, $I = m \times \dfrac{\left(\frac{l}{2}\right)^2 + 0}{3} = \dfrac{ml^2}{12}$, as here the third semi-axis has zero length. For a rectangular bar (cuboid) and an axis through its middle perpendicular to the length and breadth, l, b, respectively,

$$I = m \times \frac{\left(\frac{l}{2}\right)^2 + \left(\frac{b}{2}\right)^2}{3} = \frac{m(l^2 + b^2)}{12}.$$

For a circular disc about a central axis perpendicular to its plane,

$$I = m \times \frac{a^2 + a^2}{4} = \frac{ma^2}{2}.$$

About a diameter, $$I = m \times \frac{a^2 + 0}{4} = \frac{ma^2}{4}.$$

For a sphere about a diameter,

$$I = m \times \frac{a^2 + a^2}{5} = \frac{2}{5}ma^2.$$

EXAMPLE

A rod 6 m long is pivoted at one end and held horizontally. If the rod is released, calculate its angular velocity when it makes an angle 60° with the vertical.

Gain in kinetic energy of rod = $\frac{1}{2}I\omega^2$, where ω is the angular velocity.

$$\text{Loss in potential energy} = mgh = mg \times 3 \sin 30°,$$

since the centre of gravity is 3 m from the end of the rod.

$$\therefore \quad \tfrac{1}{2}I\omega^2 = mg \,.\, 3 \sin 30°.$$

But $$I = \frac{ml^2}{3} = m \,.\, \frac{6^2}{3}, \text{ from above.}$$

$$\therefore \quad \tfrac{1}{2} \,.\, m \,.\, \frac{6^2}{3}\,\omega^2 = mg \,.\, 3 \sin 30°$$

$$\therefore \quad \omega^2 = \frac{10 \times 3}{6 \times 2} = 2.5$$

$$\therefore \quad \omega = \sqrt{2.5} = 1.6 \text{ rad s}^{-1}.$$

Work Done by Torque

Since a torque produces rotational kinetic energy when acting on a body, it follows that the torque does work. The magnitude of the work is given by:

$$\textit{rotational work} = \textit{torque}\ (T) \times \textit{angle of rotation}\ (\theta).$$

If T is in newton-metre and θ in radian, the work is in joule.

Starting from rest, $T \times \theta$ = gain in rotational kinetic energy = $\frac{1}{2}I\omega^2$ with the usual notation. This should be compared with the linear work-energy relationship $F \times s = \frac{1}{2}mv^2$.

Kinetic Energy of Rolling Body

When a body rolls without slipping, it has translational kinetic energy due to the motion of its centre of gravity plus rotational energy about the centre of gravity.

$$\therefore \quad \text{total energy} = \tfrac{1}{2}mv^2 + \tfrac{1}{2}I\omega^2,$$

where m is the mass, v is the velocity of its centre of gravity, I is the moment of inertia about the centre of gravity, and ω is the angular velocity about the centre of gravity.

In the case of a rolling spherical or cylindrical body, the distance moved by the centre of gravity along a plane = $r\theta$, where r is the radius and θ is the angle of rotation of a fixed radius. Thus the velocity of the centre of gravity is here given by

$$v = \frac{\text{distance}}{\text{time}} = \frac{r\theta}{t} = r\omega.$$

$$\therefore \quad \text{total energy} = \tfrac{1}{2}mv^2 + \tfrac{1}{2}I\omega^2$$

$$= \tfrac{1}{2}mv^2 + \tfrac{1}{2}I\frac{v^2}{r^2}$$

$$= \tfrac{1}{2}\left(m + \frac{I}{r^2}\right)v^2.$$

Acceleration of Rolling Body

Suppose a *solid sphere* rolls without slipping down an inclined plane from rest. From the Principle of the conservation of energy,

gain in kinetic energy = loss in potential energy.

$$\therefore \quad \tfrac{1}{2}mv^2 + \tfrac{1}{2}I\omega^2 = mgs \sin \alpha \quad . \quad . \quad . \quad . \quad \text{(i)}$$

where s is the distance travelled along the plane, α is the angle of inclination of the plane to the horizontal, and I is the moment of inertia about its c.g.

$$\therefore \quad \tfrac{1}{2}mv^2 + \tfrac{1}{2}\left(\frac{I}{r^2}\right)v^2 = mgs \sin \alpha.$$

Now $\quad I = \tfrac{2}{5}mr^2$ (p. 238)

$$\therefore \quad \tfrac{7}{10}mv^2 = mgs \sin \alpha$$

$$\therefore \quad \tfrac{7}{10}v^2 = gs \sin \alpha \quad . \quad . \quad . \quad . \quad \text{(ii)}$$

Differentiating with respect to t, and noting $ds/dt = v$,

$$\therefore \quad \tfrac{7}{10} \times 2v\frac{dv}{dt} = g\frac{ds}{dt}\sin \alpha = gv \sin \alpha,$$

$$\therefore \quad \tfrac{7}{10} \times 2a = g \sin \alpha,$$

where $a = dv/dt$ = acceleration of sphere.

$$\therefore \quad a = \frac{5g}{7}\sin \alpha.$$

A thin *hollow sphere* of the same mass m as the solid sphere has a moment of inertia I given by $\tfrac{2}{3}mr^2$, where r is the radius of the sphere. Using $I = \tfrac{2}{3}mr^2$ in the above working in place of $I = \tfrac{2}{5}mr^2$, we find $a = 3g \sin \alpha/5$. This is a smaller acceleration than the case of the solid sphere, where $a = 5g \sin \alpha/7$. Thus a hollow sphere takes longer than a solid sphere of the same mass to reach the bottom of an incline, when both spheres start from rest at the same place.

Torque and Angular Acceleration

If a rigid body is made to rotate about a fixed axis O, the force F_1 on a particle of mass m_1 distant r_1 from O = mass × acceleration = $m_1r_1\alpha$, where α is the *angular acceleration* of the particle. All other particles have the same angular acceleration since the body is rigid.

$$\therefore \quad \text{total torque about O, } T = \Sigma(m_1r_1\alpha \times r_1) = \alpha\Sigma m_1{r_1}^2.$$

$$\therefore \quad T = I\alpha \qquad . \quad . \quad . \quad . \quad (1)$$

This expression for rotational acceleration is analogous to the relation $F = ma$ for the linear acceleration of a particle.

EXAMPLE

A rope is wound round the axle, radius 2 cm, of a flywheel and the free end of the rope is pulled by a constant force of 20 N. If the moment of inertia of the flywheel is 0.1 kg m², find (i) the kinetic energy of the flywheel 2 s after the force is first applied (neglect friction), (ii) the number of revolutions made by the flywheel in coming to rest if a constant opposing torque of 0.2 N m is applied to the flywheel.

(i) Torque due to 20 N force, $T = 20 \text{ N} \times 2 \times 10^{-2} \text{ m} = 0.4 \text{ N m}$.

Since $T = I\alpha$, angular acceleration $\alpha = \dfrac{T}{I} = \dfrac{0.4}{0.1} = 4 \text{ rad s}^{-2}$.

$$\therefore \quad \text{angular velocity after 2 s, } \omega = \alpha t = 4 \times 2 = 8 \text{ rad s}^{-1}$$

$$\therefore \quad \text{K.E. of flywheel} = \tfrac{1}{2}I\omega^2 = \tfrac{1}{2} \times 0.1 \times 8^2 = 3.2 \text{ J} \quad . \quad . \quad (1)$$

(ii) With a constant opposing torque of 0.2 N m.

$$\text{deceleration, } \alpha = \frac{T}{I} = \frac{0.2}{0.1} = 2 \text{ rad s}^{-2}$$

$$\therefore \quad \text{time to come to rest, } t = \frac{\omega}{\alpha} = \frac{8}{2} = 4 \text{ s.}$$

If n is the number of revolutions made during this time,

$$\therefore \quad \text{average angular velocity} = \frac{2\pi n}{4} = \frac{\omega}{2} = \frac{8}{2} = 4$$

$$\therefore \quad n = \frac{4 \times 4}{2\pi} = 2.5 \text{ rev (approx.)}$$

(*Alternatively*, torque × angle of rotation = work done. See p. 240.

$$\therefore \quad 0.2 \times \theta = \text{initial k.e.} = 3.2$$

$$\therefore \quad \theta = 16 \text{ rad}$$

$$\therefore \quad n = \frac{\theta}{2\pi} = \frac{16}{2\pi} = 2.5 \text{ rev)}$$

Angular Momentum. Conservation of Angular Momentum

In rotational dynamics, *angular momentum* is analogous to, linear momentum in translational dynamics. The angular momentum L of a moving particle of mass m about an axis O is defined by

$$L = \text{linear momentum} \times r = mvr, \qquad (1)$$

where r is the perpendicular distance from O to the direction of the linear momentum (mv) vector or the velocity (v) of the particle. Since $v = r\omega$, where ω is the angular velocity about O, it follows that, for a rigid body,

$$\text{angular momentum } L = \Sigma mr^2\omega = I\omega, \qquad (2)$$

where I is the moment of inertia of the body about O.

When no external torque acts on a rotating body, no angular acceleration is produced. In this case, the angular momentum $I\omega$ about the axis concerned remains constant. Thus a high diver, spinning in mid-air, can increase his angular velocity by coiling his body more, which diminishes his moment of inertia. The total angular momentum of two spinning bodies is also conserved in collisions, since the forces and torques on each are equal and opposite.

Planets moving round the sun S are attracted by a gravitational force which passes through S. Since this external force has no moment

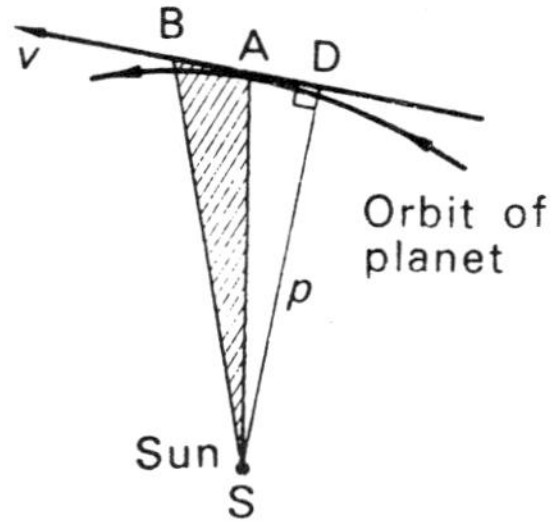

FIG. 14.6 Planetary orbit

or torque about S, it follows that the angular momentum of the planet about S is *constant*. Suppose a planet A has a mass m and velocity v and moves a *small* distance AB in a time t, Fig. 14.6. Then

$$\text{momentum} = mv,$$

and

$$\text{angular momentum about S} = mv \times \text{SD},$$

where p or SD is the perpendicular from S to BA produced.

$$\therefore \quad mv \times \text{SD} = \text{constant}.$$

$$\therefore \quad m \times \frac{AB}{t} \times SD = \text{constant.}$$

But

$$AB \times SD = 2 \times \text{area of } \Delta SAB$$

$$\therefore \quad \frac{\text{area of } \Delta SAB}{t} = \text{constant}$$

therefore area swept out per second by radius vector SA as the planet moves is proportional to the time. This is *Kepler's second law* in astronomy.

The conservation of angular momentum is also concerned in the analysis leading to the *Rutherford scattering law*. Here α-particles are scattered in various directions when they are incident on nuclei in a thin metal film. Fig. 14.7 shows an incident α-particle of mass m and velocity

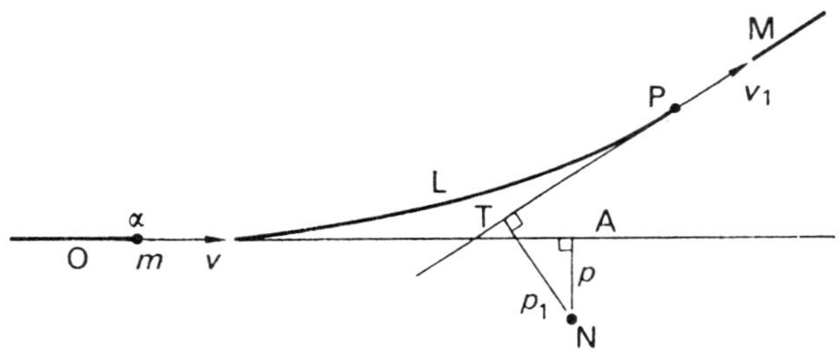

FIG. 14.7 Conservation of angular momentum—nuclear deflection

v at O, a long way from nucleus N. The angular momentum about N $= mvp$, where p is the perpendicular NA from N to the direction of the momentum. The α-particle, which carries a +ve charge, is deflected by the +ve nuclear charge as it approaches N, and travels along the path OLM. At a point P where the velocity is v_1, the angular momentum about N $= mv_1p_1$, where p_1 = NT. But the repulsive force between the nucleus and the α-particle always passes through N. Hence the momentum about N is conserved.

$$\therefore \quad mv_1p_1 = mvp$$

Since p_1 is greater than p in Fig. 14.7, it follows that v_1 is less than v.

EXERCISES 14

Circular Motion

(1) An object moves in a circular path of radius 100 m with a speed of 10 m s^{-1}. Calculate (i) the acceleration towards the centre, (ii) the angular velocity.

(2) A car of mass 1000 kg moves round a track of radius 100 m with a speed of 20 m s^{-1}. Find (i) the angular velocity, (ii) the acceleration towards the centre, (iii) the centripetal force.

(3) An object of mass 0.01 kg is whirled by a wire in a vertical circle of radius 0.8 m with a uniform speed of 4 m s^{-1}. Calculate the maximum and minimum tensions in the wire.

(4) Calculate the centripetal force on an electron moving in a circular orbit in a hydrogen atom, assuming the mass of an electron is 9×10^{-31} kg, the speed in the orbit is 2×10^{6} m s^{-1} and the radius of the orbit is 5×10^{-11} m.

(5) A mass of 2 kg is whirled in a horizontal circle by a string of length 0.5 m. What is the maximum speed if the string breaks under a tension exceeding 400 N?

(6) A bucket with 0.5 kg of water is whirled in a vertical circle of radius 1 m with a constant speed of 4 m s^{-1}. Calculate the reaction of the bucket on the water at the highest point of the circle. For what circular speed will the water just leave the bucket at the highest point?

(7) A small mass on a string of length 40 cm is whirled in a vertical circle at 5 rev s^{-1}. If it is released when the string is horizontal and the mass is moving upwards how high will the mass go above its point of release? (Take g as 10 N kg^{-1}.)

In examples 8–12 *assume* $G = 6.67 \times 10^{-11}$ *N m*^{2} *kg*$^{-2}$ *where required.*

(8) Calculate the speed necessary to keep a satellite in a circular orbit close to the surface of the earth, assuming that the radius of the earth is 6400 km and $g = 10$ m s^{-2}.

(9) Calculate the gravitational force on an electron of mass 9.1×10^{-31} kg which moves in a circular orbit of radius 5.3×10^{-11} m about a proton of mass 1.7×10^{-27} kg in a hydrogen atom. If the electron has a speed of about 2×10^{6} m s^{-1} in the orbit find whether or not the centripetal force on the electron is provided by the gravitational force.

(10) The moon has a mass about 1/81 that of the earth and a radius about 1/4 that of the earth. Compare the acceleration due to gravity at the earth's surface with that at the moon's surface.

(11) By calculating the mass of the earth and its volume, show that the mean density of the earth is about 5500 kg m^{-3}. (Assume $g = 10$ m s^{-2} and the radius of the earth = 6400 km.)

(12) A satellite is moving in a circular orbit concentric with the earth and at a height of 230 km above its surface, the plane of the orbit always passing through the poles. If the acceleration due to gravity is 9.14 m s^{-2} at this height and the radius of the earth is 6.36×10^{3} km, calculate the period of revolution of the satellite, and hence find how long it will take to go from a point vertically over an observer in latitude 45° to a point above the adjacent pole. (*O.*)

Rotational Dynamics

(13) Calculate the kinetic energy of a uniform rod, mass 0.1 kg and length 0.6 m, rotating about an axis perpendicular to its length at one end with an angular velocity of 6 rad s^{-1}. (M.I. of rod about end = $ml^2/3$ where l is the length.)

(14) Find (i) the rotational kinetic energy, (ii) the total kinetic energy of a circular disc of mass 2 kg and radius 0.4 m rolling along a horizontal plane with an angular velocity of 4 rad s^{-1}. (M.I. of disc about axis through centre perpendicular to plane = $ma^2/2$.)

(15) A uniform rod of length 6 m, pivoted at one end, is held horizontally and then released. Calculate the angular velocity of the rod as it passes the vertical. (M.I. of rod about end = $ml^2/3$.)

(16) A flywheel has a moment of inertia about its axis of rotation of 0.2 kg m^2 and a constant force of 2 N is applied tangential to the wheel of radius 0.4 m. Calculate (i) the torque about the centre of the flywheel, (ii) the angular acceleration of the flywheel, (iii) the angular velocity after 4 s, (iv) the kinetic energy of the flywheel after 4 s.

(17) A flywheel is spinning at 10 rev s^{-1} about its axis of rotation. Calculate the constant torque required to reduce the speed uniformly to 4 rev s^{-1} in 2 s, if the moment of inertia of the flywheel about its axis is 0.1 kg m^2. What is the decrease in energy of the flywheel?

(18) A gramophone record is rotating at 72 rev min^{-1} and has a moment of inertia 25×10^{-4} kg m^2 about the vertical axis through its centre. A 0.05 kg mass of putty is dropped gently onto the record at a place 0.1 m from the centre. Calculate the new rate of rotation of the record. (*Hint.* Use angular momentum.)

(19) An α-particle is projected towards a nucleus N from some distance away with a velocity of 3.0×10^6 m s^{-1}. The perpendicular distance from N to the direction of the velocity is initially 1.0×10^{-10} m and at a point X in the orbit of the particle it is 1.2×10^{-10} m. Calculate the velocity at X. Explain the principle on which your calculation is based.

Answers

1. (i) 1 m s^{-2} (ii) 0.1 rad s^{-1}
2. (i) 0.2 rad s^{-1} (ii) 4 m s^{-2} (iii) 4000 N
3. 0.3 N, 0.1 N
4. 7.2×10^{-8} N
5. 10 m s^{-1}
6. 3 N, 3.1 m s^{-1}
7. 7.9 m
8. 8 km s^{-1}
9. 3.7×10^{-4} N; not provided
10. 5 (approx.)
12. 5334 s, 667 s
13. 0.216 J
14. (i) 1.28 J (ii) 3.84 J
15. 2.2 rad s^{-1}
16. (i) 0.8 N m (ii) 4 rad s^{-2} (iii) 16 rad s^{-1} (iv) 25.6 J
17. 1.9 N m, 166 J
18. 60 rev min^{-1}
19. $2.5 \times 10^{6} \text{ m s}^{-1}$

15. Oscillations and Waves

Simple Harmonic Motion

In addition to linear and circular motion another very common type of movement found in nature is vibration. Sound for instance is caused by the particles of the medium vibrating. Electrons in the aerials of radio transmitters and receivers undergo oscillations, though these are of much greater frequency than those which cause sound waves in air. The balance wheel of a watch keeps the watch 'right' by oscillating at a constant frequency. The simplest type of oscillatory motion is called *simple harmonic motion.* The vibrations of the prongs of a tuning-fork are simple harmonic. More complicated oscillations can be analysed into a number of simple harmonic oscillations.

Simple harmonic motion (s.h.m.) can be defined as *the motion of an object whose acceleration is proportional to its distance from a fixed point and whose acceleration is always directed towards that point.* We shall now show that the projection on a fixed diameter of uniform motion in a circle is simple harmonic motion; and we shall derive s.h.m. formulae from this conception.

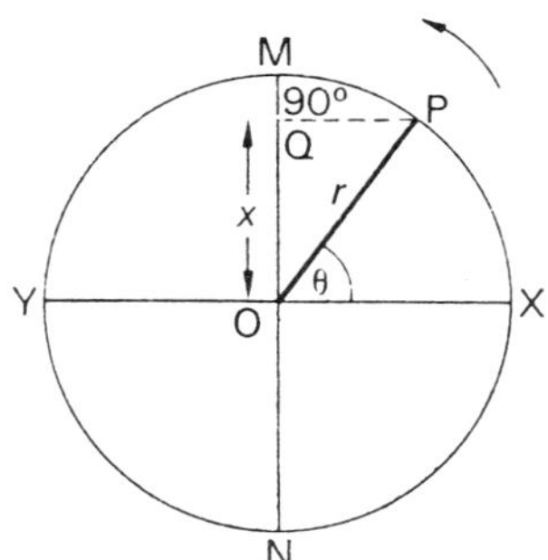

FIG. 15.1 Projection of uniform circular motion

Consider, then, a particle P moving at constant angular speed ω round a circle of centre O and radius r (Fig. 15.1). Suppose MN is a fixed diameter, and YOX a perpendicular diameter from which the angle of rotation θ of OP is measured. As P moves round the circle from X in an anticlockwise direction, the foot of the projection, Q, from P to MON moves to and fro along MON. Now the acceleration of P $= r\omega^2$, and acts along PO (p. 231). Therefore

acceleration of Q towards O

$$= \text{component along MO of acceleration } r\omega^2$$

$$= r\omega^2 \cos(90^\circ - \theta) = r\omega^2 \sin\theta.$$

But $\quad r \sin\theta = \text{OQ} = x$ say,

therefore

acceleration of Q towards O

$$= -\omega^2 \,.\, \text{OQ} = -\omega^2 x,$$

the minus sign indicating that the acceleration is in the opposite direction to the displacement.

Hence, as ω^2 is a constant, the acceleration of Q is always proportional to its distance from O and is directed towards O. Thus the motion of Q about O is simple harmonic.

Formulae for Displacement, Period, Velocity, Energy

We can now derive formulae for simple harmonic motion.

The *displacement* (distance) from O, x, is given, from triangle OQP, by

$$x = r \sin\theta.$$

But $\theta = \omega t$, where ω is the constant angular velocity and t is the time from X to P.

$$\therefore \quad x = r \sin \omega t. \quad \text{(i)}$$

If the displacement x is positive between O, M, it is negative between O, N. A graph of displacement (x) v. time (t) is shown in Fig. 15.4, and is a sine curve. The maximum displacement is r, and this is called the *amplitude* of the motion.

The time for one complete to-and-fro motion of Q is called the *period*, T. It is also the time taken by P to move once round the circle, and since 1 revolution $= 2\pi$ rad and the angular velocity of P is ω,

$$T = \frac{2\pi}{\omega}. \quad \text{(ii)}$$

The number of complete to-and-fro oscillations per second is called the *frequency*, f, of the motion. Since 1 oscillation is made in T second, then

$$f = \frac{1}{T}, \quad \text{or} \quad T = \frac{1}{f}. \quad \text{(iii)}$$

The unit of frequency is the hertz, symbol Hz. 1 Hz = 1 cycle per second.

The *velocity* v of Q along MN is the component in this direction of the velocity of P, the particle moving round the circle. Now the velocity of P is $r\omega$, and acts along the tangent to the circle at P (Fig. 15.1).

$$\therefore \quad v = r\omega \cos \theta.$$

But
$$\sin \theta = \frac{x}{r};$$

hence
$$\cos \theta = \sqrt{1 - \sin^2 \theta} = \sqrt{1 - \frac{x^2}{r^2}} = \frac{1}{r}\sqrt{r^2 - x^2}$$

$$\therefore \quad v = \omega\sqrt{r^2 - x^2}. \qquad \text{(iv)}$$

The maximum velocity, v_m, is obtained when $x = 0$, at the centre of the motion. Hence, from (iv),

$$v_m = \omega r. \qquad \text{(v)}$$

In an undamped system the total energy (the sum of the potential energy p.e. and kinetic energy k.e.) is a constant. Now when the displacement is zero the force on the oscillating mass is zero and thus the p.e. is also zero, i.e. the whole of the energy is kinetic. In this position the velocity is $r\omega$ and thus the energy is $\frac{1}{2}mr^2\omega^2$ where m is the mass of the oscillating body.

In any other position the velocity is $\omega\sqrt{r^2 - x^2}$ and the k.e. is therefore

$$\tfrac{1}{2}m\omega^2(r^2 - x^2).$$

The remainder of the energy in this position must be p.e. and so by subtracting the k.e. from the total energy we obtain the general expression for the p.e.:

$$\begin{aligned}\text{p.e. at displacement } x &= \tfrac{1}{2}mr^2\omega^2 - \tfrac{1}{2}m\omega^2(r^2 - x^2)\\ &= \tfrac{1}{2}m\omega^2x^2. \qquad \text{(vi)}\end{aligned}$$

EXAMPLE

The end of a steel strip is oscillating with an amplitude of 2 cm. If the acceleration at an instant is numerically $64x$, where x is the distance of the end from the centre of oscillation, find (i) the period, (ii) the maximum velocity, (iii) the frequency, (iv) the velocity when x is 1 cm.

Acceleration towards centre $= -64x = -\omega^2 x$, using the notation on p. 249.

$$\therefore \quad \omega^2 = 64, \quad \text{or} \quad \omega = 8.$$

(i)
$$\therefore \quad \text{period, } T, = \frac{2\pi}{\omega} = \frac{2\pi}{8} = 0.8 \text{ s}$$

(ii) Maximum velocity, v_m, $= \omega r = 8 \times 2$, as $r = 2$.

$$\therefore \quad v_m = 16 \text{ cm s}^{-1}$$

(iii) The time for 1 oscillation $= T = 0.8$ s

$$\therefore \quad \text{frequency, } f, = \frac{1}{T} = \frac{1}{0.8} = 1.25 \text{ Hz}$$

Oscillation of Mass and Spring

Consider a coiled metal spring on a smooth table, with one end attached to a fixed point A, Fig. 15.2. If a small mass m is attached to the free end O of the spring and then pulled slightly and released, the mass oscillates about its initial position O.

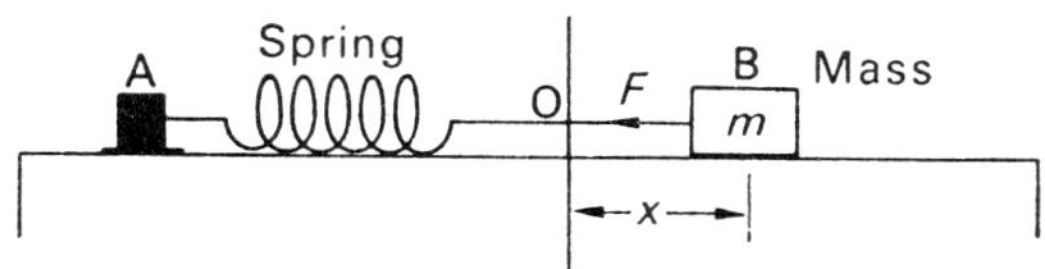

FIG. 15.2 Oscillation of spring

Suppose k is the 'force constant' of the spring, which is the force per unit extension. Then, assuming the spring extension does not exceed the elastic limit, the force F on the mass at B $= kx$. Thus the acceleration towards O, a, is given from $F = ma$, by

$$ma = -kx. \quad . \quad . \quad . \quad . \quad (1)$$

The minus indicates that the acceleration is opposite to the direction in which x is measured from O; for example, in Fig. 15.2, the acceleration of m is in the direction BO at the instant concerned, whereas x is in the direction OB.

From (1),

$$a = -\frac{k}{m}x = -\omega^2 x, \quad . \quad . \quad . \quad . \quad (2)$$

where $\omega^2 = k/m$. Thus, by definition, the motion of m is simple harmonic. The period T is given by

$$T = \frac{2\pi}{\omega} = 2\pi\sqrt{\frac{m}{k}}. \quad . \quad . \quad . \quad . \quad (3)$$

Electrical and Mechanical Analogues

A useful analogy can be made between quantities in mechanics and electricity. Thus current $I\,(=\mathrm{d}Q/\mathrm{d}t)$ is analogous to velocity $v\,(=\mathrm{d}s/\mathrm{d}t)$.

Mechanics	Electrical Analogue
velocity, v	current, I
displacement, s	quantity, Q
mass, m	inductance, L
spring constant, k	1/capacitance, $1/C$

From the differential coefficients, quantity Q is analogous to displacement s.

Further, the inductance L of a coil is a measure of its 'opposition' to growth of current in it. It is therefore analogous to mass m, which is a measure of its inertia or opposition to motion. Since $V = Q/C$ where C is capacitance, and V is analogous to 'force' and Q to 'displacement', it follows that $1/C$ is analogous to the spring constant k. The analogues are shown in the Table above.

Electrical Oscillations

In the analogues described a capacitor corresponds to a spring in mechanics. Just as spring stores an amount of mechanical potential energy, p.e. $= \frac{1}{2}kx^2$, the capacitor stores an amount of electrical potential energy $= \frac{1}{2}Q^2/C$, using the analogue table, or $\frac{1}{2}CV^2$. This result was derived on p. 171.

Similarly, an inductor is analogous to a mass m. Just as the mass stores an amount of mechanical kinetic energy, k.e. $= \frac{1}{2}mv^2$, the inductor has an amount of electrical kinetic energy $= \frac{1}{2}LI^2$, using the analogues in the Table.

Since an inductor L in series with a capacitor C is analogous to a spring-mass mechanical system, it is not surprising that a coil-capacitor in series produces electrical oscillations in an electrical circuit. In mechanical oscillations, the period

$$T = 2\pi/\omega = 2\pi/\sqrt{m/k}$$

(p. 251). Thus the period T of electrical oscillations is given by

$$T = 2\pi\sqrt{LC},$$

from the Table. Hence the *frequency*, f, is given by

$$f = \frac{1}{2\pi\sqrt{LC}}.$$

This is the frequency of radio waves from a transmitter circuit where the total capacitance is C and the total inductance is L. The same formula gives the *resonant frequency* of an inductor-capacitor circuit in a radio receiver, where 'tuning' is arranged by varying C.

As in the spring-mass mechanical system, exchanges of energy occur between the capcitor and inductor during electrical oscillations. Thus when the energy of the capacitor, $\frac{1}{2}CV^2$, is a maximum (V = maximum), the inductor energy, $\frac{1}{2}LI^2$, is zero ($I = 0$). When the inductor energy is a maximum (I = maximum), the capacitor energy is zero ($V = 0$). These analogues are of interest and in some cases aid understanding and memorization. But proofs based on analogies are not acceptable. The analogue rests on the fact that both sets of formulae can be deduced from first principles, for instance, that for the resonant frequency of an electrical circuit can be found from electrical considerations only.

Graphs of Simple Harmonic Motion

To construct graphs of simple harmonic motion (s.h.m.), we make use of the fact (proved on p. 249) that any s.h.m. can be obtained by projecting a suitable uniform circular motion on to a diameter. Consider a radius CP of length r moving round a circle in an anticlockwise direction with constant angular velocity ω (Fig. 15.3). Let the radius move

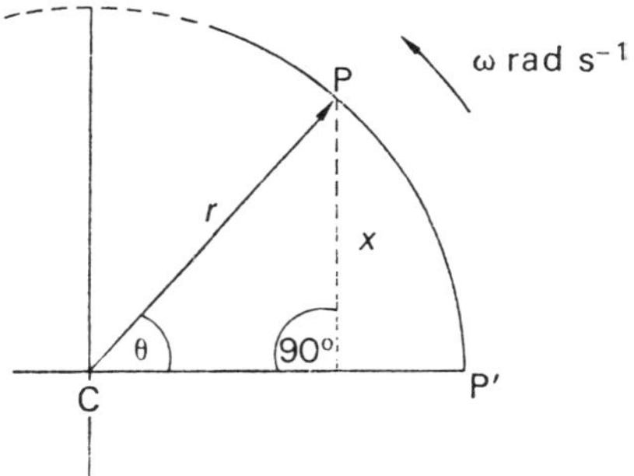

FIG. 15.3 Displacement by projection

from CP′ to CP in time t. The vertical height of P above CP′ is now given by $r \sin \theta$ and as $\theta = \omega t$ this is $r \sin \omega t$. Thus the projection on the vertical diameter ($=x$) is given by

$$x = r \sin \omega t.$$

From this we see that the quantity x has a sine relationship with time and so the graph of x against t will be a sine curve. When CP has completed one revolution the values of x will start to repeat.

The graph of x against t may be constructed in the following way: Suppose that $r = 30$ mm; Draw the axes, and to the left of the origin construct a circle (the 'circle of reference') of radius 30 mm, as shown in Fig. 15.4. Now choose values for t which are simply related to T—the most suitable being $T/12$, $2T/12$, $3T/12$ etc. For these values the angle θ (figure 15.3) will have values 30°, 60°, 90°, etc., and one cycle of the graph will be divided into twelve equal parts by time. Next, follow the instructions given beneath Fig. 15.4 to obtain the curve.

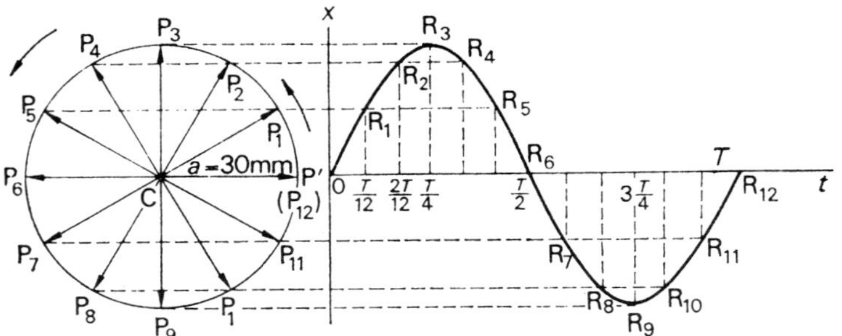

(i) Divide the circle into 12 equal parts to obtain $P_1, P_2 \ldots P_{12}$
(ii) Obtain R_1 [the plot for $t = \frac{T}{12}$] by drawing a horizontal line from P_1 to cut the line $t = \frac{T}{12}$.
(iii) Obtain R_2 by drawing the horizontal line from P_2 to cut the line $t = \frac{2T}{12}$
(iv) Continue this process to obtain positions for R up to R_{12}
(v) Join $R_1, R_2 \ldots R_{12}$ by a smooth curve

FIG. 15.4 Method of plotting sine curve

In discussing everyday examples of s.h.m. it is rare for the periodic time to be quoted; the frequency is usually used. For instance, in Britain the a.c. mains have a frequency of 50 Hz; radio stations transmit at frequencies of the order of 10^6 Hz; the sounds that we hear vary from about 20 Hz to something between 10 000 and 20 000 Hz, the upper limit depending on the person, as well as his age and health.

When the value

$$\omega = 2\pi f$$

is substituted in the equation

$$x = r \sin \omega t,$$

it transforms to

$$x = r \sin 2\pi f t,$$

which is often a more useful form.

The sine of an angle cannot exceed unity and thus the maximum value of x is r, which is called the 'peak' value. In a.c. measurements, instruments usually record the r.m.s. value. For any *sinusoidal* relationship, the r.m.s. value of x is the peak value divided by $\sqrt{2}$ (proved on p. 187).

Phase Difference. Phasors

When we started to construct the graph in the preceding section, we placed the vector CP along CP′ when t was zero. As a result, the graph passed through the origin. Had CP started in any other position the graph would not have passed through the origin but would have appeared as though it had 'slid along' the axis to some new position. Thus if the position of CP is CP″ when $t = 0$, as shown in Fig. 15.5,

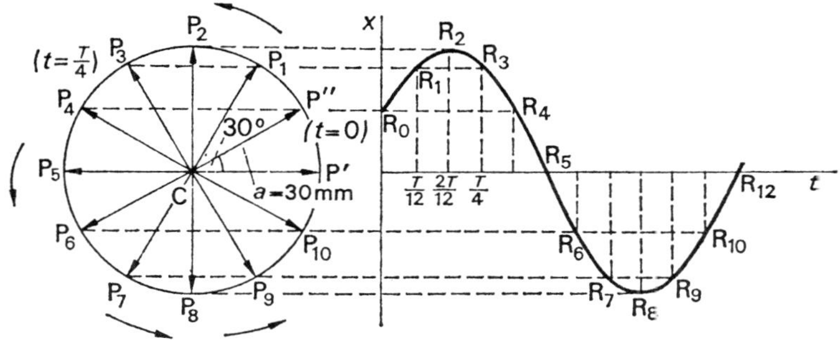

The method of construction is as for the previous figure (15.4) but the first position of the vector (i.e. at $t = 0$) is now at CP″ and thus the curve starts at R_0

FIG. 15.5 Phase in plotting sine waves

making say an angle of 30° with the t-axis, the graph would be as illustrated in that figure. This could be obtained by sliding the x-axis to the right by 30°/360° of the periodic time. In general, if the angle between CP′ and CP″ is δ degree, there will be a difference in position of the two curves which is equivalent to a shift along the time axis of $T \times \delta/360$. Notice that in the case which we have just examined, the first curve (that in Fig. 15.4) rises to a maximum *after* the second one (that in Fig. 15.5). Remember that a point more to the right in the graphs represents a later time. The relationship between the position of the curve and the time-zero is known as the '*phase*' of the disturbance and the angle between the two positions of the vectors which generate the curves is called the '*phase difference*' between them.

A vector which is rotated at a constant angular velocity to generate a sinusoidal graph by the projection method described above is known as a '*phasor*'. Note that the length of the phasor must be the peak value of the quantity concerned.

Use of Phasors in Optics

A transverse wave can be represented by a phasor with a length equal to the amplitude (this is the peak value) and whose position is determined by the '*phase angle*', ϕ. Consider the case of the diffraction of a plane wave incident on a narrow rectangular opening, PQ, of width a as shown in Fig. 15.6 (i). Suppose there are n vibrating sources between P and Q. If any source emits waves in a direction θ to the normal, the path difference between the signals arriving from P and Q at some chosen distant point will be $a \sin \theta$. Now the path difference of λ is equivalent to a phase change of 2π and hence the phase change between P and Q is

$$\frac{2\pi a \sin \theta}{\lambda}.$$

Fig. 15.6 (ii) shows the phasor diagram when

$$\frac{2\pi a \sin \theta}{\lambda} = \frac{\pi}{2} (=90°).$$

The wave from P is represented by OA; the wave from the next source by AB drawn at the phase angle ϕ to the line OA, and so on. The last position at R makes an angle of $\pi/2$ with the line OA. The *resultant* wave, due to all the sources at the chosen point, is represented by the phasor OR.

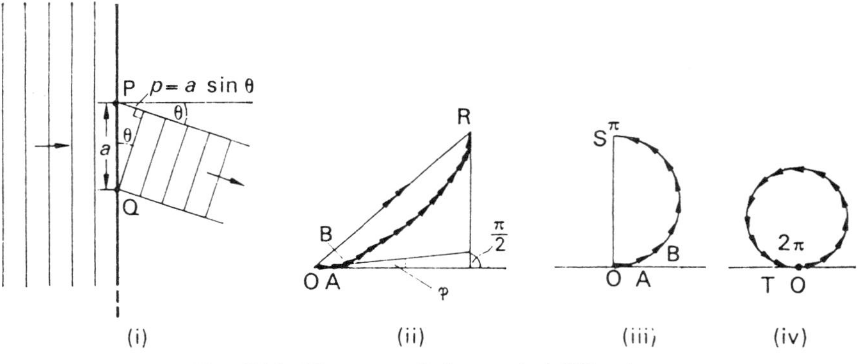

FIG. 15.6 Phasors applied to optical diffraction

Fig. 15.6 (iii) shows the phasor diagram when the phase difference between the first and last elements is $\pi(=180°)$, i.e. when

$$\frac{2\pi a \sin \theta}{\lambda} = \pi.$$

It corresponds to a direction θ greater than before. The resultant is OS. Fig. 15.6 (iv) shows the phasor diagram for the phase difference between the first and last elements of $2\pi(=360°)$.

The last vector just touches O, giving a resultant of zero. This special case corresponds to the edge of the diffraction image of the rectangular opening PQ and in this case

$$\frac{2\pi a \sin\theta}{\lambda} = 2\pi$$

$$\therefore \quad a \sin\theta = \lambda,$$

which is the path difference.

For a full treatment the student should refer to text books of Physical Optics, e.g. 'An Introduction to Physical Optics' by J. K. Robertson.

Use of Phasors in Sound. Plane Progressive Wave Equation

Suppose a simple harmonic *wave* of amplitude a, frequency f and wavelength λ travels in a constant direction Ox with a velocity V. If the displacement at O is given by

$$y = a \sin 2\pi f t,$$

then the variation of y with t can be represented by a phasor of length a and rotating anticlockwise with an angular velocity $2\pi f$.

At a point P distance x to the right of O, the phasor representing the displacement y here will lag behind the phasor for O by a phase angle δ. Since the wave takes a time x/V to reach P from O, the phasor for P is given by

$$y = a \sin 2\pi f\left(t - \frac{x}{V}\right) \quad . \quad . \quad . \quad . \quad (1)$$

This is shown in Fig. 15.7.

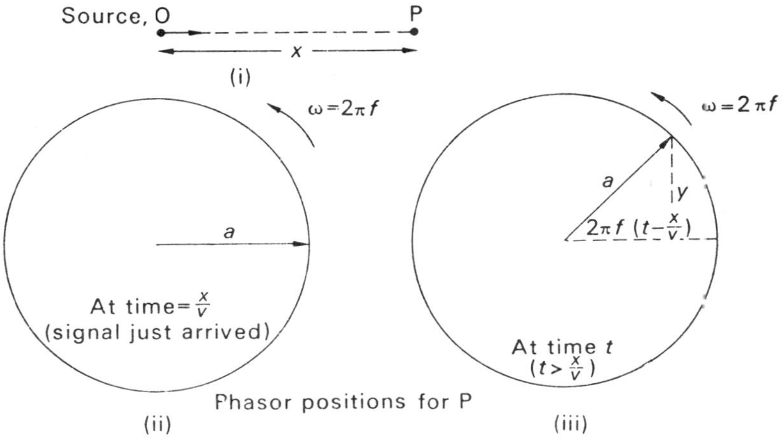

FIG. 15.7 Phasors applied to sound transmission

The expression (1) is sometimes called a 'plane progressive wave equation'. It represents the displacement y at a point distance x from some origin at a time t. Since $f = 1/T = V/\lambda$,

the form of the equation can be changed to

$$y = a \sin \frac{2\pi}{\lambda}(Vt - x). \qquad (2)$$

or to

$$y = a \sin 2\pi \left(\frac{t}{T} - \frac{x}{\lambda}\right) \qquad (3)$$

EXAMPLE

The equation of a plane progressive wave is given by:

$$y = 5 \times 10^{-4} \sin (400\pi t - 4\pi x/5),$$

where y and x are in metre and t is in second. Find (i) the amplitude, (ii) the frequency, (iii) the wavelength, (iv) the velocity, (v) the phase difference between two points on the wave 0.5 m apart.

(i) Amplitude = maximum value of $y = 5 \times 10^{-4}$ m = 0.5 mm.

(ii) By comparison with the equation $y = a \sin 2\pi(t/T - x/\lambda)$, we have

$$\frac{2\pi}{T} = 2\pi f = 400\pi$$

$$\therefore \quad f = 200 \text{ Hz}$$

(iii) Also,

$$\frac{2\pi}{\lambda} = \frac{4\pi}{5}$$

$$\therefore \quad \lambda = 2.5 \text{ m}$$

(iv)

$$\therefore \quad V = f\lambda = 200 \times 2.5 = 500 \text{ m s}^{-1}$$

(v) If two points are separated by a distance x_1, their phase difference δ is given by

$$\delta = \frac{x_1}{\lambda} \times 2\pi \text{ rad}$$

$$= \frac{0.5}{2.5} \times 2\pi = 0.4\pi \text{ rad}$$

Alternatively,

$$\delta = \frac{0.5}{2.5} \times 360° = 72°$$

Stationary Wave Equation

We have seen that a progressive wave which travels in the Ox direction is given by

$$y = a \sin 2\pi \left(\frac{t}{T} - \frac{x}{\lambda}\right). \qquad (1)$$

A wave which travels in the *opposite* direction is obtained by making x *negative*. Thus the equation is

$$y = a \sin 2\pi \left(\frac{t}{T} + \frac{x}{\lambda}\right) \quad . \quad . \quad . \quad . \quad (2)$$

Two waves of equal amplitude and frequency, which travel in opposite directions along a straight line, thus have a *resultant displacement* Y given by

$$Y = a \sin 2\pi \left(\frac{t}{T} - \frac{x}{\lambda}\right) + a \sin 2\pi \left(\frac{t}{T} + \frac{x}{\lambda}\right)$$

$$= 2a \sin 2\pi \frac{t}{T} . \cos 2\pi \frac{x}{\lambda} \qquad \text{(p. 92)}$$

$$= A \sin 2\pi \frac{t}{T}, \quad . \quad . \quad . \quad . \quad . \quad . \quad (3)$$

where $A = 2a \cos 2\pi x/\lambda$.

The *amplitude A* of the resultant wave thus varies with the distance x. At $x = \lambda/4$, $3\lambda/4$, etc., we see that $A = 0$. These points on the wave hence have no displacement. They are called *nodes* of displacement. At $x = 0$, $\lambda/2$, λ, etc., we see that $A = 2a$, $-2a$, $2a$, etc. These points on the wave hence have maximum amplitude of vibration and are called *antinodes* of displacement. See also p. 93.

The wave equation represented by (3) is called a *stationary* or *standing* wave because, in contrast to the plane progressive wave, it does not travel along Ox. Stationary (standing) waves are produced in a variety of physical phenomena.

ALTERNATING CURRENT THEORY

Pure Resistance, R

Suppose an alternating e.m.f.,

$$E = E_0 \sin \omega t,$$

is applied to a pure resistance R. Then, at any instant, the current I is given by

$$I = \frac{E}{R} = \frac{E_0}{R} \sin \omega t$$

$$\therefore \quad I = I_0 \sin \omega t, \quad . \quad . \quad . \quad . \quad . \quad . \quad (1)$$

where $I_0 = E_0/R$. Since the r.m.s. value of current $I = I_0/\sqrt{2}$ and the r.m.s. value of e.m.f. $E = E_0/\sqrt{2}$ (p. 187), it follows from $I_0 = E_0/R$ that

$$I = \frac{E}{R},$$

where I and E are r.m.s. values. Thus if the mains, 240 V (r.m.s.) is connected to a 100 Ω resistor, the current flowing

$$I(\text{r.m.s.}) = 240/100 = 2.4 \text{ A}.$$

From (1), we also note that the current I and the applied e.m.f. E are in phase, since $I = I_0 \sin \omega t$ and $E = E_0 \sin \omega t$. Thus the voltage phasor and the current phasor will coincide as is shown in Fig. 15.8 (i).

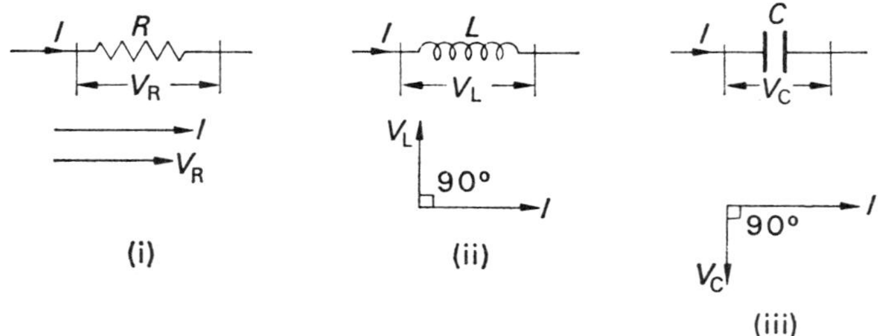

FIG. 15.8 Phasors applied to a.c. circuits

Pure Inductance, L

Suppose an alternating current $I = I_0 \sin \omega t$ flows in a pure inductance L when an alternating e.m.f. is applied. Since there is no resistance to overcome, at any instant the whole of the applied e.m.f. $E =$ the back e.m.f. developed in the inductor. Now the back e.m.f. $= L\,\mathrm{d}I/\mathrm{d}t$. From

$$I = I_0 \sin \omega t,$$

$$\therefore \quad E = \omega L I_0 \cos \omega t$$

$$\therefore \quad E = E_0 \cos \omega t, \qquad (1)$$

where

$$E_0 = \omega L I_0.$$

$$\therefore \quad E_0/\sqrt{2} = \omega L I_0/\sqrt{2}$$

$$\therefore \quad E = \omega L I,$$

where E and I are r.m.s. values. The ratio E/I is called the *reactance* of the coil, symbol X_L. It represents the 'opposition' by the coil to varying flow of current and is measured in ohm. Thus if f is the frequency of the alternating current or e.m.f.,

$$X_L = \omega L = 2\pi f L. \qquad (2)$$

Here X_L is in ohm when L is in henry (H) and frequency in Hz.

From (1),

$$E = E_0 \cos \omega t = E_0 \sin\left(\omega t + \frac{\pi}{2}\right).$$

But $$I = I_0 \sin \omega t.$$

Hence it follows that the e.m.f. (voltage) E across the coil *leads* by 90° on the current I flowing. Thus the voltage phasor will make an angle of 90° with the current phasor as shown in Fig. 15.8 (ii).

Pure Capacitance, *C*

Suppose an alternating e.m.f. $E = E_0 \sin \omega t$ is applied to a pure capacitance C. The charge Q at any instant $= CE = CE_0 \sin \omega t$. Hence the current flowing I is given by

$$I = \frac{dQ}{dt} = \omega C E_0 \cos \omega t$$

$$\therefore \quad I = I_0 \cos \omega t, \qquad (1)$$

where $$I_0 = \omega C E_0$$

$$\therefore \quad I_0/\sqrt{2} = \omega C E_0/\sqrt{2}$$

$$\therefore \quad I = \omega C E,$$

where I and E are r.m.s. values. The ratio E/I is called the *reactance* of the capacitor, symbol X_C. It represents the 'opposition' by the coil to varying current flow and is measured in ohm. Thus, since

$$E/I = 1/\omega C,$$

$$\therefore \quad X_C = \frac{1}{\omega C} = \frac{1}{2\pi f C},$$

where f is the frequency of the applied e.m.f. Here X_C is in ohm when C is in farad and f is in Hz. It follows from the equations for I and E that the voltage phasor makes an angle of 90° with the current phasor but in this case the current leads the voltage (Fig. 15.8 (iii)).

Summary of results for single 'pure' components:

1. Pure R

$$\frac{V_{\text{r.m.s.}}}{I_{\text{r.m.s.}}} = R.$$

Current and voltage in phase.

2. Pure L

$$\frac{V_{\text{r.m.s.}}}{I_{\text{r.m.s.}}} = X_L = 2\pi f L.$$

Current lags voltage by 90°.

3. Pure C

$$\frac{V_{\text{r.m.s.}}}{I_{\text{r.m.s.}}} = X_C = \frac{1}{2\pi f C}.$$

Current leads voltage by 90°.

Series Circuits

If an inductor and a resistor are connected in series, or if an inductor has resistance, there will be, in addition to the inductive voltage, a voltage I_0R across the resistance. This latter voltage is in phase with the current. The phasors representing these two voltages are shown in

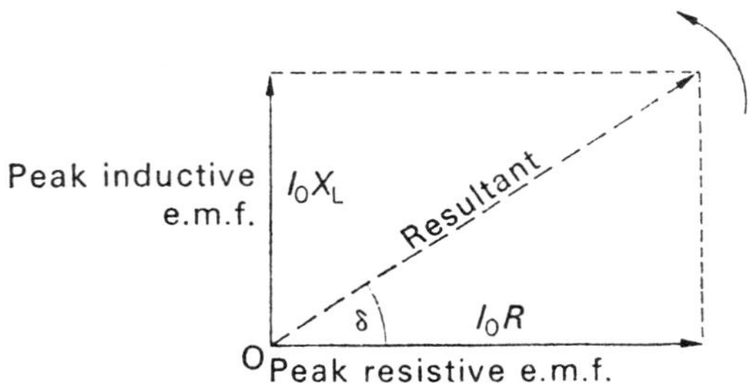

FIG. 15.9 Inductive reactance and resistance—voltage phasor diagram

Fig. 15.9 and from this diagram the resultant phasor can be obtained. Thus the resultant peak voltage V_0 is

$$I_0\sqrt{R^2 + X_L^2}.$$

From $$V_0 = I_0\sqrt{R^2 + X_L^2},$$

we see that $$\frac{V_0}{I_0} = \sqrt{R^2 + X_L^2}.$$

$\sqrt{R^2 + X_C^2}$ is called the *impedance* of the circuit, and is denoted by Z. The graphs for the variation with time of the applied e.m.f. and the current can be obtained by rotating the phasors about O in an anti-clockwise direction. Example 2, p. 264, illustrates this process.

In the case of a C—R series circuit a similar argument holds but the current leads the voltage; the impedance Z is now given by the formula $\sqrt{R^2 + X_C^2}$ (refer to Fig. 15.10). Remember also that the formula for the capacitative reactance, X_C, is

$$X_C = \frac{1}{2\pi f C}.$$

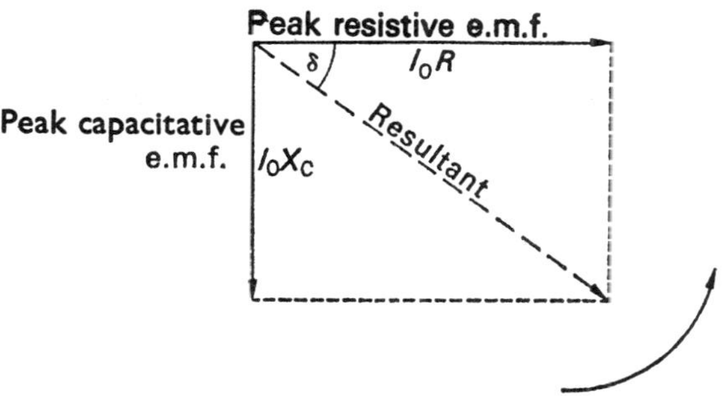

FIG. 15.10 Capacitative reactance and resistance—voltage phasor diagram

If all three types of component are present the phasor diagram becomes as shown in Fig. 15.11 (i), which can be reduced to that shown in Fig. 15.11 (ii). From this it is seen that the resultant voltage is given by

$$V_0 = I_0\sqrt{R^2 + (X_L \sim X_C)^2}$$

and hence the general expression for impedance Z is $\sqrt{R^2 + (X_L \sim X_C)^2}$ This can be used to obtain any impedance, including all the special cases referred to above.

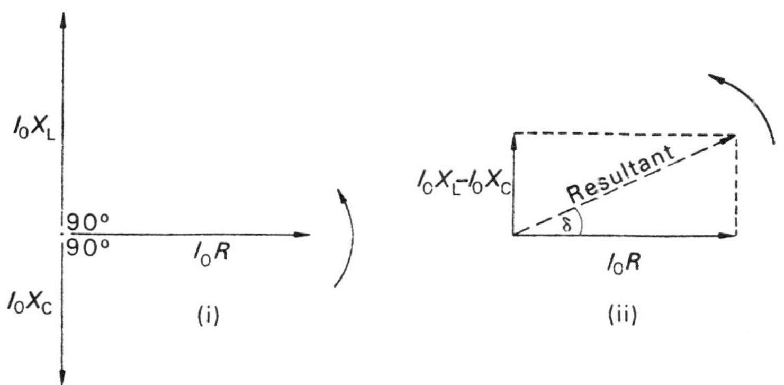

FIG. 15.11 *L-C-R* circuit—voltage phasor diagram

The phase angle between the voltage and the current, δ, is given by $\cos \delta = R/Z$. The voltage will lead if the inductive effect is greater than the capacitative effect (this is a circuit which is said to be 'nett inductive'). If the capacitative effect is the greater, i.e. the circuit is 'nett capacitative', then the current will lead the voltage by the phase angle.

EXAMPLES

1. 2000 Ω and 1 μF are connected in series and a 50 Hz, 100 V (r.m.s.) potential difference applied to the combination. Calculate the r.m.s. value of the current and the phase angle.

The reactance X_C is given by

$$X_C = \frac{1}{2\pi fC} = \frac{1}{2\pi \times 50 \times 1 \times 10^{-6}} = 3200\ \Omega\ \text{(approx.)}$$

$$\therefore \quad Z = \sqrt{X_C{}^2 + R^2} = \sqrt{3200^2 + 2000^2} = 3800\ \Omega\ \text{(approx.)}$$

$$\therefore \quad I = \frac{V}{Z} = \frac{100}{3800} = 0.026\ \text{A (approx.)} = 26\ \text{mA}$$

The phase angle δ between V and I is given by (see Fig. 15.10)

$$\tan\delta = \frac{X_C}{R} = \frac{3200}{2000} = 1.6; \quad \text{so } \delta = 58°.$$

2. An alternating e.m.f. of frequency 50 Hz and r.m.s. value 10 V is applied to a coil which has a resistance of 400 Ω and an inductance of $3/\pi$ H. Using a common axis for time, draw graphs to show how the e.m.f. and the current vary with time during half a cycle.

The inductive reactance is $2\pi fL = 2\pi \times 50 \times \dfrac{3}{\pi} = 300\ \Omega$

Hence the impedance of the coil $= \sqrt{400^2 + 300^2} = 500\ \Omega$

The r.m.s. current $= 10/500 = 0.02$ A

The peak values of e.m.f. and current, obtained by multiplying the r.m.s. values by $\sqrt{2}$, are 14.14 V and 0.028 28 A respectively.

The phase angle, δ, is given by $\cos\delta = \dfrac{400}{500} = 0.8$, hence $\delta = 36°\ 52'$.

The graphs can now be constructed as follows:

Draw the axes, leaving enough space to the left of the vertical axis to allow the circles for rotation of the e.m.f. and the current phasors to be drawn. The circle which represents the current must have radius which represents value 0.028 28 A on a suitable scale, e.g. 1 mm to represent 1 mA, so that the radius is 28.3 mm. The circle for the e.m.f. must have a radius which represents 14.14 V on another suitable scale, e.g. 4 mm to represent 1 V, so that the radius becomes 56.56 mm. The phasor for the current starts at the horizontal position and that for the e.m.f. starts at 36° 52′ to the horizontal and 'advanced' so that the e.m.f. leads the current (a nett inductive circuit). The graphs are then drawn using the methods described above and illustrated in Figs. 15.4 (for the current) and 15.5 (for the e.m.f.). The result is shown in Fig. 15.12. For clarity some of the detail of the construction for the current graph has been omitted.

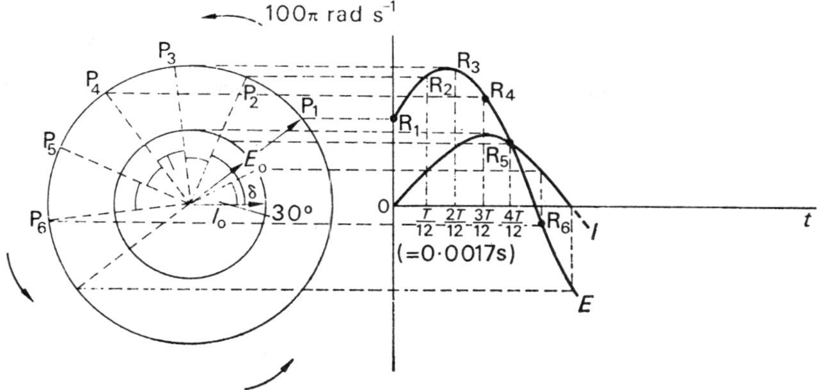

FIG. 15.12 Voltage and current growth for an inductive-resistive circuit

EXERCISES 15

S.H.M.

(1) A mass at the end of a spring vibrates through an amplitude of 2 cm and has a period of 0.1 s. Calculate (i) the frequency of the motion, (ii) the velocity of the mass 1 cm from the centre, O, of oscillation, (iii) the acceleration 1.2 cm from O, (iv) the maximum velocity, (v) the maximum acceleration.

(2) An object oscillates with a frequency of 8 Hz through an amplitude of 3 cm. Calculate (i) the period, (ii) the acceleration 2 cm from the centre of oscillation, (iii) the maximum velocity, (iv) the maximum acceleration.

(3) An object of mass 5 g oscillates with a frequency of 10 Hz through an amplitude of 4 cm. Calculate the kinetic energy of the object (i) at the centre of oscillation, (ii) at a point 3 cm from the centre.

(4) A particle vibrates with s.h.m. along a straight line. Its greatest acceleration is $5\pi^2$ cm s^{-2} and when its distance from the equilibrium position is 4 cm the velocity of the particle is 3π cm s^{-1}. Find the amplitude and period of oscillation of the particle.

(5) The prongs of a tuning-fork, frequency 320 Hz, are vibrating through an amplitude of 0.2 cm. Calculate the velocity and acceleration 0.1 cm from the centre of oscillation.

(6) A mass of 20 g executes s.h.m. with frequency 50 Hz and amplitude 10 mm. Calculate (i) the periodic time, (ii) the maximum velocity (iii) the maximum acceleration, (iv) the velocity when the displacement is 8 mm, (v) the kinetic energy for this displacement, and (vi) the potential energy at that point.

(7) A mass of 10 g executes s.h.m. with frequency 100 Hz and amplitude 13 mm. Calculate (i) the period, (ii) the maximum velocity, (iii) the maximum acceleration, (iv) the velocity when the displacement is 12 mm, (v) the kinetic energy for this displacement (vi) the potential energy at this point.

(8) A small 50 g mass is attached to the free end of a coiled spring of force constant $k = 5\ \text{N m}^{-1}$ on a smooth table (force in spring $= k \times$ extension). The other end of the spring is then fixed and the mass is pulled 10 mm and released.

Prove the motion of the mass is s.h.m. and calculate (i) the frequency of the oscillation, (ii) the maximum kinetic energy of the mass, (iii) the maximum potential energy of the spring, (iv) the kinetic energy when the spring extension is 5 mm, (v) the potential energy of the spring at this instant.

(9) A small mass of 5 g is attached to one end of a coiled spring of force constant k on a smooth table, the other end being fixed. Calculate k if the frequency of oscillation of the mass when pulled and released is 20 Hz.

If the amplitude of the motion is 5 mm, calculate the total energy of the mass and spring during the motion and explain why their total energy is constant.

(10) A particle executes s.h.m. of frequency 100 Hz and amplitude 20 mm. What is the minimum time needed for it to travel from a displacement of 5 mm to one of 10 mm?

(11) A mass of 0.2 kg oscillates with a frequency of $1/\pi$ Hz on a weightless helical spring. The amplitude is 5.0 cm. Calculate: (i) its maximum velocity, (ii) its maximum acceleration, (iii) the potential energy when the acceleration is $0.10\ \text{m s}^{-2}$, (iv) the time taken to move up from 3.0 cm below the mean position to 4.0 cm above it, (v) the velocity at 4.0 cm above the mean position.

(12) A mass of 0.5 kg is executing s.h.m. with amplitude 2.0 cm and a total energy of 100 J. Calculate (i) its maximum velocity, (ii) its periodic time, (iii) its velocity when the displacement is 1.0 cm, and (iv) the force acting on it when at a displacement of 1.0 cm.

(13) A mass of 2 kg executes s.h.m. with amplitude 10 cm and a total energy of 400 J. Calculate (i) its maximum velocity (ii) its period (iii) its velocity when the displacement is 8 cm (iv) the force acting on it at the displacement of 8 cm.

(14) A mass of 100 g undergoes s.h.m. in a field of force where the maximum force applied is 2 N, and the potential energy at this position of maximum force is 0.02 J. From the values given calculate (i) the maximum acceleration, (ii) the amplitude, (iii) the maximum kinetic energy, (iv) the maximum velocity (v) the frequency.

(15) A particle executes s.h.m. of amplitude a. Show that the minimum time taken for the particle to move from displacement a to displacement $a/2$ is twice that to move from $a/2$ to the mean position.

(16) A particle P moves to a point Q, 4 mm away in 0.1 s. What is the speed of P at Q if:
(i) P has constant velocity?
(ii) P starts from rest and has uniform acceleration?
(iii) P is executing s.h.m. with periodic time 1.0 s and is initially at rest?

(17) A particle P moves from O to Q along a linear path in 0.2 s and in so doing acquires a speed of 10 m s^{-1}. Calculate the acceleration of P when it is at Q if (i) P starts from rest and has uniform acceleration, (ii) the relationship between distance OQ ($= x$) and the acceleration of P ($= \ddot{x}$) is $\ddot{x} = -4x$.

Sinusoidal Graphs and A.C. Theory

(18) Plot the following graphs for values of t between 0 and 2 s given that $p = 2$ rad s^{-1} and $a = 10$ cm:
(i) $y = a \sin pt$
(ii) $y = a \cos pt$
(iii) $y = a \sin (pt + \pi/2)$
(iv) $y = a \sin (pt - \pi/4)$.

(19) The 240 V a.c. mains electricity supply in the laboratory is represented by the equation

$$E = E_0 \sin 2\pi ft$$

where E is the voltage at time t,

f is the frequency (= 50 Hz)

and E_0 is the peak voltage (= 340 V).
Plot two cycles of the graph showing E against t.

(20) Using the phasor diagram method, plot two cycles each for the following relationships, marking the time axis in second:
(i) $E = 100 \sin 2\pi ft$, where $f = 2$ Hz,
(ii) $I = 4 \sin 2\pi ft$, where $f = 50$ Hz,
(iii) $E = 10^{-4} \sin 2\pi ft$, where $f = 10^6$ Hz,
(iv) $y = 3 \sin 0.5t$.

(21) Sketch graphs to illustrate (i) a current lagging behind a voltage by 50°, (ii) a current leading a voltage by 50°.

(22) An inductive circuit working at 50 Hz has a peak voltage of 12 V and a peak current of 2 A. The voltage leads the current by 60°. Plot, using a common time axis, graphs of voltage against time and current against time, showing in each case two complete cycles.

(23) In a circuit working at 10 Hz the current leads the voltage by $\frac{1}{20}$ of a cycle. Draw graphs to illustrate this.

(24) Draw graphs for one and a half cycles of the relationships:
(i) $y = 10 \sin (100\pi t - \pi/6)$,
(ii) $E = 340 \sin (100\pi t + \pi/3)$.

(25) Calculate (*a*) the capacitive reactance of a 470 pF (470×10^{-12} F) capacitor, (*b*) the inductive reactance of 10 mH (10×10^{-3} H) inductor when operating at frequencies of (i) 50 Hz, (ii) 1 kHz (10^3 Hz), (iii) 1 MHz (10^6 Hz), (iv) 100 MHz.

(26) A radio transmitting circuit has a coil of inductance $L = 4 \times 10^{-4}$ H and a capacitor C of capacitance 10^{-4} μF. Calculate the frequency of the oscillations obtained when transmitting.

If the coil has a resistance of 0.2 Ω what is the total power in the circuit when the r.m.s. current is 0.5 A?

(27) Approximately what value of inductor would be required to produce resonance at a frequency of 50 MHz when in series with a capacitor of value 10 pF?

(28) If in the preceding question an inductor of value 1 mH were used in error, to what frequency would the combination resonate?

(29) A coil of inductance 5 H and negligible resistance is in series with a 1000 Ω resistance, and an a.c. voltage of 40 V, $f = 100$ Hz, is connected across them. Calculate (i) the current flowing, (ii) the voltage across the coil, (iii) the phase angle between the current and applied voltage.

(30) A capacitor of 0.1 μF is in series with a 20 000 Ω resistor, and an a.c. voltage of 40 V, $f = 50$ Hz, is connected across them. Calculate (i) the current flowing, (ii) the voltage across the capacitor, (iii) the phase angle between the current and applied voltage.

(31) A resistance of 10 Ω and a capacitance of 20 μF are connected in series and a voltage of 10 V and frequency f is applied to the combination. Calculate the current flowing when f is (i) 1 kHz and then (ii) 1 MHz, and draw a sketch showing how the current varies for the range of frequency 1 kHz to 1 MHz.

(32) A coil of inductance 20 μH (2×10^{-5} H) and negligible resistance is in series with a resistance of 10 Ω. A current of 10 mA, $f = 10^6/2\pi$ Hz, flows in the combination. Find (i) the voltage across the coil, (ii) the voltage V across the whole combination (iii) the phase angle between V and the current.

(33) An inductance made of thin wire has an impedance of 150 Ω at 50 Hz. When a 2 V accumulator is connected in series with this coil a current of $\frac{1}{45}$ A flows. The accumulator is disconnected and the coil is connected in series with a capacitor of reactance 187.5 Ω. A sinusoidal p.d. of r.m.s. value 225 V and frequency 50 Hz is applied to the combination. Calculate:

(i) the r.m.s. value of the current
(ii) the peak voltage across the inductor
(iii) the value of the inductor
(iv) the value of the capacitor.

Plot graphs with a common time-axis to show how the voltage and current vary with time.

(34) A resistance of 400 Ω, an inductance of 8 H and a capacitance of 20 μF are connected in series. A sinusoidal e.m.f. of frequency $50/\pi$ Hz and r.m.s. value 250 V is applied to the chain. Calculate the peak current and the phase angle. Hence draw graphs (using a common time axis) showing, for one and a half cycles, how voltage and current vary with time.

(35) Show that, if $\tan\phi = a/b$, then $\sin\phi = a/\sqrt{(a^2 + b^2)}$ and $\cos\phi = b/\sqrt{(a^2 + b^2)}$.

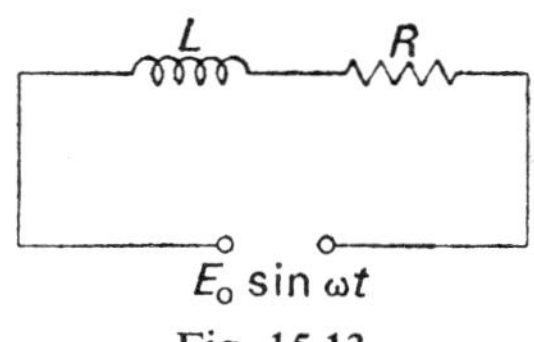

Fig. 15.13

In the circuit in Fig. 15.13, the current I flowing at time t is given by the equation

$$L\frac{dI}{dt} + RI = E_0 \sin \omega t,$$

where $E_0 \sin \omega t$ is the applied alternating voltage. Show by differentiation and substitution that $I = I_0 \sin(\omega t - \phi)$ is a solution of this equation if $\tan\phi = \omega L/R$ and $I_0 = E_0/\sqrt{(\omega^2 L^2 + R^2)}$.

Explain how I_0 and ϕ vary as ω is increased, E_0 remaining constant. (*O.*)

Wave Equation

(36) A wave is represented by $y = 10^{-2}\sin(400\pi t - \pi x)$, where y and x are in metre and t in second. Find (i) the amplitude, (ii) frequency, (iii) wavelength, (iv) velocity, (v) phase difference between two points whose distance apart are (*a*) 0.5 m (*b*) 2.2 m.

(37) The velocity of a plane progressive wave is 1600 m s^{-1}, its frequency is 100 Hz and its amplitude is 10^{-2} m. What is the wave equation?

(38) A plane progressive wave is given by $y = 10^{-3}\sin(100\pi t - 0.2\pi x)$, where y and x are in metre and t in second. Calculate the frequency and velocity of the wave. What is the displacement at a time $t = 1/300$ s where x is (i) 0, (ii) 2.5 m?

(39) A wave is represented by $y = 10^{-2}\sin(300\pi t + 0.1\pi x)$. In which direction does it travel? Calculate its frequency and velocity, and the phase difference between two points 15 m apart (y, x in metre, t in second).

(40) A wave P is represented by $y = 0.1\sin(500\pi t - 0.2\pi x)$. Another wave Q is represented by $y = 0.2\sin 500\pi t \times \cos 0.2\pi x$.

(i) Write down *two* differences between the waves P and Q.

(ii) How is Q obtained from P and another wave? Explain your answer fully.

(iii) Draw sketches of the waves P and Q.

(iv) What are the waves P and Q called, and what is the reason for their names?

Answers

1. (i) 10 Hz (ii) $1.1\ m\ s^{-1}$ (iii) $47.4\ m\ s^{-2}$
   (iv) $1.3\ m\ s^{-1}$ (v) $79\ m\ s^{-2}$

2. (i) 1/8 s (ii) $50.5\ m\ s^{-2}$ (iii) $1.5\ m\ s^{-1}$
   (iv) $75.8\ m\ s^{-2}$

3. (i) 0.016 J (ii) 0.0069 J

4. 5 cm, 2 s

5. $3.5\ m\ s^{-1}$, $4044\ m\ s^{-2}$

6. (i) 0.02 s (ii) $3.1\ m\ s^{-1}$ (iii) $987\ m\ s^{-2}$
   (iv) $1.9\ m\ s^{-1}$ (v) 0.036 J (vi) 0.063 J

7. (i) 0.01 s (ii) $8.2\ m\ s^{-1}$ (iii) $5133\ m\ s^{-2}$
   (iv) $3.1\ m\ s^{-1}$ (v) 0.05 J (vi) 0.28 J

8. (i) 1.6 Hz (ii) 2.5×10^{-4} J (iii) 2.5×10^{-4} J
   (iv) 1.9×10^{-4} J (v) 0.6×10^{-4} J

9. $k = 79\ N\ m^{-1}$, 9.9×10^{-4} J

10. 4.3×10^{-4} s

11. (i) $0.1\ m\ s^{-1}$ (ii) $0.2\ m\ s^{-2}$ (iii) 2.5×10^{-4} J
    (iv) 0.79 s (v) $0.06\ m\ s^{-1}$

12. (i) $20\ m\ s^{-1}$ (ii) 0.006 s (iii) $17.3\ m\ s^{-1}$
    (iv) 5×10^{3} N

13. (i) $20\ m\ s^{-1}$ (ii) 0.03 s (iii) $12\ m\ s^{-1}$
    (iv) 6.4×10^{3} N

14. (i) 20 m s^{-2} (ii) 0.02 m (iii) 0.02 J
(iv) 0.63 m s^{-1} (v) 5.03 Hz

16. (i) 0.04 m s^{-1} (ii) 0.08 m s^{-1} (iii) 0.077 m s^{-1}

17. (i) 50 m s^{-2} (ii) 8.45 m s^{-2}

25. (*a*) (i) $6.8 \times 10^6\ \Omega$ (ii) $3.4 \times 10^5\ \Omega$ (iii) $340\ \Omega$
(iv) $3.4\ \Omega$
(*b*) (i) $3.14\ \Omega$ (ii) $62.8\ \Omega$ (iii) $6.28 \times 10^4\ \Omega$
(iv) $6.28 \times 10^6\ \Omega$

26. 8×10^5 Hz 50 mW 27. About 1 μH 28. 1.6 kHz

29. (i) 12×10^{-3} A (ii) 38 V (iii) 72°

30. (i) 1.1 mA (ii) 34 V (iii) 58°

31. (i) 0.78 A (ii) 1.0 A

32. (i) 0.2 V (ii) 0.22 V (iii) 63.4°

33. (i) 2.0 A (ii) 424 V (iii) 0.38 H
(iv) 16.9 μF

34 0.71 A, 36.9°

36. (i) 10^{-2} m (ii) 200 Hz (iii) 2 m
(iv) 400 m s^{-1} (v) (*a*) $\pi/2$, (*b*) $\pi/5$ rad

37. $y = 10^{-2} \sin (200\pi t - \pi x/8)$

38. 50 Hz, 500 m s^{-1} (i) $+8.66 \times 10^{-3}$ m (ii) -0.5×10^{-3} m

39. $-x$ direction, 150 Hz, 3000 m s^{-1}, $3\pi/2$ rad

40. P = plane progressive, Q = stationary wave

16. Charges in Electric and Magnetic Fields. Electric Circuits

Electric Fields. Electric Intensity

We have seen that an object held above the ground has a certain amount of potential energy, equal to the work done in raising it to the point concerned. The space round the earth is called a *gravitational field* because the pull of the earth is experienced at different points, and the potential at a particular point may be defined as the work per unit mass done in raising a mass from sea-level to that point. Objects move to a lower level when released, and hence they move from points of high potential to points of low potential in the earth's gravitational field.

Similar ideas occur in electricity. The region round metal cylinders carrying static electricity, as in a cathode-ray tube for example, is called an *electric field*, because electrified particles such as electrons experience a force when moving through this region. The *electric intensity*, symbol E, at a point, is defined as the *force per coulomb* at the point concerned (compare 'gravitational intensity', p. 233). Thus E can be expressed in terms of 'newton per coulomb', symbol N C^{-1}. The force F on a test charge Q in a field of intensity E is hence given by

$$F = EQ, \quad . \quad . \quad . \quad . \quad . \quad (1)$$

and F is in newton when E is in newton per coulomb and Q in coulomb. The *direction* of E is taken as the direction which a *positive* charge would move if placed at the point.

An electron has a charge denoted numerically by e which is 1.6×10^{-19} C. In a field of $E = 1000$ N C^{-1}, then, a particle with a charge e has a force F on it given by

$$F = Ee = 1000 \times 1.6 \times 10^{-19} = 1.6 \times 10^{-16} \text{ N}.$$

This is an extremely small force. But the mass m_e of an electron, for example, is only about 9×10^{-31} kg. Hence the acceleration a of the electron in this field would be

$$a = \frac{F}{m_e} = \frac{1.6 \times 10^{-16}}{9 \times 10^{-31}} = 1.8 \times 10^{14} \text{ m s}^{-2}.$$

This enormous acceleration shows that electrons in cathode-ray tubes, and similar devices where a vacuum exists, can be accelerated to very high velocities by electric fields.

Intensity Values

The force F between two point charges Q_1, Q_2 distance r apart in a vacuum or air is given by

$$F = \frac{Q_1 Q_2}{4\pi\varepsilon_0 r^2}, \quad . \quad . \quad . \quad . \quad . \quad (1)$$

where ε_0 = permittivity of a vacuum = 8.854×10^{-12} F m^{-1}.

An approximation for use in (1) is $1/4\pi\varepsilon_0 = 9 \times 10^9$. Then

$$F = 9 \times 10^9 \frac{Q_1 Q_2}{r^2}. \quad . \quad . \quad . \quad . \quad . \quad (2)$$

In (1) or (2), F is in newton (N) when Q_1, Q_2 are in coulomb (C) and r in metre (m).

Point charge. From (1), it follows that the intensity E due to a point charge Q at a point distant r is given by

$$E = Q/4\pi\varepsilon_0 r^2,$$

since E is defined as the force per unit charge at the point.

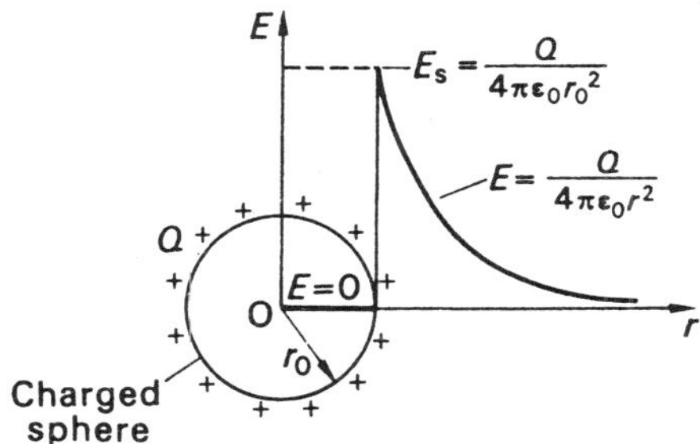

FIG. 16.1 Intensity (E) due to charged sphere

Hollow Sphere. For the intensity *outside* the sphere, we can consider the whole charge concentrated at the centre. Thus at a point distant r from the centre where $r > r_0$, the radius of the sphere,

$$E = Q/4\pi\varepsilon_0 r^2. \quad . \quad . \quad . \quad . \quad . \quad (1)$$

At the surface of the sphere, distance r_0 from the centre, the intensity E_s is given by

$$E_s = \frac{Q}{4\pi\varepsilon_0 r_0^2} \quad . \quad . \quad . \quad . \quad . \quad (2)$$

Inside the sphere, $E = 0$ . . . . . . (3)

Charged Parallel Plates. Between two close plates with equal opposite charges and having the same area, as in a parallel-plate capacitor, the intensity in the middle between the plates is given by

$$E = \frac{\sigma}{\varepsilon_r \varepsilon_0}, \quad . \quad . \quad . \quad . \quad . \quad (4)$$

where σ is the *surface density* or *charge per unit area* (Q/A) on either plate and ε_r is the relative permittivity of the medium between the plates.

Electric Potential. Relation to Intensity

The *electric potential* V at a point in an electric field is defined as the *work done per coulomb* in bringing a small positive charge from infinity (where the force is zero) to the point.

The electric intensity E at a point is the force per coulomb on a positive charge there. If the charge is moved through a small distance δr from one point to another in the direction opposite to E, then it follows that

$$\text{work per coulomb} = E \times (-\delta r)$$
$$= \text{gain in potential, } \delta V.$$

Thus, in the limit,

$$E = -\frac{\mathrm{d}V}{\mathrm{d}r}. \quad . \quad . \quad . \quad . \quad . \quad (1)$$

Thus when a p.d. V is applied to a pair of *parallel plates* distance d apart, the field intensity E between the plates is given by $E = V/d$. The unit of E is '$\mathrm{V\,m^{-1}}$' or '$\mathrm{N\,C^{-1}}$'.

Potential Due to Charged Sphere

Outside a charged sphere, the potential at a point can be considered due to the charge Q concentrated at the centre of the sphere. Consider a point distant r from the centre, where $r > r_0$, the radius of the sphere. Then the potential V is given (see p. 171) by

$$V = \frac{Q}{4\pi\varepsilon_0 r}. \quad . \quad . \quad . \quad . \quad . \quad (1)$$

See Fig. 16.2.

Inside the sphere, the potential V everywhere is constant and equal to the potential at the surface of the sphere. Since the radius is r_0,

$$V = \frac{Q}{4\pi\varepsilon_0 r_0}. \quad . \quad . \quad . \quad . \quad . \quad (2)$$

Fig. 16.2 shows how V varies from the centre of the sphere.

The intensity E can be derived from a potential formula such as (1) or (2). Thus, from (1), outside the sphere

$$E = -dV/dr = Q/4\pi\varepsilon_0 r^2.$$

Inside the sphere, $\quad E = -dV/dr = 0$

since V is constant inside the sphere (see p. 273).

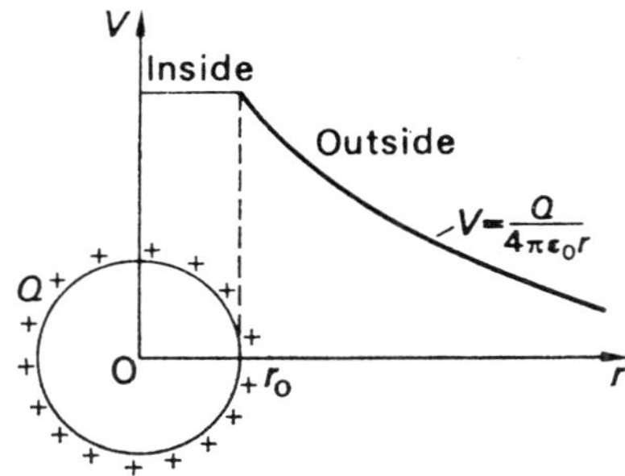

FIG. 16.2 Potential due to charged sphere

Motion of Charges in Electric Fields

(1) *Opposing Forces.* Fig. 16.3 (i) shows a charged oil-drop A between two parallel plates with a p.d. V, as in a Millikan experiment to find the charge on an electron. If A is in equilibrium, then force due to field = weight of drop. Thus

$$Eq = \frac{V}{d}q = mg, \quad . \quad . \quad . \quad . \quad (1)$$

where E = electric intensity = V/d and q is the charge on the oil-drop.

If the plates are both earthed, the drop of radius a falls with a terminal (constant) velocity v. The upward frictional force due to the air viscosity η is then $6\pi\eta av$ from Stokes' law. Since the drop has no acceleration, the resultant force on it is zero.

$$\therefore \quad 6\pi\eta av - mg = 0. \quad . \quad . \quad . \quad . \quad (2)$$

Ignoring the upthrust due to the air, the radius a can be found from equation (2). m can then be found, and by substitution in (1), the charge q can be determined.

(2) *Energy Gained.* Fig. 16.3 (ii) shows an electron, charge e, released from a hot cathode C as in a cathode-ray tube, and accelerated towards a metal A at a high potential $+V$. If the initial velocity of the

electron mass m_e at C is zero and v is the velocity on reaching A, then

$$\text{energy gained in field} = \text{charge} \times \text{p.d.}$$
$$= \text{kinetic energy at A}$$
$$\therefore \quad eV = \tfrac{1}{2}m_e v^2$$
$$\therefore \quad v = \sqrt{2\frac{e}{m_e}V}.$$

For an electron

$$e/m_e = 1.76 \times 10^{11}\ \text{C kg}^{-1}.$$

Thus if

$$V = 500\ \text{V},$$
$$v = \sqrt{2 \times 1.76 \times 10^{11} \times 500}$$
$$= 1.33 \times 10^7\ \text{m s}^{-1}\ \text{(approx.)}.$$

(3) *Field Perpendicular to Velocity.* Fig. 16.3 (iii) shows an electron beam, entering at O with a horizontal velocity v the uniform electric field E between two parallel plates of length l. The beam enters the field

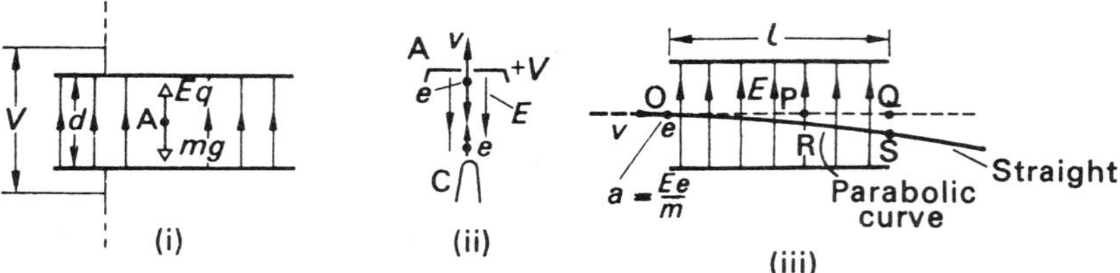

FIG. 16.3 Forces due to Electric Fields

normally to its direction. Thus the horizontal motion of the beam is unaffected by the field. Hence the time t taken to travel a distance OP, or x, $= x/v$.

During this time, an electron in the beam is acted on by a vertical force Ee. The downward acceleration

$$a = \text{force/mass} = Ee/m_e.$$

For motion in this vertical direction, the displacement

$$s = ut + \tfrac{1}{2}at^2 = \tfrac{1}{2}at^2,$$

since there is no downward component of initial velocity.

$$\therefore \quad \text{Vertical deflection at P} = \text{PR} = y = \tfrac{1}{2} \times \frac{Ee}{m_e} \times \frac{x^2}{v^2}$$

$$\therefore \quad y = \left(\frac{Ee}{2m_e v^2}\right)x^2. \qquad (3)$$

This is the equation of a *parabola*. Hence the beam moves in a parabolic arc OR.

To find the deflection QS at the edge of the plates, we put $x = l$ in (3). Thus

$$QS = \frac{Ee}{2m_e v^2} \cdot l^2. \quad . \quad . \quad . \quad . \quad . \quad (4)$$

Charges in Magnetic Fields

Magnetic fields have no effect on charges moving parallel to field direction. If B is the magnetic flux density, q is the magnitude of the charge

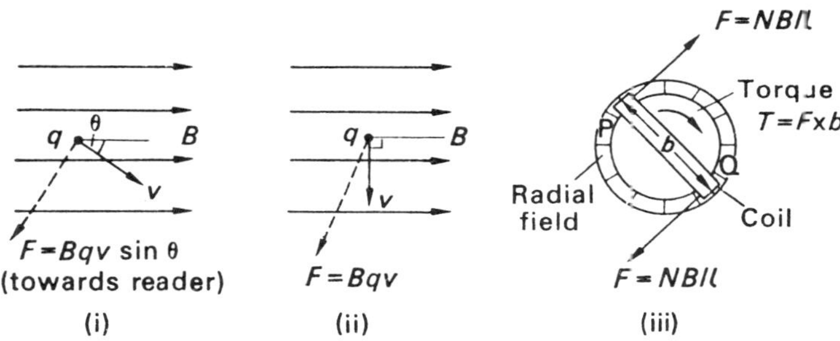

FIG. 16.4 Forces due to Magnetic Fields

and v is its velocity, then if v makes an angle θ with the field B, Fig. 16.4 (i), the force F on the charge, assumed positive, is given by

$$F = Bqv \sin \theta, \quad . \quad . \quad . \quad . \quad (1)$$

since $v \sin \theta$ is the component velocity perpendicular to the field B. If the charge moves normally to the field B as in Fig. 16.4 (ii), the force is a maximum and given by

$$F = Bqv. \quad . \quad . \quad . \quad . \quad . \quad . \quad (2)$$

The *direction* of F is given by Fleming's left-hand rule; the middle finger points in the direction of motion of *positive* charge, the forefinger in the direction of the field B and the thumb in the direction of the force F.

With a current I flowing in a conductor of length l, the formulae in (1) and (2) become

$$F = BIl \sin \theta \quad . \quad . \quad . \quad . \quad . \quad (3)$$

and

$$F = BIl. \quad . \quad . \quad . \quad . \quad . \quad . \quad (4)$$

In a *moving-coil ammeter*, the sides P and Q of a rectangular coil move in a *radial* magnetic field B. Fig. 16.4 (iii) shows a plan view. The force F on the side P $= NBIl$, where N is the number of turns, since the length of wire here is Nl if l is the length of one side. There is an equal force on the other side at Q. Since the two forces always act *normally* to PQ in a radial field, then, if PQ $= b$,

$$\text{torque (moment) of deflecting couple} = NBIl \times b$$
$$= NBIA,$$

where $A = lb =$ area of coil. See also p. 237. It can be shown that the formula is true for circular or irregular shaped narrow coils, where A is the area.

Paths in Combined Magnetic and Electric Fields

1. *B alone.* Consider the case of a horizontal electron beam, entering at P a uniform magnetic field of flux density B normal to its direction. Fig. 16.5 (i). The force F acting on an electron, charge e, is then

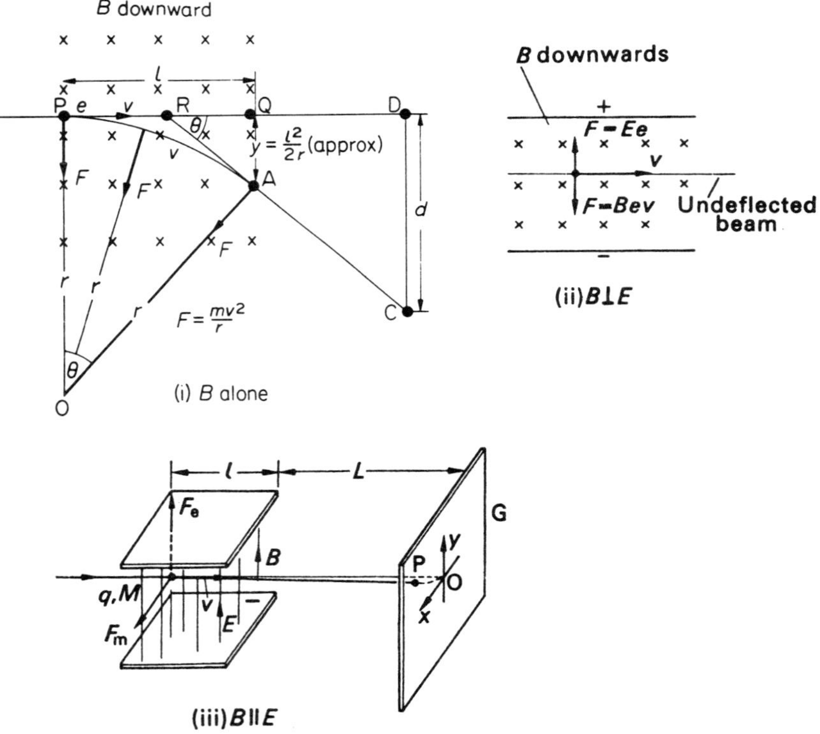

FIG. 16.5 Combined magnetic and electric fields

$F = Bev$. F acts normally to v at all parts of the beam and has a constant value. It is therefore a centripetal force, and the beam is deflected in *a circular* path PA of centre O and radius r. Thus

$$F = Bev = \frac{m_e v^2}{r}$$

$$\therefore \quad r = \frac{m_e v}{Be}. \qquad (1)$$

From (1), it follows that the radius of the circular path is proportional to the *linear momentum*, mv, of the electron.

If the curve PA is shallow, and the deflection of the beam = QA = y, then, to a good approximation, $r = l^2/2y$, by geometry. On leaving the field at A the beam travels in a straight line AC. The deflection DC = d is related to r approximately by

$$\tan\theta = \text{PQ}/r = d/\text{DR},$$

so that

$$r = \frac{\text{PQ} \times \text{DR}}{d}. \qquad (2)$$

Note that since the deflected beam PA in Fig. 16.5 (i) moves normally to the force F, no work is done by F on the electrons. Thus an electron beam gains no energy from a magnetic field in which it travels.

2. *Perpendicular (Crossed) B and E Fields.* In Sir J. J. Thomson's classic experiment on the electron, perpendicular electric and magnetic fields were applied to the beam. The forces Ee and Bev on the charges were then in the same straight line. They were arranged to be opposite in direction, and the magnitude of B was varied until *no deflection* was obtained. Fig. 16.5 (ii). In this case

$$Bev = Ee$$

$$\therefore \quad v = \frac{E}{B}. \qquad (3)$$

Thus the velocity v of the beam can be found. If

$$B = 0.1 \text{ T} \quad \text{and} \quad E = 4 \times 10^5 \text{ V m}^{-1},$$

then

$$v = 4 \times 10^5/0.1 = 4 \times 10^6 \text{ m s}^{-1}.$$

Further, from (1),

$$e/m_e = v/rB.$$

Thus knowing v, B and r (see (2)), the 'specific charge' or 'charge per unit mass' of the electron was calculated.

3. *Parallel B and E Fields.* The first 'mass spectrometer' was designed by Sir J. J. Thomson in his experiment on the positive rays in a gaseous

discharge. These 'rays' are actually *ions*, atoms from which electrons have been stripped, so that they are practically as heavy as the original atoms.

Fig. 16.5 (iii) illustrates the principle of the experiment. The fields E and B are parallel in this case. A beam of positive ions enters with horizontal velocity v midway between two parallel plates of length l, over which the fields B and E are applied. Then if q is the charge on an ion and M its mass;

due to B: acceleration in Ox direction (F_m),

$$a_x = \frac{Bqv}{M} \quad . \quad . \quad . \quad . \quad . \quad (1)$$

due to E: acceleration in Oy direction (F_e),

$$a_y = \frac{Eq}{M}. \quad . \quad . \quad . \quad . \quad . \quad (2)$$

The direction of v is normal to the magnetic force F_m and the electric force F_e. Fig. 16.5 (iii). Hence v is unaffected and the time t to travel a distance l between the plates is $t = l/v$. In this time, the velocity reached in direction Ox

$$= v_x = a_x t = (Bqv/M) \times l/v = Bql/M.$$

The charged particle then travels in a straight line to a photographic plate G at a relatively long distance L from the plates in a time $T = L/v$. Thus, neglecting the small deflection between the plates,

displacement Ox on plate,

$$x = v_x \times T = \frac{BqlL}{Mv} \quad . \quad . \quad . \quad . \quad . \quad (3)$$

Similarly,

displacement Oy on plate,

$$y = v_y \times T = \left(\frac{Eq}{M} \times \frac{l}{v}\right) \times \frac{L}{v}$$

$$= \frac{EqlL}{Mv^2}. \quad . \quad . \quad . \quad . \quad . \quad . \quad (4)$$

Eliminating v from (3) and (4), we obtain

$$x^2 = \frac{B^2 lL}{E}\left(\frac{q}{M}\right) y. \quad . \quad . \quad . \quad . \quad (5)$$

Thus ions of a given charge-mass ratio, q/M, lie on a *parabola* whose equation is given by (5); different points on the parabola correspond to ions with the same charge-mass ratio but different velocities. Using equation (5), Thomson determined the charge-mass ratio q/M of various ions. Further, a sample of pure chlorine or pure neon gas gave several particles. This showed the existence of atoms of the same chemical nature but different masses, which were called *isotopes*.

ELECTRIC CIRCUITS

Energy Formulae

In current electricity, the *energy* used in part of a circuit depends on the potential difference (p.d.) V, the current flowing I and the time t.

As we have seen on p. 2, the 'volt' is the unit of p.d.:

1 *volt is the p.d. between two points if* 1 *joule of work is done in taking* 1 *coulomb from one point to the other*. It can be seen from the definition of the volt that the work done W when a charge of Q coulomb moves between two points at a p.d. of V volt is given by

$$W = QV \text{ joule.} \qquad (1)$$

If a current I ampere flows into an electrical machine for t second, and the p.d. between the terminals is V volt, a quantity of electricity Q given by $Q = It$ coulomb flows between the terminals. Consequently the energy W supplied to the machine $= QV = IVt$ joule.

$$W = IVt. \qquad (2)$$

If the machine is an electric motor, most of the energy supplied is transformed into mechanical energy. If the machine contains a 'passive' resistor, as in the case of an electric cooker or electric fire, *all* the energy supplied is transformed into heat. Suppose R is the resistance of the filament in an electric fire. Then since $V = IR$ in this case, the heat energy = the electric energy

$$= IVt = I^2Rt = V^2t/R. \qquad (3)$$

Thus a current of 2 A flowing through at 20 Ω wire for 1 minute (60 s) produces an amount of heat

$$= 2^2 \times 20 \times 60 = 4800 \text{ J.}$$

Electrical Power

The energy used in a time t by an electrical machine which takes a current I when the p.d. across it is V

$$= IVt$$

$\therefore$ power of working,

$$P = \frac{IVt}{t}$$

$$\therefore \quad P = IV. \qquad (1)$$

In this expression P is in *watts* (W) when I is in amperes and V in volts. By definition, 1 watt = 1 joule per second rate of working.

If the machine converts all the energy into heat, which is the case in electric lamps, cookers and heaters,

$$P = I^2R \quad \text{or} \quad \frac{V^2}{R},$$

since $V = IR$ in this case.

A 60 W–240 V electric lamp filament, when operating, has thus a resistance R given, from

$$P = V^2/R,$$

by

$$60 = \frac{240^2}{R}.$$

$$\therefore \quad R = \frac{240^2}{60} = 960\ \Omega.$$

Electromotive Force

The battery or cell transforms chemical energy to electrical energy. The dynamo transforms mechanical energy to electrical energy. These machines produce at their terminals a potential difference, which is known as the *electromotive force* (e.m.f.), E, when the machine is on 'open circuit', that is, no resistor is connected to the terminals.

If we regard the cell as a source of electrical energy or power, the e.m.f. E can also be defined as the *energy per coulomb* or the *power per unit current* obtained from the cell. From this definition it follows that EI is the power when a current I flows. If a resistance R is connected to the terminals, and the cell has an *internal reistance* r ohm, then the total power in the resistances $= I^2R + I^2r$.

$$\therefore \quad EI = I^2R + I^2r$$

$$\therefore \quad E = IR + Ir$$

$$\therefore \quad E = V + v,$$

where V is the p.d. across R (external p.d.), and v is the p.d. across r (internal p.d.). When R is infinitely high (that is, there is no external resistance), no current flows and so $v = 0$. In this case $E = V =$ the terminal p.d. when the cell is on 'open circuit', as stated above.

EXAMPLE

Six accumulators of internal resistance 0.01 Ω and e.m.f. 1.9 V are charged by a 100 V supply at a current of 2 A. Calculate the series resistance required, the power dissipated as heat, and the percentage power dissipated.

$$\text{Circuit e.m.f.} = 100 - 6 \times 1.9 = 88.6\ \text{V}$$

$$\therefore \quad I = \frac{88.6}{R + 0.06} = 2,$$

where R is the required resistance. Solving,

$$\therefore \quad R = 44.24\ \Omega.$$

The power is dissipated as heat in R and in the accumulators, which together have a total resistance of $44.24 + 0.06$ or $44.3\ \Omega$.

$$\therefore \quad \text{power dissipated} = I^2 \times \text{resistance}$$

$$= 2^2 \times 44.3 = 177.2 \text{ W}$$

Now $\quad$ power supplied = power supplied by mains = IE

$$= 2 \times 100 = 200 \text{ W}$$

$$\therefore \quad \text{percentage dissipated} = \frac{177.2}{200} = 89\% \text{ (approx.)}.$$

Electromagnetic Induction. Lenz's Law

When a magnet is moved towards a coil connected to a galvanometer, an induced current is observed. The Principle of the Conservation of Energy can be used to deduce a general law concerning the direction of the induced current.

Suppose the N-pole of a magnet is pushed towards the face of a coil connected to a galvanometer G (Fig. 16.6 (i)). If the induced current flows in a clockwise direction, an attractive force is exerted on the magnet, which then moves forward faster. The increased speed produces a greater induced current, since the current is proportional to the speed, and hence a still greater force of attraction is exerted on the magnet. It can now be seen that the kinetic energy of the magnet continues to increase, and, at the same time, the electrical energy in the coil continues to increase. No work is done or energy expended on the magnet, however, and hence the growth of energy is contrary to the Principle of the Conservation of Energy. Consequently the current must flow *anticlockwise*, not clockwise as originally assumed.

Lenz's law states that 'the induced current flows in such a direction as to *oppose* the motion or change'. In this case work has always to be expended on the magnet to overcome the repulsive force due to the current, and the energy re-appears as electrical energy in the coil.

Induced Current Direction in Straight Wire

If a wire AB is perpendicular to a magnetic field B, and is moved steadily downwards in a direction perpendicular to B and to its length, an induced current is set up in AB assuming its ends are joined (Fig. 16.6 (ii)). A *motor force* F_1 then acts on AB. From the Law of Action and Reaction F_1 acts upwards, in opposition to the downward force F. From Fleming's left-hand motor rule for F_1, the induced current (and e.m.f.) must act from B to A. A *right*-hand rule can be applied to deduce the induced current and e.m.f. direction, the thumb of the right hand pointing in the direction of motion and the middle finger in the direction of the induced e.m.f.

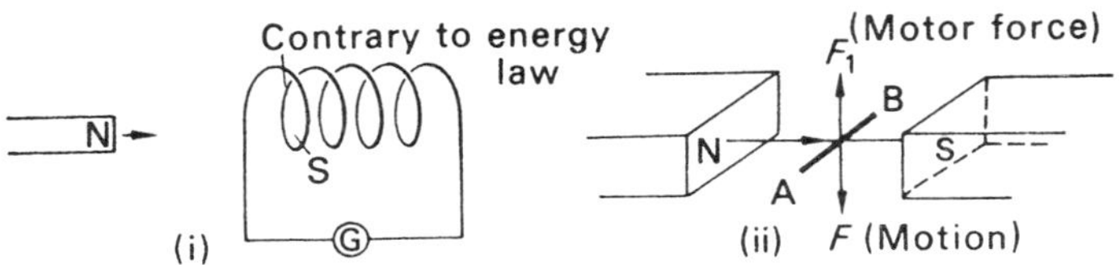

FIG. 16.6 Lenz's law and conservation of energy

Magnitude of Induced E.M.F.

The magnitude of the motor force F_1 on the wire AB is given by

$$F_1 = BIl, \quad . \quad . \quad . \quad . \quad . \quad (1)$$

where I is the induced current in ampere, B is the flux density of the field in tesla, and l is the length of the conductor in metre.

This expression follows from the definition of the magnitude of B as the size of the force per unit current per unit length on a wire held perpendicularly to the magnetic field. If the whole of the mechanical energy supplied is expended in overcoming the motor force, the total electrical energy W produced is given, from the Principle of the Conservation of Energy, by

$$W = F_1 x = BIlx,$$

where x is the distance moved by the wire in a time t. Now $x = vt$, where v is the downward uniform velocity of the wire AC.

$$\therefore \quad W = BIlvt = Blv \times It.$$

But It = quantity Q of charge produced in the circuit in this time.

$$\therefore \quad \frac{W}{Q} = Blv.$$

Since W/Q is the 'total energy per coulomb' produced by the moving wire, it follows from the definition of e.m.f. that the e.m.f. E generated is given by

$$E = Blv.$$

Thus Blv = the p.d. between the ends of the moving wire AB in Fig. 16.6 (ii).

The moving wire is regarded as a *generator* of electricity and not as a resistor. Its ends A and B are the 'poles' of the generator. A is at a higher potential than B since current would flow round the *external* circuit from A to B if, for example, the ends were joined by a wire.

EXERCISES 16

(Where necessary, assume $e = 1.6 \times 10^{-19}$ C, $e/m_e = 1.76 \times 10^{11}$ C kg^{-1}.)

Charged Particles in Fields

(1) An electron is in a field of electric intensity 2×10^6 N C^{-1}. Calculate the force on the electron.

(2) A charge of magnitude 2e is between two parallel plates which have a p.d. of 6000 V and are 20 mm apart. Calculate the force on the charge.

(3) A beam of ions with a velocity of 1.5×10^6 m s^{-1} enters a uniform magnetic field of $B = 0.1$ T which is everywhere normal to the direction of the beam. Find the radius of the path of the beam if the charge-mass ratio q/M for the ions $= 5.0 \times 10^8$ C kg^{-1}.

(4) The radius of the path of a beam of ions is 50 mm when passing through a uniform magnetic field of $B = 0.4$ T normal to the beam. Calculate the ratio q/M for the ions if the beam has a velocity of 7×10^5 m s^{-1}.

(5) Two horizontal metal plates in air are 20 mm apart and a p.d. of 12 000 V is connected across them. An oil-drop carrying a charge of 3e is in equilibrium between the plates. Calculate the mass of the oil-drop.

(6) An electron is accelerated from rest through a potential difference of 900 V. Calculate the velocity reached by the electron.

(7) A beam of ions moves in a circular orbit round a magnetic field of 0.5 T with a speed of 10^6 m s^{-1}. If the charge per unit mass of the ion is 4.0×10^7 C kg^{-1}, find the radius of the orbit.

(8) A beam of ions move in a circular orbit about a magnetic field of 0.1 T. If the ions describe 2×10^4 orbits per second, calculate their charge-mass ratio.

(9) (*a*) An electron is accelerated from rest through a potential difference of 5 kV. Calculate the velocity it acquires.

(*b*) An electron with a velocity of 10^6 m s^{-1} enters a region of uniform magnetic field of 10^{-4} T perpendicular to its direction of motion. Explain the trajectory of the electron and calculate the angle through which it is deviated by the magnetic field if it emerges again after 2×10^{-8} s.

(*c*) Explain with a diagram what must be the strength and direction of an electric field which, when superimposed on the magnetic field, will just counteract its deflecting effect, so that the electron passes through undeviated. (Take e/m to be 1.8×10^{11} C kg^{-1}.) (*O.*)

(10) Define *coefficient of viscosity*, and derive its dimensions from the definition.

A charged oil drop is prevented from falling under gravity by the vertical electric field between two horizontal metal plates charged to a potential difference of 5400 V, the distance between the plates being 15 mm. When the field is cut off the drop falls, and when travelling at constant velocity it is observed to move through 4.36 mm in 10.0 s. Taking $g = 9.81$ m s^{-2}, calculate (*a*) the radius of the drop, (*b*) the charge on the drop.

If an approximate value of 10 m s^{-2} had been taken for g and there was a 1% error in the value of the coefficient of viscosity, what percentage error would have been introduced in the calculated value of (i) the radius of the drop, (ii) the charge on it? Explain your reasoning.

(Take the density of oil to be 0.90×10^3 kg m^{-3} and the coefficient of viscosity of air to be 1.8×10^{-5} kg m^{-1} s^{-1}.) (*O.*)

Circuits

(11) Calculate (i) the filament resistance of a 60 W–240 V lamp when operating normally, (ii) the energy used in 10 min.

(12) Six dry cells, each of e.m.f. 1.5 V and internal resistance 1 Ω, are connected in series to a 9 Ω resistor. Calculate the power wasted in the cells.

(13) Resistances of 6 and 12 Ω are connected in parallel and their junctions joined to a battery of e.m.f. 12 V and internal resistance 2 Ω. Calculate the quantities of heat generated per second in the two resistances.

(14) A battery of e.m.f. 12 V and internal resistance 6 Ω is connected to a variable resistance R. Show, by calculus or otherwise, that the maximum power is developed in R when its value is 6 Ω.

(15) The current in a radio component is inversely proportional to the cube of the p.d. applied. When the p.d. is 100 V, the power dissipated is 40 W. Calculate the power dissipated when the p.d. rises to 400 V.

(16) A radio resistor of 1000 Ω can dissipate a maximum power of $\frac{1}{2}$ W. Calculate the maximum current it should carry.

(17) A narrow rectangular coil of 10 turns, length 5 cm, and width 1 cm is situated in the radial field of magnitude 0.6 T of a moving-coil meter. The field is perpendicular to the length of the coil. When a current of 8 A flows through the coil, calculate (i) the force on one side of the coil, (ii) the torque (moment of couple) on the coil.

(18) A horizontal conductor 0.8 m long is held (i) normal, (ii) at 30° to a uniform horizontal field of 0.5 T.

Calculate the induced e.m.f. in each case when the conductor moves vertically downwards through the field at a velocity of 10 m s^{-1}.

(19) Calculate the induced e.m.f. in a straight conductor of length 20 cm on the armature of a dynamo and 10 cm from the axis, if the conductor moves in a radial field of 0.50 T and the armature rotates at 1200 rev min^{-1}.

(20) A uniform magnetic field of strength 2×10^{-2} T makes an angle of 60° with the axis of a metal disc which is being rotated at 1800 r.p.m. by a motor.

Calculate the e.m.f. between a point on the rim of the wheel and a point on its hub if their diameters are 64 cm and 4 cm respectively.

If these two points are now connected to an external circuit (of low resistance) a current of 10 A flows in it. By how much will the power of the motor have to be increased if the angular velocity of the wheel is to be unchanged? (*O.*)

(21) Ten accumulators in series, each of which can be taken to have a constant e.m.f. of 2.0 V and negligible internal resistance, are charged at 5.0 A from a 50 V d.c. supply. Find (i) the value of the series resistor which must be included in the circuit, (ii) the energy taken from the supply in one hour, (iii) the useful energy put into the accumulators in one hour.

Account for the difference between your answers to (ii) and (iii). (*O.*)

Harder Examples

(22) An electron gun operates at an accelerating voltage of 1140 V and the electron beam enters the space between a pair of equal deflecting plates along the line parallel to and equidistant from the plates. A potential difference of 80 V is applied to the plates, which are 16 mm apart and 5.0 cm long. Calculate (i) the speed of the electrons as they enter the field, (ii) the time taken by an electron to traverse the field, (iii) the force acting on an electron, (iv) the acceleration caused by this force, (v) the deflection produced by passage between the plates, (vi) the emergent speed of the electrons, (vii) the deflection which would be observed in a plane perpendicular to the initial beam and 7.5 cm from the end of the plates, and (viii) the magnetic flux density which must be superposed on the electrostatic field in order to restore the beam to its undeflected path.

(23) A pair of horizontal plates 8.0 cm long and 4.0 cm apart have a p.d. of 100 V applied to them. Electrons travelling initially at 10^7 m s^{-1} enter the space midway between the plates and along a line parallel to them. Calculate the vertical displacement of the beam as it passes through the plates and the total displacement which has occurred when the beam is 16.0 cm beyond the end of the plates. What is the speed at which the electrons emerge?

(24) An electron travelling at 4×10^6 m s^{-1} enters a uniform field between a pair of equal parallel plates 20 mm apart, so that the initial direction of the velocity is along a line which is parallel to the plates and 5.0 mm from the upper plate. The latter is at a potential of +100 V whilst the lower plate is earthed. What is the maximum length of the plates if the electron is not to collide with one of them?

What voltage would have to be applied to the *lower* plate if the electron is to be deviated in the opposite direction and still just escape, assuming that the +100 V is still applied to the upper plate?

Answers

1. 3.2×10^{-13} N

2. 9.6×10^{-14} N

3. 3×10^{-2} m

4. 3.5×10^{7} C kg^{-1}

5. 2.88×10^{-14} kg

6. 1.8×10^{7} m s^{-1}

7. 0.05 m

8. 1.26×10^{6} C kg^{-1}

9. (*a*) 4.2×10^{7} m s^{-1}, (*b*) 0.36 rad, (*c*) 100 V m^{-1}

10. (*a*) 2×10^{-6} m, (*b*) 8.2×10^{-19} C, (i) 1.5%, (ii) 3%

11. (i) 960 Ω, (ii) 36 000 J

12. 2.16 W

13. $10\frac{2}{3}$, $5\frac{1}{3}$ W

15. 2.5 W

16. 2.2×10^{-3} A

17. (i) 2.4 N (ii) 0.024 N m

18. (i) 4 V (ii) 2 V

19. 1.26 V

20. 9.6×10^{-2} V, 0.96 W

21. (i) 6 Ω (ii) 9×10^{5} J (iii) 3.6×10^{5} J

22. (i) 2.0×10^{7} m s^{-1} (ii) 2.5×10^{-9} s
(iii) 8.0×10^{-16} N (iv) 8.8×10^{14} m s^{-2}
(v) 2.74 mm (vi) 2.01×10^{7} m s^{-1}
(vii) 11 mm (viii) 2.5×10^{-4} T

23. 14 mm, 70 mm, 1.06×10^{7} m s^{-1}

24. 13.5 mm, +400 V

17. Statistics and Probability

STATISTICS

Statistics is the scientific study of numbers. It is used, for example, to assess measurements in science and industry and the trends in insurance and in sales. In this chapter only an introduction to the subject is provided.

Variable and Frequency. Cumulative Frequency

We begin with an illustration of the meaning of some of the common terms used in statistics.

Consider the heights of 24 pupils in a class, correct to the nearest centimetre and arranged in numerical order from 167 cm to 173 cm in Table 1, p. 290. Column A shows the different heights, which is a *variable* x. The sum of the variable $= x_1 + x_2 + \ldots + x_7$, and is denoted by Σx; this greek symbol, representing the total or 'sum', is 'sigma'.

Column B shows that 4 pupils have a height of 168 cm and that 7 pupils have a height of 169 cm. The number of pupils corresponding to a particular height is called the *frequency*, f, of that height. The sum of the frequencies, Σf, is 24, the total number of pupils.

Column C shows the running total as the number of pupils is added, this is called the *cumulative frequency*, Column D shows the total heights of the 1, 4, 7, etc. . . . pupils, or the sum of the products fx. This sum is 4072 cm and is denoted by Σfx.

Mean, Mode, Median

The *mean* height of all the pupils is the arithmetic mean. It is obtained by adding all the heights and dividing by the total number, 24. Thus

$$\text{mean} = \frac{\Sigma fx}{\Sigma f} = \frac{4072}{24} = 169\tfrac{2}{3} = 170 \text{ cm (nearest cm).}$$

TABLE 1

A		B		C		D
Height	Variable x	No. of Pupils	Frequency f	Running Total	Cumulative Frequency (CF)	Total Heights (fx)
167 cm	x_1	1	f_1	1	f_1	167
168	x_2	4	f_2	5	$f_1 + f_2$	672
169	x_3	7	f_3	12	$f_1 + f_2 + f_3$	1183
170	x_4	6	f_4	18	—	1020
171	x_5	3	f_5	21	—	513
172	x_6	2	f_6	23	—	344
173	x_7	1	f_7	24	Σf	173
	Σx	24	Σf			$\Sigma fx = 4072$

The *mode* is the most common height, or the height which occurs most frequently. In this case it is 169 cm, as it occurs 7 times.

The *median* is the height corresponding to the 'middle' pupil. Since the number of pupils vary from 1 to 24, the middle $= (1 + 24)/2 = 12\frac{1}{2}$. In practice there is no '$12\frac{1}{2}$'th pupil, and in any case we do not know

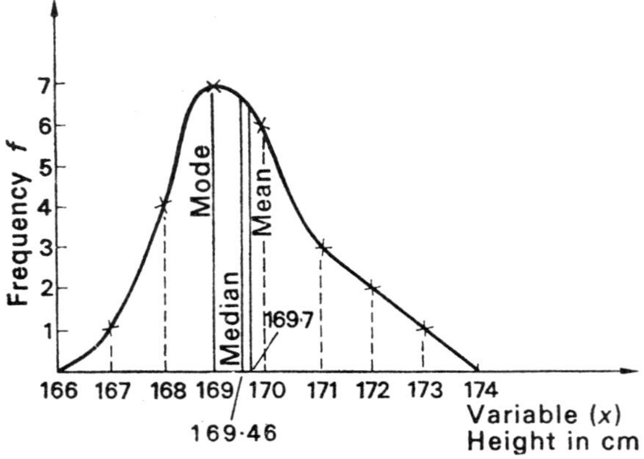

FIG. 17.1 Frequency curve

how their exact heights vary in the range 169 to 170 cm. So there is no exact median but we can estimate it. From the table, the pupil corresponding to $12\frac{1}{2}$ has a height between 169 and 170 cm, the height being nearer to 169 cm than 170 cm from the running total column.

The results obtained can be represented in the graph showing the variation of the frequency with height, or *frequency curve*. Fig. 17.1.

With a perfectly symmetrical curve, the mode, mean and median values coincide. As illustrated in Fig. 17.2, particularly when only a few cases are considered, the frequency curve may have several modes.

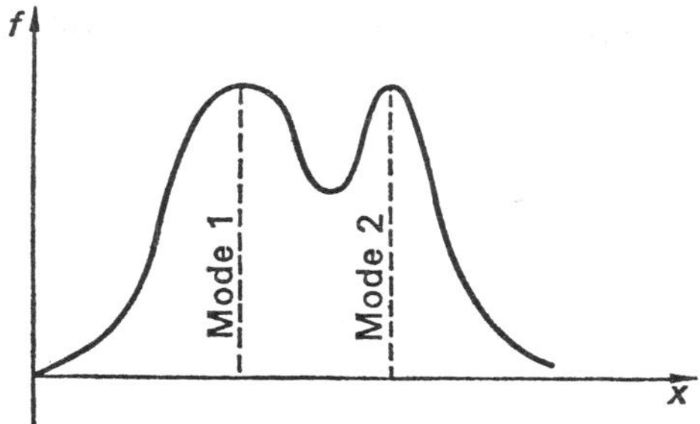

FIG. 17.2 Several modes

Continuous Distributions

A *discrete* distribution is one in which the variable x can take only values belonging to a discrete set. For example, the number of atoms decaying in equal intervals of time is a discrete variable since it must take integer values. A *continuous* distribution, on the other hand, is one in which the variable x can take every value in the range considered.

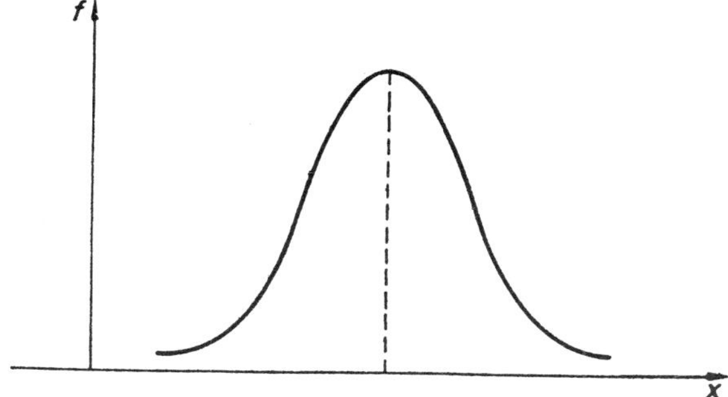

FIG. 17.3 Frequency distribution curve

The total frequency can thus be infinitely large. Fig. 17.3 illustrates a continuous distribution. This is the kind of curve obtained when a graph is plotted of the number of molecules (f) in a mass of gas against the velocity of the molecules in a given small range (x). The number of molecules in a mole of gas is about 6×10^{23}, an enormously large number. The discrete case may approximate to a continuous curve.

Cumulative Frequency Curve

From Table 1, the cumulative frequency (CF), or running total, can be plotted against the corresponding height x, Fig. 17.4. This is the cumulative-frequency curve or *ogive*. The number of pupils in the class below a particular height can be read from the curve.

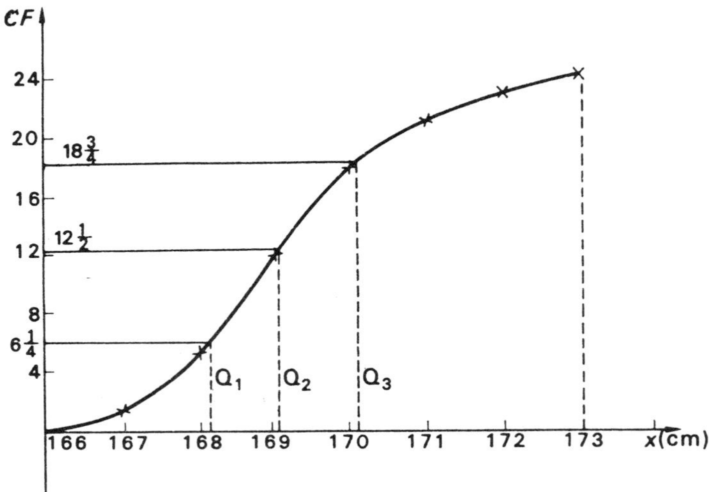

FIG. 17.4 Cumulative-frequency curve

Quartiles, Deciles, Percentiles

As already stated, the median is the height of the 'middle' pupil, that is, the total frequency has been divided into two equal parts.

When the total frequency is divided into four equal parts, the values of the variable at each of the frequencies are called *quartiles*. Fig. 17.5 shows the quartiles for the distribution of heights of boys we have considered. Since there are 24 boys, the median or second quartile Q_2 corresponds to $(1 + 24)/2$ or $12\frac{1}{2}$th boy; the first or lower quartile Q_1 to the $(1 + 24)/4$ or $6\frac{1}{4}$th boy; and the third or upper quartile Q_3 to the $\frac{3}{4}(1 + 24)$ or $18\frac{3}{4}$th boy. Fig. 17.5.

When the total frequency is divided into 10 equal parts we have *deciles*. If it is divided into 100 equal parts we have *percentiles*.

The exact values of quartiles cannot be calculated in this case. They can be estimated from Fig. 17.5, or from Fig. 17.1, p. 290. Fig. 17.5 shows that Q_1 (first quartile) lies in the range 168–169 cm, being closer to 168 cm, Q_2 is the median (169–170 cm), and Q_3 lies between 170 and 171 cm, being nearer to 170 cm. The quartiles are shown also in Fig. 17.4.

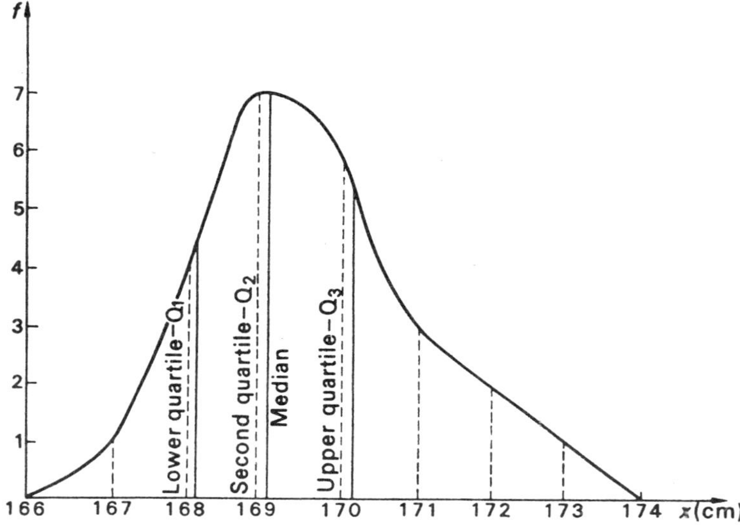

FIG. 17.5 Quartiles

Calculation of Mean by Differences

Consider the marks obtained by 30 pupils in a test for which the maximum mark is 20, as shown in Table 2, p. 294. As before, the mean can be found by adding all the marks and dividing by 30. This gives a value

$$= [8(4) + 9(5) + 10(6) + 11(7) + 12(4) + 13(3) + 14(1)]/30$$
$$= 10.5.$$

With a large number of variables, and large numbers, this calculation can be laborious. It is much easier to work from an 'estimated mean' mark. This is illustrated in Table 2. Suppose we take 10 as an estimated mean mark. First, we find the *differences* between the various marks x and the estimated mean α. As shown, these differences may be positive or negative. The differences are then all added and the average found by dividing by 30. The actual mean is then obtained by adding the average of the differences to the estimated mean. Thus

$$\text{mean} = \alpha + \frac{\Sigma f(x - \alpha)}{30} = 10 + \frac{15}{30} = 10.5.$$

This result is in agreement with the mean calculated previously.

TABLE 2

Mark	variable x	Frequency, f	Variation (estimated mean $\alpha = 10$)	$f(x - \alpha)$
8	x_1	4	$x_1 - \alpha = -2$	-8
9	x_2	5	$x_2 - \alpha = -1$	-5
10	x_3	6	$x_3 - \alpha = 0$	0
11	x_4	7	$x_4 - \alpha = 1$	7
12	x_5	4	$x_5 - \alpha = 2$	8
13	x_6	3	$x_6 - \alpha = 3$	9
14	x_7	1	$x_7 - \alpha = 4$	4

$\Sigma f(x - \alpha) = +15$

Variance and Standard Deviation

Often, the mean value of a quantity provides insufficient information about it. As an example, consider the case of a machine designed to cut steel rod into lengths of 2 m. Of course, the lengths cut are not exactly 2 m. Some may be longer and some shorter. The calculated mean should be 2 m but this would not provide any information about the accuracy of the machine. We need some measure of the *spread* of the lengths of rods.

The spread could be measured from, say, the quartile values. This is found to be insensitive to large deviations and therefore not useful. The following method, involving the *squares of differences (deviations) from the mean* $\bar{x}$, is generally adopted on theoretical grounds. It is illustrated in Table 3, which refers to values in Table 2.

TABLE 3

Mark (x)	$x - 10.5$	f	$f(x - 10.5)$	$f(x - 10.5)^2$
8	-2.5	4	-10	$+25$
9	-1.5	5	-7.5	$+11.25$
10	-0.5	6	-3.0	$+1.5$
11	$+0.5$	7	$+3.5$	$+1.75$
12	$+1.5$	4	$+6.0$	$+9.0$
13	$+2.5$	3	$+7.5$	$+18.75$
14	$+3.5$	1	$+3.5$	$+12.25$

$\Sigma f = 30$ $\Sigma f(x - 10.5)^2 = 79.5$

(1) Calculate the actual mean $\bar{x}$ of the variable x. In Table 3 the mean is 10.5.

(2) Calculate the differences, $x - \bar{x}$, for all values of x, as shown in column 2.

(3) Multiply the squares of the differences by their frequencies, f, as shown in column 5, obtained by multiplying column 4 by column 2.

(4) Calculate the mean of all these values by dividing their total by the sum of the frequencies, 30. This gives the mean of the squares of the differences or deviations, which is called the *variance*. We shall denote the variance by σ^2. The *standard deviation* is σ. Thus

$$\sigma^2 = \frac{\Sigma[f(x - \bar{x})^2]}{\Sigma f}.$$

From column 5 in Table 3,

$$\Sigma[f(x - \bar{x})^2] = 79.5.$$

Since $\Sigma f = 30,$

then $$\sigma = \sqrt{\frac{79.5}{30}} = 1.6 \text{ (approx.).}$$

The standard deviation σ is a measure of the 'spread' of the variable. With a continuous distribution from zero to infinity (see Fig. 17.3), it can be shown that about 68% of the values lie between $(\bar{x} + \sigma)$ and $(\bar{x} - \sigma)$ and that about 95% lie between $(\bar{x} + 2\sigma)$ and $(\bar{x} - 2\sigma)$. The standard deviation thus provides useful information when large samples of variables are taken, for example, in examinations where large numbers of students are concerned or in opinion polls throughout the country.

Standard Deviation Using Estimated Mean

Using differences from an estimated mean, as on p. 294, the calculation of the standard deviation can be made more quickly. It is shown shortly that

$$\sigma^2 = \frac{\Sigma f(x - \alpha)^2}{\Sigma f} - (\bar{x} - \alpha)^2, \qquad (1)$$

where x is the variable, α is an estimated mean, and $\bar{x}$ is the actual mean.

Table 4 shows how the formula is applied in calculating σ, using the marks in Table 3 and taking $\alpha = 10$. From the result obtained by adding column 5,

$$\Sigma f(x - \alpha)^2 = 87.$$

Hence from the formula in (1),

$$\sigma^2 = \frac{87}{30} - (10.5 - 10)^2 = 2.65$$

$$\therefore \quad \sigma = \sqrt{2.65} = 1.6 \text{ (approx),}$$

in agreement with our previous result above.

TABLE 4

$\alpha = 10, \quad \bar{x} = 10.5$

x	f	$x - \alpha$	$f(x - \alpha)$	$f(x - \alpha)^2$
8	4	−2	−8	16
9	5	−1	−5	5
10	6	0	0	0
11	7	1	7	7
12	4	2	8	16
13	3	3	9	27
14	1	4	4	16

$\Sigma f(x - \alpha)^2 = 87$

Proof of Standard Deviation Formula

1. $$\sigma^2 = \frac{\Sigma f(x - \bar{x})^2}{\Sigma f} = \frac{\Sigma fx^2 - \Sigma 2fx\bar{x} + \Sigma f\bar{x}^2}{\Sigma f}$$

$$= \frac{\Sigma fx^2}{\Sigma f} - 2\bar{x}\frac{\Sigma fx}{\Sigma f} + \frac{\bar{x}^2\Sigma f}{\Sigma f}$$

$$= \frac{\Sigma fx^2}{\Sigma f} - 2\bar{x}^2 + \bar{x}^2$$

$$= \frac{\Sigma fx^2}{\Sigma f} - \bar{x}^2 \quad . \quad . \quad . \quad . \quad . \quad . \quad . \quad . \quad . \quad \text{(i)}$$

2. In (i), $\bar{x}$ is an exact mean. If we take α to be an estimated mean, then

$$\frac{\Sigma f(x - \alpha)^2}{\Sigma f} = \frac{\Sigma fx^2}{\Sigma f} - 2\frac{\Sigma fx\alpha}{\Sigma f} + \frac{\Sigma f\alpha^2}{\Sigma f}$$

$$= \frac{\Sigma fx^2}{\Sigma f} - 2\alpha\frac{\Sigma fx}{\Sigma f} + \alpha^2\frac{\Sigma f}{\Sigma f}$$

$$= \frac{\Sigma fx^2}{\Sigma f} - 2\alpha\bar{x} + \alpha^2$$

$$\therefore \quad \frac{\Sigma fx^2}{\Sigma f} = \frac{\Sigma f(x - \alpha)^2}{\Sigma f} + 2\alpha\bar{x} - \alpha^2$$

From (i), $$\therefore \quad \sigma^2 = \frac{\Sigma f(x - \alpha)^2}{\Sigma f} - \bar{x}^2 + 2\alpha\bar{x} - \alpha^2$$

$$= \frac{\Sigma f(x - \alpha)^2}{\Sigma f} - (\bar{x} - \alpha)^2 \quad . \quad . \quad . \quad \text{(ii)}$$

Correlation

Correlation is a measure of the degree to which two quantities, x and y, vary with each other. If x and y are closely associated, we say they have a *high degree of correlation.* If only slightly associated they are said to have a low degree of correlation.

As an illustration, in a class studying two languages such as French and German, the same pupils will tend to be good at both or poor at both. The marks obtained in the two subjects thus have a good correlation. This can be represented on a graph, Fig. 17.6.

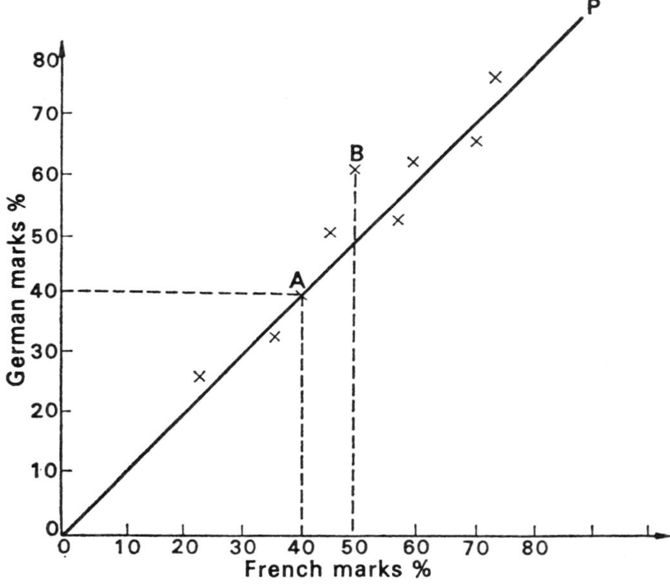

FIG. 17.6 Correlation

The point A shows that a pupil had 40% in both French and German. Point B shows that another had 50% in French and 60% in German. Most of the points are near a line OP. This is a feature of high correlation. The line OP is called the *line of regression*; it is a line which lies most evenly among the points plotted.

Some quantities will have perfect correlation. The relation between inches and centimetres, for example, is a straight line OA passing through the origin, since x in $= 2.54 \times x$ cm (1 in = 2.54 cm). This is shown in Fig. 17.7. When the physical conditions such as temperature are kept constant for a given metal such as copper, then the current I is directly proportional to the applied potential difference V (Ohm's law). This is another example of perfect correlation.

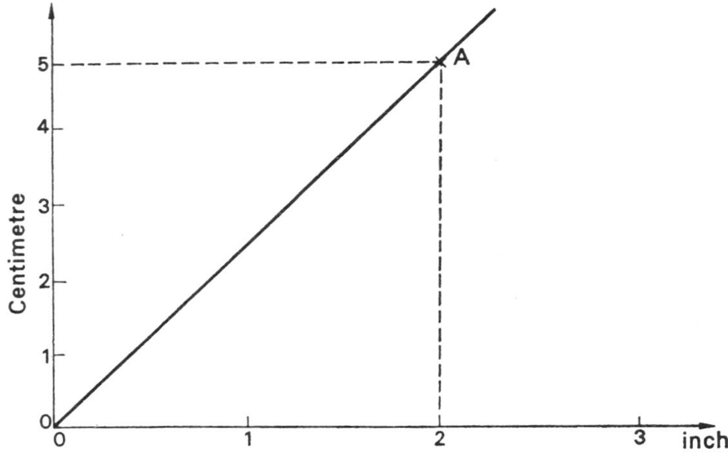

FIG. 17.7 Perfect correlation

Coefficient of Correlation

If we have two variables x and y, their correlation is measured by the *coefficient of correlation* (r). If there are n pairs of values of x and y, then, by definition,

$$r = \frac{p}{\sigma_1 \sigma_2},$$

where σ_1 and σ_2 are the respective standard deviations for x and y, and p is the *product-moment* or *covariance* of x and y defined by the relation

$$p = \frac{\Sigma(x - \bar{x})(y - \bar{y})}{n}.$$

The calculation for the coefficient of correlation r is illustrated in the following example. Suppose the marks of 6 pupils in French are denoted by x and in German by y.

x: 45, 48, 52, 55, 65, 65
y: 50, 45, 47, 68, 61, 47.

Here $n = 6$, and the respective means $\bar{x}$ and $\bar{y}$ are given by

$$\bar{x} = \frac{45 + 48 + 52 + 55 + 65 + 65}{6} = 55$$

$$\bar{y} = \frac{50 + 45 + 47 + 68 + 61 + 47}{6} = 53.$$

TABLE 5

	$x - \bar{x}$	$y - \bar{y}$	$(x - \bar{x})^2$	$(y - \bar{y})^2$	$(x - \bar{x})(y - \bar{y})$
A	− 10	− 3	100	9	+ 30
B	− 7	− 8	49	64	+ 56
C	− 3	− 6	9	36	+ 18
D	0	15	0	225	0
E	10	8	100	64	+ 80
F	10	− 6	100	36	− 60
			358	434	124

The product-moments $= (x - \bar{x})(y - \bar{y})$ and their values are calculated in column 5 of Table 5. The squares of the deviations are calculated in columns 3 and 4. Then, for the marks of the six pupils,

$$\text{coefficient of correlation } r = \frac{124}{\sqrt{358 \times 434}} = 0.3 \text{ (approx.).}$$

The correlation is thus low. If $r = 0.9$ say, the correlation is good.

Linear Relation and Perfect Correlation

Consider the set of numbers for the two variables x and y in the table below. The mean values are $\bar{x} = 4$ and $\bar{y} = 16$.

x	2	3	5	6
y	8	12	20	24
$x - \bar{x}$	−2	−1	1	2
$y - \bar{y}$	−8	−4	4	8
$(x - \bar{x})(y - \bar{y})$	16	4	4	16

From the table,

$$\Sigma(x - \bar{x})(y - \bar{y}) = 40,$$

$$\sigma_x = \sqrt{4 + 1 + 1 + 4} = \sqrt{10}$$

$$\sigma_y = \sqrt{64 + 16 + 16 + 64} = \sqrt{160}$$

$$\therefore \quad r = \frac{\Sigma(x - \bar{x})(y - \bar{y})}{\sigma_x \sigma_y} = \frac{40}{\sqrt{10 \times 160}} = 1.$$

This is perfect correlation. The result is due to the fact that the four numbers in the table satisfy the linear relationship $y = 4x$.

Rank Correlation

With many large numbers, the calculation required in Table 5 becomes tedious even with a calculator, and another measure of correlation is therefore used. This is called the *coefficient of rank correlation* or *rank coefficient.*

In calculating the rank coefficient R, each of the variables is first put in order of rank. The orders are then used to calculate R according to the relation

$$R = 1 - \frac{6\Sigma d^2}{n(n^2 - 1)},$$

where d is the difference in the ranks and n is the total number of pairs of the variables, x and y say.

The calculation for R can be illustrated by re-arranging the marks x and y in Table 5 in order of rank. Table 6 shows the results for the orders in columns 3 and 4 and the rank difference d. The value of d^2 is always positive.

TABLE 6

	x	y	x rank	y rank	rank difference d	d^2
A	45	50	6	3	3	9
B	48	45	5	6	−1	1
C	52	47	4	4	0	0
D	55	68	3	1	2	4
E	65	61	1	2	−1	1
F	65	47	1	4	−3	9

Since $n = 6$ and $\Sigma d^2 = 24$,

$$\therefore \quad R = 1 - \frac{6 \times 24}{6(36 - 1)} = 0.3 \text{ (approx.)}.$$

The rank correlation is thus a good approximation to the actual correlation r, which was calculated as 0.3 from Table 6.

PROBABILITY

Before discussing *Probability* it would be useful to summarize some of the numerical quantities and terms encountered in the subject.

Factorials. The product $5 \times 4 \times 3 \times 2 \times 1$ is written as 5! and read as 'factorial 5'. Thus

$$n! = n \times (n - 1) \times \ldots \times 3 \times 2 \times 1.$$

0! is defined as 1. This fits the pattern $2! = 2 \times 1!$ and $1! = 1 \times 0!$

Permutations (or *arrangements*)

The number of permutations of n objects is defined as the total number of ways in which they can all be arranged in order in a line.

As an example, suppose there are 3 objects, A, B and C. Then the number of permutations of all three are

ABC, ACB, BCA, BAC, CAB, CBA.

Thus there are 6 permutations of 3 objects.

If there are n objects, then there are n ways of choosing the first object, $(n - 1)$ ways of choosing the next object, and so on down to 3, 2 and 1. Thus the total number of permutations of n objects

$$= n \times (n - 1) \times \ldots \times 3 \times 2 \times 1 = n!$$

This result is usually written ${}_nP_n = n!$

The total number of permutations of r objects from n objects,

$${}_nP_r = n \times (n - 1) \times \ldots \times (n - \overline{r - 1}) = n!/(n - r)!$$

Combinations (or *selections*)

The number of combinations of r objects from a group of n objects is defined as the total number of ways of selecting r objects regardless of their order.

For example, suppose we select 2 objects, regardless of order, from the 4 objects A, B, C and D. Then the number of combinations or selections are AB, AC, AD, BC, BD, CD.

Thus there are 6 combinations. The number of combinations of 2 objects from 4 is written ${}_4C_2$. Thus ${}_4C_2 = 6$.

If r objects are selected from n objects regardless of order, this is ${}_nC_r$. But the r objects can be arranged *in order* in $r!$ ways, and the total number of arrangements is then ${}_nP_r$.

$$\therefore \quad {}_nC_r \times r! = {}_nP_r = n!/(n - r)!$$

$$\therefore \quad {}_nC_r = \frac{n!}{(n - r)!r!}.$$

Thus $${}_4C_2 = \frac{4!}{2!2!} = \frac{4 \times 3 \times 2 \times 1}{2 \times 1 \times 2 \times 1} = 6.$$

Binomial Theorem. The product

$$(x + a_1)(x + a_2) \dots (x + a_n)$$
$$= x^n + x^{n-1}(a_1 + a_2 + \dots + a_n)$$
$$+ x^{n-2}(a_1a_2 + a_2a_3 + \dots) + \dots + a_1a_2 \dots a_n.$$

If we put

$$a_1 = a_2 = \dots = a_n = a,$$

then it follows that

$$(x + a)^n = x^n + {}_nC_1x^{n-1}a + {}_nC_2x^{n-2}a^2 + \dots + {}_nC_nxa^n,$$

since $(a_1 + a_2 + \dots + a_n)$ is the number of ways of selecting any one of n things, $(a_1a_2 + a_2a_3 + \dots)$ is the number of ways of selecting any two of n things, and so on. See also p. 158.

Statistical Populations. Relative Frequency

Probability is a subject which deals with expected results. These are based on figures or values which are *samples* of the population of measurements or other attribute under investigation. In later discussions we shall draw a distinction between *discrete* numbers, that is, finite numbers, of values and an infinite number of values, leading to a continuous function. This difference can be seen most easily by means of graphs.

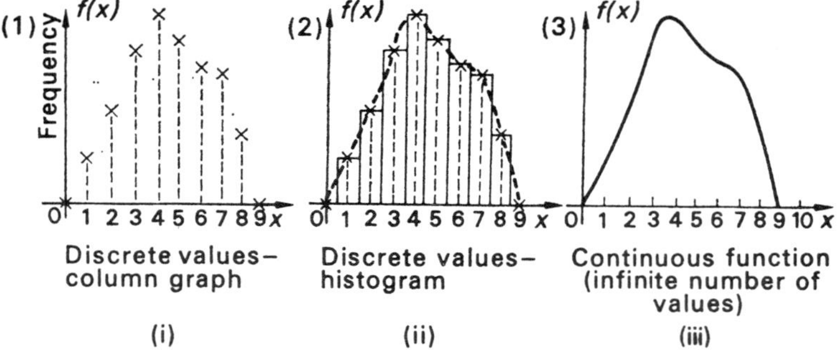

FIG. 17.8 (i) Column graph, (ii) Histogram (iii) Continuous function

Fig. 17.8 (i) shows discrete values of a variable x in a *column graph.* Fig. 17.8 (ii) shows a *histogram* of the same values. This is obtained by drawing rectangles through the points on the column graph and the midpoints of the variable x. By joining up the points with a smooth curve as shown, we obtain an approximation to the values of the function $f(x)$ for any value of x. The areas of the rectangles are proportional to the frequency values as the bases have equal lengths.

Fig. 17.8 (iii) assumes that we have an infinite number of values of the function $f(x)$ for varying values of x. In this case the function is *continuous* and all the values lie on a smooth curve. Note that a continuous function can be treated as the limiting case of a histogram when the interval between the variables is infinitesimally small.

In science we usually have discrete values but in the case of very large numbers a continuous function can be applied to the statistics. This is the case in the kinetic theory of gases, where a very large number of molecules is involved.

Relative Frequency. Mean Value

Suppose discrete values $x_1, x_2, \ldots x_n$ are taken as a sample of the population. The general term is x_1, and if its frequency is denoted by f_1, then the size N of the population is given by

$$N = \sum_{1=1}^{n} f_1.$$

The mean value m of the sample is given by

$$m = \frac{1}{N} \sum_{1=1}^{n} x_1 f_1.$$

The *relative frequency* q_1 is defined as a fraction or percentage by

$$q_1 = \frac{f_1}{N}.$$

Thus if $f_1 = 4$ and $N = 100$, $q_1 = 4/100 = 0.04 = 4\%$. We see that

$$\sum_{1=1}^{n} q_1 = \frac{\sum_{1}^{n} f_1}{N} = \frac{N}{N} = 1 = 100\%.$$

Also, the mean value m is given by

$$m = \frac{1}{N} \sum_{1}^{n} x_1 f_1 = \Sigma x_1 \frac{f_1}{N} = \Sigma x_1 q_1.$$

EXAMPLE

1. A pair of dice is rolled 100 times and the number of sixes recorded. There are 3 double sixes, 24 single sixes, and 73 throws with no six. Calculate the relative frequencies and the mean number of sixes.

No. of sixes (x_i)	Relative Frequencies q_i	$x_i q_i$
$x_1 = 0$	$q_1 = 73/100 = 0.73$	$x_1 q_1 = 0$
$x_2 = 1$	$q_2 = 24/100 = 0.24$	$x_2 q_2 = 0.24$
$x_3 = 2$	$q_3 = 3/100 = 0.03$	$x_3 q_3 = 0.06$

$$\Sigma q_i = 1.00 \qquad \Sigma x_i q_i = 0.30$$

$$\therefore \text{ mean, } m = \Sigma x_i q_i = 0.30.$$

Expected or Probable Values

If the dice in Example 1 are perfectly balanced, we should expect each die to give 1 six in 6 throws. In practice this will not happen for a small number of throws. For a large number of throws we expect roughly $\frac{1}{6}$th to be sixes; the larger the number of throws, the closer is the fraction to $\frac{1}{6}$.

The fraction $\frac{1}{6}$ is called the *probability* of throwing a six. The probability that a six is not thrown is $\frac{5}{6}$. Note that $\frac{1}{6} + \frac{5}{6} = 1$, that is, the total probability is 1.

Example 1 can be arranged as a 'probability' model in the form of a table as follows:

No. of sixes	*Probability*
0	$\frac{5}{6} \times \frac{5}{6} = \frac{25}{36}$
1	$(\frac{1}{6} \times \frac{5}{6}) + (\frac{5}{6} \times \frac{1}{6}) = \frac{10}{36}$
2	$\frac{1}{6} \times \frac{1}{6} = \frac{1}{36}$

Total probability $= \frac{25}{36} + \frac{10}{36} + \frac{1}{36} = 1$

The calculations in the probability column are made in the following way. For *no six* on die A say, the probability is $\frac{5}{6}$; for each throw of A the probability of not throwing a six with die B is $\frac{5}{6}$. Hence the total probability $= (\frac{5}{6}) \times (\frac{5}{6}) = \frac{25}{36}$.

For *one six* on die A, the probability is $\frac{1}{6}$; for no six on B, the probability is $\frac{5}{6}$. Hence the total probability $= (\frac{1}{6}) \times (\frac{5}{6}) = \frac{5}{36}$. Similarly, for no six on A and one six on B, the probability $= (\frac{5}{6}) \times (\frac{1}{6}) = \frac{5}{36}$. Hence the net probability $= 2 \times (\frac{1}{6}) \times (\frac{5}{6}) = \frac{10}{36}$.

The last case excludes the probability of throwing *two sixes*. The latter probability $= (\frac{1}{6}) \times (\frac{1}{6}) = \frac{1}{36}$.

The *mean probability* μ is the expected result from an infinite number of throws. We see that

$$\mu = \sum_1^3 x_i p_i = (0 \times \tfrac{25}{36}) + (1 \times \tfrac{10}{36}) + (2 \times \tfrac{1}{36})$$
$$= \tfrac{12}{36} = \tfrac{1}{3} = 0.33.$$

This value is reasonably near, but not exactly equal, to the value obtained in Example 1 for a finite number of throws.

Variance in Populations

For a finite number of values in a sample of a population, it follows from p. 295 that the variance s^2, and the standard deviation s, are given by

$$s^2 = \frac{1}{N}\sum_{i=1}^{n} (x_i - m)^2 f_i,$$

where m is the mean value and f_i is the frequency. Using the relative frequency q_i, this formula can be written as

$$s^2 = \sum_{i=1}^{n} (x_i - m)^2 \frac{f_i}{N}$$
$$= \sum_{i=1}^{n} (x_i - m)^2 q_i.$$

Thus if σ^2 is the variance for an *infinite* number of observations of mean value μ, and p_i is the relative frequency,

$$\sigma^2 = \sum_{i=1}^{n} (x_i - \mu)^2 p_i.$$

EXAMPLE

Compare the standard deviation s for the sample of throws described in Example 1 with the standard deviation σ expected for an infinite number of observations.

For the finite sample, p. 304,

$$s^2 = \sum_{i=1}^{3} (x_i - m)^2 q_i$$
$$= (0 - 0.3)^2 \times 0.73 + (1 - 0.3)^2 \times 0.24 + (2 - 0.3)^2 \times 0.03$$
$$= 0.27$$

For an infinite sample (probability model), $\mu = \frac{1}{3}$ and the probabilities p_i are respectively $\frac{25}{36}$, $\frac{10}{36}$ and $\frac{1}{36}$, as shown on p. 304.

$$\therefore \quad \sigma^2 = \sum_{i=1}^{3} (x_i - \mu) p_i$$
$$= (0 - \tfrac{1}{3})^2 \times \tfrac{25}{36} + (1 - \tfrac{1}{3})^2 \times \tfrac{10}{36} + (2 - \tfrac{1}{3})^2 \times \tfrac{1}{36}$$
$$= \tfrac{5}{18} = 0.2778$$

From $s^2 = 0.27$, we have $s = 0.5196$. From $\sigma^2 = 0.2778$, we have $\sigma = 0.5271$. As we take more throws of the dice, we expect s to approach σ in value.

Alternative Calculation

In examples of this kind the calculation may become unwieldy. We can simplify the working by using the relation, proved on p. 296, that

$$s^2 = \frac{1}{N}\sum_{i=1}^{n}(x_i - m)^2 f_i = \frac{1}{N}\Sigma x_i^2 f_i - m^2.$$

Thus $$s^2 = \Sigma(x_i - m)^2 q_i = \Sigma x_i^2 q_i - m^2. \qquad \text{(i)}$$

Likewise, for the probability model,

$$\sigma^2 = \Sigma x_i^2 p_i - \mu^2. \qquad \text{(ii)}$$

Using the relations (i) and (ii) for the same example as above, we proceed as follows.

Finite sample

x_i	q_i	$x_i q_i$	$x_i^2 q_i$
0	0.73	0	0
1	0.24	0.24	0.24
2	0.03	0.06	0.12

Hence, from (i),

$$s^2 = 0.36 - (0.3)^2 = 0.36 - 0.09 = 0.27$$

Infinite sample (Probability model)

x_i	p_i	$x_i p_i$	$x_i^2 p_i$
0	25/36	0	0
1	10/36	10/36	10/36
2	1/36	2/36	4/36
	1	$\mu = \frac{12}{36} = \frac{1}{3}$	14/36

Hence, from (ii),

$$\sigma^2 = \tfrac{14}{36} - (\tfrac{1}{3})^2 = \tfrac{10}{36} = \tfrac{5}{18} = 0.2778$$

Expected Values of Functions

These concepts of probability can be extended to cases where expected values can be calculated. As illustrations, consider the following example.

EXAMPLE

A gambler rolls two dice. He loses £2 if he fails to throw a six, wins £3 if he throws one six and wins £20 if he throws two sixes. Is the game fair?

No. of sixes	*Winnings* (w_i)	*Probability* (p_i)	*Expectation* ($p_i w_i$)
0	−£2	25/36	−50/36
1	+£3	10/36	+30/36
2	+£20	1/36	+20/36

Thus total expectation = $-£2 \times \frac{25}{36} + £3 \times \frac{10}{36} + £20 \times \frac{1}{36} = 0$.
Hence the game is fair in the long run.

Probability Generating Functions

Suppose A and B are the only two possible results for a particular event, for example, in a birth A will be male say and B female. In general, if a is the probability of A and b that of B, then $a + b = 1$. If a_1, b_1 and a_2, b_2 respectively are the probabilities of A and B in two different cases, a table of probabilities can be arranged as follows for the outcome:

Outcome		*Probability*
1st case	2nd case	
A	A	$a_1 \times a_2$
A	B	$a_1 \times b_2$
B	A	$b_1 \times a_2$
B	B	$b_1 \times b_2$

Thus if A is regarded as success in an event and B as failure, then

No. of successes	*Probability*
0	$b_1 b_2$
1	$a_1 b_2 + a_2 b_1$
2	$a_1 a_2$

We now see that these probabilities are the same as the coefficients of t in the function G given by

$$G = (b_1 + a_1 t)(b_2 + a_2 t)$$

$$= b_1 b_2 + (a_1 b_2 + a_2 b_1)t + a_1 a_2 t^2.$$

If the probabilities a_1, a_2 and b_1, b_2 remain the *same* for each event, then, with $a_1 = a_2 = a$ and $b_1 = b_2 = b$, we have

$$G = (b + at)^2 = b^2 t^0 + 2bat^1 + a^2 t^2.$$

Thus the coefficients of t^0, t^1 and t^2 are the respective probabilities of no success, 1 success and 2 successes. Proceeding to higher powers, then

$$G = (b + at)^n = b^n + {}_nC_1 b^{n-1} at + {}_nC_2 b^{n-2} a^2 t^2 + \ldots\ldots$$

The probability of i successes is the same as the coefficient of t^i in the binomial expansion. Thus if

$$G = \Sigma p_r t^r = p_0 + p_1 t + p_2 t^2 + \ldots,$$

then p_r will be the probability of obtaining a 'score' of r successes.

Calculation of Mean and Variance

Since $G(t) = \Sigma p_r t^r$, we can differentiate with respect to t to obtain the mean value μ. Thus

$$\frac{\mathrm{d}G(t)}{\mathrm{d}t} = \Sigma r p_r t^{r-1}.$$

Putting $t = 1$,

$$\therefore \quad \frac{\mathrm{d}G(1)}{\mathrm{d}t} = \Sigma r p_r = \mu. \quad \ldots \quad (1)$$

To find the variance σ^2, we can differentiate again. Then

$$\frac{\mathrm{d}^2G(t)}{\mathrm{d}t^2} = \Sigma r(r-1)p_r t^{r-2}.$$

Putting $t = 1$,

$$\therefore \quad \frac{\mathrm{d}^2G(1)}{\mathrm{d}t^2} = \Sigma r(r-1)p_r = \Sigma r^2 p_r - \Sigma r p_r$$

$$= \sigma^2 + \mu^2 - \mu. \quad \ldots \quad (2)$$

Using the binomial probability function, we have

$$G(t) = (b + at)^n$$

$$\therefore \quad \frac{\mathrm{d}G(t)}{\mathrm{d}t} = G'(t) = na(b + at)^{n-1}.$$

$$\therefore \quad G'(1) = na(b + a)^{n-1}.$$

Also,
$$\frac{\mathrm{d}^2G(t)}{\mathrm{d}t^2} = G''(t) = n(n-1)a^2(b + at)^{n-2}$$

$$\therefore \quad G''(1) = n(n-1)a^2(b + a)^{n-2}.$$

Now $b + a = 1$, or $a = 1 - b$. Hence, from (1),

$$\mu = G'(1) = na(b + a)^{n-1} = na. \quad \ldots \quad (3)$$

From (2),
$$n(n-1)a^2 = \sigma^2 + n^2a^2 - na$$

$$\therefore \quad \sigma^2 = na(1 - a) = nab. \quad \ldots \quad (4)$$

EXAMPLE

Apply these results to the dice-rolling situation in Example 1, p. 304.

Here
$$G(t) = \tfrac{25}{36} + \tfrac{10}{36}t + \tfrac{1}{36}t^2$$

$$= \tfrac{1}{36}(5 + t)^2$$

$$\therefore \quad \mu = G'(1) = \tfrac{1}{18}(5 + 1) = \tfrac{1}{3}, \text{ from (1)}$$

and
$$\sigma^2 = \tfrac{1}{18} + \tfrac{1}{3} - (\tfrac{1}{3})^2 = \tfrac{5}{18}, \text{ from (2).}$$

These results agree with the values found previously on p. 305.

Probability Distribution Function

Consider a quantity x which is not limited to discrete values but can vary continuously. Fig. 17.9 shows one form of variation of x, which we may call $f(x)$.

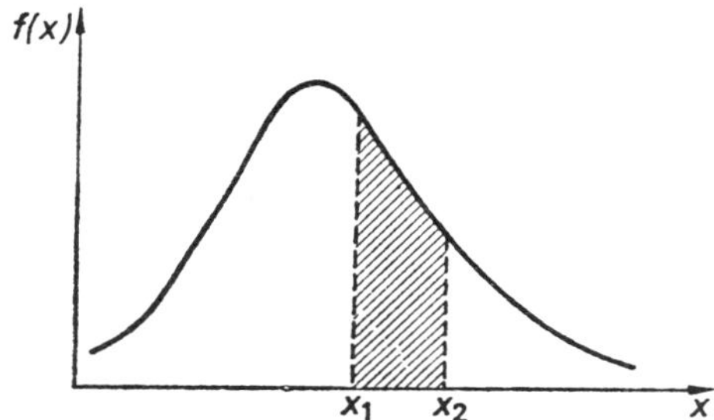

FIG. 17.9 Area and probability

If we assume that the total area under the curve is 1, the probability that the value of x lies between x_1 and x_2 is equal to the area under the curve between these ordinates. The function $f(x)$ is then the *probability density* or *distribution function.*

Normal (Gaussian) Distribution Function

In general, a physical measurement is subject to a number of independent sources of error. If a large number of values are obtained of a particular measurement, the values often obey a particular distribution, regardless of the nature of the individual errors. This distribution function is the *normal* or *Gaussian probability function.* Its equation is

$$\phi(x) = \frac{1}{\sigma\sqrt{2\pi}} \exp\left[-\tfrac{1}{2}\left(\frac{x-\mu}{\sigma}\right)^2\right],$$

where μ is the expected mean value and σ is the expected standard deviation.

Fig. 17.10 shows a normal (Gaussian) distribution. Note that:

(i) the curve is symmetrical about the mean value μ,
(ii) the curve tends to zero when x tends to $-\infty$ or $+\infty$,
(iii) the total area under the curve is 1, that is, the curve is 'normalized' so that the total probability is 1.

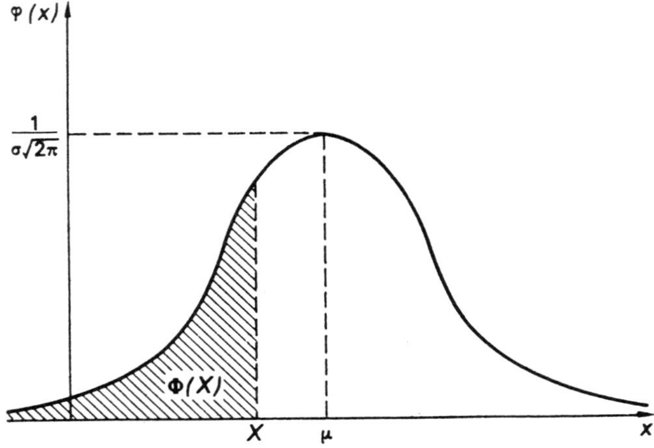

FIG. 17.10 Normal (Gaussian) Distribution

Area Under Normal Curve. Probability Values

As already indicated, the probability that x lies between values x_1 and x_2 is the area given by the integral

$$\int_{x_1}^{x_2} \phi(x)\,.\,\mathrm{d}x,$$

where $\phi(x)$ is the distribution function. This integral cannot be evaluated analytically but approximate values have been calculated by numerical methods with limits $-\infty$ to x and tabulated in books of mathematical tables. The integral is denoted by $\Phi(x)$. See Fig 17.10.

An abbreviated table of values of the probability $\Phi(x)$ is given on page 311. Note carefully that these values are obtained assuming $\mu = 0$ and $\sigma = 1$, that is, the curve is centred on the y-axis and the standard deviation is 1, as shown in Fig. 17.11. If we require $\Phi(x)$ for μ not equal to 0 and σ not equal to 1, we can still use the same table provided the substitution $x = (x - \mu)/\sigma$ is made. See Example, p. 313.

Fig. 17.12 shows approximate values of the probability that the variable will lie between the mean value $\mu = 0$ and σ, between σ and 2σ, and between 2σ and 3σ. Note that about 68% of the area falls within 1 standard deviation and that about 95% falls within 2 standard deviations.

Two other cases of the normal distribution curve are shown in Figs. 17.13 and 17.14. These correspond respectively to a large value of σ (2) and a small value of σ ($\frac{1}{2}$). The spread of values in the former case is large and narrow in the latter case.

x	$\Phi(x)$ = Probability
0.0	0.5000
0.2	0.5793
0.4	0.6554
0.6	0.7257
0.8	0.7881
1.0	0.8413
1.2	0.8849
1.4	0.9192
1.6	0.9452
1.8	0.9641
2.0	0.9773
...	...
3.0	0.9987
...	...
4.0	0.999 97

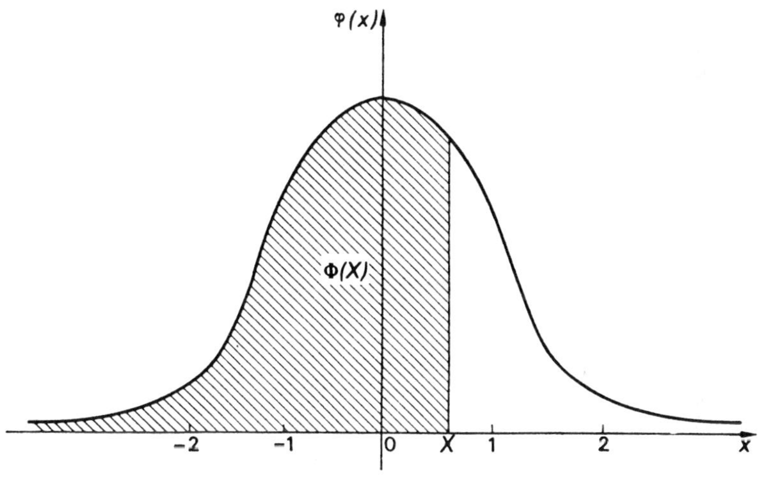

FIG. 17.11 Normal distribution; mean (μ) = 0 and s.d. (σ) = 1

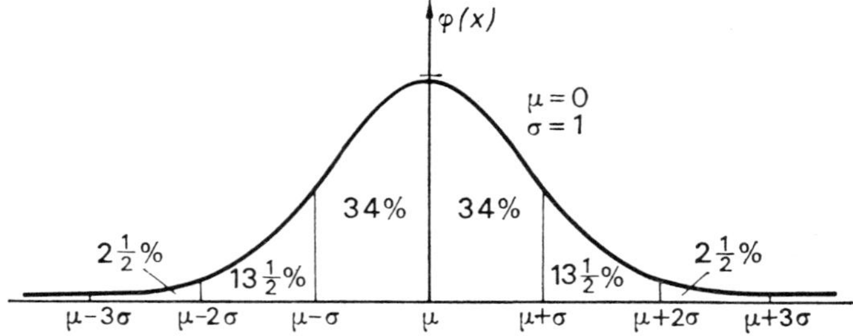

FIG. 17.12 Area distribution for Gaussian curve

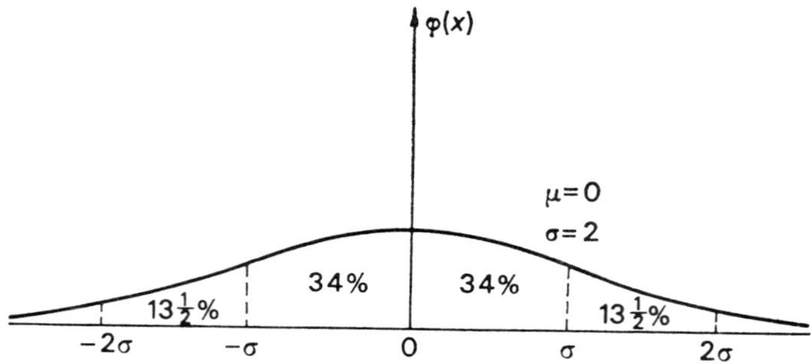

FIG. 17.13 Large spread in normal distribution

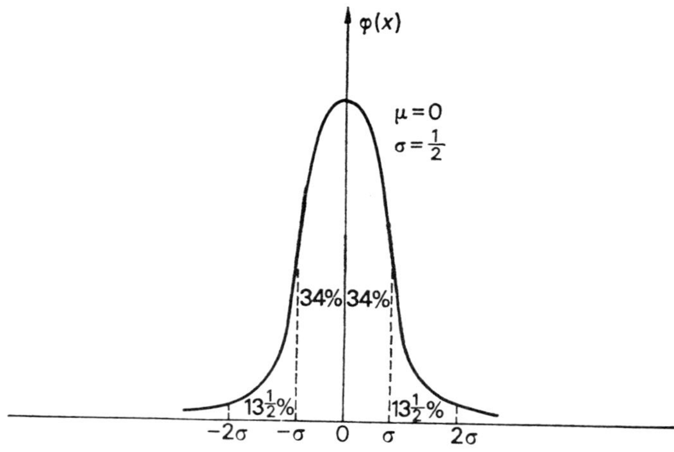

FIG. 17.14 Narrow spread in normal distribution

EXAMPLE

The mean time taken by a man to get to his office from home is 1 hour. Once in ten times the journey takes more than 5 minutes longer. What is the probability of his being more than $7\frac{1}{2}$ minutes early, assuming a Normal distribution of times? (*O.*)

The mean value of time, $\mu = 60$ min. The probability that the time takes *less* than 65 min is 9/10. Thus the area below the normal curve up to the ordinate $x = 65$ is 9/10. Hence the probability function value $\Phi(65) = 0.9$.

Converting to $\mu = 0$, then $\Phi\left(\frac{65 - 60}{\sigma}\right) = \Phi\left(\frac{5}{\sigma}\right) = 0.9$. From tables, $\Phi(x) = 0.9$ when $x = 1.2816$.

$$\therefore \quad \frac{5}{\sigma} = 1.2816$$

We require
$$p = 1 - \Phi\left(\frac{7.5}{\sigma}\right)$$

$$\therefore \quad p = 1 - \Phi(1.5 \times 1.2816)$$
$$= 1 - \Phi(1.9224)$$
$$= 0.0273, \text{ from tables of } \Phi(x)$$
$$\therefore \quad p = 2.73\%.$$

Null Tests

We often wish to test whether a set of results is consistent with a given hypothesis, for example, that the mean values of two populations are equal. For this purpose it is necessary to apply a *null test*. In such tests we make a hypothesis (*null hypothesis*) and then calculate some quantity which would be zero if this were true.

Null tests are designed to determine whether or not the deviations of the observed results from the expected values are likely to have arisen by chance. There are several null tests, for which specialist books on *Statistics* must be consulted. We shall limit ourselves to the χ^2 (chi-squared) *test*.

χ^2 Test

This test compares any set of observations with the expected values. In the form to be used, the test is applicable only to random events, not to continuous variables.

χ^2 is defined as follows:

$$\chi^2 = \sum \frac{(O - E)^2}{E},$$

where O is the observed result in each case and E is the expected result. χ^2 is derived from the Normal probability formula and depends on the number of *degrees of freedom* of the pairs of values of O and E chosen as the sample. If the expected values are derived from the mean of the observed values, the number of degrees of freedom is one less than the number of pairs of values. Tables provide probabilities P for values of χ^2 corresponding to a particular number of degrees of freedom.

A low value of P implies a low probability that discrepancies between O and E have occurred by chance. The differences between O and E are then said to be statistically significant, that is, the null hypothesis $O = E$ is probably untrue. It is undesirable to use the χ^2 test unless there are three or more observations.

EXAMPLES

1. The heights of 21 firemen were as follows:

Ht. in cm:	160–164	165–169	170–174	175–179	180–184	185–189
No. in range:	0	4	6	8	2	1

If the distribution of heights in the general population is normal with $\sigma =$ 5.0 cm, use the χ^2 test to determine whether the distribution of firemen's heights differ significantly from that of the general population.

We have

$$\text{mean height} = \frac{(4 \times 167) + (6 \times 172) + (8 \times 177) + (2 \times 182) + 187}{21}$$

$$= 174.6 \text{ cm.}$$

Since $\sigma = 5.0$ cm, we expect about 68% of the population to fall within 5 cm of the mean value, about 96% within 10 cm, and about 4% outside 10 cm. Thus a table of observed (O) and expected (E) values is as follows:

	O values		E values	$\frac{(O-E)^2}{E}$
160–164 cm	0	0	2%	2.00
165–169	4	19%	14%	1.79
170–174	6	29%	34%	0.74
175–179	8	38%	34%	0.47
180–184	2	10%	14%	1.14
185–189	1	4%	2%	2.00

$$\therefore \quad \chi^2 = \Sigma \frac{(O-E)^2}{E} = 8.14.$$

There are 5 degrees of freedom. Table shows that $P > 10\%$. Thus firemen heights do not differ significantly from that of the general population.

2. In a genetic experiment with mice, the numbers observed to be white, grey and black are respectively 31, 48, and 21. Use a null test to determine if this batch of 100 mice agree with the hypothesis that one-quarter should be white, one-half grey and one-quarter black.

From the figures given,

Colour	No. of mice		$\frac{(O - E)^2}{E}$
	Observed	Expected	
White	31	25	1.44
Grey	48	50	0.08
Black	21	25	0.64

$$\therefore \quad \chi^2 = 2.16.$$

There are 2 degrees of freedom. Tables show that P is high. The null hypothesis above is thus probably true.

EXERCISES 17

Statistics

(1) Find the mean and standard deviation of the following distribution:

x	0	1	2	3	4	5	6	7	8
f	1	3	8	12	20	18	18	8	4

(2) The following table gives the distribution of marks of 290 candidates in an examination:

Marks	0–9	10–19	20–29	30–39	40–49	50–59	60–69	70–79	80–89	90–99
No. of candidates	1	10	37	40	56	50	39	32	18	7

Calculate the mean and standard deviation.

(3) The masses of twelve sacks of sugar were measured as follows:

Mass (kg) 51, 52, 49, 53, 51, 51, 49, 50, 55, 48, 54, 53

Find their mean and standard deviation.

(4) The electrical resistance of 140 rods at constant temperature gave the following results:

Resistance (Ω)	310	311	312	313	314	315	316	317	318	319	320
Frequency	1	2	6	21	26	32	25	18	5	3	1

Calculate the mean resistance and standard deviation.

(5) The heights of similar plants were measured as follows:

Height	111–120	121–130	131–140	141–150	151–160	161–170
Frequency	2	18	30	34	15	1

Find the mean height and standard deviation.

(6) Find the variance and standard deviation of the number of seeds in the pods of a particular tree from the following results:

No. of seeds per pod	1	2	3	4	5	6	7	8
No. of pods	3	9	22	16	14	8	3	1

(7) The following results were obtained for the count of the number of large dust particles in samples of air:

No. of particles	0	1	2	3	4	5	6	7	8
Frequency	13	26	52	95	73	40	17	5	3

Find the mean and standard deviation.

Probability

(8) Three dice are thrown together for 50 throws with the following results: 3 sixes on one occasion, 2 sixes on two occasions, 1 six on twelve occasions and no sixes on thirty-five occasions. Calculate the mean value (m) and expected mean value (μ).

Calculate the expected mean for 4 dice and 5 dice respectively. Could these expected values have been guessed?

(9) In observations of the traffic flow along a road, 40% of the vehicles travelled about 100 km/h, 42% about 80 km/h, 15% about 60 km/h and 3% about 20 km/h. Calculate the parameter μ (expected mean) from this probability model.

(10) In a bridge game, I know that my opponents hold 5 trumps between them. What is the probability that the trumps are split (i) 2, 3, (ii) 4, 1, (iii) 5, 0? What is the expected number of rounds of trumps I shall have to lead to clear both hands of their trumps?

(11) A and B toss a coin alternately on the understanding that the first to obtain heads wins the toss. Show that their chances of winning are 2/3 and 1/3.

(12) Four persons are chosen at random from a group containing 3 men, 2 women and 4 children. Show that the chance that exactly two of them will be children is 10/21.

(13) In a gambling game, the possible winnings on a unit stake are 3, 2 and 1 units with probabilities of 5, 7 and 12% respectively, and the possible losings on a unit stake are 4, 1 and 2 units with probabilities of 4, 13 and 15% respectively. Show that the gambler will have an average loss per game of about 18% of his investment.

(14) Several people each toss a coin (*a*) 10 times, (*b*) 100 times, (*c*) 1000 times. Calculate in each of the 3 cases the expected standard deviation and the variance of the number of heads.

(15) In a china factory the proportion of cups rejected by inspectors is 1 in 10. What is the probability that in a given batch of 5 cups, more than three will fail inspection?

(16) Two dice, each numbered 1 to 6, are thrown and the total of the two scores recorded. What is the most likely score?

The dice are biased in favour of the 6 in each case so that the probability of scoring a 6 with either die is 1/3. What is the probability of scoring any other given number, assuming that these are all equally favoured? If (*a*) the two unbiassed dice, (*b*) two biassed dice are thrown, what is the probability in each case of scoring 8?

(17) The ratio of male births M to total births (male plus female) T, in eight counties in England in one year was as follows:

County	1	2	3	4	5	6	7	8
Ratio M/T	0.47	0.52	0.58	0.43	0.46	0.53	0.45	0.48

Find, to two significant figures, the standard deviation of these figures and compare it with its theoretical value. [In your calculation assume births of boys and girls are equally likely.] (*O.*)

Normal Distribution (*assume Normal Distributions in the following questions*)

(18) A large group of soldiers use the same target for target practice. This consists of a long plank 1 m wide, with a straight band 10 cm wide symmetrical about the centre. In one day 10 000 rounds were fired at the target. If 1500 shots hit the band, how many shots missed the target?

(19) The mean lifetime of a certain component in a radio receiver is 1000 hours. If 20% of the components have a lifetime in excess of 1100 hours, estimate how long should it be left in service if the average failure rate must be less than 1 in 1000?

(20) On average a train passes a school at 10.00 a.m. Once in a hundred days it is more than 5 min late. What is the probability on any one day that it would be over 6 min late? How often by chance would the train be more than 6 min late for two consecutive days?

(21) A gun has a mean range of 20 miles, and the range reaches over 25 miles once in every four shots. How many times will the range fall within 10 miles of the gun?

(22) In a group of 1000 children of the same age, 120 have heights above 150 cm and 200 have heights below 110 cm. How many have heights between 130 and 135 cm?

Null (Chi-squared) Test

(23) There are three shifts, A, B and C, in a factory and in a period of three months the accident rate is as follows:

A–9; B–10; C–2.

Is there a significant difference between them?

(24) A dentist divides a sample group of 100 of his patients into five age groups and compares them with the age groups of the country as a whole. Is there any significant difference between the age groups?

	0–20	21–40	41–60	61–80	80+
Dentist's patients	21	46	25	7	1
Whole population %	18	26	24	18	4

(25) A school has twice as many passes in an examination as failures and claims this as a sign of very good tuition. There are 300 pupils in the school. Is the claim justified? A parent teaching his 3 children at home has 2 passes and 1 failure and makes the same claim. Is there any justification for this claim?

(26) In an army division the heights in a normal distribution are such that the mean is 174 cm and the standard deviation is 6 cm. A sample of five men are of respective heights 180, 170, 175, 176, 173. Is this unusual?

(27) The intelligence quotients, I.Q.s, of a population with a normal distribution have a mean of 100 and a standard deviation of 15. A group of ten children have I.Q.s of 90, 80, 110, 105, 70, 115, 120, 140, 95, 99. Do they form a particularly unrepresentative group?

Answers

1. 4.54, 1.76
2. 50.8, 19.8
3. 51.3 kg, 2.05 kg
4. 315 Ω, 1.77 Ω
5. 140 cm, 10.4 cm
6. 2.28, 1.51
7. 3.30, 1.57
8. $m = 0.38$, $\mu = 0.5$; 2/3, 5/6
9. 83.2 km/h
10. (i) 5/8, (ii) 5/16, (iii) 1/16; $3\frac{7}{16}$ or 4 rounds
14. (*a*) 1.58, 2.5 (*b*) 5, 25 (*c*) 15.8, 250
15. 0.00046
16. 7, 2/15; (*a*) 5/36 (*b*) 32/225
17. 0.046, theoretical value → 0
18. 580
19. 630 h
20. 0.003, prob. $= 7 \times 10^{-6}$
21. 1 in 12.3 times
22. 96 children (approx)
23. No significance at 1% level
24. Yes, significance
25. Yes; parent claim—no
26. Not unusual
27. Not unrepresentative

EXERCISES 17A

Miscellaneous Questions on Statistics and Probability

(1) The following are the weights in ounces of a random sample of fifteen 2 lb packets of sugar delivered by an automatic packing machine:
32.11, 31.97, 32.18, 32.03, 32.25, 32.07, 32.05, 32.19, 31.98, 32.07, 31.99, 32.16, 32.03, 32.18, 32.14.

Calculate the mean and standard deviation. Assuming the distribution to be normal, estimate the percentage of underweight packets which the machine is delivering. (*O.*)

(2) To investigate the distribution of growth of runner beans, a sample distance along one row was chosen. The sample contained 500 beans whose lengths were recorded in the following frequency distribution:

Length (cm)	0–4	4–8	8–12	12–16	16–20	20–24	More than 24
No. of beans	31	72	140	159	76	15	7

The distribution has a mean of 12.0 cm and a standard deviation of 5.0 cm From the table of areas under the normal distribution curve, construct the corresponding frequency distribution which would have been expected for the mean and standard deviation, if the distribution were normal. Use the χ^2 test to decide whether it is likely that the length of the runner beans are normally distributed, with this mean and standard deviation. (*O.*)

(3) (*a*) A new factory is equipped with 10 000 light bulbs with a mean life of 150 days. Their length of life is normally distributed with a standard deviation of 20 days. How many bulbs can be expected to fail in 120 days?
(*b*) A coin is tossed 100 times and comes down heads 60 times and tails 40 times. How conclusive is this as evidence that the coin is biased? (*O.*)

(4) In a china factory the proportion of cups rejected by inspectors is 1 in 10. What is the probability that in a given batch of 5 cups more than 2 will fail inspection? (*O.*)

(5) A sample of broad beans was examined and for each bean its length and mass were measured and recorded as follows:

Bean No.	1	2	3	4	5	6	7	8	9	10
Mass (g)	0.7	1.2	0.9	1.4	1.2	1.1	1.0	0.9	1.0	0.8
Length (cm)	1.7	2.2	2.0	2.3	2.4	2.2	2.0	1.9	2.1	1.6

Plot a scatter diagram for these results and estimate the mass of a bean of length 1.8 cm. Calculate the product–moment correlation coefficient, and comment on its value.

(6) A manufacturer is producing resistances normally distributed about a mean value of 50.0 Ω with a standard deviation of 1.0 Ω. He sells them in packets of ten. Calculate:
(*a*) the percentage of resistances whose values lie more than 5% from the mean;

(*b*) the probability that a packet will contain at least one resistance whose value lies more than 5% from 50.0 Ω;

(*c*) the probability that if two resistors are chosen at random, their combined resistance in series will lie between 99 Ω and 101 Ω.

To check the constancy of his product, the manufacturer periodically extracts 100 resistors and measures them. He finds that one such sample has a mean of 50.24 Ω. Has there been any significant change in his product? (*O.*)

(7) The seeds of a certain variety of primula produce *either* red *or* yellow flowered plants. The chance of a seed producing a yellow-flowered plant is 1/3. How many seeds should I sow in order that the probability of producing at least one red-flowered plant should be greater than 9/10?

If I plant 10 seeds, what is the probability that just two plants will have yellow flowers? (Leave your answer in the form Ab^x/c^y.)

(8) A machine is used to package flour in bags to be labelled 1 kg. The mean mass of a bag can be controlled on the machine but the standard deviation remains constant at 0.03 kg. Assuming a Normal distribution, at what value should the mean be set to ensure that at least 90% of the bags have a mass of at least 1 kg?

With this value for the mean, how many of 100 bags would be expected to have a mass of more than 1.05 kg? (*O.*)

(9) To investigate the distribution of field mice in a wood, five traps were set in different parts of it and visited daily. The numbers of mice caught in each trap in 3 months were recorded as follows:

Trap	A	B	C	D	E
No. of mice caught	23	10	26	15	21

Explain the 'null hypothesis' you would use to investigate these results, and carry out a χ^2 (chi-squared) test for its validity.

Discuss briefly the relative merits in this investigation of: (*a*) killing the trapped field mice, (*b*) releasing them in the neighbourhood of the trap, (*c*) marking them before releasing them in the neighbourhood of the trap. (*O.*)

Answers

1. 32.09, 0.087; 15%
2. Yes, normally distributed
3. (*a*) 668, (*b*) significant at 5% level
4. 0.008 56
5. $m = 0.84$ g; coeff. = 0.90, good correln.
6. (*a*) 1.2%, (*b*) 0.12, (*c*) 0.52; not very significant
7. 3; $5 \times (2^8/3^8)$
8. 1.038 kg, 34 bags
9. Not significant at 5% level

Miscellaneous Worked Examples

The following solutions are given for guidance and are not intended as model answers.

1. *A baker makes cakes at a cost of 2 pence each. He finds that if he sells them at x pence each the number he sells is* $1000\,e^{-x/2}$. *At what price should he sell them to make maximum profit, and how many would he sell at this price? (There is no need for you to establish that the turning value is a maximum.) (O.)*

$$\text{Profit for each cake} = (x - 2)\text{ pence}$$

So $$\text{total profit } P = (x - 2)1000\,e^{-x/2}$$

For maximum profit, $dP/dx = 0$. By differentiation of a product,

$$\frac{dP}{dx} = (x - 2) \times 1000\,e^{-x/2} \times (-\tfrac{1}{2}) + 1000\,e^{-x/2} \times 1$$

$$= 1000\,e^{-x/2}[(-\tfrac{1}{2}(x - 2) + 1]$$

So $$\frac{dP}{dx} = 0 \text{ when } \tfrac{1}{2}(x - 2) = 1, \quad \text{or} \quad x = 2 + 2 = 4$$

So selling price per cake = 4p

and $$\text{number sold} = 1000\,e^{-4/2} = 1000 \times e^{-2} = 135$$

2. *A cricket ball of mass* 0.16 kg *is moving horizontally at* 12 m s^{-1} *when it is struck by a bat. The ball leaves the bat horizontally with a velocity of* 18 m s^{-1} *in a direction which makes an angle of 120° with that of the original velocity (as shown in Fig. 1(a)).*

If the impact lasts for 0.1 s, *what is the magnitude of the average force exerted by the bat on the ball? (A solution by accurate drawing is acceptable.) (O.)*

$$\text{Average force } F = \frac{\text{momentum change}}{\text{time}}$$

$$= \frac{\text{mass} \times \text{velocity change}}{0.1\text{ s}}$$

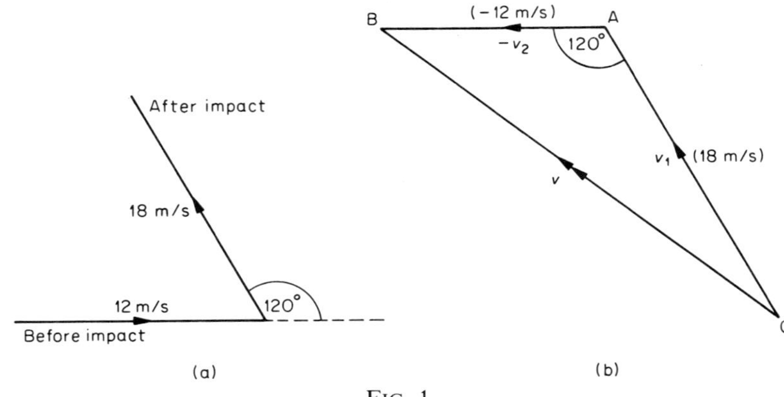

FIG. 1

Now velocity change $v = \vec{v}_1(18\text{ m/s}) - \vec{v}_2(12\text{ m/s})$

$= \text{OB}$ by vector subtraction. Fig. 1 (b).

From cosine formula applied to triangle OBA,

$$\text{OB}^2 = 18^2 + 12^2 - 2 \times 18 \times 12 \times \cos 120^\circ$$
$$= 324 + 144 - 432 \times (-\tfrac{1}{2}) = 684$$

So $$\text{OB} = v = \sqrt{684}$$

$$\therefore \quad \text{force } F = \frac{0.16 \times \sqrt{684}}{0.1} = 41.8\text{ N}$$

3. (*a*) *Define* surface tension. *Show, by the method of dimensions, that the pressure difference p across a curved spherical surface of a liquid of surface tension* γ *can be represented by* $p = A\gamma/r$, *where r is the radius of the spherical surface and A is a dimensionless constant.*

(*b*) *Describe how you would measure the surface tension of water, using the capillary-rise method. State and explain how you would expect the results to be affected if the water contained a small quantity of detergent.*

(*c*) *In some oil-fields, a dilute detergent solution at high pressure forces oil out of the pores of the containing rock, which are like very small capillary tubes. The effective surface tension* γ *is that of the oil-solution interface.*

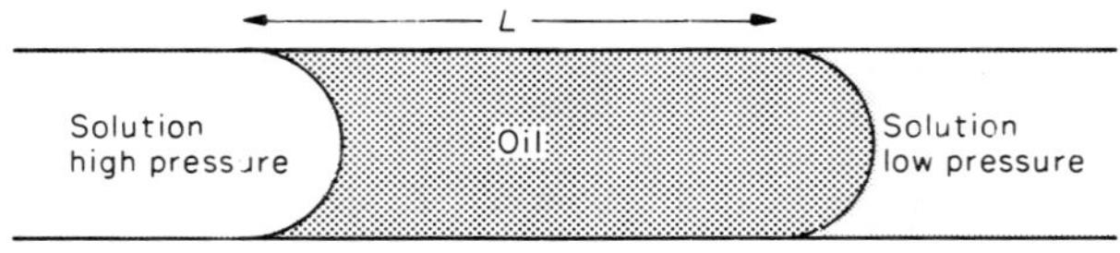

FIG. 2

(i) For the case represented in Fig. 2, show that the pressure gradient along the oil thread is $4\gamma/rL$, where r is the radius of each oil-solution interface and $A = 2$.

(ii) If $r = 5$ μm and $L = 100$ μm, find the value of γ which will give a pressure gradient of 2×10^4 Pa m^{-1}.

(iii) Discuss briefly the part played by the viscosity of the oil in the actual process of getting it out. (O.)

(a) Surface tension, γ, is the force per metre acting normally on one side of a line drawn in the surface.

$$\begin{aligned}\text{Dimensions of } \gamma &= \text{dimensions of force/dimensions of length}\\ &= \mathrm{M\,L\,T^{-2}/L = M\,T^{-2}}\end{aligned}$$

$$\begin{aligned}\text{Dimensions of pressure } p &= \text{dimensions of force/dimensions of area}\\ &= \mathrm{M\,L\,T^{-2}/L^2}\\ &= \mathrm{M\,L^{-1}\,T^{-2}}\end{aligned}$$

Suppose $p = A\gamma^x r^y$, where A is a constant and x, y are powers of γ and r. Then, by dimensions,

$$\mathrm{M\,L^{-1}\,T^{-2}} \equiv (\mathrm{M\,T^{-2}})^x\,(\mathrm{L})^y$$

Equating powers of M,L, T on both sides we have

$$x = 1,\ y = -1, \quad \text{so} \quad p = A\gamma r^{-1} = A\gamma/r$$

(b) The capillary-rise method for γ of water is described in *Advanced Level Physics* (Nelkon and Parker) or in *Modern Laboratory Physics* (Avery and Ingram). If the water contained a small quantity of detergent this would lower the surface tension, thus reducing the liquid height in a given capillary tube.

(c) (i) Since $A = 2$, $p = 2\gamma/r$ across the high pressure interface and across the low pressure interface. So

$$\text{total pressure difference across oil} = \frac{2\gamma}{r} + \frac{2\gamma}{r} = \frac{4\gamma}{r}$$

$$\therefore \quad \text{pressure gradient along oil thread} = \frac{4\gamma}{rL}$$

(ii) Since $\dfrac{4\gamma}{rL} = 2 \times 10^4$

$$\therefore \quad \gamma = \frac{rL \times 2 \times 10^4}{4} = \frac{5 \times 10^{-6} \times 100 \times 10^{-6} \times 2 \times 10^4}{4}$$

$$= \frac{10^{-5}}{4} = 2.5 \times 10^{-6}\ \mathrm{N\,m^{-1}}$$

(iii) The coefficient of viscosity η of the oil affects the volume per second flowing along the pores. In a capillary tube under a constant pressure difference,

$$\text{volume per second} \propto \frac{1}{\eta}$$

So the lower the coefficient of viscosity of the oil, the faster it will flow.

4. *A uniform electric field is maintained between two large plane parallel conducting plates, placed* 0.02 m *apart* in vacuo. *An electron enters the field midway between the plates with an initial velocity parallel to the plates of* 10^7 m s^{-1}. *Fig. 3.*

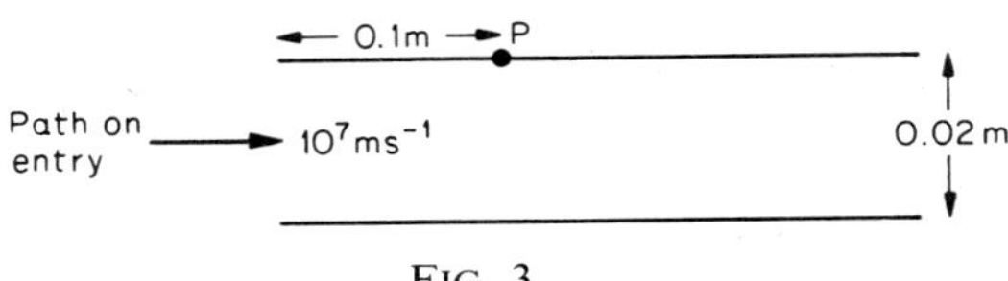

FIG. 3

(*i*) *If the potential difference, measured in volts, between the plates is V, what is the acceleration of this electron in terms of V?*

(*ii*) *If the electron strikes one of the plates at a point* P, 0.1 m *along the plate (see Fig. 3), calculate the magnitude of V and the time taken by the electron between entering the field and striking the plate.* (*O.*)

(i) With the usual notation

$$\text{acceleration } a = \frac{\text{force } F}{\text{mass } m_e} = \frac{Ee}{m_e},$$

where E = electric intensity = potential gradient $= \dfrac{V}{d}$ (d is the distance between plates).

So

$$a = \frac{V}{d} \times \frac{e}{m_e}$$

$$= \frac{V \times 1.76 \times 10^{11}}{0.02}$$

$$= 8.8 \times 10^{12}\ V \text{ m s}^{-2}$$

(ii) For *vertical* motion, $s = \frac{1}{2}at^2$, where $s = \frac{1}{2} \times 0.02 = 0.01$ m.

For horizontal motion to P, $t = \dfrac{0.1 \text{ m}}{10^7 \text{ m s}^{-1}} = 10^{-8}$ s.

So, from $s = \frac{1}{2}at^2$,

$$0.01 = \tfrac{1}{2} \times 8.8 \times 10^{12}\ V \times (10^{-8})^2$$

$$= 4.4 \times 10^{-4}\ V$$

$$\therefore \quad V = \frac{0.01}{4.4 \times 10^{-4}} = \frac{0.01 \times 10^4}{4.4}$$

$$= 22.7\ V$$

5. *(a) A 2 μF and a 4 μF capacitor are connected in series to a 12 V supply. Find (i) the total capacitance; (ii) the charge on each capacitor; (iii) the p.d. across each capacitor.*

(b) A 10 μF capacitor is charged and then discharged by connecting a 2 MΩ resistor across it. What is the time taken for the charge on the capacitor to fall to half its initial value? Sketch curves (on the same axes) to illustrate how the charge on the capacitor and the energy stored in the capacitor change with time. (O.)

(a) (i) Total capacitance C is given by

$$\frac{1}{C} = \frac{1}{2} + \frac{1}{4} = \frac{3}{4}$$

So

$$C = \frac{4}{3}\ \mu\text{F}$$

(ii) Charge on each capacitor Q = charge on *total* capacitance

$$\therefore \quad Q = CV = \frac{4}{3} \times 10^{-6} \times 12 = 1.6 \times 10^{-5}\ \text{C}$$

(iii) P.d. across each capacitor is:

$$V_1 = \frac{Q}{C_1} = \frac{1.6 \times 10^{-5}}{2 \times 10^{-6}} = 8\ \text{V}$$

$$V_2 = \frac{Q}{C_2} = \frac{1.6 \times 10^{-5}}{4 \times 10^{-6}} = 4\ \text{V}$$

(b) With the usual notation, the charge Q on the capacitor after a time t from discharge is given by

$$Q = Q_0\,\mathrm{e}^{-t/CR}$$

where Q_0 is the initial charge. When $Q = Q_0/2$, the time t is given by

$$\frac{Q_0}{2} = Q_0\,\mathrm{e}^{-t/CR}$$

$$\therefore \quad \frac{t}{CR} = \ln 2$$

or

$$t = CR \ln 2 = 10 \times 10^{-6} \times 2 \times 10^{6} \times 0.693$$

$$t = 14\ \text{s (approx)}$$

A graph of Q against t is an exponential graph. Fig. 4.
Also,

$$\text{energy } W = \frac{Q^2}{2C} = \frac{{Q_0}^2}{2C}\,\mathrm{e}^{-2t/CR}$$

So W falls exponentially with time t at a faster rate than Q. See Fig. 4.

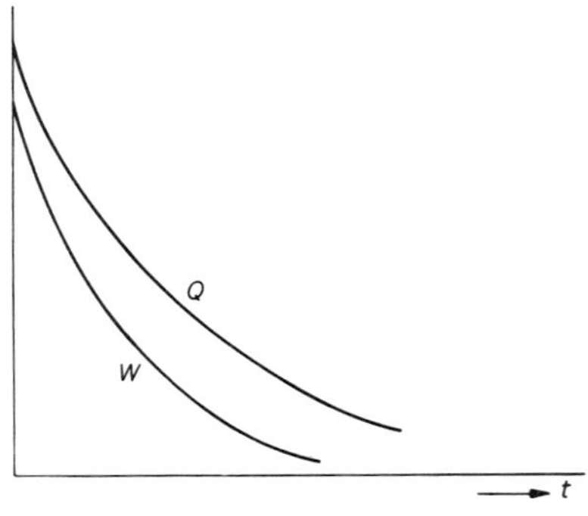

FIG. 4

6. (*a*) *The frequency control of an audiofrequency oscillator can be constructed from a capacitor (of variable capacitance C) and an inductor (of fixed inductance L) in series. If the resistance is considered negligible, and it is supposed that no power is being taken from the oscillator, show that the charge Q on the capacitor at a time t can be represented by the differential equation*

$$L\frac{d^2Q}{dt^2}+\frac{Q}{C}=0$$

and that the frequency of the electrical oscillations in the circuit is $1/2\pi\sqrt{LC}$.

(*b*) *Fig. 5 represents an air-filled 'dust-tube' which is closed at one end and has a small loudspeaker at the other end. The speaker is connected to the output of the a.f. oscillator described above. With this arrangement, each end of the tube can be regarded as a displacement node for stationary wave patterns when they occur.*

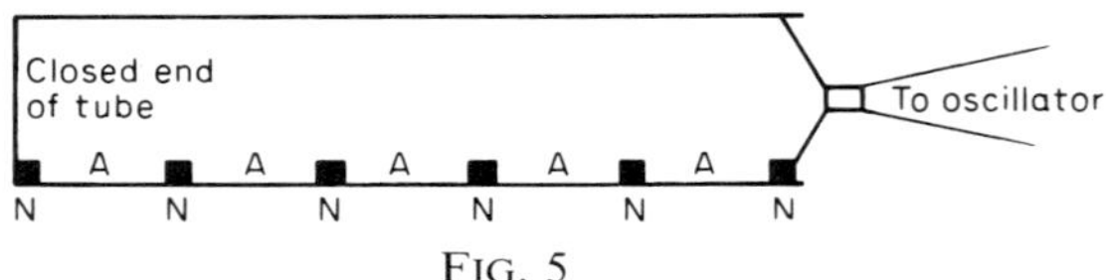

FIG. 5

(*i*) *At a certain oscillator frequency, a stationary dust-pattern with five antinodes is observed. Explain how this pattern arises.*

(*ii*) *What will be observed if the value of C is gradually increased?*

(*iii*) *Calculate the percentage increase in C required to give the next stationary wave pattern.* (*O.*)

(a) If no power is taken from the oscillator and the resistance is negligible, then, at any instant, power in C is gained from power in L. Since current I is the same in each component in a series circuit, it follows that

$$\text{p.d. across } C = \text{p.d. across } L$$

$$\therefore \quad \frac{Q}{C} = -L\frac{dI}{dt}$$

(The minus sign indicates that the p.d. across L opposes the growth of current with time.)

Now $I = \mathrm{d}Q/\mathrm{d}t$, so $\mathrm{d}I/\mathrm{d}t = \mathrm{d}^2Q/\mathrm{d}t^2$. Hence

$$L\frac{\mathrm{d}^2Q}{\mathrm{d}t^2} + \frac{Q}{C} = 0$$

Since $$\frac{\mathrm{d}^2Q}{\mathrm{d}t^2} = -\frac{1}{LC}Q = -\omega^2 Q,$$

where ω is a constant, this is a simple harmonic equation between Q and t with a frequency f of oscillation given by

$$\omega^2 = (2\pi f)^2 = \frac{1}{LC}$$

So $$f^2 = \frac{1}{4\pi^2 LC} \quad \text{and} \quad f = \frac{1}{2\pi\sqrt{LC}}$$

(b) (i) The stationary dust-pattern is due to a *stationary wave* in the air inside the tube. This is produced by the two waves travelling in opposite directions with the same frequency, one due to the sound wave from the loudspeaker and the other due to reflection at the closed end. The dust settles at the displacement nodes N after moving away from the antinodes A.

(ii) When the value of C is gradually increased, the frequency f decreases from $f = 1/2\pi\sqrt{LC}$. So, from $v = f\lambda$, where v is the velocity of sound in air, the wavelength λ increases and the stationary dust-pattern with 5 antinodes no longer applies. The dust is then seen to move and at a particular new value of λ and f, a stationary dust-pattern with 4 antinodes is seen.

(iii) With 5 antinodes A, Fig. 5, the wavelength λ_1 is given by

$$\mathrm{NN} = \frac{\lambda_1}{2} = \frac{l}{5},$$

where l is the length of the tube as shown. So $\lambda_1 = 2l/5$.

Similarly, with 4 antinodes, the new wavelength $\lambda_2 = 2l/4$.

$$\therefore \quad \frac{\lambda_2}{\lambda_1} = \frac{5}{4}$$

If C_2 is the value of C with 4 antinodes and C_1 the value with 5 antinodes, then, since $f \propto 1/\sqrt{C}$ or $\lambda \propto \sqrt{C}$, we have

$$\sqrt{\frac{C_2}{C_1}} = \frac{5}{4}$$

So $$C_2 = \frac{25}{16}C_1$$

$$\therefore \quad \text{percentage increase in } C = \frac{C_2 - C_1}{C_1} \times 100\%$$

$$= \frac{9C_1/16}{C_1} \times 100\% = 56\% \text{ (approx)}$$

7. *(a) The current through a certain circuit component is* $I_0 \sin(2\pi ft - \phi)$ *at time t when the potential applied across it is* $V_0 \sin 2\pi ft$. *Show that the mean power is* $V_{rms} \cdot I_{rms} \cos \phi$ *in terms of the root mean square values of voltage and current respectively.*

(b) A 250 V *(r.m.s.)* 50 Hz *supply is connected in turn across*

(i) a resistor of 50Ω,

(ii) a resistor of 50Ω *in series with an inductor of* $1/2\pi$ H.

Find the r.m.s. value of the current and the mean power in each case.

(c) Plot graphs of the approximate values of V against t and of I against t (on the same t-axes) for two cycles of each of these two cases. Explain how instantaneous values and the mean values of power can be derived from the graphs, and show them appropriately in each case on these same t-axes. (O.)

(a) The instantaneous power $P = IV = I_0 V_0 \sin 2\pi ft . \sin(2\pi ft - \phi)$

$$= \frac{1}{2} I_0 V_0 [\cos \phi - \cos(4\pi ft - \phi)]$$

changing the product of sines into the difference of two cosines from standard trigonometry formula.

Taken over one cycle, the average value of the term

$$\cos(4\pi ft - \phi)$$

is zero. So mean power P is given by

$$P = \frac{1}{2} I_0 V_0 \cos \phi = \frac{I_0}{\sqrt{2}} \times \frac{V_0}{\sqrt{2}} \cos \phi$$

$$= I_{rms} V_{rms} \cos \phi$$

(b) (i) From $I = V/R$, we have

$$I_{rms} = \frac{250}{50} = 5 \text{ A}$$

Also $$\text{mean power } P = \frac{V^2}{R} = \frac{250^2}{50} = 1250 \text{ W}$$

(ii) From $I = V/Z = V/\sqrt{R^2 + X_L{}^2}$, where

$$X_L = 2\pi fL = 2\pi \times 50 \times \frac{1}{2\pi} = 50\ \Omega,$$

we have

$$I = \frac{250}{\sqrt{50^2 + 50^2}} = \frac{250}{\sqrt{5000}} = 3.5 \text{ A}$$

Also, $$\text{mean power} P = I^2 R = \frac{250^2}{5000} \times 50 = 625\ W$$

(c) For plotting the graphs, see page 255. The instantaneous values of power P is found by multiplying the corresponding values of I and V, and the mean power is the average value of the power curve thus obtained.

8. (*a*) *When edge effects may be neglected, the rate of heat flow through a slab of material of cross-sectional area A in which the temperature gradient is* $\mathrm{d}\theta/\mathrm{d}x$ *is given by the equation*

$$\frac{\mathrm{d}Q}{\mathrm{d}t} = -kA\frac{\mathrm{d}\theta}{\mathrm{d}x}.$$

(*i*) *State what is represented by the term k.* (*ii*) *Name the SI unit for each of the four terms in this equation.*

(*b*) *A cylindrical container is to be designed to hold a specified volume V of a volatile liquid at the temperature of its boiling point. When the temperature of the surroundings exceeds this value some of the liquid will evaporate and so escape through a safety valve, because of the heat which is conducted through the vertical walls* (*of height h*) *and the flat roof* (*of radius r*), *all of which are of the same material and thickness* (*which is small compared with the other dimensions*).

If the circular base of the tank stands on ground through which heat transmission is negligible, show that the rate of loss of heat by evaporation will be a minimum when

$$h = r = \left(\frac{V}{\pi}\right)^{1/3}.$$

(*c*) *A tank to this specification holds* $512\ \mathrm{m}^3$ *of liquid in surroundings maintained at* 40°C. *It is made of steel plate* 6 mm *thick and of thermal conductivity* $60\ \mathrm{W\,m^{-1}\,K^{-1}}$. *If the liquid boils at* 36°C *and has a specific latent heat of vaporisation* $1.2 \times 10^6\ \mathrm{J\,kg^{-1}}$, *how much of it must be added every hour to keep the tank filled to the top?*

(*d*) *The wall and roof are now coated with a layer of asbestos* 20 mm *thick and of thermal conductivity* $0.16\ \mathrm{W\,m^{-1}\,K^{-1}}$, *all other conditions remaining unchanged. Estimate the temperature gradient in the asbestos and hence the ratio in which the rate of loss of heat by evaporation is reduced.* (*O.*)

(a) (i) k is the thermal conductivity of the material, or the energy per second passing through unit area in the steady state when the temperature gradient normal to the area is $1\ \mathrm{K\,m^{-1}}$.

(ii) SI units: $\mathrm{d}Q/\mathrm{d}t = \mathrm{J\,s^{-1}} = \mathrm{W}$; $k = \mathrm{W\,m^{-1}\,K^{-1}}$; $A = \mathrm{m}^2$; $\mathrm{d}\theta/\mathrm{d}x = \mathrm{K\,m^{-1}}$.

(b) Since k and $\mathrm{d}\theta/\mathrm{d}x$ are constants for the tank, the rate of conduction of heat, $\mathrm{d}Q/\mathrm{d}t$, through the walls and roof will be a minimum when their total surface area A is a minimum. Now area of walls $= 2\pi rh$ (cylinder) and area of roof $= \pi r^2$ (circle). So

$$A = 2\pi rh + \pi r^2$$

Now volume of liquid $V = \pi r^2 h =$ constant. So

$$h = \frac{V}{\pi r^2}$$

Substituting in the formula for A, then

$$A = 2\pi r\left(\frac{V}{\pi r^2}\right) + \pi r^2 = \frac{2V}{r} + \pi r^2$$

$$\therefore \quad \frac{\mathrm{d}A}{\mathrm{d}r} = -\frac{2V}{r^2} + 2\pi r$$

For minimum, $\mathrm{d}A/\mathrm{d}r = 0$. ($\mathrm{d}^2A/\mathrm{d}r^2 = 4V/r^3 + 2\pi$ which is +ve, showing a minimum)

$$\therefore \quad \frac{2V}{r^2} = 2\pi r, \text{ from which } r = \left(\frac{V}{\pi}\right)^{1/3}$$

Also $$h = \frac{V}{\pi r^2} = \frac{V}{\pi} \times \left(\frac{\pi}{V}\right)^{2/3} = \left(\frac{V}{\pi}\right)^{1/3} = r$$

(c) Heat per second conducted from surroundings through metal tank is numerically $kA\,\mathrm{d}\theta/\mathrm{d}x$. Now $h = r = (512/\pi)^{1/3} = 8/\pi^{1/3}$. So

$$A = 2\pi rh + \pi r^2 = 2\pi r^2 + \pi r^2 = 3\pi r^2 = 192\pi^{1/3},$$

$$k = 60 \text{ W m}^{-1}\text{ K}^{-1} \quad \text{and} \quad \mathrm{d}\theta/\mathrm{d}x = (40 - 36)/(6 \times 10^{-3}) = 4000/6 \text{ K m}^{-1}$$

So heat per second conducted to liquid

$$= 60 \times 192 \times \pi^{1/3} \times 4000/6$$
$$= 1.12 \times 10^7 \text{ J s}^{-1} \text{ (approx)}$$

$$\therefore \quad \text{heat per hour} = 1.12 \times 10^7 \times 3600 \text{ J}$$

Since 1.2×10^6 J is required for each kg,

$$\text{mass of liquid per hour for topping up} = \frac{1.12 \times 10^7 \times 3600}{1.2 \times 10^6}$$
$$= 3.4 \times 10^4 \text{ kg (approx)}$$

(d) Suppose g_a is the temperature gradient in the asbestos and g_m is the temperature gradient in the metal. Then, since $\mathrm{d}Q/\mathrm{d}t$ is numerically the same for asbestos and metal, it follows that

$$k_a g_a A = k_m g_m A,$$

where k_a, k_m are the respective thermal conductivities of asbestos and metal

So $$\frac{g_a}{g_m} = \frac{k_m}{k_a} = \frac{60}{0.16} = 375$$

Since the temperature gradient across the asbestos is so large compared to that across the metal, we may say that the temperature of the junction between the two is practically 36°C. So, to a good approximation,

$$g_a = \frac{40 - 36}{20 \times 10^{-3}} = 200 \text{ K m}^{-1}$$

Hence heat per second conducted through asbestos, if A is the total area,

$$= 0.16 \times A \times 200 = 32\,A$$

With the metal alone, heat per second conducted

$$= 60 \times A \times \frac{40 - 36}{6 \times 10^{-3}} = 4 \times 10^{4}\,A$$

So ratio in which rate of loss of heat is reduced

$$= \frac{32A}{4 \times 10^{4}A} = \frac{1}{1250}$$

Index